Frommer's®

Boston

Here's what the critics say about Frommer's:

"Amazingly easy to use. Very portable, very complete."
—*Booklist*

♦

"The only mainstream guide to list specific prices. The Walter Cronkite of guidebooks—with all that implies."
—*Travel & Leisure*

♦

"Complete, concise, and filled with useful information."
—*New York Daily News*

♦

"Hotel inform   to encyclopedic."
          Moines Sunday Register

D1293531

Other Great Guides for Your Trip

Frommer's® 99

Boston

by Marie Morris

MACMILLAN • USA

ABOUT THE AUTHOR

Marie Morris is a native New Yorker and a graduate of Harvard College, where she studied history. She has worked for the *New York Times, Boston* magazine, and the *Boston Herald,* and she covers Boston for *Frommer's New England.* She lives in Boston, not far from Paul Revere.

ACKNOWLEDGMENTS

Many thanks to Lisa Renaud, Dan Glover, and the rest of the wizards at Macmillan Travel, who made sure this book would get to you. And many more thanks to the cheerleaders and research assistants—especially my family, Kristin Goss, Beth Teitell, and Liz First Raddock—who helped make sure the manuscript got to them.

MACMILLAN TRAVEL

A Simon & Schuster Macmillan Company
1633 Broadway
New York, NY 10019

Find us online at **www.frommers.com**

ISBN: 0-02-862228-6
ISSN: 0899-322X

Editor: Dan Glover
Production Editor: Kristi Hart
Map Editor: Douglas Stallings
Design by Michele Laseau
Digital Cartography by Ortelius Design and Peter Bogaty
Page Creation by Tammy Ahrens, John Bitter, Troy Barnes, Jerry Cole, Toi Davis, Angel Perez, and Dave Pruett

SPECIAL SALES

Bulk purchases (10+ copies) of Frommer's and selected Macmillan travel guides are available to corporations, organizations, mail-order catalogs, institutions, and charities at special discounts, and can be customized to suit individual needs. For more information write to Special Sales, Macmillan General Reference, 1633 Broadway, New York, NY 10019.

Manufactured in the United States of America.

Contents

List of Maps

An Invitation to the Reader

In researching this book, we discovered many wonderful places—hotels, restaurants, shops, and more. We're sure you'll find others. Please tell us about them so that we can share the information with your fellow travelers in upcoming editions. If you were disappointed with a recommendation, we'd love to know that, too. Please write to:

Frommer's Boston
c/o Macmillan Travel
1633 Broadway
New York, NY 10019

An Additional Note

Please be advised that travel information is subject to change at any time—and this is especially true of prices. We therefore suggest that you write or call ahead for confirmation when making your travel plans. The authors, editors, and publisher cannot be held responsible for the experiences of readers while traveling. Your safety is important to us, however, so we encourage you to stay alert and be aware of your surroundings. Keep a close eye on cameras, purses, and wallets, all favorite targets of thieves and pickpockets.

What the Symbols Mean

✪ Frommer's Favorites
Our favorite places and experiences—outstanding for quality, value, or both.

The following abbreviations are used for credit cards:

AE	American Express	JCB	Japan Credit Bank
CB	Carte Blanche	MC	MasterCard
DC	Diners Club	V	Visa
DISC	Discover		

Find Frommer's Online

Arthur Frommer's Outspoken Encyclopedia of Travel (www.frommers.com) offers more than 6,000 pages of up-to-the-minute travel information—including the latest bargains and candid, personal articles updated daily by Arthur Frommer himself. No other Web site offers such comprehensive and timely coverage of the world of travel.

Welcome to Boston

The 90s have been kind to Boston. In the 1690s, the town prospered and grew into one of the colonies' most important centers of commerce. In the 1790s, the city took a leading role in the new China trade and a prominent place in the new United States. The 1890s saw the flourishing of a rich cultural tradition as the Boston Symphony Orchestra, the Museum of Fine Arts, and the Boston Public Library, among other institutions, continued their rise to international prominence.

In the 1990s, Boston has shaken off the lingering effects of the recession of the late 1980s and again become a "hot" city. It's a magnet for sightseers, history buffs, and college students, the center of the booming financial-services industry, and an increasingly popular backdrop for film and television production. As it has for hundreds of years, it offers cosmopolitan sophistication on a comfortable scale, balancing celebration of the past and pursuit of the future. It has even been featured on MTV (in "The Real World," part 6).

Boston is not perfect, of course. Even a brief visit will confirm that the city's drivers have earned their terrible reputation, and the local accents are as ear-splitting as any in Brooklyn or Chicago. Wander into the wrong part of town and you might be ordered to "pahk yuh cah" (park your car) somewhere else—pronto. And although it's the biggest college town in the world, there isn't much of a late-night scene aside from convenience stores and copy shops.

Take a few days (or weeks) to get to know Boston, or use it as a gateway to the rest of New England. The Pilgrim heritage of Plymouth, the historical and literary legacy of Lexington and Concord, the rugged coast and maritime tradition of the North Shore and Maine, the beaches of Cape Cod, and the mountains of western Massachusetts, Vermont, and New Hampshire are all within easy driving distance and well worth exploring.

Here's hoping your experience is memorable and delightful.

1 Frommer's Favorite Boston Experiences

- **A Bird's-Eye View.** On a clear day, you can see for at least 30 miles from the John Hancock Observatory or the Prudential Center Skywalk—not exactly forever, but an impressive view

Boston Orientation

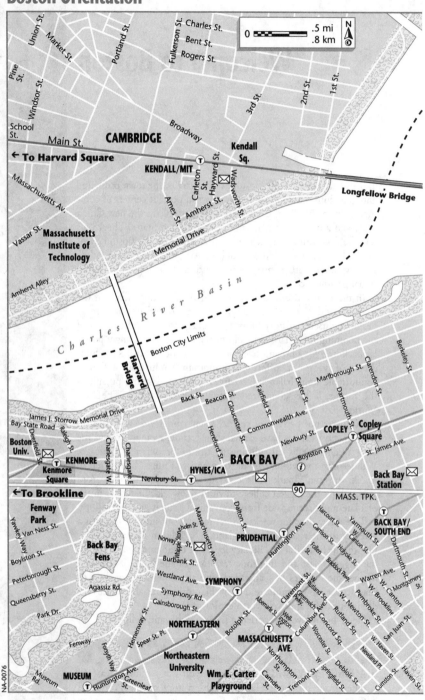

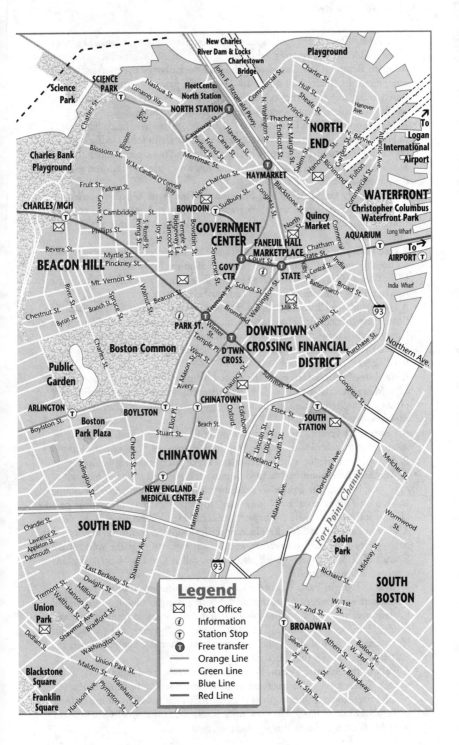

nonetheless. On a clear night, especially in winter, the cityscape looks like black velvet studded with twinkling lights.

- **A Lunch Break on the Waterfront.** Head for the harbor or the river, settle in at a restaurant or (preferably) on a park bench or a patch of grass, take off your watch, relax, and enjoy the spectacular view. Whether sailboats or ocean liners, seagulls or scullers, there's always something worth watching.

- **An Afternoon Red Sox Game.** Since 1912, baseball fans have made pilgrimages to Fenway Park, the "lyric little bandbox of a ball park" (in John Updike's words) off Kenmore Square. The seats are uncomfortable and too close together, the Red Sox last won the World Series in 1918, and you won't care a whit as you soak up the atmosphere and bask in the sun.

- **A Few Hours (at Least) at the Museum of Fine Arts.** Whether you're into Egyptian art or contemporary photography, furniture and decorative arts or the Impressionists, you're sure to find something at the MFA that tickles your interest.

- **A Free Friday Flick.** Families, film buffs, and impoverished entertainment-seekers flock to the lawn in front of the Hatch Shell on the Esplanade for free movies (*The Wizard of Oz* or *Raiders of the Lost Ark,* for example) on Friday nights in the summer. Bring something to sit on, and maybe a sweater.

- **A Quest for the Ultimate Bargain.** For some people, this is *the* quintessential Boston experience. Arrive at the legendary Filene's Basement in Downtown Crossing early, before the lunchtime crowds, and set off on a treasure hunt. Prices for the already-discounted merchandise shrink after it's been on the selling floor for 2 weeks.

- **A Newbury Street Safari.** From the genteel Arlington Street end to the cutting-edge Massachusetts Avenue end, Boston's legendary shopping destination is 8 blocks of pure temptation in the form of galleries, boutiques, jewelry and gift shops, bookstores, and more.

- **A Concert Al Fresco.** Summer nights swing to the beat of outdoor music by amateurs and professionals. A great spot for free jazz is Christopher Columbus Park, on the waterfront, where performances take place Fridays at 6:30pm.

- **A Weekend Afternoon in Harvard Square.** It's not the bohemian hangout of days gone by, but "the Square" is packed with book and record stores, clothing and souvenir shops, restaurants, musicians, students of all ages, and so many people that it's a wonder there are any left at Faneuil Hall Marketplace.

- **A Visit to Faneuil Hall Marketplace.** Specialty shops, an enormous food court, street performers, bars, restaurants, and crowds from all over the world make Faneuil Hall Marketplace (you'll also hear it called Quincy Market) Boston's most popular destination.

- **A Meal at Durgin-Park.** Dinner at this Boston institution (it opened in 1827) might start with oysters. Or it might start with a waitress slinging a handful of napkins over your shoulder, dropping a handful of cutlery in front of you, and saying, "Here, give these out." The surly service usually seems to be an act, but it's so much a part of the legend that some people are disappointed when the waitresses are nice (as they often are).

- **A Walk to the Atlantic Ocean.** Boston Harbor owes its reputation as one of the world's finest ports to its sheltered location and distance from the open sea, which batters the coastline north of the city. To get the full effect of the majestic Atlantic, get out of town. The view from Rockport, at the tip of Cape Ann, or from Marblehead, a bit farther south, is worth the trip.

Impressions

*Boston State-House is the hub of the solar system. You couldn't pry that out of a
Boston man, if you had the tire of all creation straightened out for a crowbar.*
　　　　—Oliver Wendell Holmes, *The Autocrat of the Breakfast-Table* (1858)

*The Bostonians take their learning too sadly: culture with them is an accomplishment
rather than an atmosphere; their "Hub," as they call it, is the paradise of prigs.*
　　　　—Oscar Wilde, "The American Invasion" (1887)

- **A Ride on a Duck.** A Duck Tour, that is. Board a reconditioned amphibious World War II landing craft (on Huntington Avenue behind the Prudential Center) for a sightseeing ride that includes a dip in the river—for the Duck, not you.
- **A "Ride" at the Museum of Science.** The Mugar Omni Theater, a four-story wraparound auditorium (or torture chamber, if you're prone to motion sickness), inundates you with sights and sounds and doesn't let go. Whether the film is on volcanoes or sharks, the larger-than-life images will draw you in. The museum proper (separate admission) is also a great place to explore, especially if you're traveling with children.
- **A Sky Full of Fireworks.** Twice during Independence Day festivities and again as the New Year begins, the firmament flashes in celebration. The Fourth of July fireworks are over the Charles River; the Harborfest display (in the first few days of July) and the First Night exhibition explode above the Inner Harbor.
- **A Spring Fling in the Public Garden.** Eight square blocks of paradise await you, filled with flowers, ornamental greenery, and flowering trees and shrubs. Pass through for a quick pick-me-up, take to the lagoon for a swan boat ride (or a spin on ice skates if it's cold enough), or just enjoy the ducklings. They're on view in the flesh, seasonally, and in bronze year-round.
- **A Walk Around the North End.** Boston's Little Italy (but it's never called that) has an Old World flavor you won't want to miss. Explore the shops on Salem Street, wander the narrow side streets, perhaps enjoy some pasta, and be sure to stop for coffee and a pastry at a Hanover Street cafe.
- **A Vicarious Thrill.** Without so much as lacing up a sneaker, participate in the world-famous Boston Marathon. Stretch a little so that you won't cramp up. Drink plenty of fluids. Stake out a slice of sidewalk on Commonwealth Avenue under a tree (the sun can be very draining). Cheer as the runners thunder past. Then relax and put your feet up—you've earned it.

2 The City Today

Boston embodies contrasts and contradictions—it's blue blood and blue-collar, Yankee and Irish, home to Brahmin bankers and budget-conscious graduate students. It's a proud seaport whose harbor is being reclaimed from crippling pollution. It's home to the country's first public school and to an educational system perpetually on the verge of crisis. It's a one-time hotbed of abolitionism with an intractable reputation for racism. It's a magnet for college students from all over the world and others engaged in intellectual pursuits, yet the traditional, parochial obsessions are "sports, politics, and revenge."

Boston is a living landmark that bears many marks of its colonial heritage, but where it's theoretically possible (this is an observation, not a suggestion) to spend days without going near anything built before 1960, or even going outdoors.

A CULTURED PEARL   Whether their association with the city lasts 4 years or 4 generations, most Bostonians take pride in their cultural institutions—as do residents of every municipality that boasts more than just a mall and a movie house. What makes Boston different?

Stop 10 Bostonians on the street and ask them to name their three favorite local leisure activities, and you might hear 30 different answers. Here's someone who spends every Fourth of July waiting for the annual outdoor Pops concert but has yet to set foot in Symphony Hall; her friend never skips an exhibit at the Museum of Fine Arts or a chance to sample the clam chowder at a new restaurant; here's a guy who wouldn't miss the Harvard-Yale football game but wouldn't be caught dead at Mount Auburn Cemetery (maybe that's a bad example). Like any city, Boston is what you make of it. And it has a lot of excellent potential ingredients.

Today you'll find a city of 558,400 at the heart of the Greater Boston area, which encompasses 83 cities and towns and some four million people. The hospitals and medical centers are among the best in the world, and the ongoing health-care revolution is a hot topic. The banking and financial services, computer technology, and insurance industries are thriving. The restaurant scene sizzles, with new spots opening and old favorites changing with the times or continuing to do what they've done well for generations.

WELCOME HOME   As they have for more than a century, immigrants flock to the Boston area, where the Irish, eastern European Jews, Italians, Portuguese, African Americans, Hispanics, West Indians, and, most recently, Asians have made their homes and their mark.

One pastime that unites many of the people is rooting for the city's professional sports teams, something of an uphill battle unless they're football fans. Boston is still a great sports town, but the glory days of recently demolished Boston Garden are but a memory to many current fans. That's good news for visitors, who might find that Celtics or Bruins tickets are no longer so hard to come by. Plan far in advance or budget generously if you hope to see the New England Patriots, who regularly sold out their stadium in suburban Foxboro even before they went to the Super Bowl in 1997.

CONSTRUCTION AHEAD   The most prominent feature of downtown Boston, today and for the foreseeable future, is not an architectural masterpiece or a natural wonder but an enormous construction site. The Central Artery (I-93) is being "depressed"—as are many of the people who travel into and through the city every day—in a massive project whose price recently passed $11 billion. The ultimate goals are to hide the interstate underground, turn the land it currently occupies into green space and smaller surface roads, and link the Massachusetts Turnpike (I-90) directly to Logan Airport through the Ted Williams Tunnel. (The tunnel is finished; the link is not.) The target completion date is 2004, and though the site is currently an eyesore, other parts of the city are pretty enough to help make up for it.

When the project is finished, Boston will, in a sense, have come full circle. The worst of the traffic will be hidden away, the pedestrians who originally owned the city will once again have easy access to the harbor, and the center of commerce will open onto the waterfront as it did 3 centuries ago.

3 History 101

Permanently settled in 1630 by representatives of the Massachusetts Bay Company, Boston was named for the hometown of some of the Puritans who left England to seek religious freedom in the New World. Their arrival was greeted with little of the usual strife with the natives, members of the small, Algonquian-speaking Massachuset tribe that roamed the area. They may have used the peninsula they called "Shawmut" (possibly derived from "Mushau-womuk," or "unclaimed land") as burial place, and they grew corn on some harbor islands, but they made their permanent homes farther inland.

In 1632 the little peninsula became the capital of the Massachusetts Bay Colony, and over the next decade the population increased rapidly during the great Puritan migration. Thanks to its excellent location on the deep, sheltered harbor, Boston quickly became a center of shipbuilding, fishing, and trading.

The only thing more important than commerce was religion, and the Puritans exerted such a strong influence that their legacy survives to this day. A concrete reminder is Harvard College's original 1636 mission: preparing young men to be ministers. In 1659 the town fathers officially banned Christmas (the town children apparently had second thoughts—records show the holiday was back in favor within 25 years). And another early example of puritanical stuffiness was recorded in 1673, when one Captain Kemble was sentenced to confinement in the stocks for 2 hours because he kissed his wife on their front steps on a Sunday. He had been away on a voyage for 3 years.

THE ROAD TO REVOLUTION   In 1684 the colony's charter was revoked, and the inhabitants came under tighter British control. Laws increasing taxes and restricting trading activities gradually led to trouble. The situation came to a head after the French and Indian War (known in Europe as the Seven Years' War) ended in 1763.

Having helped fight for the British, the notoriously independent-minded colonists were outraged when the Crown expected them to help pay off the war debt. The Sugar Act of 1764 imposed tariffs on sugar, wine, and coffee, mostly affecting those engaged in trade; the 1765 Stamp Act taxed everything printed, from legal documents to playing

Dateline

- 1614 Capt. John Smith maps the New England coast, names the Charles River after King Charles I of England, and calls the area "a paradise."

- 1621 A party of 11 led by Myles Standish explores Boston Harbor, visits with the Massachuset Indians, and returns to Plymouth.

- ca. 1624 William Blackstone settles on the Shawmut peninsula (on Beacon Hill) with 200 books and a Brahma bull.

- 1630 John Winthrop leads settlers to present-day Charlestown in June. The need for a better water supply soon leads them to Shawmut, which they call Trimountain. On September 7, they name it Boston in honor of the English hometown of many Puritans. On October 19, 108 voters attend the first town meeting.

- 1632 Boston becomes the capital of Massachusetts.

- 1635 Boston Latin School, America's first public school, opens.

- 1636 Harvard College founded to educate young men for the ministry.

- 1638 America's first printing press established in Cambridge.

- 1639 The country's first post office established in the home of Richard Fairbank.

- 1660 Unrepentant Quaker Mary Dyer hanged on the Common.

- 1704 America's first regularly published newspaper, the *Boston News Letter*, is founded.

- 1721 First smallpox inoculations administered at the

continues

urging of Dr. Zabdiel Boylston and Cotton Mather, over the violent objections of the populace.

- 1764 "Taxation without representation" is denounced in reaction to the Sugar Act.
- 1770 On March 5, five colonists are killed outside what is now the Old State House, an incident soon known as the Boston Massacre.
- 1773 On December 16, during the Boston Tea Party, 342 chests of tea are dumped into the harbor from three British ships by colonists poorly disguised as Indians.
- 1774 The "Intolerable Acts," which include the closure of the port of Boston and the quartering of British troops in colonists' homes, go into effect.
- 1775 On April 18, Paul Revere and William Dawes spread the word that the British are marching toward Lexington and Concord. The next day, "the shot heard round the world" is fired. On June 17, the British win the Battle of Bunker Hill but suffer heavy casualties.
- 1776 On March 17, the British evacuate Boston by ship. On July 18, the Declaration of Independence is read from the balcony of the Old State House.
- 1790s The China trade helps bring great prosperity to Boston.
- 1825 The first city census lists 58,277 people.
- 1831 William Lloyd Garrison publishes the first issue of the *Liberator*, a newspaper dedicated to emancipation.
- 1839 Boston University founded.

continues

cards, affecting virtually everyone. Boycotts, demonstrations, and riots ensued. The repeal of the Stamp Act in 1766 was too little, too late—the revolutionary slogan "No taxation without representation" had already taken hold.

The Townshend Acts of 1767 imposed taxes on paper, glass, and tea, sparking more unrest. The following year, British troops occupied Boston. Perhaps inevitably, tension led to violence. In the Boston Massacre of 1770, five colonists were killed in a scuffle with the redcoats. The first to die was a former slave named Crispus Attucks; another was 17-year-old Samuel Maverick.

TEA & NO SYMPATHY   Parliament repealed the Townshend Acts but kept the tea tax, and in 1773 granted the nearly bankrupt East India Company a monopoly on the tea trade with the colonies. The idea was to undercut the price of smuggled tea, but the colonists weren't swayed. In December, three British ships sat at anchor in Boston Harbor, waiting for their cargo of tea to be unloaded. Before that could happen, the rabble-rousing Sons of Liberty, some disguised as Indians, boarded the ships and dumped 342 chests of tea into the harbor. The Boston Tea Party became a rallying point for both sides.

The British responded by closing the port until the tea was paid for and forcing Bostonians to house the soldiers who began to flood the town. They soon numbered 4,000 in a town of 16,000. Mutual distrust ran high—Paul Revere wrote of helping form "a committee for the purpose of watching the movements of the British troops"— and when the royal commander in Boston, General Gage, learned that the patriots were accumulating arms and ammunition, he dispatched men to destroy the stockpiles.

A NEW WORLD ORDER   Troops marched from Boston toward Lexington and Concord late on April 18, 1775. William Dawes and Revere, who alerted the colonists to the British advance on their famous "midnight ride," sounded the warning to the local militia companies, the Minutemen, who mobilized for the impending confrontation. The next day, some 700 British soldiers under Major John Pitcairn emerged victorious from a skirmish in Lexington, then were routed at Concord and forced to retreat to Charlestown.

It took the redcoats almost an entire day to make the trip (along the route now marked "Battle Road"), which you can do in a car in about half an hour. Thanks in no small part to Henry Wadsworth Longfellow's poem "Paul Revere's Ride" (*Listen my children and you shall hear / Of the midnight ride of Paul Revere*), Lexington and Concord are closely associated with the beginning of the Revolution. In the early stages of the war, military activity left its mark all over eastern Massachusetts, particularly in Cambridge. Royalist sympathizers, or Tories, were concentrated so heavily along one stretch of Brattle Street that it was called "Tory Row." When the tide began to turn, George Washington made his headquarters on the same street (in a house later occupied by Longfellow that's currently open for tours). On nearby Cambridge Common is the spot where Washington took command of the Continental Army on July 3, 1775.

The British won the Battle of Bunker Hill (actually fought on Breed's Hill) in Charlestown on June 17, 1775, but at the cost of half their forces. They abandoned Boston the following March 17. On July 4, 1776, the Continental Congress adopted the Declaration of Independence. Although many Bostonians fought in the 6-year war that followed, no more battles were fought in Boston.

COMMERCE & CULTURE After the war, Boston again became a center of business; fishing, whaling, and trade with the Far East dominated the economy. Exotic spices and fruits, textiles, and porcelain were familiar luxuries in Boston and nearby Salem. The influential merchant families became known as "Boston Brahmins," and they spearheaded the cultural renaissance that continued long after the effects of the War of 1812 ravaged international shipping, and banking and manufacturing rose in importance. Boston took a back seat to New York and Philadelphia in size and influence, but the "Athens of America" became known for fine art and architecture, including the luxurious homes on Beacon Hill, and a flourishing intellectual community.

In 1822, Boston became a city. From 1824 to 1826, Mayor Josiah Quincy oversaw the landfill project that moved the waterfront away from Faneuil Hall. The market building constructed at that time was named in his honor. The undertaking was one of many, all over the city, in which hills were lopped off and deposited in the water, transforming the coastline and skyline. For example, the filling of the Mill Pond, now the area around North Station, began in 1807 and in 25 years consumed the summits of Copp's and Beacon hills.

- 1846 The first operation under general anesthesia (the removal of a jaw tumor) is performed at Massachusetts General Hospital.
- 1861 Massachusetts Institute of Technology founded.
- 1863 Boston College founded. The 54th Massachusetts Colored Regiment of the Union Army suffers heavy casualties in an unsuccessful attempt to capture Fort Wagner in the harbor of Charleston, S.C.
- 1870 Museum of Fine Arts founded.
- 1872 The Great Fire burns 65 acres and 800 buildings and kills 33 people.
- 1876 Boston University professor Alexander Graham Bell invents the telephone.
- 1878 Girls Latin School opens.
- 1881 Boston Symphony Orchestra founded.
- 1895 Boston Public Library opens on Copley Square.
- 1897 The first Boston Marathon is run. The first subway in America opens— a 1.7-mile stretch from Boylston Street to Park Street.
- 1910 John F. "Honey Fitz" Fitzgerald elected mayor.
- 1913 James Michael Curley elected mayor for the first time.
- 1918 The Red Sox celebrate their World Series victory; a championship drought (of 81 years, and counting) begins.
- 1919 A storage tank at the corner of Foster and Commercial streets ruptures, spilling 2 million gallons of raw molasses into the streets of the North End, killing 21 people and injuring 150.
- 1930s The Great Depression devastates what remains of New England's industrial base.

continues

- **1938** Guest conductor Nadia Boulanger leads the Boston Symphony Orchestra, the first woman to do so.
- **1940s** World War II and the accompanying industrial frenzy restore some vitality to the economy, particularly the shipyards.
- **1942** A fire at the Cocoanut Grove nightclub kills 491 people.
- **1946** John F. Kennedy is elected to Congress from Boston's First Congressional District.
- **1954** The first successful human-to-human organ transplant (of a kidney) is performed at Peter Bent Brigham Hospital.
- **1957** The Boston Celtics win the first of their 16 NBA championships.
- **1958** The Freedom Trail is mapped out and painted.
- **1959** Construction of the Prudential Center begins, and with it, the transformation of the skyline.
- **1962** Scollay Square is razed to make room for Government Center. Doctors at Massachusetts General Hospital carry out the first successful reattachment of a human limb, a 12-year-old boy's right arm.
- **1966** Massachusetts Attorney General Edward Brooke, a Republican, becomes the first black elected to the U.S. Senate in the 20th century.
- **1969** Students protesting the Vietnam War occupy University Hall at Harvard.
- **1974** In September (20 years after the U.S. Supreme Court made school segregation illegal), school busing begins citywide, sparking unrest in Roxbury and Charlestown.

continues

The largest project, started in 1835 and completed in 1882, was the filling of the Back Bay, the body of mud flats and marshes that gave its name to the present-day neighborhood. Beginning in 1857, much of the fill came by railroad from Needham. In the 19th century the city tripled in area, creating badly needed space.

By the mid-1800s, Ralph Waldo Emerson, Oliver Wendell Holmes, Henry Wadsworth Longfellow, Nathaniel Hawthorne, Bronson and Louisa May Alcott, John Greenleaf Whittier, Walt Whitman, Henry David Thoreau, and even Charles Dickens (briefly) and Mark Twain (more briefly) had appeared on the local literary scene. William Lloyd Garrison published the weekly *Liberator* newspaper, a powerful voice in the antislavery and social reform movements. Boston became an important stop on the Underground Railroad, the secret network developed by the abolitionists to smuggle runaway slaves into Canada.

LOCAL GLORY   During the Civil War (1861 to 1865), abolitionist sentiment was the order of the day—to such a degree that the rolls listing the names of the war dead in Harvard's Memorial Hall include only members of the Union Army. Massachusetts' contributions to the war effort included enormous quantities of firearms, shoes, blankets, tents, and men.

The famed black abolitionist Frederick Douglass, a former member of the Massachusetts Anti-Slavery Society, helped recruit the 54th and 55th Massachusetts Colored Regiments. The story of the 54th, the first army unit made up of free black soldiers, and its commander, Colonel Robert Gould Shaw, is told in the movie *Glory.*

A CAPITAL CITY   The railroad boom of the 1820s and 1830s and the flood of immigration that began soon after had made New England an industrial center, and Boston, then as now, was its unofficial capital. Thousands of immigrants from Ireland settled in the city, the first ethnic group to do so in great numbers since the French Huguenots in the early 18th century. Signs reading NO IRISH NEED APPLY became scarce as the new arrivals gained political power, and the first Irish mayor was elected in 1885.

By this time the class split in society was a chasm, with the influx of immigrants who swelled the ranks of the local working class adding to the social tension. The Irish led the way and were followed by eastern European Jewish, Italian, and

Portuguese immigrants, who had their own neighborhoods, churches, schools, newspapers, and livelihoods that intersected only occasionally with "proper" society.

Even as the upper crust was sowing seeds that would wind up enriching everyone—the Boston Symphony, the Boston Public Library, and the Museum of Fine Arts were founded in the second half of the 19th century—it was engaging in prudish behavior that gained Boston a reputation for making snobbery an art form. In 1878 the censorious Watch and Ward Society was founded (as the New England Society for the Suppression of Vice), and the phrase "banned in Boston" soon made its way into the American vocabulary. In 1889 the private St. Botolph Club removed John Singer Sargent's portrait of Isabella Stewart Gardner from public view (it's now at the museum that bears her name) because her dress was too tight.

The Boston Brahmins could keep their new neighbors out of many areas of their lives, but not politics. The forebears of the Kennedy clan had by now appeared on the scene—John F. "Honey Fitz" Fitzgerald, Rose Kennedy's father, was elected mayor in 1910—and the world was changing.

Although World War II bolstered Boston's Depression-ravaged industrial economy, the war's end touched off an economic transformation. Shipping declined, along with New England's textile, shoe, and glass industries, at the same time that students on the G.I. Bill were pouring into area colleges and universities. The rise of high technology led to new construction, changing the look of the city yet again. The 1960s saw the beginning of a building boom that continues to this day, after a lull during the recession of the late 1980s.

- **1976** The restored Faneuil Hall Marketplace opens.
- **1988** The Central Artery/Third Harbor Tunnel Project is approved.
- **1993** Thomas Menino is elected mayor, becoming the first Italian-American to hold the office.
- **1995** The New England Holocaust Memorial is dedicated. The FleetCenter opens, replacing Boston Garden as the home of the Celtics (basketball) and Bruins (hockey).
- **1996** Mayor Menino announces plans for a $45 million renovation of the buildings along the Freedom Trail.
- **1997** The renovated Old South Meeting House, an important stop on the Freedom Trail, reopens with new multimedia exhibits. Menino runs unopposed, becoming the first mayor in the city's recorded history to do so.
- **1999** The sports world comes to the Boston area in the form of the NCAA men's basketball tournament, the Major League Baseball All-Star Game, and golf's Ryder Cup.

LOSING COMMON GROUND   The mid-1970s were scarred by the incidents surrounding the Boston busing crisis, sparked by a court-ordered school desegregation plan enacted in 1974 that touched off riots, violence, and a white boycott. Because of "white flight," Boston is now what urban planners call a "doughnut city." It has a relatively large black population (25% of Boston residents are black, compared with 11% of the U.S. population) surrounded by many lily-white suburbs. It has battled its reputation for racism with varying degrees of success. One of the most integrated neighborhoods, Jamaica Plain, is linked to the least integrated, Charlestown—but only by the Orange Line of the subway. The school system has yet to fully recover from the traumatic experience of busing, but every year it sends thousands of students on to the institutions of higher learning that continue to be Boston's greatest claim to fame.

To get a sense of what Boston is (and is not) like today, hit the streets. The puritanical Bostonian is virtually extinct, but you can still uncover traces of the groups, institutions, and events that have shaped history to make Boston the complex city you see before you.

4 Famous Bostonians

Samuel Adams (1722–1803)   Perhaps best known today as the namesake of the excellent local beer, Adams was a leader of the American Revolution, and he often spoke at Faneuil Hall, where his statue now stands. An organizer of the Sons of Liberty and the Boston Tea Party, he later served as governor (1794–1797).

Larry Bird (b. 1956)   The "hick from French Lick (Indiana)" joined the Celtics in 1979 and led them to three National Basketball Association titles by 1986. Whether he was the best player in team history is open to (lengthy, contentious) debate, but he's certainly the most famous. Although he retired after the 1992 Olympics, you'll still see his no. 33 jersey around town.

Louis D. Brandeis (1856–1941)   The first Jewish justice on the United States Supreme Court, Brandeis was a public advocate for consumers and labor unions. A graduate of Harvard Law School, he practiced in Boston before his appointment to the court. Brandeis University in suburban Waltham is named for him.

Charles Bulfinch (1763–1844)   The foremost practitioner of the Federal style of architecture, Bulfinch designed the State House, St. Stephen's Church in the North End, University Hall at Harvard, the central part of Massachusetts General Hospital, and many Beacon Hill mansions. He also completed the U.S. Capitol and supervised the expansion of Faneuil Hall.

Sarah Caldwell (b. 1929)   Caldwell founded the Opera Company of Boston in 1957 and brought first-rate opera, which has had a tough time in Boston, back to the city. As stage director and operatic conductor, she has supervised more than 45 productions of traditional and contemporary works. In 1997 she received the National Medal of the Arts, the government's highest honor for artists.

Julia Child (b. 1912)   A Cambridge resident, "The French Chef" became a TV star in 1963 on Boston's WGBH. A respected author and teacher, she helped put the city on the gastronomic map even before she was immortalized on "Saturday Night Live."

John Singleton Copley (1738–1815)   Considered the first great portrait painter in North America, Copley made his reputation in Boston before relocating to London in 1775. Many of his best-known works are in the collection of the Museum of Fine Arts.

James Michael Curley (1874–1958)   A legend in Boston politics, the colorful Democratic boss served as mayor four times, as governor, as a congressman, and even as a federal prisoner (he was arrested for fraud but was later pardoned). His fame endures—contemporary-music fans might recognize him as the subject of a 1997 Mighty Mighty Bosstones song, "The Rascal King."

Ralph Waldo Emerson (1803–1882)   A central figure in the literary and philosophical "flowering of New England," Emerson was born in Boston and in his later years was known as "the sage of Concord." An ordained minister, he gained fame as a philosopher, poet, essayist, lecturer, and leader of the Transcendentalist movement. He befriended and influenced, among others, Thoreau, Hawthorne, Holmes, Whitman, Bronson and Louisa May Alcott, Longfellow, and Lowell.

Fannie Merritt Farmer (1857–1915)   The author of *The Boston Cooking School Cook Book* helped revolutionize the culinary arts by including measurements and precise directions in recipes. Her 1896 masterwork, available in a facsimile edition, is in use to this day (in revised form) as *The Fannie Farmer Cookbook*.

Arthur Fiedler (1894–1979)   The organizer of the free concert series that began on the Esplanade on July 4, 1929, Fiedler was the conductor of the Boston Pops Orchestra for 50 years. An aluminum rendering of his head is at the Esplanade end of the Arthur Fiedler Footbridge.

William Lloyd Garrison (1805–1879)   An early leader in the antislavery movement and the publisher of the weekly newspaper the *Liberator,* Garrison faced great opposition for his beliefs and activities. At one point a mob dragged him through the streets. Eventually he was honored by President Abraham Lincoln and others for his fight to abolish slavery.

John Hancock (1737–1793)   The first signer of the Declaration of Independence, Hancock, a wealthy merchant and president of the Continental Congress, played a crucial role in financing and organizing the efforts of the colonists during the Revolution. He later served as governor of Massachusetts and mayor of Boston.

John F. Kennedy (1917–1963)   Born in Brookline and educated at Harvard, Kennedy represented Boston in the U.S. House and Massachusetts in the Senate before becoming president in 1960. The youngest man and first Catholic elected to the office, he was a liberal Democrat who had many admirers and enemies. The Kennedy Library and Harvard's Kennedy School of Government celebrate his life and accomplishments.

Malcolm X (1925–1965)   In the 1940s the controversial civil rights leader and outspoken Muslim minister lived in the Roxbury section of Boston for several years, during which he worked briefly at the Parker House hotel and ran a burglary ring near Harvard Square. He also served time in Charlestown Prison and in a penal colony in Norfolk, Massachusetts, where he experienced his religious awakening and educated himself by copying the dictionary.

Frederick Law Olmsted (1822–1903)   Best known as the codesigner of New York's Central Park, Olmsted coined the term "landscape architect" to describe his work creating city gardens and parks. He conceived Boston's "Emerald Necklace," a 7-mile network of parks that includes Boston Common, the Public Garden, the Commonwealth Avenue mall, the Charles River Esplanade, the Back Bay Fens, the Arnold Arboretum, and Franklin Park.

Bobby Orr (b. 1948)   Considered the National Hockey League's best defenseman ever, Orr played for the Bruins from 1967–1976. A brilliant skater and defender as well as a potent scoring threat, "Number 4" led the team to its most recent Stanley Cup championship in 1972.

Paul Revere (1735–1818)   Immortalized in Henry Wadsworth Longfellow's poem "Paul Revere's Ride," the patriot and soldier was trained as a silversmith and also worked as a printer, engraver, and bell manufacturer. His silver, the finest of the period, is on view in many area museums and at his home in the North End, which is open to visitors.

Ted Williams (b. 1918)   The legendary Red Sox slugger was born in San Diego and retired to Florida, but it was in Boston that he achieved his stated goal: "All I want out of life is that when I walk down the street folks will say, 'There goes the greatest hitter who ever lived.'"

5 The Architectural Landscape

New York has the Statue of Liberty. Paris has the Eiffel Tower. Seattle has the Space Needle. Sydney, Australia, has the Opera House. Boston has . . . red brick.

Photo Synthesis

Boston is such a shutterbug magnet that residents have been known to offer to snap a picture of a visiting family even before being asked. Arrange Junior and Sissy in the lap of one of the area's numerous portrait sculptures, or take a step back and capture the juxtaposition of a 19th-century steeple silhouetted against a 20th-century office tower.

Say "Cheese": At the bronze **teddy bear** in front of FAO Schwarz, 440 Boylston St. (at Berkeley). Arm-in-arm or deep in thought with Mayor **James Michael Curley,** in the park on Union Street across North Street from Faneuil Hall. Pulling the cigar away from Celtics legend **Red Auerbach,** between the South Canopy of Quincy Market and the South Market building, Faneuil Hall Marketplace. Falling at the feet of a Colonial hero—pedestals support **Benjamin Franklin** (School Street, in front of Old City Hall), **Paul Revere** (Hanover Street at Clark, across from St. Stephen's Church), and **George Washington** (in the Public Garden at the foot of the Commonwealth Avenue Mall). Perched on Mrs. Mallard (or one of her babies if you fit) of *Make Way for Ducklings* fame, in the Public Garden near the corner of Beacon and Charles streets. Outdistancing the winner (or the runner-up) captured in *The Tortoise and Hare at Copley Square,* in front of Trinity Church. And at a spot so popular that the grass on the area favored by photographers had to be paved over, in front of **John Harvard,** Harvard Yard, Cambridge.

Say "Ooh": Always remember to look up for a quirky perspective on the face of the city. Capture a church against a backdrop of skyscrapers on **Tremont Street** (with the Boston Common Visitor Information Center at your back, turn left toward Park Street Church) or **Boylston Street** (in front of the Four Seasons Hotel, turn left toward the Arlington Street Church; across from Trinity Church, focus on the Hancock Tower). Kill two birds with one stone: pointing up at the Paul Revere statue on Hanover Street, you can lock in the **Old North Church** in the background, or walk around the statue for a new perspective on **St. Stephen's Church.** The Old North Church crops up all over the North End and Charlestown, as the **Hancock Tower** does throughout the Back Bay. And if your travels take you to the area around the Charles Street MBTA stop, wander out onto the **Longfellow Bridge,** especially at twilight—the views of the river are splendid, and if you hit it just right, the moon appears to shine out of the Hancock Tower.

Other building materials are widely used, of course, but in forming a mental picture of the city, most people return inexorably to red brick. It's everywhere, from the **Old North Church** (1723) to the **Boston Harbor Hotel** (1987). Those buildings bookend the central waterfront, irresistibly drawing the eye to their dramatic architecture. The church is small compared with the office towers and condo complexes nearby, but as ever, it dwarfs its closest neighbors. The hotel's landmark archway allows a peek of downtown and, often, of a flag or banner flapping in the courtyard under the huge dome.

Boston's wide variety of architecture makes it a visual treat. Fashions change, buildings disappear, urban renewal leads to questionable decisions; but everywhere you go, there's something interesting to look at.

MATERIAL GOODS Built around 1680, the **Paul Revere House** on North Square is a reminder that for Boston's first 2 centuries, buildings were mostly made

Impressions

Clear out 800,000 people and preserve it as a museum piece.
—Architect Frank Lloyd Wright (1867–1959) on Boston, 1955

of wood, and huge portions of the town regularly burned to the ground. The house is colonial in age but Tudor, rather than typically Colonial, in style. The casement windows and overhanging second floor are medieval features, and when the Reveres moved in, in 1770, the house was no longer fashionable. The one next door would have been: the **Pierce/Hichborn House,** constructed of brick around 1711, is a good example of the Georgian architecture often seen in 18th-century Boston.

After the Revolution, the Federal style dominated; it was the rage from 1780 to 1820. In Boston the new style was closely associated with architect **Charles Bulfinch** (in Salem, Samuel McIntire was similarly influential).

Bulfinch's work can be seen all over Boston, most conspicuously in the **State House** (1797) and in many Beacon Hill residences. The new Americans rejected British influence after the war and turned to classical antiquity (filtered through the Scottish architect Robert Adam) for the austere features that characterize the style: Ionic and Corinthian detailing, frequently in white against red brick or clapboard; fanlights over doors; and an almost maniacal insistence on symmetry. At **141 Cambridge St.** (1796), the first residence Bulfinch designed for Harrison Gray Otis, he even devised a room with one false door to balance the real one. Bulfinch also designed **St. Stephen's Church** (1804) in the North End, Harvard's **University Hall** (1814), and the central part of Massachusetts General Hospital, now known as **Bulfinch Pavilion** (1818). He also planned the 1805 enlargement of **Faneuil Hall,** which made it three times the size it was when it opened in 1742.

OTHER NOTABLES No other architect is as closely associated with Boston as Bulfinch, but in a brief visit you're likely to see just as much of the work of several others. Alexander Parris designed **Quincy Market** (1826), the Greek Revival centerpiece of Faneuil Hall Marketplace. It was renovated and reopened in 1976 for the Bicentennial celebration. Across town, **Trinity Church** (1877), the Romanesque showpiece in Copley Square, is H. H. Richardson's masterwork. Facing it is Charles McKim's **Boston Public Library** (1885 to 1895), an imposing structure with columns and majestic staircases influenced by the Bibliothèque Nationale in Paris.

Fascinating architectural areas lie north and south of Copley Square. To the north is the **Back Bay,** built on landfill, which permitted a logical street pattern. The grid—an anomaly in Boston—was planned in the 1860s and 1870s mostly by Arthur Gilman, and the Parisian flavor of the boulevards reflects his interest in French Second Empire style. It's also evident in Gilman's design (with Gridley J. F. Bryant) of **Old City Hall** (1862) on School Street, whose mansard roof was an early example of a style duplicated on hundreds of town houses in the Back Bay. Most of the neighborhood's lavish Victorian mansions are no longer single-family residences but are divided into apartments or used as businesses, schools, or public buildings. Heading south from Copley Square, you come to the **South End,** another trove of Victoriana whose park-studded layout owes more to London than to Paris.

PEI HEYDAY The architecture of the building boom that started in the 1960s owes a great deal to the fertile mind of a former Harvard instructor, **I. M. Pei.** His firm was responsible for much of the new construction, usually to good effect. The **Christian Science Center** (1973), the **John F. Kennedy Library** (1979), and the **West Wing of the Museum of Fine Arts** (1981) are rousing successes. The **John**

Hancock Tower (1974) is the most dramatic point in the Boston skyline, but it began its life by shedding panes of glass onto the street below (the problem has been corrected).

Government Center dates to the early 1960s and is resented by many Bostonians less for its inelegant plainness than because it replaced Scollay Square. That gritty, congested area was filled with theaters, shops, and burlesque houses, and its decrepitude and appeal are recalled with equal affection.

Government Center's greatest offense is that it surrounds **City Hall,** a utilitarian monstrosity whose numerous sins are just starting to be corrected. The vast brick wasteland of City Hall Plaza has been broken up by a small park, and there's talk of a hotel and a music hall on the plaza and a restaurant on the roof of City Hall. Until that happens, it's still possible to do a little trick: facing the building from the plaza or from Faneuil Hall, hold up the "tails" side of a nickel, upside-down. The resemblance to Monticello (Thomas Jefferson's Virginia estate) is eerie.

Visitors today should be forgiven if they look around and conclude that the city's motto is "This Is a Hard Hat Area." Construction sites litter the metropolitan area, a sign of the booming local economy and the omnipresent Central Artery project. As vacant lots are developed, historic structures are renovated, and the debate over the future of the South Boston waterfront drags on, it's heartening to see that the preferred building material on projects of every description seems to be red brick.

6 Boston Cuisine: A Gift from the Sea (& Land)

SEAFOOD Nutritionists remind us of what Bostonians already know: fish is good for you. It has become a staple on restaurant menus across the country, and Boston is one of the best places to try some. Chefs and owners of the city's best restaurants visit the docks and markets before dawn to make sure that the day's specials are just that. If you've never had fresh fish or shellfish, you're in for a treat.

You might see some unfamiliar terms. *Scrod* or *schrod* is a generic term for fresh white-fleshed fish, almost always served in fillets. Some people claim that schrod (with an *h*) is haddock, and scrod is cod, pollock, or hake. However it's spelled, scrod is served fried (often in fish-and-chips), broiled, poached, and baked. Other species of fish often seen on Boston menus (not always locally caught, but always skillfully prepared) include salmon, tuna, bluefish, flounder, sole, tilefish (another white-fleshed fish), striped bass, char, and monkfish. Local shellfish includes lobster, clams, scallops, mussels, shrimp, and oysters.

Fish appears in chowder too, but more often you'll see **clam chowder,** a staple at restaurants in every price range. New England clam chowder consists of chopped hard-shell clams, potatoes, cream, salt pork (usually), onions (usually), celery (sometimes), and milk (sometimes)—but never, ever, tomatoes. They would make the soup Manhattan clam chowder, a New York favorite that is almost impossible to find in restaurants north of Connecticut.

If you want clams but you don't want soup, at many places you can order **steamers** (soft-shell clams cooked in the shell) as an appetizer or a main dish. More common on the appetizer menu are hard-shell clams—littlenecks (small) or cherrystones (medium-sized)—served raw, like oysters. At a "raw bar," you can order clams and oysters singly or by the dozen or half-dozen. They're opened (a fascinating procedure you may be allowed to watch) and served on a bed of ice with a wedge of lemon, hot sauce, and sometimes a dish of horseradish. Technically, all hard-shell clams are quahogs (say "*co*-hogs"), but that term is usually reserved for large specimens. They're often served stuffed—the flesh is chopped, seasoned, mixed with bread crumbs, and cooked in the shells.

New England **fried clams** are particularly good. Fresh, not frozen, they come whole (with the plump belly) or in "strips" (without), lightly battered and served with french fries and coleslaw. Even greasy fried clams are ambrosial, and prepared correctly, they're a delicacy. You'll probably also see the **roll,** a hot dog bun filled with seafood. A roll is perfect if you're a light eater or on a budget; it can get expensive to order full platters of clams or other popular fillings such as seafood salad and lobster.

Mmm, **lobster.** Lobster was once so abundant off the Massachusetts coast that the resident Indians showed the Pilgrims how to use the ugly crustaceans as fertilizer. Today, the supply fluctuates by the day, boosting or depressing the price in the market and on the menu. It's expensive, so many Bostonians wait for a special occasion to have it. Order lobster boiled or steamed and you'll get a plastic bib, a nutcracker (for the claws and tail), a pick (for the legs), drawn butter (for dipping), and a bowl (for the carcass). Your server can give you pointers. If you want someone else to do the dirty work, lobster is also available stuffed, broiled, baked, in a "pie" (usually a casserole), in a cream sauce, over pasta, in salad, and in bisque (a rich, creamy soup).

BAKED BEANS & SWEETS   Traditional **Boston baked beans** originated in the days when church was an all-day affair and cooking on the Sabbath was forbidden. Typically, a crock of beans was set in a brick oven (next to a huge walk-in cooking fireplace) on Saturday to cook in the retained heat until Sunday dinner at noon.

Boston baked beans are prepared by soaking dried pea beans or navy beans in water overnight and then boiling them briefly. The cooked beans then go into a crock with dry mustard, brown sugar or molasses, some cooking water or beer, and sometimes onions, ketchup, or vinegar. The mixture is topped with strips of salt pork and cooked for about 8 hours. Made correctly, the dish that earned Boston the nickname "Beantown" is wonderful. In the sort of restaurant that serves real baked beans, you'll probably also see cornbread and **brown bread,** which is more of a steamed pudding of whole wheat and rye flour, cornmeal, molasses, buttermilk, and, usually, raisins.

If you're getting the idea that molasses is important in traditional New England cooking, you're right. Molasses fiends (this isn't for amateurs) will want to try **Indian pudding,** a heavy dish that's basically very sweet cornmeal mush topped with whipped cream or ice cream.

For **ice cream** on its own, you couldn't have come to a better place. Although the ice cream mania of 10 or 15 years ago has passed, people still gobble anything chilly year-round—frozen yogurt in a snowbank, anyone? Be aware that a milk shake in Boston (and other parts of New England) is exactly that: milk, shaken, with some flavored syrup. The concoction the rest of the world considers a milk shake is a **frappe** (say "frap") to Bostonians.

Finally, **Boston cream pie** is actually golden layer cake sandwiched around custard and topped with chocolate glaze—no cream, no pie.

7 Recommended Books, Films & TV

BOOKS   A list of authors with ties to Boston could fill a book of its own and still only scratch the surface. To get in the mood for Boston before visiting, let the impulse that inspired you to make the trip guide you around the library or bookstore. Here are a few suggestions.

For children, *Make Way for Ducklings,* by Robert McCloskey, is a classic that tells the story of Mrs. Mallard and her babies on the loose in the Back Bay. In honor of the book, bronze statues of the family are in the Public Garden. Slightly older kids might know the Public Garden as the setting of part of *The Trumpet of the Swan,* by E. B. White. An excellent historical title is *Johnny Tremain,* by Esther Forbes, a fictional boy's-eye-view account of the Revolutionary War era.

For adults, two splendid Pulitzer Prize winners chronicle the city's history. *Paul Revere and the World He Lived In* is Forbes's look at Boston before, during, and after the Revolution. J. Anthony Lukas's *Common Ground: A Turbulent Decade in the Lives of Three American Families* is the definitive account of the busing crisis of the 1970s.

Architecture buffs will enjoy *Cityscapes of Boston,* by Robert Campbell and Peter Vanderwarker, *Lost Boston,* by Jane Holtz Kay, and Susan and Michael Southworth's *A.I.A. Guide to Boston. The Proper Bostonians,* by Cleveland Amory, and *The Friends of Eddie Coyle,* by George V. Higgins, offer looks at wildly different strata of Boston society.

"Paul Revere's Ride," Henry Wadsworth Longfellow's classic but historically inaccurate poem about the events of April 18–19, 1775, is collected in many anthologies. It's a must if you plan to visit Lexington and Concord.

FILMS & TV   Television has done more than any movie to make Boston familiar to international audiences, and film is gaining fast. The Boston area isn't the nonstop backdrop that New York and Vancouver have become, but don't be surprised to stumble upon a crew or read about a location shoot in the newspapers.

As luck would have it, one of the best Boston movies ever was released in 1997, and it should be available on video by the time you read this. The extraordinary *Good Will Hunting* (starring Matt Damon, Robin Williams, Ben Affleck, and Minnie Driver) not only makes Boston and Cambridge look sensational but also perceptively explores the town-gown divide. Coauthors Affleck and Damon are boyhood friends from Cambridge, and Damon is a couple of semesters short of his Harvard degree. Not to worry—they're a lot easier to get than Academy Awards. Damon and Affleck shared the honor for best screenplay, and Williams was voted best supporting actor.

Other recent efforts filmed in the Boston area but not released at press time include *A Civil Action* (John Travolta), *The Proposition* (Madeleine Stowe and Kenneth Branagh), *The Spanish Prisoner* (Steve Martin and Campbell Scott), and *Brass Ring* (Anne Meara and Donnie Wahlberg).

Blown Away (Jeff Bridges and Tommy Lee Jones) makes the city look spectacular, especially in the scenes when the action first shifts to Boston. Classic movies that give more than a glimpse of the region include *The Witches of Eastwick* (Jack Nicholson, Cher, and Susan Sarandon), *Glory* (Denzel Washington and Matthew Broderick), *The Verdict* (Paul Newman and James Mason), and the sentimental favorite, *Love Story* (Ryan O'Neal and Ali MacGraw).

On the small screen, *Cheers* (no, the bar isn't anything like the set), *St. Elsewhere,* and *Spenser: For Hire* all used the city as a backdrop. The sixth installment of MTV's *The Real World,* which first aired in 1997, made a converted Beacon Hill firehouse its base of operations and roamed all over town. Fox's *Ally McBeal* and ABC's *The Practice* are filmed elsewhere and hadn't done much with their Boston settings at press time. But they did have a lot of people wondering where in town lawyers look like *that.*

Planning a Trip to Boston

2

This chapter addresses the practical issues that arise after you've selected a destination. Now that you've decided to visit Boston, how do you get there? How much will it cost? When should you go? How can you learn more? You'll find answers here, along with information about the climate and the events, festivals, and parades you might want to see.

1 Visitor Information & Money

VISITOR INFORMATION

The **Greater Boston Convention & Visitors Bureau** (2 Copley Place, Suite 105, Boston, MA 02116-6501; ☎ **888/ SEE-BOSTON** or 617/536-4100; fax 617/424-7664; www. bostonusa.com; e-mail visitor@bostonusa.com) offers a comprehensive visitor information kit and a "Kids Love Boston" kit. Each kit costs $5.25 and includes a travel planner, guidebook, map, and coupon book with shopping, dining, attractions, and nightlife discounts. The bureau provides information on attractions, dining, performing arts and nightlife, shopping, and travel services through its **"Boston by Phone"** service, accessible from the main phone numbers.

The **Massachusetts Office of Travel and Tourism** (100 Cambridge St., 13th floor, Boston, MA 02202; ☎ **800/227-6277** or 617/727-3201; fax 617/727-6525; www.mass-vacation.com; e-mail vacationinfo@state.ma.us) has a great Web site that even offers a "lobster tutorial." The office publishes a free *Getaway Guide* magazine that includes information about attractions and lodgings, a map, and a seasonal calendar.

For information about Cambridge, contact the **Cambridge Office for Tourism** (18 Brattle St., Cambridge, MA 02138; ☎ **800/862-5678** or 617/441-2884; fax 617/441-7736; e-mail cambtour@us1.channel1.com).

Plentiful information about the Boston area is available on the Internet. Businesses of all descriptions launch Web sites every day; you can track down useful advice by running a search from your browser, finding a site with lots of good links, or both. Here are some good places to start.

Two **Excite** sites that are packed with information and links are www.city.net/countries/united_states/massachusetts/boston and

What Things Cost in Boston	U.S. $
Taxi from airport to downtown Boston	18.00–24.00
Bus from airport to downtown Boston	6.00–8.00
MBTA subway token	.85
Double at Radisson Hotel Boston (expensive)	160.00–275.00
Double at Newbury Guest House (moderate)	105.00–140.00
Double at Longwood Inn (inexpensive)	69.00–79.00
Lunch for one at Union Oyster House (expensive)	10.00–23.00
Lunch for one at Durgin-Park (moderate)	6.00–20.00
Lunch for one at Bartley's Burger Cottage (inexpensive)	4.00–10.50
Dinner for one, without wine, at Rialto (very expensive)	20.00–45.00
Dinner for one, without wine, at Legal Seafood (expensive)	14.00–30.00
Dinner for one, without wine, at the Elephant Walk (moderate)	10.00–23.00
Glass of beer	2.75–4.50
Coca-Cola	.75–1.00
Cup of coffee	1.00 and up
Roll of ASA 100 Kodacolor film, 36 exposures	6.75–8.00
Admission to the Museum of Fine Arts	10.00
Movie ticket	4.75–7.75
Theater ticket	30.00–90.00

www.city.net/countries/united_states/massachusetts/cambridge. The excellent site run by the **Massachusetts Port Authority** (www.massport.com) lists many links for visitors, as do the cities of **Boston** (www.ci.boston.ma.us) and **Cambridge** (www.ci.cambridge.ma.us). The Convention & Visitors Bureau offers listings of visitor services that can be reached through **toll-free numbers** (www.dvm.com/users/dvm/boston). When you're ready to start planning activities, check out ✪ **Boston.com** (www.boston.com), which has links to publications; museums and other arts resources, including the Museum of Fine Arts; and an interactive tour of the Freedom Trail.

MONEY

Monetary descriptions and currency exchange information for foreign travelers appear in chapter 3.

Credit cards are accepted at most establishments in the Boston area, including many museums and other cultural attractions, so carrying large quantities of cash isn't usually necessary. When you do need folding money, you can find **Automated Teller Machines** (**ATMs**), also known as cash machines, all over Boston. Local networks typically charge a fee ($1 or $2) for access by a customer whose account is with a "foreign" bank, and your bank at home might also levy a fee. You can find ATMs at banks, shopping malls, supermarkets, the airport, and some stores.

Call your ATM network before you leave home to check out its Boston locations. **Cirrus** (☎ 800/424-7787) and **PLUS Global ATM Locator Service**

(☎ 800/843-7587) are international networks that connect with most other ATM institutions. They supply locations of machines over the phone.

If you must carry currency, U.S. dollar **traveler's checks** are the safest way to do so. They're as good as cash in most places, and they can be replaced if they are lost or stolen. Some establishments restrict the amount they will accept or cash, so purchase some traveler's checks in small denominations for convenience. Before you leave home, make a list of the serial numbers and keep it separate from the checks in case you need to replace them.

2 When to Go

Boston attracts large numbers of visitors year-round—the average occupancy rate tops 80%—and hotel rooms can occasionally be difficult to find. Make your reservations as early as possible.

The periods around college graduation (May and early June) and the major city-wide events (listed below) are especially busy. Spring and fall are popular times for conventions. Foliage season (mid-September to early November), when many leaf-peepers stay in the Boston area or pass through on the way to northern New England, has become a huge draw in recent years. The "slow" season is January through March, when many hotels offer great deals, especially on weekends. This is also the season when the city is most likely to be socked in by snow, however, and when some suburban attractions are closed for the winter.

Boston's Average Temperatures & Rainfall

	Jan	Feb	Mar	Apr	May	June	July	Aug	Sept	Oct	Nov	Dec
Temp. (°F)	30	31	38	49	59	68	74	72	65	55	45	34
Rainfall (in.)	4.0	3.7	4.1	3.7	3.5	2.9	2.7	3.7	3.4	3.4	4.2	4.9

CLIMATE

You've probably already heard the saying about New England weather—"If you don't like it, wait 10 minutes." It's not as volatile as all that, but variations from day to day can be enormous. Fall and spring are the best bets for moderate temperatures, but spring is brief (it doesn't really settle in until early May, and snow in early April isn't inconceivable). Summers are hot and sticky, especially in July and August, and winters are cold and usually snowy—bring a warm coat and sturdy boots. But you can roast in May and freeze in June, shiver in July and wish you'd packed shorts in March. Dressing in layers is always a good idea.

When in Boston, you can check the weather forecast by looking up at the short column of lights on top of the old John Hancock building in the Back Bay. (The new Hancock building is the 60-story glass tower next door.) A steady blue light means clear weather; flashing blue, cloudy; steady red, rain; flashing red, snow—except during the summer, when flashing red means the Red Sox game has been canceled.

BOSTON CALENDAR OF EVENTS

The **Greater Boston Convention & Visitors Bureau** (☎ 800/SEE-BOSTON or 617/536-4100; www.bostonusa.com) operates a regularly updated hotline that describes ongoing and upcoming events.

Impressions

If Archer had tried to imagine Ellen Olenska in improbable scenes, he could not have called up any into which it was more difficult to fit her than this heat-prostrated and deserted Boston.

—Edith Wharton, *The Age of Innocence,* 1920

I guess God made Boston on a wet Sunday.

—Raymond Chandler, 1949

The **Mayor's Office of Special Events & Tourism** (☎ 617/635-3911) can provide information about specific happenings. The "Calendar" section of the Thursday *Globe* and the "Scene" section of the Friday *Herald* are always packed with ideas.

January

- **Martin Luther King, Jr. Birthday Celebration,** various locations. Events include speeches, musical tributes, gospel celebrations, and panel discussions. Check special listings in the Thursday *Boston Globe* "Calendar" section for specifics. Third Monday of the month.
- **Chinese New Year,** Chinatown. Dragon parade (which draws a crowd no matter how cold it is), fireworks, and many raucous festivals. Special programs at the Children's Museum. Depending on the Chinese lunar calendar, the holiday falls between January 21 and February 19.
- **Boston Wine Festival,** Boston Harbor Hotel and other locations. Tastings, classes, lectures, receptions, and meals provide a lively liquid diversion in the dead of winter. Call the festival reservation line (☎ 888/660-WINE) for details. January through early April.

February

- **Black History Month,** various locations. Activities include lectures, discussions, special museum exhibits, and tours of the Black Heritage Trail led by National Park Service rangers (☎ 617/742-5415). All month.
- **Beanpot Hockey Tournament,** FleetCenter (☎ 617/624-1000). Boston College, Boston University, Harvard University, and Northeastern University vie for bragging rights and a trophy shaped like a bean pot. First two Mondays of the month.
- **School Vacation Week,** various locations. More of an occasion than an event. The slate of activities for children includes plays, special exhibitions and programs, and tours. Contact individual attractions for information on special programs and extended hours. Third week of the month.

March

- **St. Patrick's Day/Evacuation Day.** Parade, South Boston. Celebration, Faneuil Hall Marketplace. The 5-mile parade salutes the city's Irish heritage and the day British troops left Boston in 1776. Head to Faneuil Hall Marketplace for music, dancing, and food. March 17.
- **New England Spring Flower Show,** Bayside Expo Center, Dorchester. This annual harbinger of spring presented by the **Massachusetts Horticultural Society** (☎ 617/536-9280) draws huge crowds starved for a glimpse of green. Second or third week of the month.
- **Big Apple Circus,** near Museum Wharf. The New York-based "one-ring wonder" performs in a heated tent for about a month every spring to support the

Children's Museum. Visit the museum box office or contact Ticketmaster
(☎ **617/931-ARTS**). Late March through early May.

April

- **Red Sox Opening Day,** Fenway Park. Even if your concierge is a magician, this
  is an extremely tough ticket. Check with the ticket office (☎ **617/267-1700**)
  when tickets for the season go on sale in early January, or try to see the **Patriots
  Day** game, which begins at 11am. Middle of the month.
- **Swan Boats Return** to the Public Garden. Since their introduction in 1877, the
  swan boats have been a symbol of Boston. Like real swans, they go away for the
  winter. Saturday before Patriots Day.

✪ **Patriots Day,** North End, Lexington, and Concord. The events of April 18-19, 1775,
  which signified the start of the Revolutionary War, are commemorated and reen-
  acted. Lanterns are hung in the steeple of the Old North Church. Participants dressed
  as Paul Revere and William Dawes ride from the **Paul Revere House** (☎ **617/
  523-2338**) in the North End to Lexington and Concord to warn the Minutemen that
  "the regulars are out" (not that "the British are coming"—most colonists considered
  themselves British). Battles are fought on the town green in Lexington and then at the
  Old North Bridge in Concord. Contact the **Lexington Chamber of Commerce Visitor Center** (1875 Massachusetts Ave., Lexington, MA 02173; ☎ **617/862-1450**)
  or the **Concord Chamber of Commerce** (2 Lexington Rd., Concord, MA 01742;
  ☎ **508/369-3120**) for information on attending the battle reenactments. Third
  Monday of the month, which is a state holiday.

- **Boston Marathon,** Hopkinton, Massachusetts, to Boston. International stars
  and local amateurs join in the world's oldest and most famous marathon. The
  noon start means elite runners hit Boston about 2 hours later; weekend runners
  stagger across the Boylston Street finish line as much as 6 hours after that. Third
  Monday of the month.

May

- **Museum-Goers' Month,** various locations. Contact individual museums for
  details and schedules of special exhibits, lectures, and events. All month.
- **Boston Kite Festival,** Franklin Park (☎ **617/635-4505**). Kites of all shapes and
  sizes take to the air above a celebration that includes kite-making clinics, music,
  and other entertainment. Middle of the month.
- **Lilac Sunday,** Arnold Arboretum, Jamaica Plain (☎ **617/524-1717**). The only
  day of the year that picnicking is permitted at the Arboretum. From sunrise to
  sunset, wander the grounds and enjoy the sensational spring flowers, including
  more than 400 varieties of lilacs in bloom. Usually the third Sunday of the
  month.
- **Street Performers Festival,** Faneuil Hall Marketplace. Everyone but the pigeons
  gets into the act as musicians, magicians, jugglers, sword-swallowers, and artists
  strut their stuff. End of the month.

June

- **Boston Dairy Festival,** Boston Common. Cows were allowed to graze on
  Boston Common for 200 years; now they return once a year, accompanied by
  other farm animals, milking contests, and children's activities. The "Scooper
  Bowl" ice cream extravaganza takes place simultaneously on City Hall Plaza. First
  week of the month.
- **Dragon Boat Festival,** Charles River near Harvard Square, Cambridge. Teams
  of paddlers synchronized by a drummer propel boats with dragon heads and tails

as they race 500 meters. The winners go to the national championships; the spectators go to a celebration of Chinese culture and food on the shore. Second Sunday of the month.

- **Massachusetts Handicap,** Suffolk Downs (☎ **617/567-3900**). The high point of the local horse-racing season, the "MassCap" is the centerpiece of a million-dollar (in total purses) day. The prestigious main event draws some of the country's best horses. First Saturday of the month.
- **Bunker Hill Parade,** Charlestown. An observation of the Battle of Bunker Hill, June 17, 1775, which the colonists lost. The parade winds through Charlestown to the monument and ends at the Navy Yard. Sunday closest to June 17.
- ✪ *Boston Globe* **Jazz & Blues Festival,** various locations, indoors and outdoors. Big names and rising stars of the music world appear at lunchtime, after-work, evening, and weekend events, some of which are free. Contact the *Globe* (☎ **617/929-2000**) or pick up a copy of the paper for a schedule when you arrive in town. Some events require tickets purchased in advance. Third week of the month.
- **Art Newbury Street,** Newbury Street. Once a year, more than 30 galleries are open and the street is closed from the Public Garden to Massachusetts Avenue as art lovers wander through the special exhibits and enjoy the outdoor entertainment. End of the month.

July

- ✪ **Boston Harborfest,** downtown, the waterfront, and the Harbor Islands. The city puts on its Sunday best for the Fourth of July, which has become a gigantic weeklong celebration of Boston's maritime history and an excuse to get out and have fun. Events surrounding **Harborfest** (45 School St., Boston, MA 02108; ☎ **617/227-1528;** fax 617/227-1886) include concerts, guided tours, talks, cruises, fireworks, the Boston Chowderfest, and the annual turnaround of the USS *Constitution.* First week of the month (June 29 to July 4, 1999; June 28 to July 4, 2000).
- **Boston Pops Concert and Fireworks Display,** Hatch Memorial Shell on the Esplanade. Overnight camping is no longer permitted, but people wait from dawn till dark for the music to start. They also show up at the last minute—the Cambridge side of the river, near Kendall Square, is a good spot to watch the spectacular aerial show. The program includes the *1812 Overture* with actual cannon fire that coincides with the pyrotechnics. July 4.

August

- **Heritage Days,** various locations, Salem. A weeklong event with entertainment, food, and programs highlighting Salem's multicultural heritage. Contact the **Salem Office of Tourism & Cultural Affairs** (☎ **800/777-6848**) for specifics. Second or third week of the month.
- **Italian-American Feasts,** North End. These weekend street fairs begin in July, with the two biggest, the Fishermen's Feast and the Feast of St. Anthony, saved for last. The sublime (fresh seafood prepared while you wait; live music and dancing in the street) mingles with the ridiculous (carnival games and fried-dough stands) to leave a lasting impression of fun and indigestion. Last 2 weekends of the month.

September

- **Cambridge River Festival,** Memorial Drive from John F. Kennedy Street to Western Avenue. A salute to the arts, with music, dancing, children's activities, and international food on the banks of the Charles. Beginning of the month.

Wild World of Sports

The eyes of the sports world will be on the Boston area at least three times in 1999. If you hope to attend these events, you should already have tickets and room reservations (or a big budget and a friend with a futon); if you're scheduling a nonsports visit, consider a different time.

Opening-round games in the **NCAA Division I Men's Basketball Tournament** will take place March 12 and 14 at the **FleetCenter** (☎ **617/624-1000; www.fleetcenter.com**). Teams won't be announced until a week before, but as a rule, the first two rounds are likeliest to produce upset-minded underdogs.

The Major League Baseball **All-Star Game** will take place at **Fenway Park** between July 9 and 13; the exact date wasn't set at press time. It's the first time since 1961 that the Red Sox (☎ **617/267-8661;** www.redsox.com) have played host to the annual American League–National League tilt (that game ended in a 1–1 tie). The attendant festivities include a home-run-hitting contest the day before the game and a FanFest—a carnival-like event that includes interactive demonstrations—the entire previous weekend.

Golf's **Ryder Cup,** a biennial event that pits 12 of the best professionals from the United States against their counterparts from Europe, unfolds September 21 through 26 at **The Country Club** in Brookline (☎ **617/547-1999,** tournament office). Practice rounds on Tuesday and Wednesday precede Thursday's opening ceremonies and 3 days of match play. Individual tickets have already been allotted, but ticket-and-accommodations packages might still be available from **PGA Travel** (☎ **800/283-4653**). Prices start at $2,000 per person.

All of these events will probably sell out well in advance, but never say never (and in this situation, never say "cheap"). A member of the National Association of Ticket Brokers trade organization, **Best for Less,** 170 Milk St., Boston, MA 02109 (☎ **888/888-8499** or 617/350-0050), might be able to hook you up.

- **Boston Film Festival** (☎ 617/925-1378), various locations. Alternative and art films continue their turn around the festival circuit or make their premiere, sometimes accompanied by a talk by an actor or a filmmaker. Most screenings are open to the public without advance tickets. Middle of the month.

October

- **Topsfield Fair** (☎ 508/887-5000), Route 1, Topsfield. The oldest continuously running fair in the country (since 1818) offers agricultural exhibits, live musical performances in the grandstand, and an old-fashioned midway just 40 minutes north of the city. 10 days ending with Columbus Day.
- **Columbus Day Parade,** downtown and the North End. Beginning with a ceremony on City Hall Plaza at 1pm, the parade, appropriately enough, winds up in the city's Italian neighborhood, following Hanover Street to the Coast Guard station on Commercial Street. Second Monday of the month.
- **Ringling Brothers and Barnum & Bailey Circus,** FleetCenter (☎ 617/ 624-1000). The Greatest Show on Earth makes its annual 2-week visit. Middle of the month.
- ✪ **Head of the Charles Regatta,** Boston and Cambridge. High school, college, and postcollegiate rowing teams and individuals—some 4,000 in all—race in front of hordes of fans along the banks of the Charles River and on the bridges spanning

it. The Head of the Charles (☎ **617/864-8415**) always seemed to fall on the crispest, most picturesque Sunday of the season until 1996, when it was canceled because of torrential rains. It is now a 2-day event. End of the month.

Tip: The boats (called "shells") are numbered sequentially and race against the clock from a staggered start. If a higher-numbered team is ahead of one with a lower number, it's making good time.

- **Salem Haunted Happenings,** various locations. Parades, parties, a special MBTA train ride from Boston, fortune-telling, cruises, and tours lead up to a ceremony on Halloween. Contact the **Salem Office of Tourism & Cultural Affairs** (☎ **800/777-6848**) for specifics. Final 2 weeks of the month.

November

- **An Evening With Champions,** Bright Athletic Center, Allston. World-class ice skaters and local students (who once upon a time included 1994 Olympic silver medalist Nancy Kerrigan) stage three performances to benefit the Jimmy Fund, the children's fund-raising arm of the Dana-Farber Cancer Institute. Sponsored by Harvard's **Eliot House** (☎ **617/493-8172**). First weekend of the month.
- **Thanksgiving Celebration,** Plymouth (☎ **800/USA-1620**). The holiday that put Plymouth on the map is observed with a "stroll through the ages," showcasing 17th- and 19th-century Thanksgiving preparations in historic homes. **Plimoth Plantation,** where the colony's first years are re-created, wisely offers a Victorian Thanksgiving feast, for which reservations are required (☎ **508/746-1622**). Thanksgiving Day.

December

- *The Nutcracker,* Wang Center for the Performing Arts. Boston Ballet's annual holiday extravaganza is one of the country's biggest and best. This is *the* traditional way for young Bostonians (and visitors) to be exposed to culture, and the spectacular sets make it practically painless. Call **Ticketmaster** (☎ **617/931-ARTS**) as soon as you plan your trip, ask whether your hotel offers a *Nutcracker* package, or cross your fingers and visit the box office at 270 Tremont St. when you arrive. All month.
- **Christmas Tree Lighting,** Prudential Center. Carol singing precedes the lighting of a magnificent tree from Nova Scotia—an annual expression of thanks from the people of Halifax for Bostonians' help in fighting a devastating fire there in 1917. First Saturday of December.
- **Boston Tea Party Re-enactment,** Tea Party Ship and Museum, Congress Street Bridge (☎ **617/338-1773**). Chafing under British rule, the colonists rose up on December 16, 1773, to strike a blow where it would cause real pain—in the pocketbook. Middle of the month.
- **Christmas Revels,** Sanders Theater, Cambridge. This multicultural celebration of the winter solstice showcases the holiday customs of a different culture each year—recent themes have included Victorian England and the Romany Gypsies. Be ready to sing along. For information, call the **Revels** (☎ **617/621-0505**); for tickets, call the **box office** (☎ **617/496-2222**) or **Ticketmaster** (☎ **617/931-ARTS**). Last 2 weeks of the month.
- ✪ **First Night,** Back Bay and the waterfront. The concept is spreading all over the country, but the original—and still the best—arts-oriented, no-alcohol, city-wide New Year's Eve celebration is in Boston. It begins in the early afternoon and includes a parade, ice sculptures, art exhibitions, theatrical performances, and

indoor and outdoor entertainment. Some attractions require tickets, but for most you just need a First Night button, available for about $15 at visitor centers and stores around the city. For details, contact **First Night** (☎ **617/542-1399**) or check the newspapers when you arrive. It all wraps up at midnight with a spectacular fireworks display over the harbor. December 31.

3 Health & Insurance

Before you leave, be sure you are protected with adequate health insurance coverage and that you understand your insurance provider's procedures for medical treatment when you're away from home. HMOs typically require that anything other than emergency care be preapproved; be sure you have your membership card and know the phone number to call.

INSURANCE

Most travel agents sell low-cost health, loss, and trip-cancellation insurance to their vacationing clients. Rates for these short-term policies are generally reasonable, and the policies allow you to supplement existing coverage with a minimum of complications. Other forms of travel-related insurance are also available, including coverage for lost or damaged baggage. Often a single policy provided by your travel agent will protect you in all of these areas and also will provide supplementary medical coverage.

4 Tips for Travelers with Special Needs

FOR TRAVELERS WITH DISABILITIES

Boston, like all other U.S. cities, has taken the required steps to provide access for people with disabilities. Hotels must provide accessible rooms; museums and street curbs have ramps for wheelchairs. The Americans with Disabilities Act (ADA), effective in 1992, requires all forms of public transportation to provide special services to persons with disabilities.

All **MBTA buses** have lifts or kneelers; call ☎ **800/LIFT-BUS** for more information. Some bus routes are wheelchair accessible at all times; you might have to make a reservation as much as a day in advance for others. Some taxis are now equipped to handle wheelchairs—call individual taxi services to find out whether they are. In addition, there is an **Airport Handicap Van** (☎ **617/561-1769**). For reduced public transportation fares, persons with disabilities can apply to purchase a Transportation Access Pass (TAP) from the **MBTA Access Pass Office,** 10 Boylston Place, Boston, MA 02116 (☎ **617/222-5438**). The application must be completed by a licensed health-care professional.

Many of the major car-rental companies now offer hand-controlled cars for drivers with disabilities. Avis can provide such a vehicle at any of its locations in the United States with 48-hour advance notice; Hertz requires between 24 and 72 hours of advance reservation at most of its locations. **Wheelchair Getaways** (☎ **800/873-4973;** www.blvd.com/wg.htm) rents specialized vans with wheelchair lifts and other features for travelers with disabilities in more than 100 cities across the United States.

Travelers with disabilities might also want to consider joining a tour that caters specifically to them. One of the best operators is **Flying Wheels Travel,** 143 West Bridge (P.O. Box 382), Owatonna, MN 55060 (☎ **800/525-6790**). They offer various escorted tours and cruises, as well as private tours in minivans with lifts. Another good company is **FEDCAP Rehabilitation Services,** 211 W. 14th St., New York, NY 10011. Call ☎ 212/727-4200 or fax 212/721-4374 for information about membership and summer tours.

An excellent source of information is **Very Special Arts Massachusetts,** 2 Boylston St., Boston, MA 02116 (☎ 617/350-7713; fax 617/482-4298; TTY 617/350-6836; www.vsamass.org; e-mail vsamass@aol.com). It has a comprehensive Web site, and it publishes *Access Expressed! Massachusetts: A Cultural Resource Directory* ($5), which includes general access information and specifics about more than 200 arts and entertainment facilities in the state. The **Massachusetts Coalition for Citizens with Disabilities,** 20 Park Plaza, Suite 603, Boston, MA 02116 (☎ 800/55VOTER or 617/482-1336, voice or TDD) is also helpful.

FOR GAY & LESBIAN TRAVELERS

The **Gay and Lesbian Helpline** (☎ 617/267-9001) offers information Monday through Friday from 4 to 11pm, Saturday from 6 to 8:30pm, and Sunday from 6 to 10pm. You can also contact the **Boston Alliance of Gay and Lesbian Youth** (BAGLY) (☎ 800/422-2459; www.bagly.org). *In Publications,* 258 Shawmut Ave., Boston, MA 02118 (☎ 617/426-8246), and *Bay Windows,* 1523 Washington St., Boston, MA 02118 (☎ 617/266-6670), publish weekly newspapers that concentrate on upcoming gay-related events, news, and features. The weekly *Boston Phoenix* publishes a monthly supplement, "One in 10," and has a gay-interest area in its Web site (www.bostonphoenix.com). The *Pink Pages,* 66 Charles St., Boston, MA 02114 (☎ 800/338-6550), is a guide to gay- and lesbian-owned and gay-friendly businesses that's available for $10.05; it also has a comprehensive Web site (www.pinkweb.com/boston.index.html).

FOR SENIORS

Boston-area businesses offer many discounts to seniors with identification. Hotels, restaurants, museums, and movie theaters offer special deals. Discounts are usually offered in restaurants and theaters only at off-peak times, but museums and other attractions offer reduced rates at all times. Seniors can ride the **MBTA** subways for 20¢ (a 65¢ savings), and local bus fares for seniors are 15¢ (a 45¢ savings). On zoned and express buses and on the commuter rail, the senior citizen fare is half the regular fare. On the commuter rail, proof of age is a valid driver's license or passport, but for the subway and buses, you need an MBTA **senior citizen card.** Call in advance for information on purchasing the card, which is available at the Downtown Crossing MBTA station (☎ 617/722-5438) weekdays from 8:30am to 4:15pm.

The **American Association of Retired Persons,** or AARP, 601 E St. NW, Washington, D.C., 20049 (☎ 800/424-3410; www.aarp.org), offers discounts on car rentals, accommodations, airfares, and sightseeing. It's open to anyone 50 or older.

A **Golden Age Passport** gives you free lifetime admission to all recreation areas run by the federal government, including parks and monuments. It's available at any National Park Service site that charges admission.

In addition, most of the major domestic airlines, including American, United, Continental, US Airways, and TWA, offer discount programs for senior travelers—be sure to ask whenever you book a flight.

You might also be interested in the programs for those 60 and older organized by **Elderhostel, Inc.,** 75 Federal St., Boston, MA 02110 (☎ 617/426-8056;

www.elderhostel.org). Participants generally live in a college dorm, take courses at the college in the morning, and explore the city in the afternoon. And **Grand Circle Travel,** 347 Congress St., Boston, MA 02210 (☎ **800/221-2610** or 617/350-7500), organizes educational and adventure vacations for people 50 and up. Although both of these companies have Boston addresses, they run programs all over the country.

FOR FAMILIES

Children (usually under 17, sometimes under 12) can stay free in their parents' hotel room, when using existing bedding. Most hotels charge for cots, and some charge for cribs. Many hotels have family package deals that offer a suite, breakfast, and parking, plus discount coupons for museums and restaurants. The **Greater Boston Convention & Visitors Bureau,** 2 Copley Place, Suite 105, Boston, MA 02116-6501 (☎ **888/SEE-BOSTON** or 617/536-4100; fax 617/424-7664; www.bostonusa.com) sells a "Kids Love Boston" kit ($5.25) with a guidebook, travel planner, map, and discount coupon book.

FOR STUDENTS

Students don't actually rule Boston—it just feels that way sometimes. Museums, theaters, concert halls, and other attractions often offer discounts for college and high-school students with valid identification. During the summer months, students can rent rooms in college dorms on some campuses. Check with the schools for information. Visiting students might want to check campus bulletin boards; many events are open to them. The weekly *Boston Phoenix* also lists activities for students.

5 Getting There

BY PLANE

Most major domestic carriers serve Boston. Be prepared to show at least one form of photo identification that matches the name on your ticket when you board.

The major airlines flying into **Logan International Airport** are **American** (☎ 800/433-7300), **Continental** (☎ 800/523-3273), **Delta** (☎ 800/221-1212), **Midway** (☎ 800/446-4392), **Northwest** (☎ 800/225-2525), **TWA** (☎ 800/221-2000), **United** (☎ 800/241-6522), and **US Airways** (☎ 800/428-4322). Most of the major international carriers also fly into Boston.

The domestic discount airline **Southwest** (☎ 800/435-9792) can be a good choice for those who have more time than money. Southwest flies into T. F. Green Airport, outside Providence, RI, about 50 miles south of Boston. **Bonanza** (☎ 800/556-3815) offers bus service between the airport and Boston's South Station daily from 9am to 9pm; the fare is $15 one-way, $27 round-trip.

FINDING THE BEST AIRFARE To purchase a ticket quickly and without much hassle, go through your travel agent. To get the best price, you'll need to shop around, probably on your own. Fares change constantly; they vary from airline to airline and even from day to day at the same airline. Try to schedule your travel for weekdays during the busy summer season and avoid major holiday periods, when fares go up. Staying over a Saturday night usually means a lower price. Call around, or ask your travel agent to call around, as far in advance as possible. And be flexible if you can—shifting by a day or two can sometimes mean great savings, but you have to ask.

In general, the lowest fares are economy (also known as tourist) or APEX (Advance Purchase Excursion). Economy has no restrictions; APEX requires you to reserve and pay for the ticket 7, 14, 21, or 30 days in advance and stay for a minimum number of days. As a rule, the lower the price, the more trouble and expense it is to change plans. APEX fares are usually nonrefundable, and there is a charge for changing dates. However, the savings are considerable.

Another way to find the cheapest fare is by using the Internet to do the searching for you. There are too many companies now to mention, but a few of the better-respected ones are **Travelocity** (**www.travelocity.com**), **Microsoft Expedia** (**www.expedia.com**), and **Yahoo's Flifo Global** (**http://travel.yahoo.com/travel**). Each has its own little quirks—Travelocity, for example, requires you to register with them—but they all provide variations of the same service. Just enter the dates you want to fly and the cities you want to visit, and the computer looks for the lowest fares. The Yahoo site has a feature called "Fare Beater," which checks flights on other airlines or at different times or dates in hopes of finding an even cheaper fare. Expedia's site e-mails you the best airfare deal once a week if you so choose. Travelocity uses the SABRE computer reservations system that most travel agents use, and it has a "Last Minute Deals" database that advertises really cheap fares for those who can get away at a moment's notice.

Great last-minute deals are also available directly from the airlines themselves through a free e-mail service called **E-savers.** Each week, the airline sends you a list of discounted flights, usually leaving the upcoming Friday or Saturday, and returning the following Monday or Tuesday. You can sign up for all the major airlines at once by logging on to **Epicurious Travel** (http://travel.epicurious.com/travel/c_planning/02_airfares/email/signup.html). Or you can go to each airline's Web site:

- **Air Canada:** www.aircanada.ca
- **American Airlines:** www.americanair.com
- **Canadian Airlines:** www.cdnair.ca
- **Continental Airlines:** www.flycontinental.com
- **TWA:** www.twa.com
- **Northwest Airlines:** www.nwa.com
- **US Airways:** www.usairways.com

A **charter** flight can be a good option if you choose the company carefully. Tour operators book a block of seats and then offer them at substantial reductions. You must book and pay in advance, and you might lose your full payment or be hit with a penalty if you cancel—or if the company goes out of business. Check with the Better Business Bureau before you pay to make sure that the company is reliable. A charter company that serves Boston from most major European cities is **Travac,** 989 Sixth Ave., New York, NY 10018 (☎ **800/872-8800** or 212/695-8101; fares-by-fax menu ☎ 888-872-8327).

Consolidators (also known as "bucket shops") buy blocks of tickets from airlines and resell them, often at rates below the official ones. As with charter companies, check with the Better Business Bureau. You might want to explore the possibilities of **Travel Avenue,** 10 S. Riverside Plaza, Suite 1404, Chicago, IL 60606 (☎ **800/333-3335**), a national agency. Its tickets are often cheaper than those at most shops, and it charges only a $25 fee on international tickets, rather than taking the usual 10% commission from an airline. Travel Avenue rebates most of that to you—hence the lower fares. The nationwide airline reservation and ticketing service **1-800-FLY-4-LESS** specializes in finding the lowest fares. For information on available consolidator airline tickets for last-minute travel, call ☎ **800/359-4537.** When fares are high and planning time is short, such a service is invaluable.

To fly **standby,** you wait at the airport for an empty seat on your flight. Because of security concerns, this option is less often available than it once was. After all reserved seats are accounted for, you might be able to board at great savings. If not, you go home and try again, or book a regular flight.

LOGAN INTERNATIONAL AIRPORT   Boston's airport, in East Boston at the end of the Sumner, Callahan, and Ted Williams tunnels, is one of the most accessible in the country, just 3 miles across the harbor from the downtown area. At the moment, it's in the throes of a massive overhaul called "Logan 2000"; but you probably won't be spending much time there, and everything is clearly marked.

You can get to the city by cab, bus, or subway, via underwater tunnels, or by boat. The **subway** is fast—Government Center is just 10 minutes away—and costs only 85¢ per ride. Free **shuttle buses** run from each terminal to the Airport station on the MBTA Blue Line from 5:30am to 1am every day, year-round. The Blue Line stops at Aquarium (for the waterfront) and at State Street and Government Center, downtown points where you can exit or transfer to the other lines.

Some hotels have their own **limos** or **shuttle vans;** ask about them when you make your reservations. A **cab** from the airport to downtown costs about $18 to $24. (See "Getting Around," in chapter 4, for more information on taxis.)

The ride into town takes from 10 to 40 minutes, depending on the time of day and how congested the approaches to the tunnels are. If you must travel during rush hour or on Sunday afternoon, allow extra time, or plan to take the subway and pack accordingly.

The trip to the downtown waterfront in a weather-protected boat takes 7 minutes, dock to dock. Courtesy buses from all the airport terminals run to the Logan ferry dock. The **Airport Water Shuttle** (☎ 617/330-8680) runs to Rowes Wharf on Atlantic Avenue every 15 minutes from 6am to 8pm on weekdays, and every 30 minutes on Friday until 11pm, Saturday from 10am to 11pm, and Sundays and national holidays (except January 1, July 4, Thanksgiving, and December 25) from 10am to 8pm. The one-way fare is $10 for adults and children 12 and up, $5 for senior citizens, free for children under 12.

Harbor Express (☎ 617/376-8417) runs between the airport and Long Wharf 24 times a day on weekdays between 5:30am and 9pm (Friday until 11pm), and less frequently on weekends. There's no service on Thanksgiving and December 25. The one-way fare is $10.

The Massachusetts Port Authority (☎ **800/23LOGAN;** www.massport.com) coordinates **bus service** between the airport and Gate 25 at Boston's South Station, as well as suburban hubs in Braintree, Framingham, and Woburn. You can also try the **Share-A-Cab booths** at each terminal and save up to half the fare. To arrange **limousine** service, call ahead for a reservation, especially at busy times. Your hotel can recommend a company, or try **Carey Limousine Boston** (☎ **800/336-4646** or 617/623-8700) or **Commonwealth Limousine Service** (☎ **800/558-LIMO** outside Massachusetts, or 617/787-5575).

If you prefer to rent (hire) a car, the following agencies offer shuttle service from the airport to their offices: **Alamo** (☎ 800/327-9633), **Avis** (☎ 800/831-2847),

Gridlock Alert

The **Central Artery/Third Harbor Tunnel project,** or "Big Dig," has begun, and while the Central Artery (the John F. Fitzgerald Expressway) is being moved underground, traffic patterns in the area change almost daily. Paradoxically, that means streets, attractions, and businesses are well labeled, but that's because they're sometimes nearly impossible to find in the maze of jersey barriers and construction sites. If possible, avoid the Central Artery altogether by choosing alternate routes. The **Ted Williams Tunnel** part of this undertaking, which will eventually connect the Pike to the airport, is complete; the connection is part of the rest of the project, and until it's finished, the tunnel is open on weekdays to commercial traffic only (at the risk of a hefty fine). Check the message boards on the major highways leading into town to see whether the tunnel is open to you when you need to reach the airport and points north from the south or west.

Budget (☎ 800/527-0700), **Enterprise** (☎ 800/325-8007), **Hertz** (☎ 800/654-3131), **National** (☎ 800/227-7368), and **Thrifty** (☎ 800/367-2277). Boston levies a $10 surcharge on car rentals that goes toward the construction of a new convention center.

FLYING WITH FILM & LAPTOPS Traveling with electronic devices and film (exposed or not) can take extra time in this age of heightened security, so plan accordingly. X-ray machines won't affect film up to ASA 400, but you might want to request an inspection by hand anyway. A visual check for computers is standard practice in most airports—you'll probably be asked to switch it on, so be sure that the batteries are charged (and don't forget to turn it off). You may use your computer in flight, but not during take-off and landing because of possible interference with cockpit controls. In many cases, airport security guards will also ask you to turn on electronic devices (including camcorders and personal stereos) to prove that they are what they appear to be, so make sure that batteries are charged and working for those items as well.

BY CAR

Driving to Boston is not difficult. (Driving *in* Boston is another story altogether.) The major highways leading to and from Boston are **I-95** (Massachusetts Route 128), which connects Boston to highways in Rhode Island, Connecticut, and New York to the south, and New Hampshire and Maine to the north; **I-90,** the Massachusetts Turnpike, an east-west toll road that links up with the New York State Thruway; **I-93/U.S. 1,** extending north to Canada and leading to the Northeast Expressway, which enters downtown Boston; and **I-93/Route 3,** the Southeast Expressway, which connects Boston with the south, including Cape Cod.

The Massachusetts Turnpike ("Mass Pike") extends into the center of the city and connects with the Central Artery (the John F. Fitzgerald Expressway), which is linked to the Northeast Expressway. If you want to avoid Central Artery construction, exit at the Prudential Center in the Back Bay. The Southeast Expressway is a busy commuter route, so try to avoid it at rush hour.

The approach to Cambridge is either **Storrow Drive** or **Memorial Drive,** which run along each side of the Charles. Storrow Drive has a Harvard Square exit that leads you across the Anderson Bridge to John F. Kennedy Street and into the square;

Memorial Drive intersects with Kennedy Street. Turn away from the bridge to reach the square.

Boston is 218 miles from New York; the driving time is about 4½ hours. The 992-mile drive from Chicago to Boston should take around 21 hours; from Washington, D.C., it takes about 8 hours to cover the 468 miles.

The **American Automobile Association** (☎ **800/AAA-HELP;** www.aaa.com) provides its members with maps, itineraries, and other travel information, and it arranges free towing if you break down. Be aware that the Mass Pike is a privately operated road that arranges its own towing; if you break down there, wait in the car until one of the regular patrols arrives.

It's impossible to say this often enough: When you reach your hotel, leave your car in the garage and walk or use public transportation. Use the car for trips to the suburbs, the North Shore, or Plymouth; if you must drive in town, ask at the front desk for a route around or away from the construction area.

BY TRAIN

Boston has three rail centers: **South Station** at 700 Atlantic Ave., **Back Bay Station** at 145 Dartmouth St., and **North Station** on Causeway Street. **Amtrak** (☎ **800/USA-RAIL** or 617/482-3660; www.amtrak.com) serves South Station and Back Bay Station. At South Station you can take the Red Line to Cambridge or to Park Street, the central hub of the **MBTA** (☎ **617/222-3200;** www.mbta.com), where you can make connections to the Green, Blue, and Orange lines. The Orange Line connects Back Bay Station with Downtown Crossing (where there's a walkway to Park Street station) and other points. The MBTA **commuter rail** runs to Ipswich, Rockport, and Fitchburg from North Station, and to points south of Boston, including Plymouth, from South Station.

Amtrak runs to South Station from New York and points south and in between, with stops at Route 128 and Back Bay Station. Express trains make the trip from New York in about 4 hours; others take 4½ to 5 hours or longer. All-reserved Northeast Direct service predominates; fares range from $95 to $128 round-trip. The round-trip unreserved fare is about $86. From Washington, D.C., count on 8½ hours; Northeast Direct fares run from $132 to $172 round-trip. Unreserved fares range from $122 to $156. Traveling time from Chicago is 22 hours (sleepers are available), and the fares range from $128 to $198 round-trip. All of these fares are subject to change and can fluctuate depending on the time of year. During slow times, excursion fares might be available. Discounts are not available Friday and Sunday afternoon. Always remember to ask for the discounted rate.

Once a somewhat scary destination, South Station was renovated and restored in the late 1980s, and it's now a beautiful, airy facility with a newsstand, a bookstore kiosk, a florist, a bakery, and a wide range of food choices. The 1-ton clock above the main entrance is the only remaining hand-wound tower clock in New England. It is wound once a week from a small room behind the 14-foot-diameter clock face.

BY BUS

The **South Station Transportation Center** (a fancy name for the bus terminal) is at 700 Atlantic Ave., right next to the train station, and it's the city's bus-service hub. It's served by the following bus lines: **Greyhound** (☎ 800/231-2222 or 617/526-1801; www.greyhound.com), **American Eagle** (☎ 800/453-5040 or 508/993-5040), **Bonanza** (☎ 800/556-3815 or 617/720-4110), **Brush Hill**

(☎ 617/986-6100), **Concord Trailways** (☎ 800/639-3317 or 617/426-8080), **Peter Pan** (☎ 800/237-8747 or 617/426-8554), **Plymouth & Brockton** (☎ 617/773-9401 or 508/746-0378), and **Vermont Transit** (☎ 800/451-3292).

Following are some sample fares and times on Greyhound (and Peter Pan, which serves some of the same destinations) to Boston from other major cities: New York, $53 to $65 round-trip, 4½ to 5 hours. Washington, D.C., $80 to $100 round-trip, 11 hours. Chicago, $159 to $210 round-trip, 22½ to 27 hours. Fares are subject to change. Greyhound occasionally discounts tickets purchased several weeks in advance.

For Foreign Visitors

3

American fads and fashions have spread across the world, making the United States seem like familiar territory long before you arrive. Perhaps you even have friends or relatives studying in the Boston area. Nevertheless, there are many peculiarities and uniquely American situations that any foreign visitor will encounter. Be sure to consult chapter 2 for general advice, too.

1 Preparing for Your Trip

ENTRY REQUIREMENTS

Immigration laws are a hot political issue in the United States, and the following requirements might have changed somewhat by the time you plan your trip. Check at any U.S. embassy or consulate for current information and requirements.

DOCUMENT REGULATIONS Citizens of **Canada** and **Bermuda** may enter the United States without visas, but they need to show proof of nationality, the most common and hassle-free form of which is a passport.

The U.S. State Department has a Visa Waiver Pilot Program under which citizens of some countries may enter the country without a visa for stays of fewer than 90 days of holiday travel. At press time they included **Andorra, Argentina, Australia, Austria, Belgium, Brunei, Denmark, Finland, France, Germany, Iceland, Ireland, Italy, Japan, Liechtenstein, Luxembourg, Monaco, the Netherlands, New Zealand, Norway, San Marino, Slovenia, Spain, Sweden, Switzerland,** and the **United Kingdom.** (The program as applied to the United Kingdom refers to British citizens who have the "unrestricted right of permanent abode in the United Kingdom"—citizens from **England, Scotland, Wales, Northern Ireland,** the **Channel Islands,** and the **Isle of Man,** and not, for example, citizens of the British Commonwealth of Pakistan.)

Citizens from these countries need only a valid passport and a round-trip air or cruise ticket in their possession upon arrival. If they first enter the United States, they may then visit Mexico, Canada, Bermuda, and the Caribbean islands and return to the United States without needing a visa. Further information is available from any U.S. embassy or consulate.

Citizens of countries other than those specified above, those traveling to the U.S. for reasons or lengths of time outside the restrictions of the visa waiver program, or those who require waivers of inadmissibility must have two documents:

- A **valid passport,** with an expiration date at least 6 months later than the scheduled end of the visit to the United States. (Some countries are exceptions to the 6-month validity rule. Contact any U.S. embassy or consulate for complete information.)
- A **tourist visa,** available from the nearest U.S. consulate. To obtain a visa, the traveler must submit (in person or by mail) a completed application form with a 1½-inch-square photo and the required application fee. There might also be an issuance fee, depending on the type of visa and other factors.

Usually you can obtain a visa right away or within 24 hours, but the process might take longer during the summer rush period (June to August). If you cannot go in person, contact the nearest U.S. embassy or consulate for directions on applying by mail. Your travel agent or airline office might also be able to provide you with visa applications and instructions. The U.S. consulate or embassy that issues your visa will determine whether you will be issued a multiple- or single-entry visa. The Immigration and Naturalization Service officers at your U.S. port of entry will make an admission decision and determine your length of stay.

Foreign driver's licenses are recognized in Massachusetts, although you might want to get an international driver's license if your home license is not written in English.

MEDICAL REQUIREMENTS   Inoculations are not needed to enter the United States unless you are coming from, or have stopped over in, areas known to be suffering from epidemics, particularly cholera or yellow fever.

If you have a disease requiring treatment with medications containing narcotics or drugs requiring a syringe, carry a valid signed prescription from your physician to allay suspicions that you are smuggling drugs.

CUSTOMS REQUIREMENTS   Every adult visitor may bring in, free of duty, 1 liter of wine or hard liquor, 200 cigarettes or 100 cigars (but no cigars from Cuba) or 3 pounds of smoking tobacco, and $100 worth of gifts. The exemptions are offered to travelers who spend at least 72 hours in the United States and who have not claimed them within the preceding 6 months. It is altogether forbidden to bring into the country foodstuffs (particularly cheese, fruit, cooked meats, and canned goods) and plants (vegetables, seeds, tropical plants, and so on). Foreign tourists may bring in or take out up to $10,000 in U.S. or foreign currency with no formalities; larger sums must be declared to customs on entering or leaving.

INSURANCE

There is no nationwide health system in the United States. Because the cost of medical care is extremely high, we strongly advise every traveler to secure health insurance coverage before setting out.

You might want to take out a comprehensive travel policy that covers sickness or injury costs (medical, surgical, and hospital); loss or theft of your baggage; trip-cancellation costs; guarantee of bail in case you are arrested; and costs of accident, repatriation, or death. Such packages (for example, "Europe Assistance" in Europe) are sold by automobile clubs at reasonable rates, as well as by insurance companies and travel agencies.

MONEY

CURRENCY AND EXCHANGE   The American monetary system has a decimal base: one U.S. **dollar** ($1) = 100 **cents** (100¢). Dollar bills commonly come in $1

The Bostonians are really, as a race, far inferior in point of anything beyond mere intellect to any other set upon the continent of North America. They are decidedly the most servile imitators of the English it is possible to conceive.
　　　　　　　　　　　　　　　　　　　　—Edgar Allan Poe, 1849

We are Boston, Glasgow is Cleveland.
　　　　　　　　　　　　　—John McKay, Lord Provost of Edinburgh, 1985

(a "buck"), $5, $10, $20, $50, and $100 denominations. Bills larger than $20 are not welcome for small purchases and are not accepted in most taxis or movie theaters. The slang term "break" (as in "Can you break a 20?") means "make change for."

There are six denominations of coins: 1¢ (1 cent or a "penny"), 5¢ (5 cents or a "nickel"), 10¢ (10 cents or a "dime"), 25¢ (25 cents or a "quarter"), 50¢ (50 cents or a "half-dollar"), and $1. The $1 piece is not in common use and is typically dispensed only by post-office vending machines when you purchase more than a few stamps.

The foreign exchange bureaus so common in Europe are rare even in airports in the United States and nonexistent outside major cities. Try to avoid having to change foreign money, or traveler's checks in currency other than U.S. dollars, at a small-town branch, or even a branch in a big city.

CREDIT CARDS　　The method of payment most widely used is the credit card: Visa (BarclayCard in Britain), MasterCard (EuroCard in Europe, Access in Britain, Chargex in Canada), American Express, Diners Club, Discover, and Carte Blanche. You can save yourself trouble by using "plastic money" rather than cash or traveler's checks in most hotels, restaurants, and retail stores, and many food and liquor stores. You need a credit card to rent a car in Massachusetts.

TRAVELER'S CHECKS　　It's cheaper and faster to get cash at an automatic teller machine (ATM) than to fuss with traveler's checks. If you do bring them, traveler's checks denominated in U.S. dollars are readily accepted at most hotels, restaurants, and large stores.

SAFETY

GENERAL　　Tourist areas are generally safe, but U.S. urban areas tend to be less safe than those in Europe or Japan. Visitors should always stay alert, particularly in large cities like Boston. Avoid deserted areas, especially at night. Don't go into any city park at night, even to jog or skate, unless there is an event that attracts crowds—for example, Boston's concerts and films on the Esplanade. Generally speaking, you can feel safe in areas where there are many people and many open establishments.

Avoid carrying valuables with you on the street, and don't display expensive cameras or electronic equipment. Sling your pocketbook diagonally across your body and keep a hand on it, and place your wallet or billfold in an inside pocket. Make sure that your wallet and other valuables are not easily accessible—if possible, keep them on your person, and *never* in the outside pocket of a backpack. In theaters, restaurants, and other public places, keep your possessions in sight.

Remember also that hotels are open to the public, and in a large hotel security might not be able to screen everyone entering. Always lock your room door—don't assume that once inside your hotel you are automatically safe and no longer need to be on your guard.

DRIVING   The best way to protect yourself is to be aware of your surroundings. Question your rental agency about personal safety, or ask for a brochure of traveler safety tips when you pick up your car. Ask for written directions, or a map with the route clearly marked, showing how to get to your destination. If possible, arrive and depart during daylight hours.

Park in well-lighted, well-traveled areas if possible. Always keep your car doors locked, whether the car is attended or unattended. Look around you before you get out of your car, and never leave any packages or valuables in sight. If someone attempts to rob you or steal your car, do not try to resist—report the incident to the police department immediately by dialing ☎ **911.** This is a free call, even from pay phones.

Recently more and more crime in all U.S. cities has involved cars and drivers, notably "carjacking"—forcing the occupants out and stealing the car. If you drive off a highway into a doubtful neighborhood, be sure to keep the doors locked and the windows rolled up, and leave the area as quickly as possible. If you have an accident, even on the highway, stay in your car with the doors locked until you assess the situation or until the police arrive. If you are bumped from behind on the street or are involved in a minor accident with no injuries and the situation appears to be suspicious, motion to the other driver to follow you to the nearest police precinct, well-lighted service station, or all-night store. *Never* get out of your car in such situations.

If you see someone on the road who indicates a need for help, do not stop. Take note of the location, drive on to a well-lighted area, and telephone the police.

2 Getting to the United States

Travelers from overseas can take advantage of the **APEX** (**Advance Purchase Excursion**) fares offered by all the major U.S. and European carriers. Most itineraries will take you through another American city, but some airlines do serve Boston directly: **American** and **TWA** from Paris; **British Airways, Virgin Atlantic,** and **Delta** from London; **Aer Lingus** from Dublin; **Lufthansa** from Frankfurt; **Northwest** from Amsterdam; **Icelandair** from Reykjavik; and **Swissair** from Geneva and Zurich. Prices vary with market activity; fares between October and March are almost always lower than in the summer.

Some large American airlines (for example, TWA, American, Northwest, United, and Delta) offer travelers on their trans-Atlantic or trans-Pacific flights special discount tickets under the name **Visit USA,** allowing travel between any U.S. destinations at minimum rates. They are not on sale in the United States, and you must purchase them before you leave your foreign point of departure. This system is the best, easiest, and fastest way to see the United States at low cost. Obtain information well in advance from your travel agent or the office of the airline concerned, because the conditions attached to the tickets can be changed without notice.

The visitor arriving by air, no matter what the port of entry, should cultivate a good measure of patience and resignation before setting foot on U.S. soil. Getting through immigration control might take as long as 2 hours on some days, especially on summer weekends. Add the time it takes to clear customs, and you'll see that you should allow for long delays in planning connections between international and domestic flights—an average of 2 to 3 hours at least.

In contrast, travelers arriving by car or by rail from Canada find border-crossing formalities streamlined almost to the vanishing point. Air travelers from Canada,

Bermuda, and some places in the Caribbean can sometimes go through customs and immigration at the point of departure, which is much quicker and less painful. Air Canada (☎ **800/776-3000**) serves Boston from Halifax, Montreal, and Toronto; Canadian Airlines/Air Atlantic (☎ **800/426-7000**), from Vancouver only.

For further information about travel to and arrival in Boston, see "Getting There" in chapter 2.

3 Getting Around the United States

Flying is the fastest, and most expensive, mode of travel within the United States. For a list of carriers that serve Boston, see "Getting There" in chapter 2.

Traveling by **car** (or perhaps **bicycle**) is the best way to see the country outside of the major cities, especially if you have time to explore. The major roads are excellent, and the secondary routes that branch off them can lead you to the small towns and natural wonders that help make the United States such a multifaceted destination.

BY TRAIN   International visitors can buy a **USA Railpass,** good for 15 or 30 days of unlimited travel on **Amtrak** (☎ **800/USA-RAIL**). The pass is available through many foreign travel agents. Prices in 1998 for a 15-day pass are $260 off-peak (mid-October to late May) and $375 during peak travel periods; a 30-day pass costs $350 off-peak and $480 in peak months. (With a foreign passport, you can also buy passes at Amtrak offices in some U.S. cities, including Boston, San Francisco, Los Angeles, Chicago, New York, Miami, and Washington, D.C.) Reservations are generally required, and you should make them for each part of your trip when you purchase the pass (you can change them later at no cost).

Visitors should be aware of the limitations of long-distance rail travel in the United States. With a few notable exceptions (for instance, the Northeast Corridor between Boston and Washington, D.C.), service is rarely up to European standards. Delays are common, routes are limited and often infrequently served, and fares are rarely significantly lower than discount airfares.

BY BUS   The cheapest way to travel in the United States is by bus. The country's nationwide bus line, **Greyhound** (☎ **800/231-2222;** www.greyhound.com), offers an Ameripass for unlimited travel. Prices in 1998 were $199 for 7 days, $299 for 15 days, $400 for 30 days, and $599 for 60 days. Bus travel in the United States can be both slow and uncomfortable, so this option is not for everyone.

FAST FACTS: For the Foreign Traveler

Automobile Organizations   Auto clubs supply members with maps, suggested routes, guidebooks, accident and bail-bond insurance, and emergency road service. The major auto club in the United States, with offices nationwide, is the **American Automobile Association,** or AAA (☎ **800/222-4357;** www.aaa.com). Members of some foreign auto clubs have reciprocal arrangements with AAA and may use its services at no charge. If you belong to an auto club, inquire about AAA reciprocity before you leave. AAA can provide you with an International Driving Permit validating your foreign license, and you might be able to join the association even if you are not a member of a reciprocal club. In addition, some automobile rental agencies now provide the same services; inquire about their availability when you reserve your car.

Business Hours   Banks are open weekdays from 8:30 or 9am to 3 or 4pm, and sometimes Saturday morning; most offer 24-hour access to Automated Teller Machines (ATMs). Business offices generally are open weekdays from 9am to 5pm. Stores and other businesses are open 6 days a week, with most open on Sunday as well; department stores usually stay open until 9pm at least 1 night a week.

Climate   See "When to Go," in chapter 2.

Currency   See "Preparing for Your Trip," at the beginning of this chapter.

Currency Exchange   A reliable choice is **Thomas Cook Currency Services, Inc.** (160 Franklin St.; ☎ **800/287-7362**), which has been in business since 1841 and offers a wide range of services. It sells commission-free foreign and U.S. traveler's checks, drafts, and wire transfers, and it also does check collections (including Eurochecks). **BankBoston** has many currency exchange locations, including Logan Airport, Terminal C (☎ **617/569-1172**) and Terminal E (☎ **617/567-2313**), and 1414 Massachusetts Ave., Harvard Square, Cambridge (☎ **617/556-6050**). Other places in Boston at which to change money are the **Boston Bank of Commerce,** 133 Federal St. (☎ **617/457-4400**) and **Ruesch International,** 45 Milk St. (☎ **617/482-8600**). Many hotels offer currency exchange; check when you make your reservation.

Drinking Laws   The legal drinking age in Boston is 21. In many bars, particularly near college campuses, you might be asked for identification if you appear to be under 30 or so. Liquor sales are not allowed in stores on Sunday (but bars, taverns, and restaurants take up the slack).

Electric Current   The United States uses 110-120 volts, 60 cycles, compared with 220–240 volts, 50 cycles, in most of Europe. Besides a 100-volt converter, small appliances of non-American manufacture, such as hair dryers or shavers, will require a plug adapter, with two flat, parallel pins.

Embassies/Consulates   Embassies are in the national capital, Washington, D.C. Some consulates are located in major cities, and most countries have a mission to the United Nations in New York City.

Listed here are the embassies and Boston and New York consulates of Australia, Canada, Ireland, New Zealand, and Britain. If you are from another country, you can get the telephone number of your embassy by calling Washington, D.C., directory assistance (☎ **202/555-1212**).

The embassy of **Australia** is at 1601 Massachusetts Ave. NW, Washington, DC 20036 (☎ **202/797-3000**). The **honorary consulate** in Boston is at 20 Park Plaza, Suite 457, Boston, MA 02116 (☎ **617/542-8655**). The **consulate in New York** is in the International Building, 630 Fifth Ave., New York, NY 10111 (☎ **212/408-8400**).

The embassy of **Canada** is at 501 Pennsylvania Ave. NW, Washington, DC 20001 (☎ **202/682-1740**). The **consulate in Boston** is at 3 Copley Place, Suite 400, Boston, MA 02116 (☎ **617/262-3760**). The **consulate in New York** is at 1251 Avenue of the Americas, New York, NY 10020 (☎ **212/596-1600**).

The embassy of the **Republic of Ireland** is at 2234 Massachusetts Ave. NW, Washington, DC 20008 (☎ **202/462-3939**). The **consulate in Boston** is at 535 Boylston St., 3rd floor, Boston, MA 02116 (☎ **617/267-9330**). The **consulate in New York** is at 345 Park Ave., 17th floor, New York, NY 10154 (☎ **212/319-2555**).

The embassy of **New Zealand** is at 37 Observatory Circle NW, Washington, DC 20008 (☎ **202/328-4848**). The **consulate in New York** is at 780 3rd Ave., Suite 1904, New York, NY 10017 (☎ **212/832-4038**).

The embassy of the **United Kingdom** is at 19 Observatory Circle NW, Washington, DC 20008 (☎ **202/588-7800**). The **consulate in Boston** is at Federal Reserve Plaza, 600 Atlantic Ave., 25th floor, Boston, MA 02210 (☎ **617/ 248-9555**). The **consulate in New York** is at 845 Third Ave., New York, NY 10022 (☎ **212/745-0200**).

Emergencies   Call ☎ **911** for fire, police, and ambulance. If you encounter such travelers' problems as sickness, accident, or lost or stolen baggage, call the **Travelers Aid Society,** 17 East St., Boston, MA 02111 (☎ **617/542-7286**), which specializes in helping travelers, whether American or foreign. It has a branch at Logan Airport's Terminal E (☎ **617/567-5385**).

Gasoline (Petrol)   One U.S. gallon equals 3.75 liters; 1.2 U.S. gallons equal 1 Imperial gallon. Several grades (and price levels) of gasoline are available at most gas stations. Each gas company has a different name for the various levels of octane; most fall into the "regular," "super," and "plus" categories. Unleaded gas with the highest octane is the most expensive, but most rental cars take the least expensive, regular unleaded.

Holidays   Banks, government offices, and post offices are closed (some stores, restaurants, and museums are open) on the following national holidays: **New Year's Day** (January 1), **Martin Luther King Jr. Day** (third Monday in January), **Presidents' Day** (third Monday in February), **Memorial Day** (last Monday in May), **Independence Day** (July 4), **Labor Day** (first Monday in September), **Columbus Day** (second Monday in October), **Veterans Day** (November 11), **Thanksgiving** (fourth Thursday in November), and **Christmas** (December 25). The Tuesday following the first Monday in November is **Election Day** and is a legal holiday in presidential election years. The next one is in 2000.

In Massachusetts, state offices are closed for **Patriots Day** on the third Monday in April and on March 17 for **Evacuation Day.**

Legal Aid   The well-meaning foreign tourist will probably never become involved with the American legal system. However, you should know a few things just in case. If you are pulled over for a minor infraction (for example, of the highway code, such as speeding), never attempt to pay the fine directly to a police officer; you might wind up arrested on the much more serious charge of attempted bribery. Pay fines by mail, or directly into the hands of the clerk of the court. If accused of a more serious offense, it's wise to say and do nothing before consulting a lawyer. Under U.S. law, an arrested person is allowed one telephone call to a party of his or her choice. Call your embassy or consulate.

Mail   Post offices are scattered throughout the city; they're keyed on the map in chapter 1. **Postcard stamps** cost 20¢ for delivery in the United States, 40¢ for Canada, and 50¢ for other international addresses. **Letter stamps** for up to 1 ounce in the United States are 32¢; for half-ounce letters to Canada, 46¢; to other international addresses, 60¢.

If you want your mail to follow you on your vacation and you aren't sure of your address, it can be sent to you, in your name, c/o General Delivery, Fort Point Station, Boston, MA 02205 (☎ **617/654-5325**). The station is at 25 Dorchester Ave., behind South Station. The addressee must pick up the mail in person and produce proof of identity (a driver's license or passport, for example).

Medical Emergencies   If you become ill, consult your hotel desk staff or concierge for referral to a physician. For an ambulance, dial ☎ **911.** Also see "Doctors" in the "Fast Facts" section in chapter 4.

Newspapers/Magazines   National newspapers include the *New York Times, USA Today,* and the *Wall Street Journal.* National news weeklies include *Newsweek, Time,* and *U.S. News & World Report.* The major newspapers in Boston are the *Boston Globe,* the *Boston Herald,* and the weekly *Boston Phoenix.*

Radio/Television   Nationally, there are four commercial over-the-air television networks—ABC, CBS, NBC, and Fox—along with the Public Broadcasting System (PBS) and the cable news network CNN. In big cities, viewers have a choice of dozens of channels (including basic cable), most of them transmitting 24 hours a day. Most hotels have at least basic cable, and many offer access to "premium" movie channels that show uncut theatrical releases. For the major radio and television stations in Boston, see "Fast Facts: Boston" in chapter 4.

Safety   See "Safety" in "Preparing for Your Trip," above.

Taxes   In the United States there is no VAT (value-added tax) or other indirect tax at a national level. Every state, and each city in it, is allowed to levy its own local tax on all purchases, including hotel and restaurant checks, airline tickets, and so on. Massachusetts's 5% sales tax is not levied on food, prescription drugs, newspapers, or clothing worth less than $175, but there seems to be a tax on everything else. The lodging tax in Boston and Cambridge is 12.45%; the meal tax (which also applies to take-out food) is 5%; the gasoline tax (included on the price at the pump) is 10%.

Telephone/Telegraph/Telex   The telephone system in the United States is run by private corporations. Rates, especially for long-distance service, can vary widely, even on calls made from public telephones. Local calls in the Boston area usually cost 25¢. If you expect to make a lot of phone calls, **prepaid calling cards** are convenient if not particularly economical. They're available at visitor information centers and many stores, usually in multiples of $5.

Generally, hotel surcharges on long-distance and local calls are astronomical. You are usually better off using **public pay telephones,** which are clearly marked in most public buildings and private establishments as well as on the street. Outside metropolitan areas, public telephones are more difficult to find. Stores, gas stations, and bars are your best bet.

Most long-distance and international calls can be dialed directly from any phone. For calls to Canada and other parts of the United States, dial 1 followed by the area code and the seven-digit number. For international calls, dial 011 followed by the country code, city code, and telephone number.

For **reversed-charge** or **collect** calls, and for **person-to-person calls,** dial 0 (zero, not the letter *O*) followed by the area code and number you want; an operator will then come on the line, and you should specify that you are calling collect, or person to person, or both. If your operator-assisted call is international, ask for the overseas operator.

Calls to area codes 800, 888, and 877 are toll-free. However, calls to numbers in area codes 700 and 900 (chat lines, bulletin boards, "dating" services, etc.) can be very expensive—usually a charge of 95¢ to $3 or more per minute, and they sometimes have minimum charges that can run as high as $15 or more.

For local directory assistance ("Information"), dial ☎ **411;** for long-distance information dial 1, then the area code and **555-1212.**

Like the telephone system, **telegraph** and **telex** services are provided by private corporations such as ITT, MCI, and, above all, Western Union. You can bring your telegram to the nearest Western Union office (there are hundreds across the country) or dictate it over the phone (☎ **800/325-6000**). You can also telegraph money, or have it telegraphed to you, over the Western Union system.

Telephone Directory   Two kinds of telephone directories are available. Many hotels provide a set for each room, and they are usually also available at the front desk.

The general directory is the **white pages,** in which private and business subscribers are listed in alphabetical order. The inside front cover lists emergency numbers for police, fire, and ambulance, and other vital numbers (the Coast Guard, poison-control center, crime victims' hotline, and so on). The first few pages are devoted to community-service numbers, including a guide to long-distance and international calling, complete with country codes and area codes.

The second directory, printed on yellow paper (and called the **yellow pages**), lists local services, businesses, and industries by type of activity, with an index at the back. The listings cover not only such obvious items as automobile repairs by make of car, or drugstores (pharmacies), often by geographical location, but also restaurants by type of cuisine and geographical location, bookstores by special subject and/or language, places of worship by religious denomination, and other information that the tourist might otherwise not readily find.

Time   Noon in Boston or New York City (Eastern Time) is 6pm in Cape Town, 5pm in London, 11am in Chicago, 9am in Vancouver or Los Angeles, and—1 day ahead—5am in Auckland and 3am in Sydney.

Daylight saving time is in effect from the first Sunday in April through the last Saturday in October (the change is made at 2am). Daylight saving time moves the clock 1 hour ahead of standard time.

Tipping   This is part of the American way of life, based on the principle that good service is rewarded. Many service employees, in particular waiters, rely on tips for the bulk of their earnings. Here are some rules of thumb (if you receive extraordinary service, consider tipping a bit more):

Bartenders, 10% to 15%; **bellhops,** at least $1 per piece, $5 or more for a lot of baggage; **cab drivers,** 15% to 20% of the fare; **cafeterias, fast-food restaurants,** no tip; **chambermaids,** $2 a day; **checkroom attendants** (restaurants, theaters), $1 per garment; **movie theater employees,** including ushers, no tip; **doormen** (hotels or restaurants), not obligatory; **gas station attendants,** no tip; **hairdressers,** 15% to 20%; **skycaps or redcaps** (airport and railroad station), at least 50¢ per piece, $5 or more for a lot of baggage; **restaurants, nightclubs,** 15% to 20% of the check; **sleeping-car porters,** $3 to $5 per night; **valet parking attendants,** $1 or $2.

Toilets   Foreign visitors often complain that public toilets are hard to find in most U.S. cities. True, there are none on the streets, but you can usually find one in a visitor information center, shopping center, bar, restaurant, hotel, museum, department store, or service station—and it will probably be clean. The cleanliness of toilets at railroad and bus stations might be open to question. Some restaurants and bars, including those in Boston's tourist areas, display a sign saying toilets are for the use of patrons only. Paying for a cup of coffee or a soft drink qualifies you as a patron.

4

Getting to Know Boston

Boston bills itself as "America's Walking City," and walking is by far
the easiest way to get around. Legend has it that the streets were laid
out along cow paths, but the layout owes more to 17th-century
London and to Boston's original shoreline. To orient yourself, it
helps to look at the big picture. This chapter provides an overview
of the city's layout and neighborhoods. It also lists information and
resources you might need while you're away from home. As you
familiarize yourself with Boston's geography, it might help to iden-
tify the various neighborhoods and landmarks on the free map provided with this guide.

1 Orientation

VISITOR INFORMATION

You'll probably want to begin exploring at one of the city's **visitor
information centers.** The staff members are knowledgeable and
helpful, and you can pick up free maps, brochures, listings of special exhibits, and schedules and find out the admission fees for the
historic attractions.

The **Boston National Historic Park Visitor Center,** at 15 State
St. (☎ **617/242-5642**), across the street from the Old State House
and the State Street T station, is a good place to start your excursion. National Park Service rangers staff the center, dispense information, and lead free tours of the Freedom Trail. The audiovisual
show about the trail provides basic information on 16 historic sites.
The center is accessible by stairs and ramps and has rest rooms and
comfortable chairs. Open daily from 9am to 5pm except January 1,
Thanksgiving Day, and December 25.

The Freedom Trail, a line of red paint or red brick on or in the
sidewalk, begins at the **Boston Common Information Center,** at
146 Tremont St. on the Common. The center is open Monday
through Saturday from 8:30am to 5pm, and Sunday from 9am to
5pm. The **Prudential Information Center,** on the main level of
the Prudential Center, is open Monday through Saturday from 9am
to 8pm, and Sunday from 11am to 6pm. The **Greater Boston
Convention & Visitors Bureau** (☎ **888/SEE-BOSTON** or
617/536-4100) operates both centers.

In Cambridge, there's an information kiosk (☎ **617/497-1630**)
in the heart of Harvard Square, near the T entrance at the

Impressions

For we must consider that we shall be as a city upon a hill. The eyes of all people are
upon us. . . .
                    —John Winthrop, "A Model of Christian Charity" (sermon), 1630

I do not speak with any fondness, but the language of coolest history, when I say that
Boston commands attention as the town which was appointed in the destiny of nations
to lead the civilization of North America.
                    —Ralph Waldo Emerson, *The Natural History of the Intellect,* 1893

intersection of Massachusetts Avenue, John F. Kennedy Street, and Brattle Street.
It's open Monday through Saturday from 9am to 5pm, and Sunday from 1 to 5pm.

PUBLICATIONS   The city's newspapers offer the most up-to-date information
about events in the area. The "Calendar" section of the Thursday *Boston Globe* lists
festivals, street fairs, concerts, films, speeches, and dance and theater performances.
The Friday *Boston Herald* has a similar, smaller insert called "Scene." Both papers
briefly list events in their weekend editions. The arts-oriented *Boston Phoenix,*
published on Thursday, has extensive entertainment and restaurant listings.

Where, a monthly magazine available free at most hotels throughout the city, lists
information about shopping, nightlife, attractions, and current shows at museums
and galleries.

Newspaper boxes around both cities dispense free copies of the weekly *Tab,*
which lists neighborhood-specific event information; the twice-monthly *Improper*
Bostonian, with extensive event and restaurant listings; and *Stuff@Night,* an offshoot of the *Phoenix* with selective listings and extensive arts coverage. Available on
newsstands, *Boston* magazine is a lifestyle-oriented monthly with cultural and
restaurant listings.

CITY LAYOUT

When Boston was established as the first permanent European settlement in the
region in 1630, it was one-third the size it is now. Parts of the city still reflect its
original layout, a seemingly haphazard plan that leaves even longtime residents tear-
ing their hair. Old Boston is littered with alleys, dead ends, one-way streets, streets
that change names, and streets named after extinct geographical features. On the
plus side, every wrong turn **downtown,** in the **North End,** or on **Beacon Hill** is a
chance to see something interesting you might otherwise have missed.

Much of the city's landscape was transformed by landfill projects of the 19th century, which altered the shoreline and created the **Back Bay,** where the streets proceed in orderly parallel lines. After you've spent some frustrating time in the older
part of the city, this simple plan will seem ingenious.

The most "main" street downtown is **Washington Street.** The causeway that
connected the Boston peninsula to the mainland in the 17th and 18th centuries ran
along this street, then called Orange (in honor of the British royal family). By 1824
the entire street had been renamed after George Washington; as another tribute,
streets (except Massachusetts Avenue) change their names when they cross Washington Street: Bromfield becomes Franklin, Winter becomes Summer, Stuart
becomes Kneeland.

In Chinatown, several blocks inland, Washington intersects **Beach Street,** which
used to be harborfront property. Vestiges of the old waterfront crop up in other odd

places. **Dock Square,** at Congress and North streets, is a reminder of the days when ships could deliver their cargo directly to the market on the first floor of Faneuil Hall.

Beacon Hill is also named after a long-ago topographical feature. It seems like a big enough hill—until you see the pillar behind the State House that rises 60 feet into the air, a reminder of its original height, before earth was taken from the top of the hill to be used as landfill. In their loftier days, Beacon, Copp's, and Fort hills gave the Shawmut peninsula the name Trimountain, rendered today as "Tremont." Copp's and Fort hills sloped down to the town dock at Dock Square.

When the hills were pulled down to fill in the coves that made up the shoreline, the layout of some new streets was somewhat willy-nilly. Not so in the Back Bay, where the streets (laid out on landfill) not only line up but even go in alphabetical order, starting at the Public Garden with Arlington, then Berkeley, Clarendon, Dartmouth, Exeter, Fairfield, Gloucester, and Hereford (and then Massachusetts). In the **South End,** also mostly landfill, the grid is less pristine but still pretty logical. Street names change from West to East when they cross Washington Street, and many of the names are those of the towns with train service from what is now South Station (for example, Concord, Worcester, and Springfield), which had just started when the streets were being christened.

MAIN ARTERIES & STREETS   The most prominent feature of downtown Boston is **Boston Common,** whether in person, on a map, or from atop the John Hancock Tower or the Prudential Center. The land for the Common was set aside in 1640, when it had only three trees. The Common is bordered by **Park Street,** which is 1 block long (but looms large in the geography of the T), and four important thoroughfares. **Tremont Street** originates at Government Center and runs through the Theater District into the South End and Roxbury. **Beacon Street** branches off Tremont at School Street and curves around, passing the golden dome of the State House at the apex of Beacon Hill and the Public Garden at the foot, and slicing through the Back Bay and Kenmore Square on its way into Brookline. At the foot of the hill, Beacon crosses **Charles Street,** the fourth side of the Common and the main street of Beacon Hill. Near Massachusetts General Hospital, Charles crosses **Cambridge Street,** which loops around to Government Center and turns into Tremont Street.

On the far side of Government Center, I-93 (also known as the Fitzgerald Expressway) separates the North End from the rest of the city. **Hanover Street** is the main street of the North End; at the harbor it intersects with **Commercial Street,** which runs along the waterfront from the North Washington Street bridge (the route to Charlestown, also known as the Charlestown bridge) until it gives way to Atlantic Avenue at Fleet Street. **Atlantic Avenue** completes the loop around the North End and runs more or less along the waterfront past South Station.

Boylston Street is the fifth side of the Common. It runs next to the Public Garden, through Copley Square and the Back Bay, and on into the Fenway. To get there it has to cross **Massachusetts Avenue,** or "Mass. Ave.," as it's almost always called (you might as well get into the habit now). Mass. Ave. is 9 miles long, extending as far as Lexington, and cutting through Arlington and Cambridge before hitting Boston at Storrow Drive, then Beacon Street, Marlborough Street, and Commonwealth Avenue. "**Comm. Ave.**" starts at the Public Garden and runs through Kenmore Square, past Boston University, and into the western suburbs. Farther along Mass. Ave., Symphony Hall is at the corner of **Huntington Avenue.** Huntington begins at Copley Square and passes Symphony Hall, Northeastern University, and the Museum of Fine Arts before crossing into Brookline.

FINDING AN ADDRESS   There's no rhyme or reason to the street pattern, compass directions are virtually useless, and there aren't enough street signs. The best way to find an address is to call ahead and ask for directions, including landmarks, or leave extra time for wandering around. If the directions involve a T stop, be sure to ask which exit to use—most stations have more than one.

STREET MAPS   In addition to the map provided with this guide, free maps of downtown Boston and the rapid transit lines are available at visitor information centers around the city. The **Greater Boston Convention & Visitors Bureau** (2 Copley Place, Suite 105, Boston, MA 02116; ☎ **888/SEE-BOSTON** or 617/536-4100; fax 617/424-7664; www.bostonusa.com; e-mail visitor@bostonusa.com) distributes a visitor information kit ($5.25) that includes a map, travel planner, guidebook, and discount coupon book. *Where* magazine, available free at most hotels, has maps of central Boston and the T.

Gousha's *Boston Fast Map* ($4.95), *Streetwise Boston* ($5.95), and *Artwise Boston* ($5.95) are sturdy, laminated maps available at most bookstores. Less detailed but more fun is MapEasy's *GuideMap to Boston* ($5.50), a hand-drawn map of the central areas and major attractions.

NEIGHBORHOODS IN BRIEF

The Waterfront   The Waterfront faces not the ocean but the Inner Harbor. Although for purposes of city government it's considered part of the North End, this neighborhood has a different feel. The narrow area along Atlantic Avenue and Commercial Street, once filled with wharves and warehouses, now abounds with luxury condos, marinas, restaurants, offices, and hotels. Also on the waterfront are the New England Aquarium and embarkation points for harbor cruises and whale-watching expeditions.

The North End   Crossing under I-93 from downtown on the way to the waterfront brings you to one of the city's oldest neighborhoods, the North End. Home to waves of immigrants in the course of its history, it has been predominantly Italian for 70 years or so, but the balance is shifting. It's now about half Italian-American and half newcomers, many of them young professionals who walk to work in the Financial District. Nevertheless, you'll hear Italian spoken in the streets and find a wealth of Italian restaurants, cafes, and shops. Nearby, and technically part of the North End, is the **North Station** area. With the September 1995 opening of the FleetCenter, the restaurants and clubs closer to Beacon Hill really started jumping. In spite of the increased traffic, this area isn't yet a good place to wander around alone at night.

Charlestown   One of the oldest areas of Boston, this is where you'll see the Bunker Hill Monument and USS *Constitution* ("Old Ironsides"), as well as one of the city's best restaurants, Olives. Off the beaten track, Charlestown is an almost entirely white residential neighborhood with a well-deserved reputation for insularity.

Faneuil Hall Marketplace/Haymarket   Employees aside, actual Boston residents tend to be in short supply at Faneuil Hall Marketplace (also called Quincy Market after the central building). An irresistible draw for out-of-towners and suburbanites, the cluster of restored market buildings bounded by Government Center, State Street, the Waterfront, and the North Station area is the city's most popular attraction. You'll find restaurants, bars, a food court, specialty shops, and Faneuil Hall itself. Haymarket, just off the Central Artery, is home to an open-air produce and fish market on Fridays and Saturdays.

Government Center   Love it or hate it, Government Center introduced modern design into the red-brick facade of traditional Boston architecture. Flanked by Beacon Hill, Downtown Crossing, and Faneuil Hall Marketplace, it is home to state and federal office towers and to City Hall.

Financial District   Bounded loosely by State Street, Downtown Crossing, Summer Street, and Atlantic Avenue, the Financial District is the banking, insurance, and legal center of the city.

Downtown Crossing   The intersection that gives Downtown Crossing its name is at Washington Street where Winter Street becomes Summer Street, and Filene's and Macy's face off across the pedestrian mall. This shopping and business district lies between the Common, the Theater District, the Financial District, and Government Center.

Chinatown   The third-largest Chinese community in the country resides near the Theater District in a small but growing area jammed with Asian restaurants, groceries, and gift shops. As the "Combat Zone," or red-light district, shrinks under pressure from the business community, Chinatown is expanding to fill the area between Downtown Crossing and the Mass. Turnpike extension.

The South End   Cross Stuart Street or Huntington Avenue heading south and you'll soon find yourself in a landmark district packed with Victorian row houses and little parks. Known for its ethnic, economic, and cultural diversity, the South End has a large gay community and some of the best restaurants in the city. With the gentrification of the 1980s, Tremont Street (particularly the end closest to downtown) gained a cachet it hadn't known for almost a century. *Note:* Don't confuse the South End with South Boston, another insular, predominantly Irish-American residential neighborhood.

Beacon Hill   Narrow, tree-lined streets and architectural showpieces, mostly in Federal style, make up this tiny residential area in the shadow of the State House. Louisburg Square and Mount Vernon Street, two of the loveliest (and most exclusive) spots in Boston, are on Beacon Hill. Bounded by Government Center, Boston Common, and the river, it's also home to Massachusetts General Hospital, on the nominally less tony north side of the neighborhood.

Back Bay   Perpetually fashionable since its creation out of landfill a century ago, the Back Bay overflows with gorgeous architecture and chic shops. It is bounded by the Public Garden, Mass. Ave., the river, and to the south by either Huntington Avenue or St. Botolph Street, depending on who's describing it to you. Students dominate the area near Mass. Ave. but grow scarce as property values rise approaching the Public Garden. Commonwealth Avenue is largely residential, and Newbury Street is largely commercial; both are excellent places to walk around.

Huntington Avenue   Not an actual neighborhood, Huntington Avenue starts at Copley Square and separates Copley Place from the Prudential Center before heading southwest into the suburbs. It's home to a number of landmarks, including the Christian Science Center, Symphony Hall (at the corner of Mass. Ave.), Northeastern University, and the Museum of Fine Arts. Parts of Huntington can sometimes be a little risky, so if you're leaving the museum at night, stick to the car or the Green Line, and travel in a group.

Kenmore Square   The white-and-red Citgo sign that dominates the skyline above the intersection of Commonwealth Avenue, Beacon Street, and Brookline Avenue tells you you're approaching Kenmore Square. Its shops, bars, restaurants, and clubs are a magnet for students from adjacent Boston University. The college-town atmosphere goes out the window when the Red Sox are in town and baseball fans pour into the area on the way to historic Fenway Park, 3 blocks away.

2 Getting Around

BY PUBLIC TRANSPORTATION

The **Massachusetts Bay Transportation Authority,** or MBTA (☎ 617/222-3200; www.mbta.com), is known as the T, and its logo is that letter in a circle. It runs subways, trolleys, and buses in Boston and many suburbs, as well as the commuter rail, which extends as far as Providence, Rhode Island.

DISCOUNT PASSES   The **Boston Visitor Passport** (☎ 617/222-5218) is one of the best deals in town. You get unlimited travel on all subway lines and local buses and Zones 1A and 1B of the commuter rail system, plus discounts on museums, restaurants, and entertainment. The cost is $5 for 1 day, $9 for 3 consecutive days, and $18 for 7 consecutive days. Passes are for sale at the Airport, Government Center, Harvard, Alewife and Riverside T stations, North Station, South Station, Back Bay Station, the Boston Common and Prudential Center information centers, and Quincy Market. Your hotel might also be able to provide you with the Visitor Passport.

BY SUBWAY   The subways and Green Line trolleys will take you around Boston faster than any other mode of transportation except walking. You might find this hard to believe when you're trapped in a tunnel during rush hour, but it's true. The oldest system in the country, the T dates to 1897, and recent and ongoing improvements have made it pretty reliable. The ancient Green Line is the most unpredictable—leave extra time if you're taking it to a vital appointment. And remember, downtown stops are so close together that it's often faster to walk.

The subways are color-coded and are called the Red, Green, Blue, and Orange lines. The commuter rail to the suburbs shows up on system maps in purple (but it's rarely called the Purple Line). The local fare is 85¢—you'll need a token—and can be as much as $2.25 for some surface line extensions on the Green and Red lines. Route and fare information and timetables are available at Park Street station (under the Common), which is the center of the system. Signs reading INBOUND and OUTBOUND refer to the direction of trains in relation to Park Street.

Service begins at around 5:15am and shuts down between 12:30 and 1am, systemwide. The only exception is New Year's Eve, or First Night, when service is free after 8pm and closing time is 2am.

The Green Line is not wheelchair accessible, but most stations on other lines are. They are indicated on system maps. To learn more, call the **Office for Transportation Access** (☎ 800/533-6282 or 617/222-5123; TDD 617/222-5415).

BY BUS   The **MBTA** (☎ 617/222-3200) runs buses and "trackless trolleys" (identifiable by their electric antennae but otherwise indistinguishable from buses) that provide service around town, and to and around the suburbs. The local routes you're likeliest to need are **no. 92** and **no. 93,** which run between Haymarket and Charlestown; **no. 1,** along Mass. Ave. from Dudley Square in Roxbury through the Back Bay and Cambridge to Harvard Square; and **no. 77,** along Mass. Ave. north of Harvard Square to Porter Square, North Cambridge, and Arlington.

The local bus fare is 60¢; express buses are $1.50 and up. Exact change is required. Many buses are equipped with lifts for wheelchairs (☎ 800/LIFT-BUS).

Planning Pointer

Wait to buy your Visitor Passport until you're ready to start sightseeing (at the airport or front desk, if you plan to plunge in immediately). This will allow you to coordinate trips to businesses that offer discounts with the days you're eligible.

BY CAR

If you plan to confine your visit to Boston and Cambridge, there's absolutely no reason to have a car, and it's probably more trouble than it's worth. If you're driving to Boston, leave the car in the hotel garage, and use it for day trips or to visit Cambridge, if you're feeling flush—you'll probably pay to park there too. If you're not motoring and you decide to take a day trip (see chapter 11), you'll probably want to rent a car. Here's the scoop.

RENTALS The major car-rental firms have offices in Boston and at Logan Airport, and some have branches in Cambridge. Rentals that originate in Boston and Cambridge are subject to a $10 convention center surcharge. If you're traveling at a busy time, reserve a car well in advance. Companies with offices at the airport include **Alamo** (☎ 800/327-9633), **Avis** (☎ 800/831-2847), **Budget** (☎ 800/527-0700), **Enterprise** (☎ 800/325-8007), **Hertz** (☎ 800/654-3131), **National** (☎ 800/227-7368), and **Thrifty** (☎ 800/367-2277). Most companies have cars for nonsmokers, but you'll have to ask. And be aware that a hefty drop-off charge is standard for most companies if you rent in one city and return in another.

To reserve a car when you're in town, call the toll-free number. Most companies have several outlets in the area; ask for the one nearest your hotel.

Expect to pay at least $40 a day for a midsize car from a national chain. If you are a member of AAA, a frequent-flyer program, or a professional association, you might be eligible for discounts.

To rent from the major national chains, you must be at least 25 years old and have a valid driver's license and credit card. If you don't have a credit card, make alternative arrangements well in advance; some companies require that you meet strict eligibility requirements. Read the rental agreement carefully, and know what your obligations are (for example, returning the car with a full tank, or paying through the nose for the company to refill it).

Your rental fee does not include insurance; but you might be covered under the insurance on your car at home. Many credit cards offer automatic coverage. Check before you pick up the rental car. Otherwise, be prepared to pay for Collision Damage Waiver or Loss Damage Waiver. Without coverage you could be liable for the full retail price of the car if it is damaged or stolen.

BOSTON DRIVERS Everything you've heard is true. Boston drivers deserve their notoriety, and even though the truly reckless are a tiny minority, it pays to be careful. Never assume that another driver will behave as you might expect, especially when it comes to the rarely used turn signal. Watch out for cars that leave the curb and change lanes without signaling, double- and triple-park in the most inconvenient places imaginable, and travel the wrong way down one-way streets.

PARKING It's difficult to find your way around Boston and practically impossible to find parking in some areas. Most spaces on the street are metered (and patrolled until 6pm on the dot every day except Sunday) and are open to nonresidents for 2 hours or less between 8am and 6pm. The penalty is a $20 ticket, but

Boston Transit

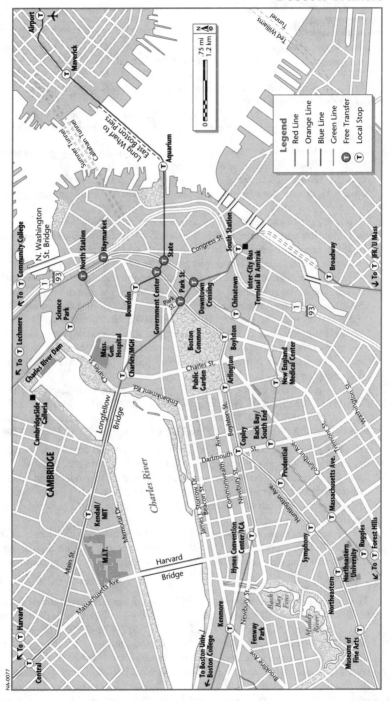

should you blunder into a tow-away zone, retrieving the car will cost you at least $50 and a lot of running around. Read the sign or meter carefully. In some areas parking is allowed only at certain hours. Rates vary in different sections of the city (usually $1 an hour downtown); bring plenty of quarters. Time limits range from 30 minutes to 2 hours.

To save yourself some aggravation, leave the car in a parking lot or garage and walk. Most lots cost no more than $20 for a full day, and there's often a lower flat rate if you enter and exit before certain times or if you park in the evening. Some restaurants offer reduced rates at nearby garages; ask when you call for reservations.

The two largest garages are under **Boston Common** and under the **Prudential Center.** The reasonably priced city-run garage under the Common (☎ 617/954-2096) at Charles Street accepts vehicles less than 6 feet, 3 inches tall. The garage at the Prudential Center (☎ 617/267-1002) has entrances on Boylston Street, Huntington Avenue, and Exeter Street, and at the Sheraton Boston Hotel & Towers. Parking is discounted if you make a purchase at the Shops at Prudential Center. A similar deal is offered at the garage at **Copley Place** (☎ 617/375-4488), off Huntington Avenue.

Good-sized garages can be found at **Government Center** off Congress Street (☎ 617/227-0385), at the **New England Aquarium** (☎ 617/723-1731), at 75 State St. (☎ 617/742-7275), near the Hynes Convention Center on **Dalton Street** (☎ 617/247-8006), and at **Zero Post Office Square** (☎ 617/423-1430).

SPECIAL DRIVING RULES   When traffic permits, drivers are allowed to make a right turn at a red light after stopping, unless a sign is posted saying otherwise (as it often is downtown). Seat belts are mandatory for adults and children, and infants and children under 5 must be strapped into car seats. You can't be stopped just for having an unbelted adult in the car, but a youngster on the loose is considered reason enough to pull you over.

Two state laws to be aware of, if only because the frequency with which they're broken will take your breath away: Pedestrians in the crosswalk have the right of way, and vehicles already in a rotary (traffic circle or roundabout) have the right of way.

BY TAXI

Taxis are expensive and not always easy to find—seek out a cab stand (often found in front of hotels), or call a dispatcher. To call ahead for a cab, try the **Independent Taxi Operators Association,** or ITOA (☎ 617/426-8700), **Town Taxi** (☎ 617/536-5000), or **Checker Taxi** (☎ 617/536-7000).

The fare structure is as follows: The first quarter of a mile (when the flag drops) costs $1.50, and each additional eighth of a mile is 25¢. "Wait time" is extra, and the passenger pays all tolls, as well as the $1.50 airport fee (on trips leaving Logan only). Charging a flat rate is not allowed within the city; the Police Department publishes a list of distances to the suburbs that establishes the flat rate for those trips. If you want to report a problem or have lost something in a cab, you can contact the Police Department's **Hackney Hotline** (☎ **617/536-8294**).

BY BICYCLE

Bring your own bike or rent one—you'll fit right in. Unless you're a real pro, though, you'll probably want to stay off the city streets until you're comfortable with the layout and traffic patterns. Boston has more than 50 miles of marked bike paths, including the 17.7-mile Dr. Paul Dudley White loop around the Charles River from the Museum of Science to Watertown and back.

For information about renting a bike, see "Biking" in chapter 7. If you bring or rent a bike, be sure to lock it as securely as possible when leaving it unattended, even for a short time.

FAST FACTS: Boston

Airport See "Getting There," in chapter 2.

American Express The main local office is at 1 Court St. (☎ **617/723-8400**), close to the Government Center and State Street MBTA stops. It's open Monday through Friday from 8:30am to 5:30pm. The Cambridge office, just off Harvard Square at 39 John F. Kennedy St. (☎ **617/661-0005**), is open Monday through Friday from 9am to 5pm and Saturday from 11am to 3pm.

Area Code For Boston and the immediate suburbs, it's **617**; for other nearby suburbs, **781, 508,** or **978.**

Baby-sitters Many hotels maintain lists of reliable sitters; check at the front desk or with the concierge. In an emergency, try **Parents in a Pinch,** 45 Bartlett Circle, Brookline, MA 02446 (☎ **617/739-KIDS**), weekdays from 8am to 5pm. It carefully screens child-care providers and will share references with parents who request them. The referral fee of $30 for an evening or half day, or $40 for a full day, is charged to your credit card (AE, MC, V). The provider fee of $8 per hour for one child, plus 50¢ for each additional child (with a 4-hour minimum), as well as transportation and authorized expenses, must be paid by cash or check directly to the provider.

Camera Repair Try **Bromfield Camera & Video,** 10 Bromfield St. (☎ **800/723-2628** or 617/426-5230), or the **Camera Center,** 107 State St. (☎ **800/924-6899** or 617/227-7255).

Car Rentals See "Getting Around," earlier in this chapter.

Climate See "When to Go," in chapter 2.

Dentists The desk staff or concierge at your hotel might be able to provide the name of a dentist. The **Metropolitan District Dental Society** (☎ **508/ 651-3521**) can point you toward a member of the Massachusetts Dental Society.

Doctors The desk staff or concierge at your hotel should be able to direct you to a doctor, but you can also try one of the many area hospital referral services. Among them are **Beth Israel Deaconess Health Information Line** (☎ 617/667-5356), **Brigham and Women's Hospital Physician Referral Service** (☎ 800/294-9999), **Massachusetts General Hospital Physician Referral Service** (☎ 800/711-4MGH), and **New England Medical Center Physician Referral Service** (☎ 617/636-9700).

Driving Rules See "Getting Around," earlier in this chapter.

Drugstores   See "Pharmacies," below.

Embassies/Consulates   See "Fast Facts" in chapter 3.

Emergencies   Call ☎ **911** for fire; ambulance; or the Boston, Brookline, or Cambridge police. This is a free call from pay phones. For the state police, call ☎ **617/523-1212.**

Eyeglass Repair   Cambridge Eye Doctors has offices in downtown Boston at 100 State St. (☎ **617/742-2076**) and 300 Washington St. (☎ **617/426-5536**). In Cambridge, **For Eyes Optical** has a branch at 56 John F. Kennedy St. (☎ **617/876-6031**).

Hospitals   Here's hoping you won't need to evaluate Boston's reputation for excellent medical care. In case you do: **Massachusetts General Hospital,** 55 Fruit St. (☎ **617/726-2000,** or 617/726-4100 for children's emergency services), and **New England Medical Center,** 750 Washington St. (☎ **617/636-5000,** or 617/636-5566 for emergency services), are closest to downtown Boston. At the Harvard Medical Area on the Boston–Brookline border are, among others, **Beth Israel Deaconess Medical Center,** 330 Brookline Ave. (☎ **617/667-7000**); **Brigham and Women's Hospital,** 75 Francis St. (☎ **617/732-5500**); and **Children's Hospital,** 300 Longwood Ave. (☎ **617/355-6000,** or 617/355-6611 for emergency services). In Cambridge are **Mount Auburn Hospital,** 330 Mount Auburn St. (☎ **617/492-3500,** or 617/499-5025 for emergency services), and **Cambridge Hospital,** 1493 Cambridge St. (☎ **617/498-1000**).

Hotlines   AIDS Hotline (☎ **800/235-2331** or 617/536-7733), **Poison Control Center** (☎ **617/232-2120**), **Rape Crisis** (☎ **617/492-7273**), **Samaritans Suicide Prevention** (☎ **617/247-0220**), **Samariteens** (☎ **800/252-8336** or 617/247-8050).

Information   See "Visitor Information," earlier in this chapter. For telephone directory assistance, dial ☎ **411.**

Liquor Laws   The legal drinking age is 21. In many bars, particularly near college campuses, you might be asked for ID if you appear to be under 30 or so. At sporting events, everyone purchasing alcohol is asked to show ID. Alcohol is sold in liquor stores and a few supermarkets and convenience stores. Liquor stores (and the liquor sections of supermarkets) are closed on Sundays, but alcohol may be served in restaurants and bars. Some suburban towns, notably Rockport, are "dry."

Lost Property   The T divides its Lost and Found into **buses** (☎ **617/222-5607**); **commuter rail** (☎ **617/222-3600**); and individual subway lines: **Blue** (☎ **617/222-5533**), **Green** (☎ **617/222-5221**), **Orange** (☎ **617/222-5403**), and **Red** (☎ **617/222-5317**). If you lose something in a taxi, call the cab company or the Police Department's **Hackney Hotline** (☎ **617/536-8294**).

Luggage Storage/Lockers   The desk staff or concierge at your hotel might be able to arrange storage for you. Lockers are available at the airport; you can check your luggage during the day at South Station, but not at all at Back Bay Station.

Maps   See "City Layout," earlier in this chapter.

Newspapers/Magazines   The *Boston Globe* (☎ **617/929-2000**) and *Boston Herald* (☎ **617/426-3000**) are published daily. The *Boston Phoenix* (☎ **617/536-5390**), a weekly, emphasizes arts coverage and publishes extensive entertainment and restaurant listings. **Boston** magazine (☎ **617/262-9700**) is a lifestyle-oriented monthly.

Pharmacies (Late-Night)   The pharmacy at the **CVS** in the Porter Square Shopping Center, off Mass. Ave. in Cambridge (☎ **617/876-5519**), is open 24 hours, 7 days a week. The pharmacy at the **CVS** at 155–157 Charles St. in Boston (☎ **617/523-1028**), next to the Charles T stop, is open until midnight. Some emergency rooms can fill your prescription at the hospital's pharmacy.

Police   Call ☎ **911** for emergencies.

Post Office   The main post office at 25 Dorchester Ave. (☎ **617/654-5326**), behind South Station, is open 24 hours, 7 days a week. Other post offices throughout the city are keyed on the map in chapter 1.

Radio   AM stations include WBZ (news, Bruins games), 1030; WEEI (sports, Red Sox games), 850; WILD (urban contemporary, soul), 1090; and WRKO (talk, sports, Celtics games), 680. FM stations include WBCN (rock, Patriots games), 104.1; WBOS (soft rock), 92.9; WBUR (public radio, classical music), 90.9; WCRB (classical music), 102.5; WFNX (alternative rock), 101.7; WGBH (public radio, classical music, jazz), 89.7; WJMN (pop, urban contemporary), 94.5; WKLB (country), 99.5; WODS (oldies), 103.3; and WZLX (classic rock), 100.7.

Rest Rooms   The visitor center at 15 State St. has a public rest room, as do most tourist attractions, hotels, department stores, and public buildings. There are rest rooms at the CambridgeSide Galleria, Copley Place, Prudential Center, and Quincy Market shopping areas. One of the few public rest rooms in Harvard Square is in the Harvard Coop.

Safety   On the whole, Boston is a safe city for walking. As in any large city, stay out of parks (including the Esplanade) at night unless you're in a crowd, and in general, trust your instincts—a dark, deserted street is probably deserted for a reason. Specific areas to avoid at night include Boylston Street between Tremont and Washington streets, and Tremont Street from Stuart to Boylston streets. Public transportation in the areas you're likely to be is busy and safe, but service stops between 12:30 and 1am.

Taxes   The 5% sales tax is not levied on food, prescription drugs, newspapers, or clothing worth less than $175, but there seems to be a tax on almost everything else. The lodging tax is 12.45% in Boston and Cambridge; the meal tax (which also applies to takeout food) is 5%; and the gasoline tax (included on the price at the pump) is 10%. There is also a tax on alcohol based on alcoholic content.

Taxis   See "Getting Around," earlier in this chapter.

Television   Stations include Channel 2 (WGBH), public television; Channel 4 (WBZ), CBS; Channel 5 (WCVB), ABC; Channel 7 (WHDH), NBC; Channel 25 (WFXT), Fox; Channel 38 (WSBK), UPN; and Channel 56 (WLVI), WB. Cable TV is available throughout Boston and the suburbs.

Time Zone   Boston is in the Eastern time zone. Daylight saving time begins on the first Sunday in April and ends on the last Sunday in October.

Transit Info   The **MBTA** (☎ **617/222-3200;** www.mbta.com) runs the subways and local buses. The **Massachusetts Port Authority** (☎ **800/23LOGAN;** www.massport.com) coordinates public transportation to and from the airport.

Weather   Call ☎ **617/936-1234** for forecasts.

5 Accommodations

Boston has one of the busiest hotel markets in the country, with occupancy rates soaring and renovations and new construction going on all over town. With enough planning and flexibility, you probably won't have much difficulty finding a suitable place to stay in or near the city, but it's always a good idea to **make a reservation.** Try to book far in advance for the vacation months of **July and August,** the busy **spring and fall** convention seasons, and the college graduation season in **May and early June.**

Boston regularly lands in the top 10 on lists of the most expensive destinations for business travelers, but that doesn't mean you have to break the bank. At many hotels, **rates are lower on weekends** than on weeknights, when corporate and convention travelers fill rooms. Bargain hunters who don't mind cold and the possibility of snow (sometimes *lots* of snow) will want to aim for **January through March,** when you can find great deals, especially on weekends. As with travel plans, it helps to **be flexible** in selecting dates—a hotel that's full of conventioneers one week might be courting business a few days later.

When choosing a hotel, ask a lot of questions about rates and the amenities that matter to you. Members of **auto clubs, professional organizations,** and **frequent-flyer programs** might be eligible for **discounts or other perks** such as free parking, but these amenities generally won't be offered unless you ask. The same goes for special rates some hotels offer to **senior citizens** and to **students with ID cards.** And if you don't need a pool, a health club, room service, or other perks, consider less luxurious (and less expensive) lodgings. If you have allergies or special requests—a bed board, a room that faces a particular direction, accommodations for your pet—make arrangements in advance.

Parking is available at most hotels (usually for a fee) and motels; some have arrangements with nearby garages. See "By Car" in the "Getting Around" section, in chapter 4, for help in deciding whether you'll need a car in Boston and Cambridge.

If you're traveling alone, single rates are almost always lower. Weekend and other package deals can knock the price down considerably. These listings cover **Boston, Cambridge, Brookline,** and a few other suburbs; chapter 11 includes suggestions for daytrippers who want to plan an overnight visit.

Where There's Smoke . . .

Accommodations reserved for nonsmokers—often in blocks as large as several floors—are so common that we no longer single out hotels that offer them. However, nonsmokers should not assume that they'll get a smoke-free room without specifically requesting one. As smokers are squeezed into fewer and fewer rooms, the ones they are allowed to use become saturated with the smell of smoke, even in hotels that are otherwise antiseptic. To avoid this disagreeable situation, be sure that everyone who handles your reservation knows that you need a smoke-free room.

A NOTE ON TAXES   The **state hotel tax** is **5.7%.** As of January 1, 1998, **Boston and Cambridge** (as well as Worcester and Springfield) levy a **2.75% convention center tax** on top of the **4% city tax,** bringing the total tax to 12.45%. If you're on a tight budget, remember that **Brookline,** covered in our "Mass. Ave. to Brookline" section, is not subject to the tax, and its rate remains **9.7%** (5.7% for the state, 4% for the city). If you plan to stay there and visit downtown Boston, however, remember to budget at least an extra $1.70 a day for T fare. Not all suburbs have a local tax, so some towns charge only the 5.7% state tax.

MORE SUGGESTIONS   The **Greater Boston Convention and Visitors Bureau** has a new **Hotel Hot Line** (☎ 800/777-6001) that can help make reservations even during the busiest times. It's staffed weekdays until 8pm, weekends until 4pm. The bureau, 2 Copley Place, Suite 105, Boston, MA 02116 (☎ 888/SEE-BOSTON or 617/536-4100; fax 617/424-7664; www.bostonusa. com), also sells **visitor information kits** ($5.25) for people traveling with and without children; they include a travel planner, city map, guidebook, and discount coupon book.

The **Massachusetts Office of Travel and Tourism,** 100 Cambridge St., 13th floor, Boston, MA 02202 (☎ 800/227-6277 or 617/727-3201; fax 617/727-6525; www.mass-vacation.com; e-mail vacationinfo@state.ma.us) publishes a free **"Getaway Guide"** magazine divided into six regional sections that list accommodations and attractions. It includes a map and a seasonal calendar.

BED & BREAKFASTS   Whether you're uncomfortable with the idea of a big, impersonal chain hotel or just can't afford one, a B&B can be a good option. Home accommodations are usually less expensive than hotels and often more comfortable; most are near public transportation. Expect to pay at least $60 a night for a double in the summer, more during special events. Breakfast is usually included in the room rate. The following organizations can help match you with a suitable host in Boston, Cambridge, or the Greater Boston area:

- **Bed and Breakfast Associates Bay Colony Ltd.,** P.O. Box 57166, Babson Park Branch, Boston, MA 02157-0166 (☎ 800/347-5088 or 781/449-5302; fax 781/449-5958; www.bnbboston.com; e-mail info@bnbboston.com), lists more than 150 bed-and-breakfasts and inns in the metropolitan Boston area and throughout eastern Massachusetts, including Cape Cod. The agency also arranges long-term lodging and lists furnished apartments and house-sharing opportunities. A member of the B&B National Network, it can help arrange reservations elsewhere in the United States and in Canada.
- **Bed and Breakfast Agency of Boston,** 47 Commercial Wharf, Boston, MA 02110 (☎ 800/CITY-BNB or 617/720-3540, from the United Kingdom 0800/89-5128; fax 617/523-5761), offers accommodations in waterfront lofts

Boston Accommodations

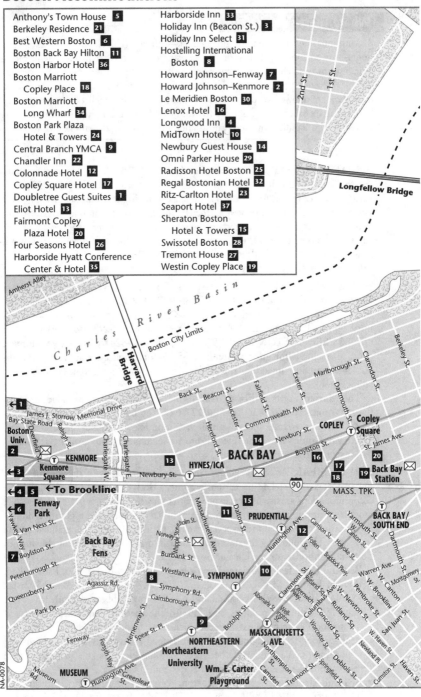

Anthony's Town House **5**
Berkeley Residence **21**
Best Western Boston **6**
Boston Back Bay Hilton **11**
Boston Harbor Hotel **36**
Boston Marriott
  Copley Place **18**
Boston Marriott
  Long Wharf **34**
Boston Park Plaza
  Hotel & Towers **24**
Central Branch YMCA **9**
Chandler Inn **22**
Colonnade Hotel **12**
Copley Square Hotel **17**
Doubletree Guest Suites **1**
Eliot Hotel **13**
Fairmont Copley
  Plaza Hotel **20**
Four Seasons Hotel **26**
Harborside Hyatt Conference
  Center & Hotel **35**

Harborside Inn **33**
Holiday Inn (Beacon St.) **3**
Holiday Inn Select **31**
Hostelling International
  Boston **8**
Howard Johnson–Fenway **7**
Howard Johnson–Kenmore **2**
Le Meridien Boston **30**
Lenox Hotel **16**
Longwood Inn **4**
MidTown Hotel **10**
Newbury Guest House **14**
Omni Parker House **29**
Radisson Hotel Boston **25**
Regal Bostonian Hotel **32**
Ritz-Carlton Hotel **23**
Seaport Hotel **37**
Sheraton Boston
  Hotel & Towers **15**
Swissotel Boston **28**
Tremont House **27**
Westin Copley Place **19**

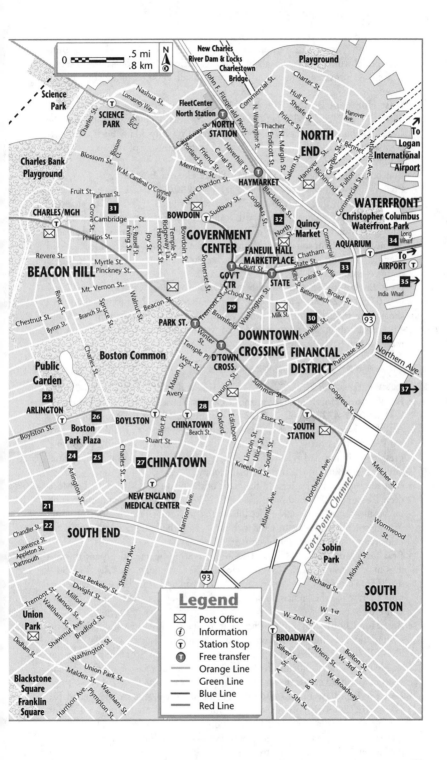

and historic homes in Boston and Cambridge. Nightly, weekly, monthly, and special winter rates are available. Listings include 155 rooms and 60 suites, as well as furnished studios and apartments, all within walking distance of downtown.

- **Host Homes of Boston,** P.O. Box 117, Waban Branch, Boston, MA 02168-0001 (☎ **617/244-1308;** fax 617/244-5156), lists 45 homes throughout the city and suburbs and emphasizes personalized hospitality. Many hosts speak foreign languages, and all provide breakfast. A minimum stay of at least 2 nights is required.

- **Bed & Breakfast Reservations North Shore/Greater Boston/Cape Cod,** P.O. Box 35, Newtonville, MA 02460-0001 (☎ **800/832-2632** outside MA, or 617/964-1606; fax 617/332-8572; www.bnbinc.com; e-mail bnbinc@ix.netcom.com), matches visitors with carefully inspected accommodations in Greater Boston and areas north of Boston; on Cape Cod; and in selected areas in Maine, New Hampshire, and Vermont. Some lodgings are classified as "kid friendly," making this a good choice for families. A minimum stay of at least 2 nights is required.

- **New England Bed and Breakfast,** P.O. Box 1426, Waltham, MA 02454 (☎ **617/244-2112**), offers home accommodations in the suburbs that are a short drive from Boston and within walking distance of public transportation. This organization offers residences for nonsmokers and will make an appropriate match if you have allergies.

1 Best Bets

- **Best Historic Hotel:** The ✪ **Fairmont Copley Plaza Hotel,** 138 St. James Ave. (☎ **800/527-4727**), built in 1912 on the original site of the Museum of Fine Arts, has entertained almost every president since William Howard Taft, including President Kennedy, who visited regularly for the fish chowder. At press time, President Clinton had yet to join the party. There's a display of historic memorabilia in a cabinet in the majestic main lobby.

- **Best for Business Travelers:** In the heart of the Financial District, ✪ **Le Meridien Boston,** 250 Franklin St. (☎ **800/543-4300**), has well-equipped rooms for business travelers, a full-service business center, and a great health club. And, so that you'll know what to wear without leaving the hotel, a weather report is delivered to your room every evening.

- **Best for a Romantic Getaway:** The intimate atmosphere and elegant furnishings make the suites at the ✪ **Eliot Hotel,** 370 Commonwealth Ave. (☎ **800/44-ELIOT**), a great spot for trysting. And if you and your beloved need some time apart, close the French doors—you can be in separate rooms but still maintain eye contact.

- **Best Hotel Lobby for Pretending That You're Rich:** As you walk around the ground floor of the ✪ **Boston Harbor Hotel,** 70 Rowes Wharf (☎ **800/752-7077**), make believe you just tied up your yacht out front and are keeping an eye on it. Then suddenly "remember" an important meeting in the Financial District and head across the street.

- **Best for Families:** The ✪ **Doubletree Guest Suites,** 400 Soldiers Field Rd. (☎ **800/222-TREE**), offers two rooms for the price of one, with two TVs and a refrigerator, and a nice pool. The location, straddling Boston and Cambridge, is especially good if you're coming from the west—you leave the turnpike before downtown traffic shatters the truce in the back of the minivan.

- **Best for Travelers with Disabilities:** The ✪ **Royal Sonesta Hotel,** 5 Cambridge Pkwy., Cambridge (☎ **800/SONESTA**), trains its staff in disability awareness and offers 11 wheelchair-accessible rooms, some of which adjoin standard units, and 16 rooms for guests with hearing impairments. A wheelchair ramp for use in conference rooms is available. The **Westin Copley Place Boston,** 10 Huntington Ave. (☎ **800/WESTIN-1**), has 48 fully accessible rooms that adjoin standard units.
- **Best Moderately Priced Hotels:** The ✪ **Newbury Guest House,** 261 Newbury St. (☎ **617/437-7666**), and its sister property, the ✪ **Harborside Inn,** 185 State St. (☎ **617/723-7500**), would be good deals even if they weren't ideally located. And room prices include continental breakfast.
- **Best Service:** Hands down, the ✪ **Four Seasons Hotel,** 200 Boylston St. (☎ **800/332-3442**), wins. The chain's standards are sky-high, and the friendly and efficient staff here meets and exceeds them.
- **Best Hotel Pool:** The enormous **Sheraton Boston Hotel & Towers,** 39 Dalton St. (☎ **800/225-2008**), is a little impersonal because of its size, but it has a great indoor-outdoor pool with a retractable dome.
- **Best Views:** Several hotels offer impressive views of their immediate surroundings, but for a picture-postcard panorama of Boston and Cambridge, head to the upper floors of the **Westin Copley Place Boston** (see above).
- **Best Hotels for Baseball Fans:** Devotees of the national pastime can rub shoulders with major leaguers at the **Boston Marriott Copley Place,** 110 Huntington Ave. (☎ **800/228-9290**), and the **Sheraton Boston Hotel & Towers** (see above), the standard addresses for teams in town to take on the Red Sox.

2 Downtown

The downtown area includes the **Freedom Trail** and the historic neighborhoods defined in chapter 4 as the **Waterfront, Faneuil Hall,** the **Financial District, Downtown Crossing,** and **Beacon Hill.** Accommodations in the moderate and inexpensive price categories are mostly bed-and-breakfasts. Consult the businesses listed at the beginning of this chapter, or try Beacon Hill's **Eliot and Pickett Houses,** 6 Mount Vernon Place, Boston, MA 02108 (☎ **617/248-8707**), whose 20 guest rooms are extremely popular, especially in the high season.

THE WATERFRONT & FANEUIL HALL MARKETPLACE

At all hotels in these neighborhoods, **ask for a room on a high floor**—you'll want to be as far as possible from the noise and disarray of the ongoing Central Artery construction.

VERY EXPENSIVE

✪ **Boston Harbor Hotel.** 70 Rowes Wharf (entrance on Atlantic Ave.), Boston, MA 02110. ☎ **800/752-7077** or 617/439-7000. Fax 617/330-9450. www.bhh.com. 230 units. A/C MINIBAR TV TEL. $255–$510 double; from $365 suite. Extra person $50. Children under 18 stay free in parents' room. Weekend packages available. AE, CB, DC, DISC, MC, V. Valet parking $26; self-parking $22 weekdays. MBTA: Blue Line to Aquarium, or Red Line to South Station. Pets accepted.

The Boston Harbor Hotel is one of the finest in town, and certainly the prettiest, whether you approach its landmark six-story-high archway from land or sea (the Airport Water Shuttle stops here). The 16-story red-brick hotel is within walking distance of downtown and the waterfront attractions, and it prides itself on offering top-notch service to travelers pursuing both business and pleasure.

Guest rooms look out on the harbor or the skyline (rooms with city views are less expensive), and all have windows that open. Each room is a luxurious bed- and living-room combination, with mahogany furnishings that include an armoire, a desk, and comfortable chairs. Some suites have private terraces. Standard guest-room amenities include three telephones, dataports, hair dryers, robes, slippers, and umbrellas. A museum-quality collection of paintings, drawings, prints, and nautical charts enhances the grand public spaces of the hotel, which is part of a 12-year-old hotel-office-retail-condominium complex.

Dining/Diversions: The excellent **Rowes Wharf Restaurant** overlooks the harbor, as does **Intrigue,** the ground-floor cafe. It opens at 5:30am for breakfast (carry-away and sit-down); serves lunch, dinner, and afternoon tea; and has seasonal outdoor seating. The **Rowes Wharf Bar** serves cocktails and light fare.

Amenities: Video rentals; health club and spa with 60-foot lap pool; whirlpool; sauna, steam, and exercise rooms; salon for facials, massage, manicures, pedicures, and spa treatments. State-of-the-art business center with professional staff; conference rooms; concierge; 24-hour room service; dry cleaning and laundry; newspaper delivery; in-room massage; twice-daily maid service; baby-sitting available; express checkout; valet parking; courtesy car. Eighteen rooms for people with disabilities.

✪ **Regal Bostonian Hotel.** At Faneuil Hall Marketplace, Boston, MA 02109. ☎ **800/ 343-0922** or 617/523-3600. Fax 617/523-2454. www.regal-hotels.com/boston. 152 units. A/C MINIBAR TV TEL. $245–$325 double; $265–$345 deluxe; $295–$375 Regal Class; $500–$775 suite. Extra person $20. Children under 19 stay free in parents' room. Rollaway $20. Weekend and other packages available. AE, DC, DISC, JCB, MC, V. Parking $20. MBTA: Green or Blue Line to Government Center, or Orange Line to Haymarket.

Across North Street from Faneuil Hall Marketplace, the relatively small Regal Bostonian offers excellent service and features that make it competitive with larger hotels. The newly redecorated guest rooms vary in size; all boast top-of-the-line furnishings and amenities, including on-demand video, 26-inch TVs, safes, terry robes, and two-line phones with dataports. The bathrooms are a primper's paradise, with hair dryers, heat lamps, heated towel racks, and both overhead and European-style handheld shower sprays. Many rooms have French doors that open onto small private balconies. Some suites have double vanities and separate dressing areas, working fireplaces, or Jacuzzis. Hotel-wide soundproofing means you won't be forced to choose between quiet and a nice view, but some of the scenery is anything but soothing. The marketplace is busy from early till late, the Central Artery construction is nearby, and on Friday and Saturday the noisy Haymarket vendors are in place by 7am.

The hotel, acquired by Regal Hotels International in 1996, is in an unusual building. The four- and seven-story red-brick structure consists of two wings. One wing, an old warehouse building with exposed beams, dates from 1824 and is furnished in traditional style; the other, built in 1890, has more contemporary appointments. Public spaces are decorated with artwork on loan from the Bostonian Society.

Dining: On the fourth-floor rooftop is the glass-enclosed **Seasons** restaurant. The lounge in the glass-walled lobby serves champagne by the glass and affords a great view of the scene at the marketplace.

Amenities: VCRs; complimentary health-club and swimming-pool privileges at the excellent Sky Club, 4 blocks away; conference rooms; concierge; 24-hour room service; dry cleaning and laundry; newspaper delivery; in-room massage; twice-daily maid service; secretarial services available; express checkout; valet parking; complimentary morning limousine service. Rooms for people with disabilities are available.

EXPENSIVE

The newest hotel on the Waterfront—technically in South Boston, next to the World Trade Center—is the independent **Seaport Hotel,** 164 Northern Ave., Boston, MA 02210 (☎ **888/WTC-HOTEL** or 617/385-4100). The 427-unit hotel was scheduled to open in May 1998 after several years of meticulous planning, and it has all the features you'd expect in this price range. If you don't have business at the World Trade Center or a hankering for seafood, it's not exactly centrally located, but it does offer shuttle service to the airport and downtown.

Boston Marriott Long Wharf. 296 State St., Boston, MA 02109. ☎ **800/228-9290** or 617/227-0800. Fax 617/227-2867. www.marriott.com/marriott/BOSLW. 400 units. A/C TV TEL. Apr–Nov $189–$269 double; Dec–Mar $159–$229 double; $450–$490 suite. Weekend packages from $214 per night. AE, DC, DISC, JCB, MC, V. Parking $25. MBTA: Blue Line to Aquarium.

The terraced red-brick exterior of this long, narrow, seven-story hotel looks nothing like the ocean liner it supposedly resembles, but it is one of the most recognizable sights on the harbor. The location is the chief appeal of this otherwise ordinary Marriott: it's a stone's throw from the New England Aquarium, convenient to downtown and waterfront attractions, and just two subway stops from the airport.

Rooms are large and the decor varies; all have a choice of king-size or double beds, two phones, and a table and chairs in front of the window. The Central Artery construction is directly under the windows of the rooms near the street. Ask to be as close to the water as possible, and you'll have good views of the wharves and waterfront.

The seventh floor is the Concierge Level, with complimentary continental breakfast, cocktails, and hors d'oeuvres served in a private lounge, and private exercise facilities.

Dining: Oceana Restaurant, with a 180° expanse of glass wall fronting the harbor; cafe and lounge; bar and grill.

Amenities: Indoor pool with an outdoor terrace; exercise room; whirlpools; saunas; game room; business center; conference rooms; concierge; room service until 11pm; dry cleaning; newspaper delivery; twice-daily maid service; express checkout; valet parking. Eighteen rooms for people with disabilities.

MODERATE

✪ **Harborside Inn.** 185 State St., Boston, MA 02109. ☎ **617/723-7500.** Fax 617/670-2010. 54 units. A/C TV TEL. $135–$155 double, winter $105–$125 double; $250 suite, winter $175 suite. Rates include continental breakfast. Rates might be higher during special events. Extra person $10. AE, CB, DC, DISC, MC, V. No parking available. MBTA: Blue Line to Aquarium.

Under the same management as the Newbury Guest House in the Back Bay, the Harborside Inn offers a similarly enticing combination of value, location, and service. The renovated 1858 warehouse is perfectly situated for sightseers and thrifty business travelers alike, across the street from Faneuil Hall Marketplace and the waterfront, and a short walk from most addresses in the Financial District. Guest rooms, which have hardwood floors, Oriental rugs, queen-size beds, and Victorian-style furniture, surround an atrium; those with city views are more expensive. All are nicely appointed and have some features you'd expect at pricier hotels, including free local phone calls and voice mail. Rooms on the top floors of the eight-story building have lower ceilings but better views. On the ground floor are a small exercise room and the cafe, where the buffet breakfast is served—the finishing touch that makes this one of the best deals in Boston.

FINANCIAL DISTRICT/DOWNTOWN CROSSING

Besides being great for **corporate travelers,** hotels in this area can be even more convenient than those nearer the water—they're that much closer to the major **shopping areas** and the start of the **Freedom Trail.**

VERY EXPENSIVE

✪ **Le Meridien Boston.** 250 Franklin St. (at Post Office Sq.), Boston, MA 02110. ☎ **800/543-4300** or 617/451-1900. Fax 617/423-2844. www.lemeridien.com. 326 units. A/C MINIBAR TV TEL. $285–$335 double; $475–$800 suite. Weekend rates from $159. Extra person $30. AE, CB, DC, DISC, MC, V. Valet parking $29, $13 Fri–Sat; self-parking $28, $8 Fri–Sat. MBTA: Red Line to Downtown Crossing or South Station, or Blue or Orange Line to State.

This is the city's premier business hotel. If you don't need to leave the Financial District, you might not even need to leave the premises—ask for a Business Traveler room (with a fax machine, an oversized desk, halogen lighting, and a coffeemaker) and arrange a power lunch in the elegant Julien restaurant. Vacationing visitors are near the waterfront and downtown attractions but not all that close to public transportation. Whatever your purpose, you'll find the service by the multilingual staff superb.

Guest rooms have 153 different configurations, including dramatic loft suites with first-floor living rooms, a bedroom in the loft area, and bathrooms on both levels. All rooms have two telephones (one in the bathroom), as well as hair dryers. The glass mansard roof (not part of the original design) surrounds the top three stories, where a number of rooms have large sloped windows and extraordinary views. The nine-story granite-and-limestone building is an architectural marvel. It's the old Federal Reserve Bank building, designed by R. Clipston Sturgis in 1922 in the style of a 16th-century Roman palace. The bank's original grand marble staircase now leads to the dining areas; two murals by N. C. Wyeth grace the walls of the bar; and the lobby features ornately carved marble fireplaces and floor-to-ceiling arched windows.

Dining/Diversions: Julien serves lunch and dinner daily; the bar features live piano music 6 nights a week. The less formal **Café Fleuri** serves three meals daily, the Saturday "Chocolate Bar Buffet" (September through May), and Sunday jazz brunch. **La Terrasse** is the seasonal outdoor cafe.

Amenities: Forty-foot indoor pool; well-equipped health club with whirlpool and sauna; full-service business center with library and full-time staff; conference rooms; concierge; 24-hour room service; dry cleaning and laundry; newspaper delivery; twice-daily maid service; express checkout; valet parking; courtesy car to Newbury Street; daily weather report. Fifteen rooms for people with disabilities.

Swissôtel Boston (The Lafayette). 1 Avenue de Lafayette, Boston, MA 02111. ☎ **800/621-9200** or 617/451-2600. Fax 617/451-0054. www.swissotel.com. 454 units. A/C MINIBAR TV TEL. $235–$260 double; $440–$595 suite or Swiss Butler Executive Level; $2,500 Presidential Suite. Extra person $25. Children under 12 stay free in parents' room. Weekend packages available. AE, CB, DC, DISC, JCB, MC, V. Valet parking $26; self-parking $22 weekdays, $8 weekends. MBTA: Red Line to Downtown Crossing, or Green Line to Boylston. Small pets accepted.

This centrally located 22-story hotel lives two lives. It's a busy convention and business destination during the week, and the excellent weekend packages make it popular with sightseers. The dichotomy carries over to its exterior, a plain facade that contrasts with both the opulence within and the commotion of adjacent Washington Street. In the luxurious second-floor lobby, European style takes over, with antique and contemporary furnishings, and elegant accents such as Waterford crystal chandeliers and imported marble columns.

Guest rooms cluster around four atriums with semiprivate lobbies, creating the effect of several small hotels in one. Each room has a sitting area with a desk, a settee, and king- or twin-size beds. The suites are either L-shaped rooms with sitting areas, or living rooms with connecting bedrooms. All rooms have three telephones with dataports, fax machines, and coffeemakers. On the Executive Level, a Swiss butler performs traditional valet functions, acts as a private concierge, and even runs errands.

Dining: Café Suisse serves three meals daily and Sunday brunch. The lounge in the atrium offers cocktails, vintage wines by the glass, and light meals.

Amenities: Fifty-two-foot indoor pool; health club; exercise room; saunas; sun terrace; high-tech business center; conference rooms; 24-hour room service; dry cleaning; valet service; nightly turndown.

EXPENSIVE

Omni Parker House. 60 School St., Boston, MA 02108. ☎ **800/THE-OMNI** or 617/227-8600. Fax 617/742-5729. www.omnihotels.com. 550 units. A/C MINIBAR TV TEL. $185–$325 double; $260 minisuite; from $295 parlor suite. Children under 18 stay free in parents' room. Weekend packages available. AE, CB, DC, DISC, MC, V. Valet parking $24; self-parking $17. MBTA: Green Line to Government Center, or Red Line to Park St.

The Parker House offers a great combination of nearly 150 years of history and $60 million in renovations. It has operated continuously longer than any other hotel in America—since 1855—and a massive overhaul scheduled to be completed by August 1998 upgraded it throughout and added a business center and an exercise facility. Guest rooms now have minibars, two-line phones, modem hookups, hair dryers, and irons and ironing boards. They're not huge, but they are thoughtfully laid out and nicely appointed; many have views of Old City Hall or Government Center. The pattern on the bedspreads—so gaudy that it's elegant—is a reproduction of the original, and the lobby of the 14-story hotel still boasts its original American oak paneling.

Over the years, the Parker House has entertained many famous guests and even had some famous employees—Malcolm X and Ho Chi Minh both worked here. The room that's now Parker's Bar hosted the best-known group of guests: Henry Wadsworth Longfellow, Oliver Wendell Holmes, Ralph Waldo Emerson, Nathaniel Hawthorne, and sometimes even Charles Dickens, who made up a literary salon called the Saturday Club.

Dining/Diversions: Parker's Restaurant serves three meals daily, including Parker House rolls, which were invented here; **Parker's Bar,** open from midday to early morning, has live piano music Monday through Saturday nights.

Amenities: Health club; staffed business center; newly refurbished and expanded conference rooms; concierge; room service until 11pm; dry cleaning and laundry; newspaper delivery; in-room massage; secretarial services available; express checkout; valet parking. Rooms for people with disabilities are available.

BEACON HILL
EXPENSIVE

Holiday Inn Select Boston Government Center. 5 Blossom St., Boston, MA 02114. ☎ **800/HOLIDAY** or 617/742-7630. Fax 617/742-4192. 303 units. A/C TV TEL. From $200 double. Extra person $20. Rollaway $20. Children under 18 stay free in parents' room. Weekend and corporate packages and 10% AARP discount available. AE, DC, DISC, JCB, MC, V. Parking $18. MBTA: Red Line to Charles/MGH.

At the base of Beacon Hill, near Massachusetts General Hospital, this utilitarian hotel rises 15 stories above a shopping plaza with a supermarket, shops, and restaurants. It's leading the chain's charge into the battle for the business traveler—rooms, which were renovated in 1994, are furnished in contemporary style and have fax machines, dataports, coffeemakers, hair dryers, and ironing boards. Each room has a picture-window view of the city or the State House (or the parking lot—ask to be as high up as possible). Executive rooms, on the 12th and 14th floors, have two phones, terry robes, evening turndown service, and minirefrigerators, and rates there include continental breakfast and access to a private lounge.

Dining: Foster's Bar & Grille serves three meals daily.

Amenities: Outdoor heated pool; small exercise room; sundeck; business center; 15th-floor conference rooms; coin laundry; concierge; room service until 10pm; dry cleaning and laundry; newspaper delivery; secretarial services available; express checkout. Rooms for people with disabilities are available.

3 Back Bay

The first section of listings for this area includes hotels in the plush territory near **Boston Common** and the **Public Garden,** and in the rapidly improving **Theater District.** The second section lists accommodations closer to **Copley Square** and the **Hynes Convention Center.** The first group is closer to downtown, but bear in mind that nothing in central Boston is all that far from anything else.

BOSTON COMMON/PUBLIC GARDEN/THEATER DISTRICT
VERY EXPENSIVE

✪ **Four Seasons Hotel.** 200 Boylston St., Boston, MA 02116. ☎ **800/332-3442** or 617/338-4400. Fax 617/423-0154. www.fourseasons.com/locations/Boston/index.html. 288 units. A/C MINIBAR TV TEL. $385–$610 double; from $950 1-bedroom suite; from $1,900 2-bedroom suite. Extra person $40. Weekend packages available. AE, CB, DC, DISC, JCB, MC, V. Valet parking $27. MBTA: Green Line to Arlington. Pets accepted.

Many hotels offer exquisite service, a beautiful location, elegant guest rooms and public areas, a terrific health club, and wonderful restaurants. No other hotel in Boston—indeed, in New England—combines every element of a luxury hotel as seamlessly as the 14-year-old Four Seasons. If I were traveling with someone else's credit cards, I'd head straight here.

Overlooking the Public Garden, the 16-story red-brick-and-glass hotel incorporates the traditional and the contemporary, in architecture and in attitude. Each spacious room is elegantly appointed and has a striking view, with a breakfront that conceals a 19-inch TV and minibar. All rooms have bay windows that open, climate control, three two-line phones with computer and fax capability, hair dryers, terry robes, and a safe. Children receive bedtime snacks and toys. Small pets are accepted and treated as generously as their traveling companions, with a special menu and amenities. Larger accommodations range from Executive Suites, with enlarged alcove areas for entertaining or business meetings, to luxurious one-, two-, and three-bedroom deluxe suites.

Dining/Diversions: The elegant restaurant **Aujourd'hui,** one of Boston's best, serves contemporary American cuisine; the **Bristol Lounge** is open for lunch, afternoon tea, dinner, and breakfast on Sunday, and it features live entertainment nightly.

Amenities: In general, if you want it, you'll get it. VCRs; free video rentals; indoor heated 51-foot pool and whirlpool with a view of the Public Garden; spa with weight machines, StairMasters, treadmills, private masseuse, Jacuzzi, and sauna. (Residents of the condominiums on the upper floors of the hotel share the pool and spa.) Excellent business center; conference rooms; concierge; 24-hour room service; dry cleaning and laundry; newspaper delivery; in-room massage; twice-daily maid service; baby-sitting available; express checkout; valet parking; complimentary shoeshine; complimentary limousine service to downtown Boston addresses. Rooms for people with disabilities are available.

The Ritz-Carlton. 15 Arlington St., Boston, MA 02117. ☎ **800/241-3333** or 617/536-5700. Fax 617/536-1335. www.ritzcarlton.com/location/NorthAmerica/Boston/main.htm. 278 units. A/C MINIBAR TV TEL. $265–$415 double; $345–$2,000 1-bedroom suite; $710–$915 2-bedroom suite. Ritz-Carlton Club $320–$650 one-bedroom suite; $820–$1,025 2-bedroom suite. Extra person $20. Weekend packages available. AE, CB, DC, DISC, JCB, MC, V. Valet parking $24. MBTA: Green Line to Arlington. Small pets accepted.

Overlooking the Public Garden, the Ritz-Carlton has attracted both the "proper Bostonian" and the celebrated guest since 1927. The 17-story hotel has the highest staff-to-guest ratio in the city, including white-gloved elevator operators. Although the pricier Four Seasons has better amenities, notably the on-premises pool and business center, the status-conscious consider the Ritz—well, ritzier.

The guest rooms have French provincial furnishings, crystal chandeliers, two telephones (one in the bathroom), safes, closets that lock, and climate control; some have windows that open. Bathrooms are finished in Vermont marble, and terry robes are provided. You'll pay more for rooms with a view. Fresh flowers grace the suites, many of which have wood-burning fireplaces.

Floors 15, 16, and 17 make up the Club Level, with gorgeous views and the use of the Ritz-Carlton Club, which has its own concierge and serves complimentary breakfast, afternoon tea, hors d'oeuvres, and after-dinner sweets.

Dining/Diversions: The Dining Room and **The Bar at the Ritz** are as legendary for their clientele as for their food and drink. There is also a rather cramped cafe, and a lounge that serves the city's best afternoon tea, then cognac, cordials, caviar, and desserts. On weekend evenings, there's live jazz. **The 17th-floor Roof,** open seasonally, offers dinner and dancing to the Ritz-Carlton Orchestra.

Amenities: Well-equipped fitness center with sauna and massage room; use of pool at the nearby Candela of Boston spa; conference rooms; beauty salon; gift shop; concierge; 24-hour room service; dry cleaning and laundry; newspaper delivery; twice-daily maid service; baby-sitting and secretarial services available; complimentary limousine service; complimentary shoeshine.

EXPENSIVE

Boston Park Plaza Hotel. 64 Arlington St., Boston, MA 02116. ☎ **800/225-2008** or 617/426-2000. Fax 617/423-1708. 960 units (some with shower only). A/C TV TEL. $175–$265 double; $375-$2,000 suite. Extra person $20. Children under 18 stay free in parents' room. Senior discount; weekend and family packages available. AE, CB, DC, DISC, MC, V. Valet parking $23; self-parking $19. MBTA: Green Line to Arlington.

Built as the great Statler Hilton in 1927, this hotel is proud of its history and equally proud of its renovations—it's the antithesis of generic, with a slightly old-fashioned atmosphere exemplified by the cavernous, ornate lobby. Yet it offers all the modern comforts and does a hopping convention business. Room size and decor vary greatly (some rooms are quite small); all rooms have two phones, coffeemakers, and hair dryers. The lobby of the 15-story hotel is a little commercial hub, with a travel agency, a currency exchange, Amtrak and airline ticket offices, and a pharmacy.

Dining/Diversions: On the ground floor are four restaurants—**Café Rouge, Red Herring, Legal Sea Foods,** and its offspring, **Legal C Bar**—and two lounges, **Swans Court** and the cozy **Captain's Bar.**

Amenities: Health club with heated pool; business center; newly renovated conference rooms; hairdresser; beauty salon; concierge; 24-hour room service; dry cleaning and laundry; express checkout; valet parking.

Radisson Hotel Boston. 200 Stuart St. (at Charles St. South), Boston, MA 02116. ☎ **800/333-3333** or 617/482-1800. Fax 617/451-2750. 356 units. A/C TV TEL. $160–$275 double. Extra person $20. Cot $20. Cribs free. Children under 18 stay free in parents' room. Weekend and theater packages available. AE, DC, DISC, JCB, MC, V. Parking $12. MBTA: Green Line to Boylston, or Orange Line to New England Medical Center.

A top-to-bottom renovation completed in 1997 left the centrally located Radisson in great shape. The 24-story hotel was already quite nice, and a recent push to attract business travelers has made it even more so. The tastefully decorated guest rooms are among the largest in the city. Each room has a private balcony (with great views from the higher floors), a sitting area, a king-size bed or two double beds, a 25-inch TV with on-command movies, a hair dryer, a coffeemaker, an iron, an ironing board, and two phones. Business-traveler rooms on the top three floors come with upgraded amenities and access to a private lounge.

Dining/Diversions: The 57 Restaurant & Bar serves traditional American food; the **Theatre Café** is more casual. The **57 Theatre** (☎ **800/233-3123**) is an intimate venue that lends itself to one-person shows.

Amenities: Heated indoor pool with sundeck and exercise room; newly expanded staffed business center; conference rooms; concierge; room service until 11pm; dry cleaning and laundry; newspaper delivery; express checkout; valet parking.

Tremont House Hotel. 275 Tremont St., Boston, MA 02116. ☎ **800/331-9998** or 617/426-1400. Fax 617/482-6730. 322 units (some with shower only). A/C TV TEL. $159–$269 double; $399–$599 suite. Extra person $20. Children under 17 stay free in parents' room. Weekend packages and 10% AAA discount available. AE, DC, DISC, MC, V. Valet parking $20. MBTA: Green Line to Boylston, or Orange Line to New England Medical Center.

The Tremont House is as close to Boston's theaters as you can be without actually attending a show, and convenient to downtown and the Back Bay. The neighborhood is improving, and a recently completed $10 million renovation expanded some rooms and spruced up all of them. The good-sized rooms have modern furnishings, coffeemakers, and hair dryers. The 15-story brick building, formerly the landmark Hotel Bradford, captures the style that prevailed when the hotel was built in 1924. The original gold-leaf decorations and crafted ceilings in the huge lobby and ballrooms have been restored and the original marble walls and columns refurbished.

Dining/Diversions: La Famiglia Giorgio restaurant serves huge portions of hearty Italian food. Weekend club-goers have two options in the hotel. **The Roxy** features Top 40 and international music, and the **Jukebox's** recorded dance music is a favorite with suburbanites.

Amenities: Conference rooms, secretarial services, dry cleaning and laundry, newspaper delivery, express checkout, and valet parking. There are 14 rooms for people with disabilities.

COPLEY SQUARE/HYNES CONVENTION CENTER
VERY EXPENSIVE

The Colonnade Hotel. 120 Huntington Ave., Boston, MA 02116. ☎ **800/962-3030** or 617/424-7000. Fax 617/424-1717. 285 units. A/C MINIBAR TV TEL. $315 double; $450–$1,400 suite. Children under 12 stay free in parents' room. Weekend packages available. AE, CB, DC, DISC, MC, V. Parking $20. MBTA: Green Line E train to Prudential. Pets accepted.

The swimming pool and "rooftop resort" are probably this hotel's best-known features, with excellent service a close runner-up. Adjacent to Copley Place and the

Prudential Center, the independently owned Colonnade is a slice of Europe in the all-American shopping mecca of the Back Bay. You might hear a dozen languages spoken by the guests and employees of this 10-story concrete-and-glass hotel, where the friendly, professional staff is known for its personalized service. The elegance of the quiet, high-ceilinged public spaces carries over to the large guest rooms, which have contemporary oak or mahogany furnishings, marble bathrooms, two phones (one in the bathroom), robes, on-demand movies, hair dryers, and windows that open. Suites have dining rooms and sitting areas, and the "author's suite" features autographed copies of the work of celebrated (or at least published) literary guests.

Dining/Diversions: Brasserie Jo, the first branch of the Chicago hot spot, opened in May 1998 and serves French-Alsatian cuisine. There's also a bar with live entertainment and swing dancing on Friday and Saturday nights.

Amenities: Seasonal "rooftop resort" with heated outdoor pool and sundeck; well-equipped fitness room; children's programs; business center; conference rooms; car-rental desk; concierge; 24-hour room service; dry cleaning and laundry; newspaper delivery; baby-sitting available; express checkout; valet parking; courtesy car; currency exchange.

✪ **The Fairmont Copley Plaza Hotel.** 138 St. James Ave., Boston, MA 02116. ☎ **800/527-4727** or 617/267-5300. Fax 617/247-6681. www.fairmont.com/boston.html. E-mail: boston@fairmont.com. 373 units. A/C MINIBAR TV TEL. $329–$409 double; $429–$1,500 suite. Extra person $30. AE, CB, DC, JCB, MC, V. Valet parking $24. MBTA: Green Line to Copley, or Orange Line to Back Bay. Pets accepted.

"Meet me in the Oak Bar at the Plaza"—only in New York, right? Not if the Fairmont Hotel Group has anything to say about it. The San Francisco–based chain acquired the *grande dame* of Boston hotels in 1996 and immediately set about turning it into a true "grand hotel," in line with Fairmont's most famous property, New York's Plaza (home of the original Oak Bar). With superb service and plush accommodations, the Boston branch is off to a flying start.

Built in 1912, the six-story Renaissance-revival hotel faces Copley Square, with Trinity Church and the Boston Public Library on either side. The large guest rooms underwent renovation and restoration from 1996 to 1998. Furnished with reproduction Edwardian antiques, they reflect the elegance of the opulent public spaces. In-room features include oversized desks, climate control, coffeemakers, phones with dataports, and irons and ironing boards. Bathrooms have hair dryers, terry robes, and oversized towels.

Dining/Diversions: There are two restaurants, the **Oak Room** and **Copley's,** and two lounges, the **Oak Bar** and **Copley's Bar.**

Amenities: VCRs; fitness center; well-equipped business center; conference rooms; beauty salon; gift shop; concierge; 24-hour room service; dry cleaning and laundry; newspaper delivery; in-room massage; twice-daily maid service; baby-sitting available; express checkout; valet parking; currency exchange; complimentary shoeshine. Rooms for people with disabilities are available.

✪ **The Lenox Hotel.** 710 Boylston St., Boston, MA 02116. ☎ **800/225-7676** or 617/536-5300. Fax 617/236-0351. www.lenoxhotel.com. 212 units. A/C TV TEL. From $245 double; executive corner room with fireplace $275; fireplace suite $475. Extra person $20. Cots $20. Cribs free. Children under 18 stay free in parents' room. Corporate and weekend packages available. AE, CB, DC, DISC, JCB, MC, V. Parking $28. MBTA: Green Line to Copley.

The Lenox Hotel was the latest thing when it opened in 1900, and as it approaches its second century, the 11-story hotel has upgraded its decor and furnishings to echo that turn-of-the-century splendor. The $20 million renovation spiffed up everything from the ornate lobby to the spacious, luxurious rooms. Building on its

⊕ Family-Friendly Hotels

The Boston area's moderately priced chain hotels probably have the most practice at accommodating young guests—you can't go wrong with a Howard Johnson's or a Holiday Inn—but their higher-end competitors put on a good show.

Units at the **Doubletree Guest Suites** (see p. *76*) have an extra room in which to spread out, and they cost far less than adjoining rooms at any other hotel this nice. You can use the coffeemaker and refrigerator to eat breakfast in the room, then feast on lunch and dinner.

The "Weekend with the Kids" package at the **Four Seasons Hotel** (*see p. 66*) ensconces young visitors—and their parents—in an executive suite, where they can get children's videos for the VCR, milk and cookies delivered by room service (which offers a special kids' menu), child-size bathrobes, and any needed child accessories. The concierge has food packets for the ducks and squirrels at the Public Garden.

In the Back Bay, the **Colonnade Hotel** (see p. *68*) offers a family weekend package that includes parking; breakfast for two adults; up to four passes (two adult, two children) to an attraction of your choice; and a fanny pack for younger guests that holds sunglasses, a pad and pen, a yo-yo, and a toy duck.

At Cambridge's **Charles Hotel** (see p. *78*), the adjoining WellBridge Health and Fitness Center sets aside time for family swimming. The Harvard Square scavenger hunt is fun, as is the room service menu, which includes pepperoni pizza. Phone the "Children's Storyline" to hear four bedtime tales for guests under 7.

Also in Cambridge, the **Royal Sonesta Hotel** (see p. *79*) fills the vacation months with Summerfest, which includes complimentary use of bicycles, Polaroid cameras, the health club and indoor/outdoor pool, boat rides along the Charles River, and plenty of ice cream.

---

great location, the hotel courts business travelers with in-room fax machines, two-line speakerphones, dataports, and function space. The high-ceilinged guest rooms have sitting areas with custom-designed wood furnishings, marble bathrooms, terry robes, hair dryers, and irons and ironing boards. Fifteen corner rooms have wood-burning fireplaces, and rooms on the top two floors have excellent views.

Dining: Anago, one of Boston's newest fine-dining destinations, serves lunch, dinner, and Sunday brunch, and provides the hotel's food services. **The Upstairs Grille** serves breakfast; the **Samuel Adams Brew House** serves lunch and dinner and has a dozen brews on tap.

Amenities: Small exercise room; children's TV channel; conference rooms; barber shop; concierge; room service until midnight; valet laundry; newspaper delivery; express checkout; nightly turndown; secretarial services available; valet parking. Rooms for people with disabilities and wheelchair lift to the lobby are available.

The Westin Copley Place Boston. 10 Huntington Ave., Boston, MA 02116. ☎ **800/WESTIN-1** or 617/262-9600. Fax 617/424-7483. www.westin.com/listings/index.html. 800 units. A/C MINIBAR TV TEL. $189–$305 double; $350–$1,500 suite. Extra person $25; $20 Guest Office; $30 junior suites and Executive Club Level. Weekend packages available. AE, CB, DC, DISC, JCB, MC, V. Valet parking $24. MBTA: Green Line to Copley, or Orange Line to Back Bay. Small pets accepted.

Towering 36 stories in the air above Copley Square, the Westin attracts convention-goers, sightseers, and dedicated shoppers. Skybridges link the hotel to Copley Place and the Prudential Center complex, and Copley Square is across the street from the pedestrian entrance. The multilingual staff emphasizes quick check-in.

The spacious guest rooms have comfortable oak and mahogany furniture, coffeemakers, two phones, dataports, hair dryers, and windows that open. You might not notice any of that at first, because you'll be captivated by the view. Qualms you might have had about choosing a huge chain hotel will fade as you survey downtown Boston, the airport and harbor, or the Charles River and Cambridge. Executive Club Level guests have private check-in and a lounge that serves complimentary continental breakfast and hors d'oeuvres.

Dining/Diversions: The Palm, a branch of the famous New York–based chain, serves lunch and dinner—steak, chops, and jumbo lobsters. The excellent seafood restaurant **Turner Fisheries** features live jazz Tuesday through Saturday after 8pm. The **Lobby Lounge** is a great spot to meet for drinks and people-watching.

Amenities: Indoor pool; health club with Nautilus equipment and saunas; business center with computer rentals and secretarial services; conference rooms; car-rental desk; tour desk; beauty salon; in-room safes; concierge; 24-hour room service; dry cleaning and laundry; newspaper delivery; twice-daily mail service; baby-sitting; express checkout; valet parking; free morning coffee in lobby. Forty-eight guest rooms for people with disabilities adjoin standard rooms.

EXPENSIVE

Boston Back Bay Hilton. 40 Dalton St., Boston, MA 02115. ☎ **800/874-0663,** 800/HILTONS, or 617/236-1100. Fax 617/867-6104. www.hilton.com/hotels/BOSBHHF/index.html. 341 units. A/C TV TEL. $210–$270 double; $400 minisuite; $600 1-bedroom suite; $800 2-bedroom suite. Packages and AAA discount available. Extra person $20. AE, CB, DC, DISC, MC, V. Parking $17. MBTA: Green Line B, C, or D train to Hynes/ICA. Small pets accepted.

The motto at this hotel across the street from the Prudential Center complex is "We mean business," and as if to prove it, at press time the Back Bay Hilton was in the midst of a $5 million expansion to add 44 executive rooms. The project, scheduled to be completed in July 1998, coincides with a $5 million upgrade of the existing rooms. Vacationing families will also find the hotel convenient and comfortable.

Rooms are large and have modern furnishings, with either one king-size or two double beds, windows that open, coffeemakers, hair dryers, and irons and ironing boards. Soundproofing helps keep the level of street noise down.

Dining/Diversions: Boodles Restaurant draws businesspeople for grilled steaks and seafood, and **Boodles Bar** offers nearly 100 American microbrews. There is a lounge and a nightclub, **Club Nicole,** which attracts a young crowd.

Amenities: Heated indoor pool; well-equipped 24-hour fitness center; sundeck; business center; conference rooms; concierge; room service until midnight; dry cleaning and laundry; newspaper delivery; express checkout; currency exchange.

Boston Marriott Copley Place. 110 Huntington Ave., Boston, MA 02116. ☎ **800/228-9290** or 617/236-5800. Fax 617/236-5885. www.marriott.com/marriott/BOSCO. 1,147 units. A/C TV TEL. $225–$319 double; $450-$1,050 suite. Children stay free in parents' room. Weekend and other packages available. AE, DC, DISC, JCB, MC, V. Valet parking $23; self-parking $19. MBTA: Orange Line to Back Bay, or Green Line E train to Prudential. Pets accepted.

Yes, 1,147 units. This 38-story tower feels somewhat generic, but it does offer something for everyone—it's part of upscale Copley Place, with complete business facilities in the heart of Boston's shopping wonderland.

The guest rooms, renovated in 1995, have Queen Anne-style mahogany furniture, including a desk and table and either two armchairs or an armchair and an ottoman. Other features include full-length mirrors, hair dryers, ironing boards, and phones with dataports. Ultrasuites feature individual whirlpool bathtubs. One suite even has a grand piano. Guests in Concierge Level rooms have a private lounge where complimentary continental breakfast, cocktails, and hors d'oeuvres are served.

Dining/Diversions: Champions, the city's best-known sports bar, is a fun place to watch TV and eat bar food and burgers. There are two restaurants, a sushi bar, and a lounge that offers live entertainment 5 nights a week.

Amenities: Heated indoor pool; well-equipped health club with exercise room, whirlpools, saunas; full-service business center with personal computers; conference rooms with Internet access; car-rental desk; tour desk; concierge; 24-hour room service; valet laundry; valet parking. Rooms for people with disabilities are available.

Copley Square Hotel. 47 Huntington Ave., Boston, MA 02116. ☎ **800/225-7062** or 617/536-9000. Fax 617/236-0351. 143 units. A/C TV TEL. $175–$215 double; $327 suite. Children under 18 stay free in parents' room. Packages and senior discount available. AE, DISC, JCB, MC, V. Parking $18 (in adjacent garage). MBTA: Green Line to Copley, or Orange Line to Back Bay.

The Copley Square Hotel offers a great location along with the advantages and drawbacks of its relatively small size. Built in 1891, the seven-story hotel extends attentive service that's hard to find at the nearby megahotels, without those giants' abundant amenities. If you don't need to engineer a corporate takeover from your room, it's a good deal. Each attractively decorated room has a queen-size or king-size bed or two double beds, and a distinct layout (some are on the small side). All rooms have hair dryers, coffeemakers, safes, and phones with modem hookups and guest voice mail. There is a 24-hour currency exchange in the lobby. Guests are treated to afternoon tea in the lobby and have access to the health club at the nearby Westin.

The hotel has three dining options: **Speeder & Earl's** serves breakfast, and **Café Budapest** and the **Original Sports Saloon** serve lunch and dinner.

Sheraton Boston Hotel & Towers. 39 Dalton St., Boston, MA 02199. ☎ **800/325-3535** or 617/236-2000. Fax 617/236-1702. www.sheraton.com/sheraton/html/Properties/ Hotels_and_Resorts/430.html. 1,125 units. A/C TV TEL. $229–$319 double; suites from $400. Children under 17 stay free in parents' room. Weekend packages available. 25% discount for students, faculty, and retired persons with ID, depending on availability. AE, CB, DC, DISC, JCB, MC, V. Valet parking $24; self-parking $18. MBTA: Green Line B, C, or D train to Hynes/ICA, or E train to Prudential. Small pets accepted.

Its central location, range of accommodations, lavish convention facilities, and huge pool make this 29-story hotel one of the most popular in the city. It offers business and leisure travelers just about everything except the personalized service a smaller hotel can provide, including direct access to the Hynes Convention Center and the Prudential Center. A $65 million renovation project, scheduled to be completed in mid-1999, will upgrade the bathrooms, install individual climate control in every room, and reconfigure the lobby and convention space. It's being executed by closing off one tower at a time, virtually eliminating inconveniences to guests.

Standard rooms, which were redecorated in 1995 and 1996, are fairly large, with traditional mahogany and cherry furnishings, coffeemakers, and hair dryers. Many suites have a phone in the bathroom, a wet bar, and a refrigerator. Club Level guests get free local calls, no access charges on long-distance calls, and admission to a lounge where complimentary breakfast and hors d'oeuvres are served. The luxurious 26th-floor Sheraton Towers offer private check-in, some antique furnishings, and upgraded amenities, including Egyptian cotton sheets and goose-down comforters. The lounge affords Towers guests a great view, complimentary breakfast, afternoon tea, and hors d'oeuvres and beverages.

Dining/Diversions: The lobby restaurant serves three meals daily. The clubby **Punch Bar** serves after-dinner drinks, cordials, and a breathtaking selection of cigars.

Amenities: Heated indoor/outdoor pool with retractable dome, pavilion, Jacuzzi, and sauna; large, well-equipped health club; conference rooms; car-rental desk; concierge; 24-hour room service; dry cleaning and laundry; newspaper delivery; in-room massage; express checkout; valet parking; courtesy car. Rooms for people with disabilities are available.

MODERATE

Chandler Inn Hotel. 26 Chandler St. (at Berkeley St.), Boston, MA 02116. ☎ **800/ 842-3450** or 617/482-3450. Fax 617/542-3428. www.chandlerinn.com. E-mail: inn3450@ix.netcom.com. 56 units. A/C TV TEL. Apr to mid-June $89–$99 double; Marathon weekend $129–$139 double; mid-June to mid-Nov $99-$109 double weekdays, $109–$119 double weekends; mid-Nov to March $79–$89 double. Rates include continental breakfast. Extra person $10–$20. Children under 12 stay free in parents' room. AE, CB, DC, DISC, MC, V. No parking available. MBTA: Orange Line to Back Bay.

The Chandler Inn is technically in the South End, near the Boston Center for the Arts, but so convenient to the Back Bay and such a good deal that you won't mind the slightly lower-budget address. The guest rooms in the eight-story inn were recently redecorated and recarpeted—and, most important, air-conditioned. They're still nothing fancy, but if your needs are basic, you'll be fine. And the staff is friendly and helpful. This is a practical choice for bargain hunters who don't care about a tony address and a lot of extras.

The MidTown Hotel. 220 Huntington Ave., Boston, MA 02115. ☎ **800/343-1177** or 617/262-1000. Fax 617/262-8739. 159 units. A/C TV TEL. $109–$179 double. Extra person $15. Children under 18 stay free in parents' room. 10% AARP discount available; government employees' discount subject to availability. AE, DC, DISC, MC, V. Free parking. MBTA: Green Line E train to Prudential, or Orange Line to Mass. Ave.

Even without free parking, this two-story hotel would be a good deal. It's on a busy street within easy walking distance of Symphony Hall, the Museum of Fine Arts, and the Back Bay attractions. The newly renovated rooms are bright and attractively outfitted, and some have connecting bedrooms for families. For business travelers, the phones have dataports, and photocopying and fax services are available at the front desk. The heated outdoor pool is open from Memorial Day through Labor Day. **Tables of Content,** an American cafe, is open from 7am to 10pm.

✪ **Newbury Guest House.** 261 Newbury St. (between Fairfield and Gloucester), Boston, MA 02116. ☎ **617/437-7666.** Fax 617/262-4243. 32 units (some with shower only). A/C TV TEL. $105–$140 double; winter $95–$125 double. Rates include continental breakfast. Rates might be higher during special events. Extra person $10. AE, CB, DC, DISC, MC, V. Parking $10 (reservation required). Minimum 2 nights on weekends. MBTA: Green Line to Copley, or B, C, or D train to Hynes/ICA.

After just a little shopping in the Back Bay, you'll appreciate what a find this cozy inn is—a bargain on Newbury Street. It's a pair of brick town houses built in the 1880s and combined into a refined guest house. It offers comfortable furnishings, a pleasant staff, nifty architectural details, and—*such* a deal—a buffet breakfast served in the ground-level dining room, which adjoins a brick patio. The Hagopian family opened the B&B in 1991, and it operates near capacity all year, drawing business travelers during the week and sightseers on weekends. Rooms aren't huge but are nicely appointed. At these prices in this location, there's only one caveat: reserve early.

Impressions

This isn't Boston! This is a free country!
            —*Let's Dance* (film starring Betty Hutton and Fred Astaire), 1950

Boston is no place to rekindle a romance.
            —*The Parent Trap* (film starring Hayley Mills), 1961

INEXPENSIVE

Berkeley Residence YWCA. 40 Berkeley St., Boston, MA 02116. ☎ **617/482-8850.** Fax 617/482-9692. 200 units (none with bathroom). $42 single; $64 double; $75 triple. Rates include breakfast. Long-term stay (4-week minimum) $136 per week, including breakfast and dinner daily. JCB, MC, V. Parking $16 in public lot 1 block away. MBTA: Green Line to Arlington, or Orange Line to Back Bay.

This pleasant, conveniently located hotel/residence for women offers a dining room, a patio garden, pianos, a library, and laundry facilities. The guest rooms are basic, containing little more than beds, but they are well maintained and comfortable—definitely not luxurious, but not cells either. The public areas were renovated in 1997. Guests have access to the pool and exercise room at the YWCA 2 blocks away.

4 Mass. Ave. to Brookline

Hotels in this area are close to **Fenway Park,** the hospitals at the **Longwood Medical Area,** and several **colleges and museums.** Some are in Boston, some in **Brookline,** which starts about 2 blocks beyond Kenmore Square. Brookline lodgings are not subject to the **2.75% convention center tax** that applies in Boston.

MASS. AVE. & THE FENS
VERY EXPENSIVE

✪ **Eliot Hotel.** 370 Commonwealth Ave. (at Mass. Ave.), Boston, MA 02215. ☎ **800/ 44-ELIOT** or 617/267-1607. Fax 617/536-9114. E-mail: HotelEliot@aol.com. 91 units. A/C MINIBAR TV TEL. $245–$295 1-bedroom suite for 2; $400–$475 2-bedroom suite. Extra person $20. Children under 12 stay free in parents' room. AE, DC, MC, V. Valet parking $20. MBTA: Green Line B, C, or D train to Hynes/ICA. Small pets accepted.

This exquisite hotel combines the flavor of Yankee Boston with European-style service and amenities. It feels more like a classy apartment building than a hotel, with features that attract tycoons as well as honeymooners. Built in 1925, the nine-story building underwent a complete renovation from 1990 to 1994. The spacious suites have antique furnishings, traditional English-style chintz fabrics, and authentic botanical prints. French doors separate the living rooms and bedrooms, and modern conveniences, such as Italian marble bathrooms, dual-line telephones with dataports, a personal fax machine, and two TVs, are standard. Many suites also have a pantry with a microwave.

The hotel is near Boston University and MIT (across the river), and the location on tree-lined Commonwealth Avenue contrasts pleasantly with the bustle of Newbury Street, a block away.

Dining: Breakfast is served in the hotel's elegant new restaurant, **Clio.** At dinner, Clio specializes in contemporary French and American cuisine.

Amenities: VCRs; safe-deposit boxes; concierge; room service until midnight; dry cleaning and laundry; newspaper delivery; twice-daily maid service; baby-sitting

Hotels from Mass. Ave. to Brookline

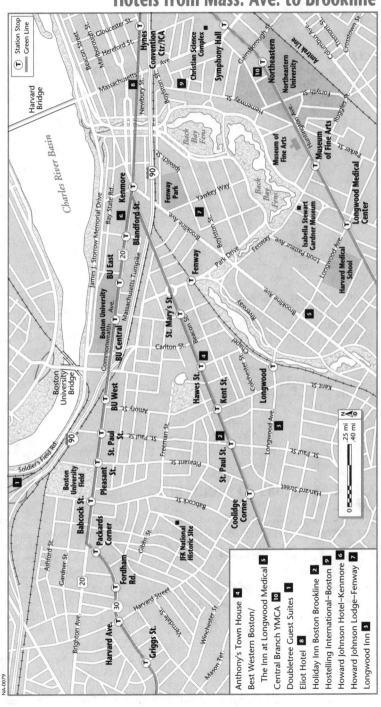

Station Stop
Green Line

Harvard Bridge

Charles River Basin

Boston University Bridge

Soldier's Field Rd.

Hynes Convention Ctr/ICA

Christian Science Complex

Symphony Hall

Back Bay Fens

Museum of Fine Arts

Northeastern University

Amtrak Line

Kenmore

Fenway Park

Yawkey Way

Back Bay Fens

Isabella Stewart Gardner Museum

Longwood Medical Center

Harvard Medical School

BU East

Blandford St.

BU Central

Boston University

St. Mary's St.

Fenway

Carlton St.

Longwood

Hawes St.

Kent St.

St. Paul St.

Coolidge Corner

BU West

St. Paul St.

Boston University Field

Pleasant St.

Babcock St.

Packards Corner

JFK National Historic Site

Fordham Rd.

Harvard Ave.

Griggs St.

N
.25 mi
.40 mi

Anthony's Town House 4
Best Western Boston/
The Inn at Longwood Medical 5
Central Branch YMCA 10
Doubletree Guest Suites 1
Eliot Hotel 8
Holiday Inn Boston Brookline 2
Hostelling International–Boston 9
Howard Johnson Hotel–Kenmore 6
Howard Johnson Lodge–Fenway 7
Longwood Inn 3

NA-0079

75

and secretarial services available; express checkout; valet parking. Rooms for people with disabilities are available.

INEXPENSIVE

Central Branch YMCA. 316 Huntington Ave., Boston, MA 02115. ☎ **617/536-7800.** 67–150 units, depending on season (8 with bathroom). TV. Late June to Aug $39 single; $58 single with bathroom; $60 double; $80 triple; $95 quad. AE, DISC, MC, V. Rates include breakfast. No parking available. MBTA: Green Line E train to Northeastern.

The "Y" is about 15 minutes from downtown, near Symphony Hall and the Museum of Fine Arts. During the winter, adjacent Northeastern University sometimes leases the guest rooms for student housing; plans for the 1998–99 school year were not set at press time, so definitely call ahead. The modern (but not air-conditioned) accommodations for men and women 18 years of age and over are basic but not overly institutional. Rooms have televisions and maid service, and rates include use of the pool, gym, weight room, fitness center, and indoor track. There is also a cafeteria on the premises. Luggage and an ID are required for check-in.

Hostelling International-Boston. 12 Hemenway St., Boston, MA 02115. ☎ **800/HOST222** or 617/536-9455. Fax 617/424-6558. www.tiac.net/users/hienec/. E-mail: bostonhostel@juno.com. 205 beds. Members $18 per bed; nonmembers $21 per bed. JCB, MC, V. MBTA: Green Line B, C, or D train to Hynes/ICA.

This hostel near Symphony Hall and the Berklee College of Music caters to students, youth groups, and other travelers in search of comfortable, no-frills lodgings. It has two full dine-in kitchens, 19 bathrooms, a coin laundry, and a large common room. The public areas, remodeled in 1997 and 1998, contain meeting and workshop space. Accommodations are dorm-style, with three to six beds per room. The hostel provides a "sheet sleeping sack," or you can bring your own (sleeping bags are not permitted). The staff organizes cultural, educational, and recreational programs on the premises and throughout the Boston area.

Note: To get a bed during the summer season, you must be a member of Hostelling International-American Youth Hostels. For information and an application, contact HI-AYH, P.O. Box 37613, Washington, DC 20013 (☎ **202/ 783-6161;** www.hiayh.org). If you are not a U.S. citizen, apply to your home country's hosteling association.

KENMORE SQUARE TO BROOKLINE
EXPENSIVE

✪ **Doubletree Guest Suites.** 400 Soldiers Field Rd., Boston, MA 02134. ☎ **800/ 222-TREE** or 617/783-0090. Fax 617/783-0897. www.doubletreehotels.com/DoubleT/ Hotel41/57/57Main.htm. 310 units. A/C MINIBAR TV TEL. $169–$249 double. Extra person $20. Children under 19 stay free in parents' room. Weekend packages from $119 per night. AAA discount available. AE, CB, DC, DISC, JCB, MC, V. Parking $14 Sun–Thurs, $7 Fri–Sat.

This hotel is one of the best deals in town—every unit is a two-room suite with a living room, bedroom, and bathroom. Business travelers can entertain in their rooms, and families can spread out, making this a good choice for both. Overlooking the Charles River adjacent to the Allston/Cambridge exit of the Massachusetts Turnpike, the hotel is convenient to Cambridge and the bike and jogging path that runs along the river, but it isn't in an actual neighborhood. There's complimentary van service to and from attractions and business areas in Boston and Cambridge.

The suites, which were renovated in 1996, surround a 15-story atrium. Rooms are large and attractively furnished, and most bedrooms have king-size beds and a writing desk. Living rooms feature full-size sofa beds, a dining table, and a good-sized refrigerator. Each suite has a coffeemaker, two TVs, and three telephones (one in the bathroom).

Dining/Diversions: Scullers Grille and **Scullers Lounge** serve meals from 6:30am to 11pm. The celebrated **Scullers Jazz Club** has two nightly shows.

Amenities: Heated indoor pool; exercise room; whirlpool; sauna; game room; conference rooms; laundry room; concierge; room service until 10pm; dry cleaning and laundry; newspaper delivery; in-room massage; twice-daily maid service; baby-sitting and secretarial services available; express checkout; van service. Suites for people with disabilities on each floor.

MODERATE

Best Western Boston/The Inn at Longwood Medical. 342 Longwood Ave., Boston, MA 02115. ☎ **800/528-1234** or 617/731-4700. TDD 617/731-9088. Fax 617/731-6273. 170 units, 14 with kitchenette. A/C TV TEL. $129–$189 double; $250 suite; $199 kitchenette unit. Extra person $15. Children under 18 stay free in parents' room. AE, CB, DISC, MC, V. Parking $14. MBTA: Green Line D or E train to Longwood.

Next to Children's Hospital in the Longwood Medical Area (Beth Israel Deaconess and Brigham and Women's hospitals, the Dana-Farber Cancer Institute, and the Joslin Diabetes Center are nearby), this six-story hotel is a good base for those with business at the hospitals. It's also near museums, colleges, and Fenway Park, and about 15 minutes from downtown Boston by public transportation.

The guest units are quite large, and equipped with coffeemakers and hair dryers. Hotel facilities include a restaurant, a lounge, meeting rooms, and valet laundry service. The hotel abuts the Longwood Galleria business complex, with a food court, retail stores, and a fitness center available to hotel guests for $10 a day or $35 a week.

Holiday Inn Boston Brookline. 1200 Beacon St., Brookline, MA 02446. ☎ **800/HOLIDAY** or 617/277-1200. Fax 617/734-6991. 225 units. A/C TV TEL. $145–$170 double; $200–$350 suite. Extra person $10. Children under 18 stay free in parents' room. AE, DC, DISC, JCB, MC, V. Parking $9. MBTA: Green Line C train to St. Paul St.

Just 15 minutes from downtown on the subway, this sparkling hotel is more than just another Holiday Inn. Built around a colorful atrium with a small indoor pool plus whirlpool, sundeck, and exercise room, it offers recently redecorated rooms that are large and well appointed, with coffeemakers, hair dryers, and irons and ironing boards. Laundry service is available. Ten rooms are equipped for guests with disabilities. The six-story hotel has a restaurant and a lounge, and the bustling Coolidge Corner neighborhood is a 10-minute walk away.

Howard Johnson Hotel–Kenmore. 575 Commonwealth Ave., Boston, MA 02215. ☎ **800/654-2000** or 617/267-3100. Fax 617/424-1045. 180 units. A/C TV TEL. $125–$225 double. Extra person $10. Children under 18 stay free in parents' room. Senior and AAA discount available. AE, CB, DC, DISC, JCB, MC, V. Free parking. MBTA: Green Line B train to Blandford St. Pets accepted.

If the location doesn't get you, the pool and free parking might. This eight-story hotel is surrounded by the Boston University campus, with the T to downtown out front and Kenmore Square and Fenway Park nearby. Rooms are standard-issue Howard Johnson's—comfortable, but nothing fancy—and some are small. The hotel has a glass-enclosed elevator, which goes to the rooftop lounge and provides a good view of the area. The indoor swimming pool and skylighted sundeck on the roof are open year-round from 11am to 9pm.

Howard Johnson Lodge Fenway. 1271 Boylston St., Boston, MA 02215. ☎ **800/654-2000** or 617/267-8300. Fax 617/267-2763. 94 units. A/C TV TEL. $115–$185 double.

Extra person $10. Children under 18 stay free in parents' room. Family packages, senior and AAA discounts available. AE, CB, DC, DISC, JCB, MC, V. Free parking. MBTA: Green Line B, C, or D train to Kenmore; 10-minute walk. Pets accepted.

This is as close to Fenway Park as you can get without buying a ticket. If you're not visiting during baseball season, this motel on a busy street in a commercial-residential neighborhood is convenient to the Back Bay colleges, the Museum of Fine Arts, and the Isabella Stewart Gardner Museum. When the Red Sox are playing, guests contend with crowded sidewalks and raucous baseball fans who flood the area. There's an outdoor pool, open from 9am to 7pm in the summer, and some rooms are outfitted with a microwave oven and a refrigerator. On the premises are a steak house and a popular lounge that has live jazz entertainment.

INEXPENSIVE

Anthony's Town House. 1085 Beacon St., Brookline, MA 02446. ☎ **617/566-3972.** 12 units (none with private bathroom). A/C TV. $48–$78 double. Extra person $10. Weekly rates available. No credit cards. Free parking. MBTA: Green Line C train to Hawes St.

One mile from Boston's Kenmore Square, about 15 minutes from downtown by subway, and 2 blocks from a busy commercial strip, this four-story brownstone guest house has been operated by the Anthony family since 1944. The turn-of-the-century restored town house is listed on the National Register of Historic Places. Each floor has three rooms and a shared bathroom with enclosed shower. Rooms have Queen Anne- and Victorian-style furnishings, and the large front rooms have bay windows with comfortable lounge chairs.

Longwood Inn. 123 Longwood Ave., Brookline, MA 02446. ☎ **617/566-8615.** Fax 617/738-1070. 22 units, 17 with bathroom (some with shower only). A/C TEL. Apr–Nov $69–$79 double; Dec–Mar $59–$69 double. 1-bedroom apt (sleeps 4 plus) $89 summer, $79 winter. Weekly rates available. No credit cards. Free parking. MBTA: Green Line D train to Longwood, or C train to Coolidge Corner.

In a residential area near the Brookline border 3 blocks from Boston, this three-story Victorian guest house offers comfortable accommodations at modest rates. Guests have the use of a fully equipped kitchen and common dining room, coin laundry, and TV lounge. The apartment has a private kitchen and balcony. Tennis courts, a running track, and a children's playground at the school next door are open to the public. Public transportation is easily accessible, and the Longwood Medical Area and busy Coolidge Corner neighborhood are within walking distance.

5 Cambridge

A city so close to Boston that they're usually thought of as a unit, Cambridge has its own attractions, its own colleges, and its own excellent hotels. If your visit involves more than sightseeing in Boston, Cambridge is a good base for day trips, and when you get back to the hotel, you'll still have plenty to do. The MBTA Red Line links Cambridge and Boston, and some hotels provide shuttle service. Even more than in Boston, getting a room during the college graduation season of May and early June is difficult, so plan accordingly.

VERY EXPENSIVE

✪ **The Charles Hotel.** 1 Bennett St., Cambridge, MA 02138. ☎ **800/882-1818** outside MA, or 617/864-1200. Fax 617/864-5715. 252 units. A/C MINIBAR TV TEL. $239–$315 double; $389–$2,000 suite. Extra person $20. Children under 18 stay free in parents' room. Weekend packages available. AE, CB, DC, DISC, JCB, MC, V. Valet parking $18; self-parking $16. MBTA: Red Line to Harvard. Pets accepted.

The Charles Hotel is a phenomenon—an instant classic. The nine-story brick hotel a block from Harvard Square has been *the* place for both business and leisure travelers to Cambridge since it opened in 1985. Much of its fame derives from its excellent restaurants, jazz bar, and day spa, and the service is, if anything, equally exalted.

Antique blue-and-white New England quilts, handcrafted between 1865 and 1885, hang in the lobby's oak staircase and at the entrance to each floor. In the guest rooms, the style is contemporary country, with custom-designed adaptations of early American Shaker furniture and down quilts. Bathrooms have telephones, TVs, hair dryers, and scales. All rooms have large windows that open, three phones, dataports, and state-of-the-art Bose Wave radios. And it wouldn't be Cambridge if your intellectual needs went unfulfilled—you can order books over the phone, and a Charles staffer will pick them up at WordsWorth Books and bill your room.

There are five terrific weekend packages, including a workout weekend for two with a full day of pampering at the spa for about $500. The $1,000 spa weekend includes spa and salon treatments and gourmet low-calorie meals.

Dining/Diversions: Rialto, one of the best restaurants in greater Boston, serves Mediterranean cuisine by award-winning chef Jody Adams. **Henrietta's Table** offers New England country cooking. The renowned **Regattabar** features live jazz Tuesday through Saturday nights.

Amenities: Video rentals; glass-enclosed pool, Jacuzzi, sun terrace, and exercise room at the WellBridge Health and Fitness Center. Beauty treatments are available at the European-style Le Pli Day Spa. Conference rooms; facilities for teleconferencing; car-rental desk; concierge; 24-hour room service; dry cleaning and laundry; newspaper delivery; in-room massage; twice-daily maid service; baby-sitting and secretarial services available; express checkout; valet parking. Thirteen rooms for people with disabilities; rooms with special amenities for female travelers.

✪ Royal Sonesta Hotel. 5 Cambridge Pkwy., Cambridge, MA 02142. ☎ **800/SONESTA** or 617/491-3600. Fax 617/661-5956. www.sonesta.com. 400 units. A/C MINIBAR TV TEL. $195–$300 double; $400–$600 suite. Children under 18 stay free in parents' room. AE, CB, DC, DISC, JCB, MC, V. Parking $16. MBTA: Green Line to Lechmere; 10-minute walk.

This luxurious hotel is in a curious location—it's close to only a few things but convenient to everything, making it a good choice for both businesspeople and families. The CambridgeSide Galleria Mall is across the street, and the Museum of Science is around the corner on the bridge to Boston (which is closer than Harvard Square). In the other direction, MIT is a 10-minute walk. Most of the spacious rooms have a lovely view of the river or the city, and all have two phones, plus hair dryers. Everything is custom designed and renovated regularly. A great new perk: cellular phone service linked to your guest room phone. Original contemporary artwork—including pieces by Andy Warhol and Frank Stella—hangs throughout the public spaces and guest rooms.

Dining: Davio's, a branch of the Newbury Street favorite, serves three meals daily and has an outdoor patio overlooking the Charles River. The casual **Gallery Café** also has a patio.

Amenities: Heated indoor/outdoor pool with retractable roof; well-equipped health club; Jacuzzi; sauna; sundeck; business center; conference rooms; concierge; room service until 1am (2am on weekends); dry cleaning and laundry; baby-sitting available; express checkout; valet parking. Eleven wheelchair-accessible rooms, 16 for those with hearing impairments; staff trained in disability awareness.

Cambridge Accommodations

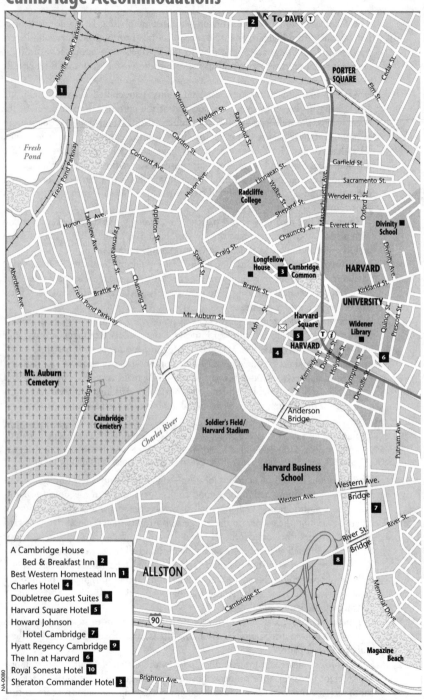

A Cambridge House
  Bed & Breakfast Inn **2**
Best Western Homestead Inn **1**
Charles Hotel **4**
Doubletree Guest Suites **8**
Harvard Square Hotel **5**
Howard Johnson
  Hotel Cambridge **7**
Hyatt Regency Cambridge **9**
The Inn at Harvard **6**
Royal Sonesta Hotel **10**
Sheraton Commander Hotel **3**

NA-0080

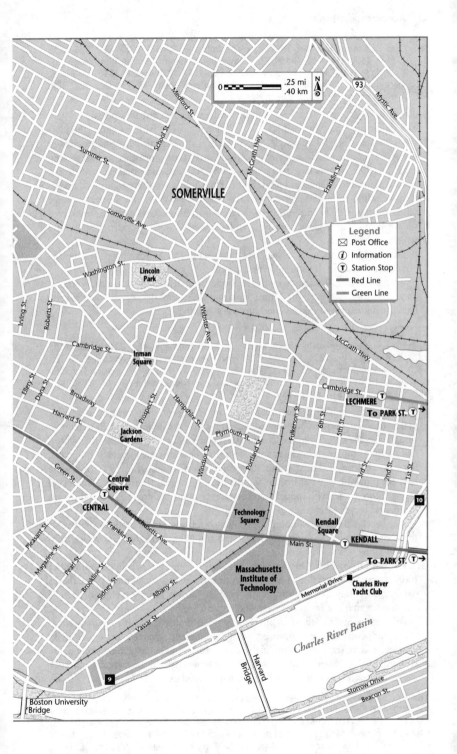

Sheraton Commander Hotel. 16 Garden St., Cambridge, MA 02138. ☎ **800/325-3535** or 617/547-4800. Fax 617/868-8322. www.sheraton.com/sheraton/html/Properties/ Hotels_and_Resorts/607.html. 175 units. A/C TV TEL. $159–$279 double; $330–$550 suite. Extra person $20. Children under 18 stay free in parents' room. AE, CB, DC, DISC, JCB, MC, V. Free parking. MBTA: Red Line to Harvard.

This six-story hotel in the heart of Cambridge's historic district opened in 1927, and it's exactly what you'd expect of a traditional hostelry within sight of the Harvard campus. The Colonial-style decor begins in the elegant lobby and extends to the guest rooms, which aren't huge but are attractively furnished; all were renovated in 1996. Rooms have two phones with dataports, coffeemakers, hair dryers, irons and ironing boards, and night lights. The Club Level offers additional amenities, including in-room fax machines, free local phone calls, and a private lounge where complimentary continental breakfast and afternoon hors d'oeuvres are served on weekdays. Suites have two TVs, and some have wet bars, refrigerators, and whirlpools.

Dining: The restaurant serves three meals daily and Sunday brunch. The cafe serves lighter fare in the afternoon and evening.

Amenities: Small fitness center; sundeck; conference rooms; laundry room; concierge; room service until 11pm; dry cleaning and laundry; newspaper delivery; baby-sitting available; express checkout; valet parking.

EXPENSIVE

Hyatt Regency Cambridge. 575 Memorial Dr., Cambridge, MA 02139. ☎ **800/ 233-1234** or 617/492-1234. Fax 617/491-6906. www.hyatt.com. 469 units. A/C TV TEL. $210–$295 double weekdays, $119–$224 weekend; $300–$795 suite. Extra person $25. Children under 18 stay free in parents' room. Weekend packages available. AE, DC, DISC, JCB, MC, V. Valet parking $17; self-parking $16.

This dramatic red-brick hotel, a prominent feature of the Cambridge skyline, makes up for its not-exactly-central location with its appointments and architecture. Across the street from the Charles River and not far from the Allston/Brighton exit of the turnpike, it encloses a 16-story atrium with glass elevators, fountains, trees, and balconies. The spacious guest rooms were renovated in 1997, and some have breathtaking views of Boston and the river. All have coffeemakers. Families are especially welcome, with special rates for parents whose children sleep in a different room, and bicycles for rent.

The hotel is about 10 minutes from downtown Boston by car and convenient for those visiting colleges—it's between Harvard and MIT, and across the bridge from Boston University.

Dining/Diversions: On the rooftop, the revolving, glass-enclosed **Spinnaker Italia** restaurant serves dinner and Sunday brunch, and it has a lounge where there's dancing on Friday and Saturday nights and live jazz on Sunday evenings. There is a restaurant that overlooks the river, and a sports bar.

Amenities: Seventy-five-foot indoor lap pool; health club with Jacuzzi, sauna, and whirlpool; sundeck; business center; conference rooms; car-rental desk; concierge; room service until midnight; dry cleaning and laundry; newspaper delivery; express checkout; valet parking; complimentary shuttle service; currency exchange. Twenty-four rooms for people with disabilities.

The Inn at Harvard. 1201 Massachusetts Ave. (at Quincy St.), Cambridge, MA 02138. ☎ **800/458-5886** or 617/491-2222. Fax 617/491-6520. www.doubletreehotels.com/ DoubleT/Hotel100/109/109Main.htm. 109 units (some with shower only). A/C TV TEL. $169–$269 double; $450 presidential suite. Extra person $10. Children under 19 stay free in parents' room. Packages and senior, AAA, and AARP discounts available. AE, CB, DC, DISC, MC, V. Valet parking $20. MBTA: Red Line to Harvard.

At first glance, the Inn at Harvard looks almost like a dormitory—it's adjacent to Harvard Yard, and its red brick and Georgian-style architecture would fit nicely on campus. Inside, there's no mistaking it for anything other than an elegant hotel, popular with business travelers and university visitors. The four-story, skylighted atrium opens from the "living room," where you'll find antique tables mixed with contemporary furniture, backgammon and chess tables, bookshelves stocked with current periodicals, newspapers, and Harvard University Press publications, and a small, upscale restaurant. The elegantly decorated guest rooms have cherry furniture, and each has a lounge chair or two armchairs around a table, a work area, windows that open, and an original painting from the Fogg Art Museum. Each room has two phones, one with a computer modem hookup. Some rooms have dormer windows and window seats.

Dining: The Atrium Dining Room serves seasonal New England fare at breakfast, lunch, dinner, and afternoon tea.

Amenities: Conference rooms; safe-deposit boxes; room service; dry cleaning and laundry; newspaper delivery; secretarial services available; express checkout; valet parking. Six wheelchair-accessible rooms.

MODERATE

A Cambridge House Bed & Breakfast Inn. 2218 Massachusetts Ave., Cambridge, MA 02140. ☎ **800/232-9989** or 617/491-6300; 800/96-2079 in the United Kingdom. Fax 617/868-2848. www.acambridgehouse.com. E-mail: innach@aol.com. 16 units (some with shower only). A/C TV TEL. $139–$275 double. Rates include breakfast. Extra person $35. AE, DISC, MC, V. Free parking. MBTA: Red Line to Porter.

A Cambridge House is a beautifully restored 1892 Victorian home listed in the National Register of Historic Places. The three-story building is on a busy stretch of Cambridge's main street (Mass. Ave.), set back from the sidewalk by a lawn. Rooms vary widely in size; all are warmly decorated with Waverly-Schumacher fabrics and period antiques. Most have fireplaces and four-poster canopy beds with down comforters. Complimentary beverages and fresh pastries are served by the fireplace in the library or parlor, and a generous buffet breakfast is offered every morning.

Best Western Homestead Inn. 220 Alewife Brook Pkwy., Cambridge, MA 02138. ☎ **800/491-4914** or 617/491-8000. Fax 617/491-4932. www.bwhomestead.com/22025.html. 69 units. A/C TV TEL. Mid-Mar to Oct $109–$220 double; Nov to mid-Mar $79–$170 double. Rates include continental breakfast. Rates might be higher during special events. Extra person $10. Children under 18 stay free in parents' room. AE, CB, DC, DISC, JCB, MC, V. Free parking. MBTA: Red Line to Alewife, 10-minute walk.

The gritty commercial neighborhood is nothing to write home about, but this four-story motel is a comfortable and convenient oasis for motorists. Guest rooms are spacious, with contemporary or reproduction colonial furnishings, and are at least one floor up from the busy street. All have hair dryers and irons and ironing boards. There's an indoor pool with a Jacuzzi, and a 2½-mile jogging trail around Fresh Pond is across the street. Laundry service (weekdays only), meeting facilities for up to 45 people, and rental-car pickup and drop-off are available. There's a restaurant next door, and a shopping center with a 10-screen movie theater nearby. Boston is about a 15-minute drive or a 30-minute T ride away; Lexington and Concord are less than 30 minutes away by car.

Harvard Square Hotel. 110 Mount Auburn St., Cambridge, MA 02138. ☎ **800/458-5886** or 617/864-5200. Fax 617/864-2409. www.doubletreehotels.com/DoubleT/Hotel100/108/108Main.htm. 73 units. A/C TV TEL. $125-$180 double. Extra person $10. Children under 17 stay free in parents' room. Corporate rates, AAA and AARP discounts available. AE, DC, DISC, JCB, MC, V. Parking $16. MBTA: Red Line to Harvard.

Smack in the middle of Harvard Square, this hotel is a favorite with visiting parents and budget-conscious business travelers in search of a comfortable, unpretentious atmosphere. In early 1996 the six-story brick hotel was completely refurbished, and the guest rooms were redecorated in contemporary style. All have dataports, voice mail, hair dryers, and irons and ironing boards; some overlook Harvard Square. Fax and copy services and complimentary newspapers (weekdays only) are available at the front desk, and dry cleaning and laundry service are also available. There are four wheelchair-accessible rooms. Guests have dining privileges at the Inn at Harvard—like the Harvard Square Hotel, managed by Doubletree Hotels Corporation—and the Harvard Faculty Club.

Howard Johnson Hotel Cambridge. 777 Memorial Dr., Cambridge, MA 02139. ☎ **800/654-2000** or 617/492-7777. Fax 617/492-6038. 205 units. A/C TV TEL. $119–$235 double. Extra person $10. Cribs free. Children under 18 stay free in parents' room. AARP and AAA discounts available. AE, CB, DC, DISC, JCB, MC, V. Free parking. Pets accepted.

An attractive, modern hotel with a swimming pool and sundeck, this 16-story tower is across the street from the Charles River, not far from the major college campuses and the Massachusetts Turnpike, and a 10-minute drive from downtown Boston. Each room has a picture window, giving guests who are up high enough a panoramic view of the Boston skyline. Rooms have modern furnishings, and some have a private balcony. Prices vary with the size of the room, the floor, and the view. Laundry service and conference rooms are available.

Also at the hotel are the **Bisuteki Japanese Steak House,** where dinners are prepared at the table in the hibachi style of "firebowl" cooking, and **Dionysos,** a Greek-American restaurant that serves a full American breakfast.

6 At the Airport

A new 10-story, 600-room **Hilton Hotel** (☎ **800/HILTONS;** www.hilton.com) is scheduled to open at construction-choked Logan Airport sometime in 1999.

Harborside Hyatt Conference Center & Hotel. 101 Harborside Dr., Boston, MA 02128. ☎ **800/233-1234** or 617/568-1234. Fax 617/567-8856. www.hyatt.com. 270 units. A/C TV TEL. From $214 double. Children under 12 stay free in parents' room. AE, CB, DC, DISC, JCB, MC, V. Parking $10. MBTA: Blue Line to Airport, then take shuttle bus. By car, follow signs to Logan Airport and take Harborside Dr. past the car-rental area and tunnel entrance.

This striking 14-story waterfront hotel, which opened in 1993, has unobstructed views of the harbor and city skyline. It caters to the convention trade; sightseers whose budget for transportation doesn't include a fair amount of time (on the shuttle bus and subway) or money (on ferries, parking, or cabs) will be better off closer to downtown.

The guest rooms have all the amenities you'd expect from a deluxe hotel, plus such extras as coffeemakers, irons and ironing boards, luxury bathrooms, and fine wood furnishings. The building has some quirky features: the turret is a lighthouse (the airport control tower manages the beacon so that it doesn't interfere with runway lights), and fiber-optic stars change color in the ceiling of the reception area.

Dining: The restaurant serves three meals and has floor-to-ceiling windows that allow for spectacular views.

Amenities: Indoor heated pool; health club with Jacuzzi and sauna; business center; conference rooms; concierge; room service until 2am; dry cleaning and laundry; secretarial services available; express checkout; ferries to Rowes Wharf and Long Wharf dock outside; 24-hour airport shuttle service.

7 Highway Hot Spots

Staying outside of downtown can save you some money, some aggravation, or both. Here are three options—two in **Dorchester** off the Southeast Expressway (Exit 12 southbound, Exit 13 northbound), close to the Kennedy Library; one in **Waltham** at Exit 27A off Route 128.

Susse Chalet Boston Inn. 900 Morrissey Blvd., Boston, MA 02122. ☎ **800/886-0056** or 617/287-9200. Fax 617/282-2365. www.bostonhotel.com. 172 units. A/C TV TEL. $74-$82 double; suite $125. Extra person $5. AE, CB, DC, DISC, MC, V. Free parking. MBTA: Red Line to JFK/UMass, then take free shuttle bus.

The Susse Chalet Boston properties (see the Lodge listing, below) are inexpensive but not cheap—they have high standards and low prices. The Inn is a five-story building with large guest rooms, including rooms for people with disabilities. The newest rooms are on the fifth floor, which was added in 1998. Ask—beg if you have to—to be on the side of the building that faces away from the interstate. Rooms have a full, double, or king-sized bed, and all have hair dryers, dataports, and access to free local calls. There are coin-operated washers and dryers, and a seasonal outdoor swimming pool.

Susse Chalet Boston Lodge. 800 Morrissey Blvd., Boston, MA 02122. ☎ **800/5-CHALET** or 617/287-9100. Fax 617/265-9287. www.bostonhotel.com. 175 units. A/C TV TEL. $70-$80 double. Extra person $5. AE, CB, DC, DISC, MC, V. Free parking. MBTA: Red Line to JFK/UMass, then take free shuttle bus.

This three-story motor lodge offers utilitarian lodgings at reasonable prices. Here, too, ask to face away from traffic. The newly redecorated rooms have hair dryers and dataports. An outdoor swimming pool is open in the warmer months. Guests have the use of the facilities in the adjacent Susse Chalet Boston Inn (see above).

The Westin Waltham–Boston. 70 Third Ave., Waltham, MA 02454. ☎ **800/WESTIN-1** or 617/290-5600. Fax 617/290-5626. www.westin.com/listings/index.html. 346 units. A/C MINIBAR TV TEL. $129-$215 double. Extra person $20. Children stay free in parents' room. Weekend packages, senior and AAA discounts available. AE, CB, DC, DISC, JCB, MC, V. Free parking.

This dramatic glass structure is on a hilltop overlooking Route 128, centrally located for travelers with business in the surrounding high-tech heartland. The guest rooms in the eight-floor tower have two telephones, hair dryers, ironing boards and irons, business-size desks, message retrieval, and windows that open. The business center offers secretarial services and business equipment rentals; for deal-making on a smaller scale, Guest Office rooms offer amenities such as in-room printer-fax-copiers; office supplies; and free access to toll-free, local, and credit-card calls. Hourly shuttle service to Logan Airport ($17 per person), currency exchange, and 24-hour room service are available. There are 18 rooms for people with disabilities, and a health club with an indoor pool, whirlpool, sauna, and fitness room. Also on the premises are a restaurant, a lounge, and a pub.

8 Nearby Resorts

Complete vacation packages are available at these resort hotels, all within a half-hour drive of the city. All offer free parking and easy highway access.

Colonial Hilton and Resort. 427 Walnut St., Lynnfield, MA 01940. ☎ **800/HILTONS** or 617/245-9300. Fax 617/245-0842. www.hilton.com/hotels/WAKHIHF/index.html. 280 units. A/C TV TEL. $129-$169 double. Extra person $10. Children stay free in parents' room. Packages and senior discounts available. AE, DC, DISC, MC, V.

Just off I-95 on the Lynnfield-Wakefield border, this 220-acre luxury resort hotel has an 18-hole golf course, indoor and outdoor tennis courts, racquetball courts, an indoor basketball court, an Olympic-size swimming pool, and a health club. The largest and most luxurious rooms are in the 11-story tower. On a hilltop overlooking the golf course is the Colonial at Lynnfield Restaurant, specializing in prime rib and New England fare; there's also another casual restaurant. Rooms for people with disabilities are available.

Renaissance Bedford Hotel. 44 Middlesex Tpk., Bedford, MA 01730. ☎ **800/HOTELS-1** or 781/275-5500. Fax 781/275-3042. www.renaissancehotels.com/BOSSB. 284 units. A/C MINIBAR TV TEL. Sun–Thurs $170–$200 double; Fri–Sat $125–$155 double. Extra person $15. Children under 19 stay free in parents' room. Weekend packages and senior discount available. AE, CB, DC, DISC, JCB, MC, V.

The sights in Lexington and Concord are convenient to this three-story hotel, which neatly makes the transition from a primarily business destination during the week to a family resort on weekends. There's also plenty to do without leaving the property. The country lodge-style building on landscaped, wooded grounds has a business center, recently renovated meeting and function space, a fitness center, an indoor pool, a whirlpool, a sauna, and indoor and outdoor tennis courts. A restaurant and lounge are in the hotel; there is also 24-hour room service. A complimentary shuttle transports guests to destinations within 5 miles, including the Burlington Mall. All rooms have two phones and hair dryers. Larger rooms have king-size beds; a few units have twin beds. Several suites have sofas and conference tables. A newspaper and coffee arrive at your room with your wake-up call. There are 11 rooms for people with disabilities.

Tara's Ferncroft Conference Resort. 50 Ferncroft Rd., Danvers, MA 01923. ☎ **800/ THE-TARA** or 978/777-2500. Fax 978/750-7959. 367 units. A/C TV TEL. $89–$210 double; $190–$550 suite. Extra person $15. Children under 12 stay free in parents' room. Weekend packages and 20% AARP discount available. AE, CB, DC, DISC, MC, V.

This popular business destination is a great spot for a golf vacation. Robert Trent Jones designed the 18-hole championship course, and the rooms high above Route 1 (at I-95) look out on the course or the surrounding countryside.

If golf isn't your game, there are tennis, racquetball, basketball, and cross-country skiing facilities; an indoor and an outdoor pool; and a health and fitness center with cardiovascular room, Nautilus room, aerobics studio, sauna, and masseuse. The eight-story resort has a concierge, a staffed business center, and meeting and function space. All rooms have a sofa, a desk, heat controls, a coffee maker, a hair dryer, and an iron and ironing board. "Top of the Tara" rooms offer additional amenities, including whirlpools. There are 23 rooms for people with disabilities.

The hotel is 30 minutes from Boston, about 20 minutes from Gloucester and Rockport, and even closer to Salem. There are four restaurants on the property, and room service lasts until midnight.

Dining 6

When we first tackled this assignment, a friend laughed and said, "From 1940 to 1970, you could have used the same dining guide every year—now you could probably do a new one every 6 months or so." The restaurant scene in Boston is one of the most dynamic in the country, with hot spots opening and former hot spots closing almost as often as blockbuster movies, and top chefs and their protégés turning up everywhere.

One ingredient found at almost all area restaurants—trendy and classic, expensive and cheap, typical American (whatever that is) and ethnic—is seafood. Ipswich and Essex clams, Atlantic lobsters, Wellfleet oysters, mussels, cod, haddock, and flounder are available in every imaginable form. Chowder fans who have never had fresh clams are in for a treat.

You'll find vegetarian offerings on almost every menu in every price range. With the recent trend toward "fusion" cuisine, many restaurants use unexpected accents—Asian and Southwestern are especially widespread—in food of all descriptions, with considerably more success in some kitchens than in others. And as in any college community, there are many little restaurants that serve various ethnic cuisines.

The guiding thought for this chapter, without regard to price, was "If this were your only meal in Boston, would you be delighted with it?" All of the restaurants listed fit, in one way or another, under the wide umbrella of "delightful." They're divided by neighborhood and listed alphabetically under the following main-course price ranges: **Very Expensive,** $18 to $35; **Expensive,** $12 to $20; and **Moderate,** $8 to $15. The **Inexpensive** category includes restaurants charging less than $10 for a meal. Wine, appetizers, soups, salad, dessert, and coffee can easily double the total bill, and in the top restaurants, dinner for two might come to more than $125. Note that the price of lobster at market and at most restaurants fluctuates daily.

1 Best Bets

- **Best Spot for Romance:** The soft lighting, well-spaced tables, and cushy surroundings at **Icarus,** 3 Appleton St. (☎ 617/426-1790), make it the perfect place for trysting. And because it's underground, there's no view to distract you from your beloved.

Boston Dining

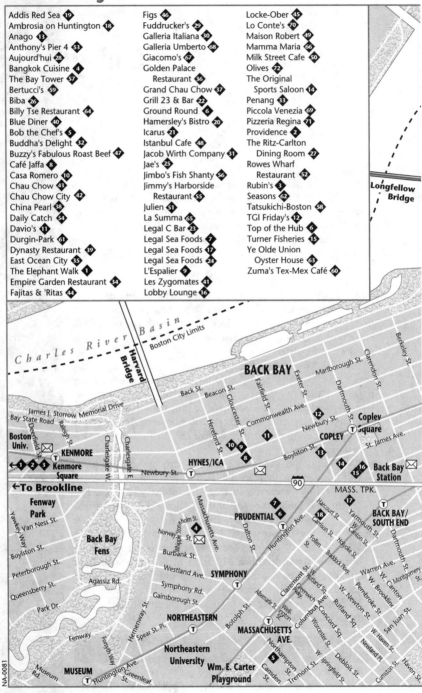

Addis Red Sea **19**
Ambrosia on Huntington **18**
Anago **13**
Anthony's Pier 4 **53**
Aujourd'hui **28**
Bangkok Cuisine **4**
The Bay Tower **57**
Bertucci's **59**
Biba **26**
Billy Tse Restaurant **64**
Blue Diner **40**
Bob the Chef's **5**
Buddha's Delight **32**
Buzzy's Fabulous Roast Beef **47**
Café Jaffa **8**
Casa Romero **10**
Chau Chow **43**
Chau Chow City **42**
China Pearl **38**
Daily Catch **54**
Davio's **11**
Durgin-Park **61**
Dynasty Restaurant **39**
East Ocean City **35**
The Elephant Walk **1**
Empire Garden Restaurant **34**
Fajitas & 'Ritas **44**

Figs **46**
Fuddrucker's **29**
Galleria Italiana **30**
Galleria Umberto **68**
Giacomo's **67**
Golden Palace
  Restaurant **36**
Grand Chau Chow **37**
Grill 23 & Bar **22**
Ground Round **6**
Hamersley's Bistro **20**
Icarus **21**
Istanbul Cafe **48**
Jacob Wirth Company **31**
Jae's **25**
Jimbo's Fish Shanty **56**
Jimmy's Harborside
  Restaurant **55**
Julien **51**
La Summa **65**
Legal C Bar **23**
Legal Sea Foods **7**
Legal Sea Foods **17**
Legal Sea Foods **24**
L'Espalier **9**
Les Zygomates **41**
Lobby Lounge **16**

Locke-Ober **45**
Lo Conte's **70**
Maison Robert **49**
Mamma Maria **66**
Milk Street Cafe **50**
Olives **72**
The Original
  Sports Saloon **14**
Penang **33**
Piccola Venezia **69**
Pizzeria Regina **71**
Providence **2**
The Ritz-Carlton
  Dining Room **27**
Rowes Wharf
  Restaurant **52**
Rubin's **3**
Seasons **62**
Tatsukichi-Boston **58**
TGI Friday's **12**
Top of the Hub **6**
Turner Fisheries **15**
Ye Olde Union
  Oyster House **63**
Zuma's Tex-Mex Café **60**

88

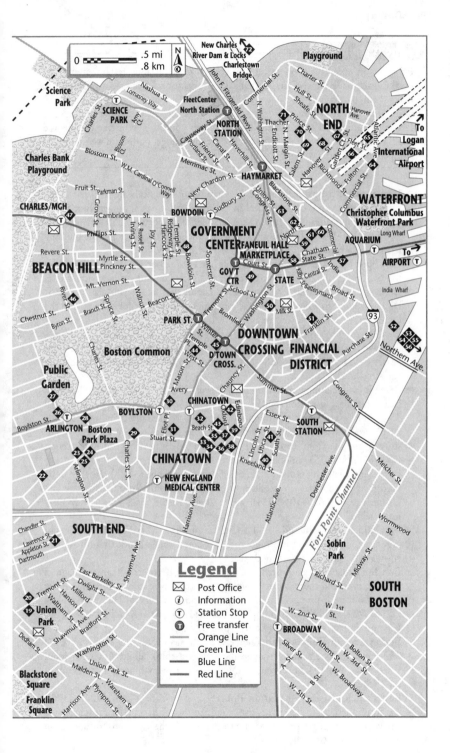

Time is Money

Lunch is an excellent, economical way to check out a fancy restaurant without breaking the bank. At restaurants that take reservations, it's always a good idea to make them, particularly for dinner, and for lunch as well at the better restaurants. A quirk of Bostonian restaurant-goers is their apparent reluctance to dine out if it's not Friday or Saturday. If you're flexible about when you indulge in fine cuisine and when you go for pizza and a movie, opt for the low-budget option on weekends and pamper yourself on a weeknight.

- **Best Spot for a Business Lunch:** Numerous business deals are finalized at the private clubs in town, but for deal-making out in the open, put on your three-piece suit and head to **Julien,** in Le Meridien Boston, 250 Franklin St. (☎ **617/451-1900**). It has always been a prime business location—the building used to be a bank.
- **Best Spot for a Celebration:** Cool your heels at the bar at **Dalí,** 415 Washington St., Somerville (☎ **617/661-3254**), and toast your good news with sangria while you wait for a table. (Finally, a restaurant that makes you glad it doesn't take reservations.) The dishes on the tapas menu are perfect for sharing, and the atmosphere is lively and festive.
- **Best Decor:** The luxurious banquettes, gorgeous paintings and flowers, and picture windows overlooking the Public Garden make **Aujourd'hui,** in the Four Seasons Hotel, 200 Boylston St. (☎ **617/451-1392**), feel like an extremely elegant tree house.
- **Best View:** The dining room at the **Bay Tower,** 60 State St. (☎ **617/723-1666**), isn't the highest in Boston, but its view is the most impressive. From the palatial 33rd floor, everyone in the room (not just people near the windows) can see what's afoot on the waterfront and at the airport. A close second is the 52nd-story panorama from **Top of the Hub,** 800 Boylston St., Prudential Center (☎ **617/536-1775**), especially at dusk.
- **Best Wine List:** Organized by characteristics (from light to rich) rather than by vintage or provenance, the excellent offerings at the **Blue Room,** 1 Kendall Sq., Cambridge (☎ **617/494-9034**), are arranged in the most user-friendly way imaginable.
- **Best Value: The Helmand,** 143 First St., Cambridge (☎ **617/492-4646**), looks expensive but isn't. And it's so good that it could single-handedly turn Afghan cuisine into the next ethnic-food craze.
- **Best for Kids:** The wood-fired brick ovens of the **Bertucci's** chain are magnets for little eyes, and the pizza that comes out of them is equally enthralling. Picky parents will be happy here, too. Try the locations at Faneuil Hall Marketplace (☎ **617/227-7889**), 43 Stanhope St. (☎ **617/247-6161**), and 21 Brattle St., Harvard Square, Cambridge (☎ **617/864-4748**).
- **Best American Cuisine: Providence,** 1223 Beacon St., Brookline (☎ **617/232-0300**), might actually change the way you think about American food. Chef-owner Paul O'Connell puts a unique twist on everything that comes out of his kitchen.
- **Best French Cuisine:** At **Maison Robert,** 45 School St. (☎ **617/227-3370**), the atmosphere is as impressive as the food. You won't find better French cuisine anywhere in the city—in fact, when visiting French chefs come to town, Maison Robert is their first choice.

- **Best Bistro:** A friend who knows both Paris and Boston swears by **Les Zygomates,** 129 South St. (☎ 617/542-5108), where you can enjoy the flavor of the Left Bank in a congenial American setting.
- **Best Italian Cuisine:** "Cuisine" suggests a level of refinement, and **Mamma Maria,** 3 North Sq. (☎ 617/523-0077), has it. The restaurant offers remarkable Northern Italian fare in the red-sauce paradise of the North End.
- **Best Seafood: Legal Sea Foods,** 800 Boylston St., in the Prudential Center (☎ 617/266-6800), does one thing and does it exceptionally well. It's a chain for a great reason—people can't get enough of the freshest seafood in the area.
- **Best Steakhouse:** In some areas—delis, late-night activity, sane drivers—New York eclipses Boston. In this category, Bostonians can point to **Grill 23 & Bar,** 161 Berkeley St. (☎ 617/542-2255), and dare New Yorkers to top it. Whether you eat meat twice a day or twice a year, you'll want to return soon.
- **Best Pizza:** Considering how well pizza travels, it's surprising that the branches of **Pizzeria Regina** throughout the Boston area can't seem to get it quite right. For the real thing, head to the North End original, at 10½ Thacher St. (☎ 617/227-0765).
- **Best Investment (of Time and Money):** As you enter **L'Espalier,** 30 Gloucester St. (☎ 617/262-3023), even if it's early, you might hear the valet-parking attendant say, "Enjoy your evening." Thanks to the grand cuisine and solicitous service, you certainly will.
- **Best Late-Night Dining:** Maybe that should be *only* late-night dining. If you're starving in the wee hours, you'll be glad to know that the fry cooks at **Buzzy's Fabulous Roast Beef,** 327 Cambridge St. (☎ 617/242-7722), work 24/7. **The Blue Diner,** 150 Kneeland St. (☎ 617/338-4639), keeps round-the-clock hours on weekends, and if you have a car, make like a college student and road-trip to the **International House of Pancakes** at 1850 Soldiers Field Rd. in Brighton (☎ 617/787-0533).
- **Best Outdoor Dining:** Good food in a comfortable open-air setting sounds easy but apparently isn't, judging by the number of restaurants that can't manage both. The planets were perfectly aligned when **Upstairs at the Pudding,** 10 Holyoke St., Cambridge (☎ 617/864-1933), opened its peaceful, verdant terrace.
- **Best People-Watching:** Take the genteel route and park yourself in the **Bristol Lounge** at the Four Seasons Hotel, 200 Boylston St. (☎ 617/351-2071). Or check out the freak show in and around the Harvard Square **Au Bon Pain** (near the Harvard T station).
- **Best Afternoon Tea:** At the **Ritz-Carlton,** 15 Arlington St. (☎ 617/536-5700), afternoon tea is an elegant and traditional affair. You'll want to sit up and act like a lady or gentleman while you enjoy scones and Devonshire cream, among other treats.
- **Best Brunch:** The insane displays at many of the top hotels are well worth the monetary and caloric compromises, but if you're looking for a delicious meal that won't destroy your budget and waistline, join the throng at the **S&S Restaurant,** 1334 Cambridge St., Cambridge (☎ 617/354-0777).
- **Best for Pretheater Dinner:** Snappy service is the rule all over Chinatown. Start your evening at **East Ocean City,** 27 Beach St. (☎ 617/542-2504), and you'll be both prompt and well fed.
- **Best Picnic Fare:** On the way to a concert or movie on the Esplanade, stop for food to go at **Figs,** 42 Charles St. (☎ 617/742-3447), a minuscule pizzeria that's an offshoot of its sister restaurant, Olives. The upscale fare isn't cheap, but you

get what you pay for—and you get to eat long, long before the people waiting for a table.

- **Best Barbecue: The Original Sports Saloon,** in the Copley Square Hotel, 47 Huntington Ave. (☎ **617/536-9000**), is about the size of a large bus and perilously close to a Hungarian restaurant (Café Budapest). Somehow it still cranks out the best barbecue in town.
- **Best Raw Bar:** After just a few moments of gobbling fresh seafood and being hypnotized by the shuckers at **Ye Olde Union Oyster House,** 41 Union St. (☎ **617/227-2750**), you might find yourself feeling sorry for the people who wound up with the pearls instead of the oysters.
- **Best Place for a Classic Boston Experience: Durgin-Park,** 340 Faneuil Hall Marketplace (☎ **617/227-2038**), has packed 'em in since 1827. From tycoon to tourist, everyone is happy here except the famously crotchety waitresses. It's a classic, not a relic.
- **Best, Period:** If you have only one meal during your visit, make it dinner at **Rialto,** in the Charles Hotel, 1 Bennett St., Cambridge (☎ **617/661-5050**).

2 Restaurants by Cuisine

AFGHAN
The Helmand, Cambridge (M)

AMERICAN
Anago, Back Bay (VE)
Aujourd'hui, Public Garden (VE)
Bartley's Burger Cottage, Cambridge (I)
The Bay Tower, Faneuil Hall (VE)
Grill 23 & Bar, Back Bay (VE)
House of Blues, Cambridge (M)
Jacob Wirth Company, Theater District (M)
Locke-Ober, Downtown Crossing (VE)
Milk Street Café, Financial District (I)
The Original Sports Saloon, Back Bay (E)
Providence, Brookline (E)
Rowes Wharf Restaurant, Waterfront (VE)
Salamander, Cambridge (VE)
Seasons, Faneuil Hall (VE)
Top of the Hub, Back Bay (VE)

ASIAN
Ambrosia on Huntington, Back Bay (VE)
Billy Tse Restaurant, Waterfront (M)
Jae's, Theater District (E)
Salamander, Cambridge (VE)

BARBECUE
East Coast Grill, Cambridge (E)
The Original Sports Saloon, Back Bay (E)
Redbones, Cambridge (M)

CAJUN
Bob the Chef's, Mass. Ave. & the Fens (M)

CAMBODIAN
The Elephant Walk, Kenmore Square to Brookline (M)

CANTONESE
Chau Chow, Chinatown (M)
East Ocean City, Chinatown (M)
Grand Chau Chow, Chinatown (M)

CARIBBEAN
Green Street Grill, Cambridge (M)

VE = Very Expensive   E = Expensive   M = Moderate   I = Inexpensive

CHINESE

Billy Tse Restaurant, Waterfront (M)
Buddha's Delight, Chinatown (M)
Empire Garden Restaurant, Chinatown (M)

CONTINENTAL

Locke-Ober, Downtown Crossing (VE)
Upstairs at the Pudding, Cambridge (VE)

CUBAN

Chez Henri, Cambridge (E)

DELI

Rubin's, Brookline (M)
S&S Restaurant, Cambridge (I)

ECLECTIC

Biba, Public Garden (VE)
The Blue Room, Cambridge (E)
Hamersley's Bistro, South End (VE)
Icarus, South End (VE)
Les Zygomates, Financial District (E)
Olives, Charlestown (VE)
Providence, Brookline (E)

ETHIOPIAN

Addis Red Sea, South End (M)

FRENCH

Ambrosia on Huntington, Back Bay (VE)
Chez Henri, Cambridge (E)
The Elephant Walk, Kenmore Square to Brookline (M)
Julien, Financial District (VE)
L'Espalier, Back Bay (VE)
Les Zygomates, Financial District (E)
Maison Robert, Government Center (VE)
Ritz-Carlton Dining Room, Public Garden (VE)

GERMAN

Jacob Wirth Company, Theater District (M)

INDIAN

Bombay Club, Cambridge (M)

ITALIAN

Daily Catch, Waterfront (M)
Davio's, Back Bay (E)
Galleria Italiana, Theater District (E)
Galleria Umberto, North End (I)
Giacomo's, North End (E)
La Groceria Ristorante Italiano, Cambridge (M)
La Summa, North End (M)
Lo Conte's, North End (M)
Mamma Maria, North End (VE)
Piccola Venezia, North End (M)
Upstairs at the Pudding, Cambridge (VE)

JAPANESE

Tatsukichi-Boston, Faneuil Hall (M)

KOREAN

Jae's, Theater District (E)

KOSHER

Milk Street Café, Financial District (I)
Rubin's, Brookline (M)

MALAYSIAN

Penang, Chinatown (M)

MEDITERRANEAN

Casablanca, Cambridge (E)
Julien, Financial District (VE)
Rialto, Cambridge (VE)

MEXICAN

Casa Romero, Back Bay (E)

MIDDLE EASTERN

Algiers Coffeehouse, Cambridge (I)
Café Jaffa, Back Bay (I)

NEW ENGLAND

Durgin-Park, Faneuil Hall (M)
L'Espalier, Back Bay (VE)
Ye Olde Union Oyster House, Faneuil Hall (E)

PORTUGUESE

Casa Portugal, Cambridge (M)

SEAFOOD

Anthony's Pier 4, Waterfront (E)
Daily Catch, Waterfront (M)
East Coast Grill, Cambridge (E)
East Ocean City, Chinatown (M)
Giacomo's, North End (E)
Jimbo's Fish Shanty, Waterfront (I)
Jimmy's Harborside Restaurant, Waterfront (E)
Legal Sea Foods, Back Bay (E)
Rowes Wharf Restaurant, Waterfront (VE)
Turner Fisheries, Back Bay (E)
Ye Olde Union Oyster House, Faneuil Hall (E)

SOUTHERN/SOUTHWESTERN

Bob the Chef's, Mass. Ave. & the Fens (M)
Border Café, Cambridge (M)
East Coast Grill, Cambridge (E)

SPANISH

Dalí, Cambridge (E)

SUSHI

Jae's, Theater District (E)
Sakura-Bana, Financial District (M)
Tatsukichi-Boston, Faneuil Hall (M)

TEX-MEX

Fajitas & 'Ritas, Downtown Crossing (I)
Zuma's Tex-Mex Café, Faneuil Hall (I)

THAI

Bangkok Cuisine, Mass. Ave. & the Fens (M)

TURKISH

Istanbul Café, Beacon Hill (M)

VEGETARIAN

Buddha's Delight, Chinatown (M)

VIETNAMESE

Buddha's Delight, Chinatown (M)

3 On the Waterfront

VERY EXPENSIVE

Rowes Wharf Restaurant. In the Boston Harbor Hotel, 70 Rowes Wharf (entrance on Atlantic Ave.). ☎ **617/439-3995.** Reservations recommended. Main courses $11.25–$17.50 at lunch, $25–$35 at dinner. Breakfast $10.75–$13.25. Sun buffet brunch $42. AE, CB, DC, DISC, MC, V. Mon–Sat 6:30–11am, Sun 7–10am; Mon–Sat 11:30am–2:30pm, Sun brunch 10:30am–2pm; Mon–Sat 5:30–11pm, Sun 5:30–10pm. Valet parking available. MBTA: Blue Line to Aquarium, or Red Line to South Station. REGIONAL AMERICAN/SEAFOOD.

Tucked away on the second floor of the Boston Harbor Hotel, the wood-paneled Rowes Wharf Restaurant feels almost like a private club. Sink into the richly uphol-stered chairs as you take in the breathtaking picture-window view of the harbor—a good match for the cuisine, which is among the best in the city. Chef Daniel Bruce uses local ingredients when possible, prepared in deceptively simple ways that accent natural flavors without overwhelming them. The signature appetizer is lus-cious Maine lobster meat seasoned and formed into a sausage, grilled, sliced, and served in a light cream sauce with lobster claw meat and lemon pasta. Or try polen-ta topped with flavorful wild mushrooms. Entrees include pan-roasted Nova Scotia salmon, Maine lobster with chorizo and sweet corn pudding, and pecan-smoked filet mignon grilled and served with whiskey sauce. Desserts vary with the inspira-tion of the chef—there's usually an excellent sorbet sampler. Symbols on the break-fast and lunch menus indicate items low in fat, sodium, and calories; at dinner a separate "Harbor Lites" menu is available.

EXPENSIVE

Anthony's Pier 4. 140 Northern Ave. ☎ **617/423-6363.** Reservations recommended for dinner. Jackets requested for men at dinner. Main courses $10–$25 at lunch, $14–$30 at dinner. AE, CB, DC, MC, V. Mon–Sat 11:30am–11pm, Sun and holidays 12:30–10:30pm. Closed Dec 25. MBTA: Red Line to South Station, 20-minute walk. SEAFOOD.

Long considered one of New England's outstanding places for special-occasion dining, Anthony's Pier 4 has lost a few feet off its fastball. It's still in an amazing location, though, and if you don't order anything too fancy, you can have an enjoyable meal. The restaurant is at the end of a pier, with glass walls facing the water that allow clear views of the traffic on the water. There's outdoor dining in the summer. To start, you're served celery, carrots, and cheese and crackers, then hot popovers. If you have room for more appetizers, the clam chowder is good. Stick to the basic offerings—simple preparations of fresh New England seafood, Dover sole from the English Channel (flown over especially for Anthony's), roast beef, and lobster. Ask your server for dessert recommendations, or try the excellent chocolate mint pie or baked Alaska. If you can't make the trek from South Station, you can park free on the wharf, and cabs are usually around.

Jimmy's Harborside Restaurant. 242 Northern Ave. ☎ **617/423-1000.** Reservations recommended at dinner. Main courses $11–$29. AE, CB, DC, MC, V. Mon–Sat noon–4pm; daily 4–9:30pm. Closed Dec 25. Valet parking available. MBTA: Red Line to South Station, 25-minute walk. SEAFOOD.

This Boston landmark—the sign out front reads "Home of the Chowder King"—offers tasty seafood and fine views of the harbor to businessmen at lunch and tourists at dinner. Long the main competitor of Anthony's Pier 4, Jimmy's has pulled ahead in the rivalry by not trying to do too much. Dinners include appetizer (perhaps the Chowder King's fish chowder, with generous chunks of whitefish), salad, potato, dessert, and beverage. This is a good place to try Atlantic lobster or a "shore dinner" of New England seafood. The à la carte menu includes prime rib and Jimmy's famous finnan haddie (smoked haddock in cream sauce). There are special dinners for children, and complimentary hors d'oeuvres in the lounge while you wait for your table. There's meter parking on Atlantic Avenue, and getting a cab is usually not difficult.

MODERATE

Billy Tse Restaurant. 240 Commercial St. ☎ **617/227-9990.** Reservations recommended at dinner on weekends. Main courses $5–$20; lunch specials $5.50–$7.50. AE, DC, DISC, MC, V. Mon–Thurs 11:30am–11:30pm, Fri–Sat 11:30am–midnight, Sun 11:30am–11pm. MBTA: Blue Line to Aquarium, or Green or Orange Line to Haymarket. CHINESE/PAN-ASIAN.

A pan-Asian restaurant on the edge of the Italian North End might seem incongruous, but this casual, economical spot isn't what it seems to be—an ordinary Chinese restaurant. Excellent renditions of the usual dishes are available, and for a wonderful surprise, the kitchen has a flair for fresh seafood. The pan-Asian selections are just as enjoyable. Start with one of the wonderful soups, sinfully good crab rangoon, or fried calamari with garlic and pepper. Move on to main dishes that range from seven kinds of fried rice to scallops with garlic sauce to the house special fried noodles, topped with shrimp, calamari, and scallops in a scrumptious sauce. Be sure to ask about the daily specials—bitter Chinese broccoli, when it's available, is deftly prepared. Lunch specials, served until 4pm, include vegetable fried rice or vegetable lo mein. You can eat in the comfortable main dining room or near the bar, which has French doors that open to the street. Despite being directly opposite a trolley stop, Billy Tse doesn't have an especially touristy clientele—the neighborhood patrons obviously welcome a break from pizza and pasta.

① Family-Friendly Restaurants

Like chocolate and champagne, well-behaved children are welcome almost everywhere, and we've seen youngsters comporting themselves better than many adults at some of the nicest restaurants in town. If your kids aren't willing or able to sign a good-conduct pledge, here are some suggestions.

The ✪ **Bertucci's** chain of pizzerias appeals to children and adults equally, with wood-fired brick ovens that are visible from many tables, great rolls made from pizza dough, and pizza and pastas that range from basic to sophisticated. There are convenient branches at Faneuil Hall Marketplace (☎ 617/227-7889); at 43 Stanhope St. (☎ 617/247-6161), around the corner from the Hard Rock Cafe; and in Cambridge at 21 Brattle St., Harvard Square (☎ 617/864-4748).

The **Ground Round** chain of family restaurants has a lively branch at the Prudential Center, 800 Boylston St. (☎ 617/247-0500). You'll find free popcorn on the table, cartoons on a wall screen, video games, and crayons. On special days, kids pay a penny a pound for their entree.

Fuddrucker's, another family-oriented chain, serves burgers and other grilled items in the Theater District at 137 Stuart St. (☎ 617/723-3833), not far from the Common and the Public Garden. Order at the counter, hit the condiment bar, and make as much noise as you want—this is also a rowdy business lunch spot. There are children's dinner specials Monday through Thursday evenings.

TGI Friday's, 26 Exeter St., at Newbury Street (☎ 617/266-9040), made its reputation by catering to singles. All that pairing off apparently led to children, who are now courted as well. They receive a kids' package with balloons, crayons, a coloring book, peanut butter and crackers, and surprises wrapped in the chain's signature red-and-white stripes.

The **Bristol Lounge,** in the Four Seasons Hotel, 200 Boylston St. (☎ 617/351-2071), looks almost too nice to have a kids' menu (with appetizers, plain main courses, desserts, and beverages). The staff is unflappable and accommodating, and high chairs and sticker fun books are available.

Daily Catch. 261 Northern Ave. ☎ **617/338-3093.** Reservations accepted only for parties of 8 or more. Main courses $10–$18. AE. Sun–Thurs noon–10:30pm, Fri–Sat noon–11pm. MBTA: Red Line to South Station, 25-minute walk. SOUTHERN ITALIAN/SEAFOOD.

Make sure that your fellow travelers accompany you to this Fish Pier institution, because you're going to emanate garlic for at least a day and you might as well have someone to share it with. This is a basic storefront, where the staff sometimes seems overwhelmed and it can take forever to get a table, but the food is terrific. There are Sicilian-style calamari (squid stuffed with bread crumbs, raisins, pine nuts, parsley, and tons of garlic), freshly shucked clams, mussels in garlic-flavored sauce, broiled and fried fish, and shellfish. Calamari is prepared at least eight ways—even the standard garlic-and-oil pasta sauce has ground-up squid in it. If you've never tasted it before, try the fried version as an excellent appetizer. And if you really want to try something different, order the squid ink pasta puttanesca. All food is prepared to order, and some dishes are served in the frying pans in which they were cooked.

The other two branches of this minichain don't accept credit cards or reservations. The original Daily Catch, in the **North End** at 323 Hanover St. (☎ 617/523-8567), keeps the same hours as the Fish Pier location. The **Brookline** restaurant, at 441 Harvard St. (☎ 617/734-5696), opens at 5pm nightly.

INEXPENSIVE

Jimbo's Fish Shanty. 245 Northern Ave. ☎ **617/542-5600.** Main courses $6–$14. AE, DC, MC, V. Mon-Thurs 11:30am–9:30pm, Fri–Sat 11:30am–10pm, Sun noon–8pm. MBTA: Red Line to South Station, 25-minute walk. SEAFOOD.

Bring your sense of humor to this jam-packed restaurant, where model trains run overhead on tracks suspended from the low ceiling, road signs hang everywhere, and the wait staff is incredibly informal. Under the same management as Jimmy's Harborside across the street, Jimbo's serves decent portions of good, fresh seafood to office workers, tourists, and bargain hunters. Feel free to ask your server for a suggestion—someone who starts off calling you "pal" or "honey" isn't holding back. You can also order skewers threaded with fish or beef, and pasta dishes (at dinner only) with varied sauces, including a lobster cream version. The decadent desserts generally involve ice cream and chocolate—save room.

4 The North End

Boston's Italian-American enclave has dozens of restaurants; many are tiny and, to keep the tables turning over, don't serve dessert and coffee. Hit the cafes for coffee concoctions and fresh pastry in an atmosphere where lingering is welcome—as is smoking. Favorites include **Dolce Vita,** 237 Hanover St. (☎ **617/720-0422**), **Caffè Graffiti,** 307 Hanover St. (☎ **617/367-2494**), and **Caffè Vittoria,** 296 Hanover St. (☎ **617/227-7606**). There's also table service at **Mike's Pastry,** 300 Hanover St. (☎ **617/742-3050**), which is better known for a bustling takeout business and its cannoli—President Clinton's favorite.

VERY EXPENSIVE

✪ **Mamma Maria.** 3 North Sq. ☎ **617/523-0077.** Reservations recommended. Main courses $18–$28. AE, DC, DISC, MC, V. Daily 5–10pm. Valet parking available. MBTA: Green or Orange Line to Haymarket. NORTHERN ITALIAN.

In a townhouse overlooking North Square and the Paul Revere House, this is a traditional-looking restaurant that offers innovative cuisine and a level of sophistication far removed from the North End's familiar hey-whaddaya-want service. The menu changes seasonally; you can usually start with excellent *pasta fagioli* (bean-and-pasta soup) or risotto, and the daily pasta special is always a good bet. The excellent entrees are unlike anything else in this neighborhood, except in size—portions are more than generous. The fork-tender osso buco is almost enough for two, but you'll want it all for yourself. Or try roasted chicken with lightly steamed green beans, garlic poached to bring out its sweetness, and a hunk of potato casserole. You can't go wrong with pasta on this part of the menu either, and the fresh seafood specials are marvelous. The pasta, bread, and desserts are homemade, and the shadowy, whitewashed rooms make this a popular spot for getting engaged—we have to assume the kitchen staff regularly fields offers.

EXPENSIVE

Giacomo's. 355 Hanover St. ☎ **617/523-9026.** Reservations not accepted. Main courses $15–$24. No credit cards. Mon–Thurs 5–10pm, Fri–Sat 5–10:30pm, Sun 4–10pm. MBTA: Green or Orange Line to Haymarket. ITALIAN/SEAFOOD.

Fans of Giacomo's seem to have adopted the Postal Service's motto—they brave snow, sleet, rain, and gloom of night. The line forms early, especially on weekends. No reservations, cash only, a tiny dining room with an open kitchen—what's the secret? Well, the food is terrific and there's plenty of it—and don't underestimate the we're-all-in-this-together atmosphere. The fried calamari appetizer is almost grease-less, and you can take the chef's advice or put together your own main dish from the list of daily ingredients on a board on the wall. Salmon in pesto cream sauce with fettuccine is a keeper, as is any dish with shrimp. Nonseafood offerings such as butternut squash ravioli in mascarpone cheese sauce are equally memorable. Service is friendly but incredibly swift, and lingering is not encouraged—but unless you have a heart of stone, you won't want to take up a table when people are standing outside in 90-degree heat or an ice storm waiting for your seat.

For those who don't consider privation fun, the **South End Giacomo's** at 431 Columbus Ave. (☎ **617/536-5723**) takes reservations and credit cards (AE, MC, V) and offers valet parking. But it doesn't have the same cramped-kitchen atmosphere, and you can't say you waited an hour for a meal (however delicious) that took 40 minutes.

MODERATE

La Summa. 30 Fleet St. ☎ **617/523-9503.** Reservations recommended. Main courses $11–$17. AE, CB, DC, MC, V. Daily 4:30–10:30pm. MBTA: Green or Orange Line to Haymarket. ITALIAN.

Fleet Street is one of the busiest side streets in the North End, but because La Summa isn't on the restaurant rows of Hanover and Salem streets, it maintains a cozy neighborhood atmosphere. Unlike some neighborhood places, it's friendly to outsiders—you'll feel welcome even if the waiter doesn't greet you by name. La Summa is worth seeking out for the wonderful homemade pasta and desserts, and most of the more elaborate entrees are tasty, too. You might start with ravioli—almost always available as a special, stuffed with cheese and meat (on the same plate, not in the same wrapper)—or stick to the excellent salad that's included with each meal and save room for sweets. A main dish of lobster ravioli will have you thanking the first person who thought to cook a crustacean. Or try any seafood special or the veal stuffed with artichoke hearts and sun-dried tomatoes—a better choice than the rigatoni, chicken, and broccoli, which is sometimes on the dry side. The desserts, especially the tiramisu, are terrific.

Lo Conte's. 116 Salem St. ☎ **617/720-0339** or 617/720-3550. Reservations recommended at dinner. Main courses $10.50–$17. AE, DC, DISC, MC, V. Sun–Thurs 11:30am–10pm, Fri–Sat 11:30am–11pm. MBTA: Green or Orange Line to Haymarket. SOUTHERN ITALIAN.

This is a neighborhood place, with chummy service and large portions of excellent food. The house-special chicken, broccoli, and ziti (a dish you'll find on menus more than chicken parmigiana) is the best in town. Photos of Italy cover the walls of the two glorified-storefront dining rooms, where it gets quite noisy on busy nights. Salads and appetizers aren't cheap, but portions are large and quality is generally high. The house salad dressing is tangy and packed with cheese, and eggplant rolatini, when it's available as a special, is out of this world. (The cold antipasto appetizer is more cold than appetizing.) Main dishes are divided into pasta, chicken, veal, seafood, and "House Specials"—all terrific. And the daily specials actually taste as good as they sound. If they involve seafood, go for it.

Piccola Venezia. 263 Hanover St. ☎ **617/523-3888.** Reservations not accepted. Main courses $10–$20; lunch specialties $5.25–$8. AE, DISC, MC, V. Daily 11am–10pm; lunch menu Mon–Fri 11am–4pm. MBTA: Green or Orange Line to Haymarket. ITALIAN.

The glass front wall of Piccola Venezia ("little Venice") shows off the exposed-brick dining room, decorated with prints and photos and filled with happy patrons.

North End & Charlestown Dining

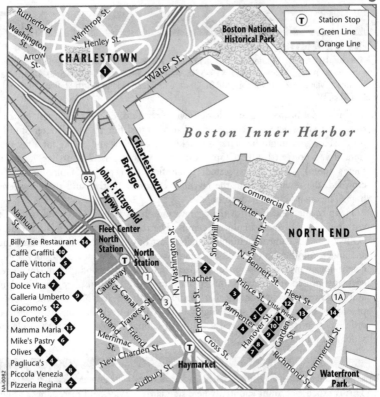

Portions are large and the homey food tends to be heavy on red sauce, though more sophisticated dishes are available. The delicious sautéed mushroom appetizer is solidly in the latter category; a more traditional starter is the tasty *pasta e fagioli* (bean-and-pasta soup). Then dig into spaghetti and meatballs, chicken parmigiana, eggplant rolatini, or pasta puttanesca. This is a good place to try traditional Italian-American favorites such as polenta (home-style, not the yuppie croutons available at so many other places), *baccala* (reconstituted salt cod), or the house specialty, tripe.

INEXPENSIVE

Galleria Umberto. 289 Hanover St. ☎ **617/227-5709.** Reservations not accepted. All items $2.75 or less. No credit cards. Mon–Sat 11am–2pm. MBTA: Green or Orange Line to Haymarket. ITALIAN.

The long, fast-moving line of businesspeople and tourists tips you off to the fact that this cafeteria-style spot is a real bargain. And the food is good, too. You can fill up on a couple of slices of pizza, but if you're feeling adventurous, try the *arancini* (a rice ball filled with ground beef, peas, and cheese). The calzones—ham and cheese, spinach, spinach and cheese, or spinach and sausage—and potato croquettes are also tasty. Study the cases while you wait, and be ready to order at once when you reach the head of the line. Have a quick lunch and get on with your sightseeing.

5 Charlestown

VERY EXPENSIVE

✪ **Olives.** 10 City Sq., Charlestown. ☎ **617/242-1999.** Reservations accepted only for parties of 6 or more. Main courses $19–$30. AE, DC, MC, V. Tues–Fri 5:30–10pm, Sat 5–10:30pm. Valet parking available. MBTA: Orange or Green Line to North Station; 10-minute walk. ECLECTIC.

This informal bistro near the Charlestown Navy Yard, one of the hottest spots in town, just keeps getting more popular. Patrons often line up shortly after 5pm to get a table—you might be better off making five friends and calling for a reservation. If you don't arrive by 5:45pm, expect to wait at least 2 hours (at the bar if there's room). Once you're seated, you'll find many of the tables small and crowded, the service uneven, the ravenous customers festive, and the noise level high. The open kitchen adds to the din.

Happily, the food is worth the aggravation. Todd English, chef and co-owner with his wife, Olivia, is a culinary genius. The regularly changing menu includes "Olives Classics," one meltingly delicious tart of olives, caramelized onions, and anchovies. Another, spit-roasted chicken flavored with herbs and garlic, oozes succulent juices into old-fashioned mashed potatoes. The wood-grilled lamb over eggplant-infused risotto with tomato-and-mint salsa is an inspired combination, and the sweet lady celebrating her birthday at the next table (in other words, practically sitting with us) spoke highly of the Cuban steak. For dessert, when you order your entree you'll be asked if you want falling chocolate cake with raspberry sauce and vanilla ice cream. Say yes.

6 Faneuil Hall/Government Center/Financial District

This is expense-account country, where standards, service, and prices are sky-high (as is one of the restaurants). You'll also find excellent places that cater to office workers on a budget.

VERY EXPENSIVE

The Bay Tower. 60 State St. ☎ **617/723-1666.** Reservations recommended. Jacket required for men in dining room. Main courses $18–$35. AE, CB, DC, MC, V. Mon–Thurs 5:30–10pm, Fri 5:30–11pm, Sat 5–11pm. Validated parking available. MBTA: Blue or Orange Line to State, or Green Line to Government Center. CREATIVE AMERICAN.

Let's cut to the chase: Would you pay this much at a restaurant with a view of a brick wall or a street corner? Of course not. Is it worth it? Absolutely. One of the most beautiful dining rooms in Boston, the 33rd-floor Bay Tower has glass walls facing a glorious panorama of Faneuil Hall Marketplace, the harbor, and the airport. The terraced table area is arranged so that every seat has a view, and the shiny (polished, not mirrored) surfaces lend a casino-like air to the candlelit room.

The menu, an intriguing variety of traditional and contemporary dishes, changes seasonally. You might start with lobster bisque, shrimp cocktail, or a goat-cheese-and-artichoke napoleon. Entrees include the usual meat, chicken, and seafood, often with a twist. Pan-seared veal is served with fava bean cassoulet, fresh pasta, and a morel mushroom sauce; for those with more traditional tastes, Dover sole meunière is filleted at the table. Special dietary preparations are available on request, and there's always at least one vegetarian entree. As you might expect at a restaurant where many people come just for sweets, drinks, and dancing, desserts are wonderful, with an emphasis on chocolate. There is a $12 minimum in the lounge after 9:30pm on Friday and Saturday.

Julien. In Le Meridien Boston, 250 Franklin St. ☎ **617/451-1900.** Reservations recommended. Main courses $14.50–$18.75 at lunch, $26–$33 at dinner. Business Lunch $26. Sun buffet brunch $41. AE, CB, DC, MC, V. Mon–Fri noon–2pm; Mon–Thurs 6–10pm, Fri–Sat 6–10:30pm. MBTA: Blue or Orange Line to State, or Red Line to Downtown Crossing. FRENCH/MEDITERRANEAN.

Julien is in one of the most beautiful rooms in the city, under a vaulted, gilt-edged ceiling and five crystal chandeliers. Listen closely and you can almost hear the business deals going down, especially at lunch. The seasonal menus emphasize fresh regional products. Specialties to start include terrine of fresh homemade foie gras with truffles, and Maine lobster salad on a bed of diced vegetables. The sautéed tuna steak with brochette of asparagus and wild mushrooms is an excellent choice, as is the salmon soufflé, and the lamb loin with spinach mousse, served with olive-and-thyme-flavored potatoes, is also delicious. The desserts are among the best (and most expensive) in town. The wine list offers selections from top French, American, German, and Italian wineries. The Business Lunch includes a soup or salad, a choice of entrees, and coffee or tea.

Café Fleuri, Le Meridien's atrium-style informal dining room, serves lunch on weekdays and Sunday brunch at 11 and 11:30am and 1 and 1:30pm. On Saturday afternoons from September through May, the "Chocolate Bar Buffet" takes over.

✪ **Maison Robert.** 45 School St. ☎ **617/227-3370.** www.maisonrobert.com. Reservations recommended. Main courses $9–$22 at lunch, $17–$32 at dinner. Le Café fixed-price menu $18 or $25; à la carte main courses $14–$28. AE, CB, DC, MC, V. Mon–Fri 11:45am–2:30pm; Mon–Sat 5:30–10pm. Valet parking available at dinner. MBTA: Red Line to Park St. or Green Line to Government Center. INNOVATIVE FRENCH.

This world-class French restaurant has been a legend in Boston since it opened in Old City Hall in 1971. Like many excellent restaurants, it's family-owned and operated—proprietors Lucien and Ann Robert are executive chef Andrée Robert's parents, and nephew Jacky Robert took over in the kitchen in 1996 after many years as a top chef in San Francisco (including 10 years at Ernie's).

Maison Robert has only improved since Jacky Robert returned. The formal dining room was already spectacular, with majestic crystal chandeliers and tall windows. The food equals the setting, classic but dramatic, with unexpected but welcome Asian influences. You might start with a tender, airy Roquefort soufflé, or lobster and Sauterne cream soup with trumpet mushrooms. Entrees include options you would expect and pleasant surprises—filet mignon is a meat-lover's delight, Dover sole is served *à la Meunière,* and ostrich medallions are marinated in Asian spices and served with a leek salad. Desserts are impressive, ranging from excellent soufflés to heart-stopping chocolate concoctions to upside-down apple tart, served warm with cinnamon sabayon.

On the ground floor is the cozy **Ben's Café.** It's more casual and less expensive than the upstairs room, but also thoroughly French. In the summer, cafe seating spills onto the lovely terrace next to the landmark statue of Benjamin Franklin.

Seasons. In the Regal Bostonian Hotel, at Faneuil Hall Marketplace. ☎ **617/523-4119.** Reservations recommended. Main courses $14–$21 at lunch, $26–$42 at dinner; breakfast items $3.75–$13.75. AE, CB, DC, JCB, MC, V. Mon–Fri 6:30–10:30am and 11:30am–2pm; Sat–Sun 7am–noon; Sun–Thurs 6–10pm, Fri–Sat 6–11pm. Valet parking available. MBTA: Green or Blue Line to Government Center, or Orange Line to Haymarket. NEW AMERICAN.

On the fourth-floor rooftop of the Regal Bostonian Hotel, Seasons offers stunning views of Faneuil Hall Marketplace. Executive chef Michael Taylor's equally interesting menu changes (you guessed it) seasonally. You might try an Asian-influenced dish such as miso-crusted tuna with a scallion pancake and baby spinach, or a slab of pepper-seared beef tenderloin with potato-beet gratin. Lunch, less expensive and equally enjoyable, might consist of a braised lamb shank or a salad with enough protein (shrimp, roast chicken, even veal) to be a complete meal. Like the rest of the menu, the dessert list is short but high-quality. The wine list is entirely American and encyclopedic, with 50 chardonnays, 65 cabernet sauvignons, and some rare selections from top producers.

Seasons draws a business crowd for breakfast and lunch, but there's no dress code. Whether that's a plus depends on your attitude toward an evening out—you might find yourself seated between people dressed for the theater and people dressed for the movie theater.

EXPENSIVE

✪ **Les Zygomates.** 129 South St. ☎ **617/542-5108.** www.winebar.com. Reservations recommended. Main courses $12–$20. Prix fixe lunch $11, prix fixe dinner $19. AE, CB, DC, DISC, MC, V. Mon–Fri 11am–1am, Sat–Sun 6pm–1am. Valet parking available at dinner. MBTA: Red Line to South Station. FRENCH/ECLECTIC.

Pick your way across the construction wasteland near South Station to this delightful bistro and wine bar. It's worth the trouble. Over the bar in the high-ceilinged, brick-walled room is a great selection of wine, available by the bottle, the glass, and the "taste" (2 oz.). The efficient staff will guide you to a good accompaniment for chef and co-owner Ian Just's delicious food. Salads are excellent, lightly dressed, and garden-fresh, and main courses are hearty and filling but not heavy. A large piece of pan-fried catfish is flaky and light, and flank steak with garlic mashed potatoes and sautéed vegetables is succulent. The supply of bread at every place setting is constantly replenished. For dessert, try not to fight over the lemon mousse, a cloud of citrus and air. And Sunday through Thursday nights, you can linger over a glass of wine and listen to live jazz.

Ye Olde Union Oyster House. 41 Union St. (between North and Hanover sts.). ☎ **617/227-2750.** Reservations recommended. Main courses $9–$19 at lunch, $15–$28 at dinner. AE, CB, DC, DISC, MC, V. Sun–Thurs 11am–9:30pm, Fri–Sat 11am–10pm. Lunch menu until 5pm Sun–Thurs, until 6pm Fri–Sat. Union Bar: 11am–3pm lunch, 3–11pm late-supper fare. Bar open until midnight. MBTA: Green or Orange Line to Haymarket. NEW ENGLAND/SEAFOOD.

America's oldest restaurant in continuous service, the Union Oyster House opened in 1826, and the booths and oyster bar haven't moved since. The food is tasty, traditional New England fare, popular with tourists on the adjacent Freedom Trail. At the crescent-shaped bar on the lower level of the cramped, low-ceilinged building, "where Daniel Webster drank many a toddy in his day," try the sampler, a mixed appetizer of hot or cold oysters, clams, and shrimp. Oyster stew made with fresh milk and country butter makes a good beginning. Follow with a broiled or grilled dish such as scrod or salmon, or perhaps seafood primavera, fried seafood, or grilled pork loin. A complete shore dinner with chowder, steamers, lobster, salad, corn, and dessert is an excellent introduction to local favorites. Low-calorie menu selections, introduced in 1994, are popular too. For dessert, try gingerbread with whipped cream. Ask to be seated at John F. Kennedy's favorite booth (number 18), which is marked with a plaque.

MODERATE

✪ **Durgin-Park.** 340 Faneuil Hall Marketplace. ☎ **617/227-2038.** Reservations not accepted. Main courses $5–$18, specials $16–$25. AE, CB, DC, DISC, MC, V. Daily 11:30am–2:30pm; Mon–Thurs 2:30–10pm, Fri–Sat 2:30–10:30pm, Sun 2:30–9pm. MBTA: Green or Blue Line to Government Center, or Orange Line to Haymarket. NEW ENGLAND.

Sunday Brunch

Many restaurants serve an excellent Sunday brunch, but for true decadence, head to a top hotel for a buffet of monstrous proportions. Do *not* make elaborate dinner plans.

Aujourd'hui, in the Four Seasons Hotel, 200 Boylston St. (☎ **617/451-1392**), serves a bountiful New England buffet in a lovely dining room with a view of the Public Garden. Pâtés, salads, smoked and steamed fish, roast sirloin, chicken, lobster, egg dishes, waffles, and a fabulous assortment of desserts make up the meal. It's served from 11:30am to 2:30pm, and reservations are recommended. Adults eat for $44, children for $19.

Overlooking the waterfront, the **Rowes Wharf Restaurant,** in the Boston Harbor Hotel, 70 Rowes Wharf (☎ **617/439-3995**), offers a traditional American buffet of fresh and smoked seafood, carved prime rib and rack of lamb, garden salad, soused shrimp, and regional specialty items. You can also try omelettes made to order, Belgian waffles, freshly baked pastries, and desserts. When you make reservations, be sure to ask for a table overlooking the harbor. Hours are from 10:30am to 2pm, and there is a dress code (no jeans or sneakers). Adult $42, child $21.

Café Fleuri at Le Meridien Boston, 250 Franklin St. (☎ **617/451-1900**), is in a gorgeous garden court. The hot and cold buffet is just as impressive, with a selection of dishes befitting the hotel's French background. The desserts are especially fabulous. The price includes a sparkling wine cocktail. Seatings are at 11 and 11:30am and 1 and 1:30pm. Adult $41, child $20.50.

The **Ritz-Carlton,** 15 Arlington St. (☎ **617/536-5700**), serves brunch in the beautiful main dining room. You can choose delicacies such as oysters on the half shell, gravlax, seafood mousse, sturgeon, assorted pâtés, soup, roast beef carved to order, crêpes, omelettes to order, quiche, salads, and hot and cold vegetables. There's a dessert table with pastries, fruit tarts, cakes, cheese, and fruit. Reservations are necessary and are taken for 10:45am to 2:30pm. Jackets are requested for men, and jeans and sneakers are not allowed. Adult $47, child $26.

For huge portions of delicious food, a rowdy atmosphere where CEOs share tables with students, and famously cranky waitresses who can't seem to bear the sight of any of it, people have been flocking to Durgin-Park since 1827. It's everything it's cracked up to be—a tourist magnet that attracts hordes of locals, where everyone's disappointed when the waitresses are nice (they often are). Approximately 2,000 people a day find their way to the line that stretches down a flight of stairs to the first floor of Faneuil Hall Marketplace's North Market building. The queue moves quickly, and you'll probably wind up seated at a long table with other people (smaller tables are available).

The food is wonderful, and there's plenty of it—prime rib the size of a hubcap, giant lamb chops, piles of fried seafood, roast turkey that might fill you up till Thanksgiving. Steaks and chops are broiled on an open fire over wood charcoal. Fresh seafood arrives twice daily, and fish dinners are broiled to order. Vegetables come à la carte; if you want to try Boston baked beans, now's the time. For dessert, the strawberry shortcake is justly celebrated, and molasses lovers (this is not a dish for dabblers) will want to try Indian pudding—molasses and cornmeal baked for hours and served with ice cream.

If you're having "dinner" (otherwise known as lunch; the evening meal is "supper"), beat the crowd by arriving when the restaurant opens. Or start out at the ground-floor Gaslight Pub, which has a private staircase that leads upstairs.

Tatsukichi-Boston. 189 State St. ☎ **617/720-2468.** Reservations recommended. Main courses $10–$22; lunch specials from $8. AE, CB, DC, DISC, JCB, MC, V. Restaurant Mon–Fri 11:45am–2:30pm; Sun–Thurs 5-10pm, Fri–Sat 5--11pm; VIP karaoke lounge Tues–Sat 7pm–1am. Validated parking available. MBTA: Blue Line to Aquarium. JAPANESE/SUSHI.

A block away from Faneuil Hall Marketplace, this award-winning restaurant is a favorite with the Japanese community and other fans of the cuisine. At half of the tables, patrons sit on chairs; at the rest, they kneel on an elevated platform. There's an excellent sushi bar. If you prefer your food cooked, choose from an extensive array of authentic Japanese dishes, including sukiyaki, *shabu shabu* (beef and vegetables cooked in seasoned boiling water), teriyaki, and *kushiage* (meat, seafood, and vegetables on skewers, lightly battered, breaded, and quickly fried, served with special dipping sauces). At lunch, the *unagi-don* (grilled eel) is as tasty as it is scary-sounding. There are private tatami rooms and a newly remodeled karaoke lounge (the cover charge is $7.50 for dinner guests, half the usual rate).

INEXPENSIVE

Milk Street Café. 50 Milk St. ☎ **617/542-2433** (menu line) or 617/542-FOOD. Most items under $8. No credit cards. Mon–Fri 7am–3pm. MBTA: Blue Line to State. CREATIVE AMERICAN/KOSHER.

In the heart of the Financial District, this popular spot offers fresh, homemade fare that's often but not exclusively vegetarian. The restaurant is kosher, but most customers are neither kosher nor vegetarian. They come for the excellent food—soups, salads, hot entrees, quiches, sandwiches on homemade bread, and salad plates. The veggie melts, Middle Eastern plates, and fruit and cheese platters are very popular. At breakfast there are scones, bagels, muffins, pastries, fruit salad, fresh-squeezed juices, herbal teas, and coffee. Try to arrive after rush hour if you want to start your day in a calm environment.

A second Milk Street Café, in the park at Zero Post Office Square (☎ **617/350-7275**), is open weekdays from 7am to 6pm (5pm in fall and winter). Located in a copper-roofed, glass-enclosed kiosk, it's strictly kosher and does a lively take-out business. Offerings include salads, meat sandwiches (on bread and rolled up in pita), fish dishes, fruit, and pastries.

Zuma's Tex-Mex Café. 7 N. Market St., Faneuil Hall Marketplace. ☎ **617/367-9114.** Main courses $5–$14. AE, CB, DC, DISC, MC, V. Mon-Thurs 11:30am–11pm, Fri–Sat 11:30am–midnight, Sun noon–10pm. MBTA: Green or Blue Line to Government Center, or Green or Orange Line to Haymarket. TEX-MEX.

Because of its great location, Zuma's could probably get away with serving so-so food and still draw enormous crowds. Happily, its Southwestern cuisine is excellent, with guacamole and salsa cruda made from scratch, and tortilla chips cut and fried throughout the day right in the dining room. The casual, friendly spot is even popular with local office workers, who congregate at the noisy bar (the table area is marginally quieter). Portions are large, especially considering the low prices. An appetizer of calamari fried in a spicy batter is big enough for three, and the noisy fajitas constantly flying out of the kitchen are substantial and delectable. The firecrackers, or fried jalapeños stuffed with shrimp and cheese, are marked with a skull on the menu and are not for the uninitiated. The key lime pie and the margaritas (including a neon version) deserve their acclaim. And you can order lunch to go.

Their hotels are bad. Their pumpkin pies are delicious. Their poetry is not so good.
—Edgar Allan Poe, *Broadway Journal*, 1845

7 Downtown Crossing

VERY EXPENSIVE

Locke-Ober. 3 and 4 Winter Place. ☎ **617/542-1340.** Reservations required. Main courses $8–$24.50 at lunch, $17–$40 at dinner. AE, CB, DC, DISC, MC, V. Mon–Fri 11:30am–3pm; Mon–Sat 3–10pm. Valet parking available after 6pm. MBTA: Red or Orange Line to Downtown Crossing. AMERICAN/CONTINENTAL.

"Locke's" is *the* traditional Boston restaurant, a power-broker favorite since 1875. In a tiny alley off the Winter Street pedestrian mall, this dark, wood-paneled restaurant feels like a men's club, with exquisite service, stained-glass windows, crystal chandeliers, and silver buffet covers on the long, mirrored downstairs bar, which dates from 1880. Women won't feel unwelcome, but this is definitely not a "girls' night out" place; for one thing, anyone on a diet will be sorely tempted. This is old-fashioned food—the famous Jonah crab cakes or steak tartare to start, then superb grilled salmon with horseradish sauce, Wiener schnitzel à la Holstein, or an excellent veal chop. The signature dish is lobster Savannah, which calls for the meat of a 3-pound lobster diced with pepper and mushrooms, bound with cheese and sherry sauce, stuffed into the shell, and baked. If your heart doesn't stop on the spot, you won't be hungry again for a long time. The dessert menu lists about two dozen items, and as you might expect, the chocolate mousse is a dish for the ages.

INEXPENSIVE

Fajitas & 'Ritas. 25 West St. (between Washington and Tremont sts.). ☎ **617/426-1222.** Most dishes under $9. AE, DISC, MC, V. Sun–Thurs 11:30am–10pm, Fri–Sat 11:30am–2am. MBTA: Red or Green Line to Park St., or Orange Line to Downtown Crossing. TEX-MEX.

This entertaining storefront restaurant might not be the most authentic in town, but it's one of the most fun. You order by filling out a slip, checking off your choices of fillings and garnishes to go with your nachos, quesadillas, burritos, and, of course, fajitas. There's nothing exotic, just the usual beef, chicken, shrimp, beans, and so forth. A member of the somewhat harried staff relays your order to the kitchen and returns with big portions of fresh food—this place is too busy for anything to be sitting around for very long. As the name indicates, 'ritas (margaritas, ordered from a list of about a dozen options using the same checkoff system as the food) are a house specialty.

8 Chinatown

This small, crowded area offers a number of good places to dine, but the most entertaining and delicious introduction to the neighborhood is dim sum (see the box below). Many restaurants are open every day from midmorning till 3am or later. The menus are geared to American palates, but sometimes there's a second menu for Chinese patrons (often written in Chinese). Ask for it, or tell your waiter you want your meal Chinese style.

MODERATE

Buddha's Delight. 5 Beach St. ☎ **617/451-2395.** Main courses $6–$12. No credit cards. Sun–Thurs 11am–10pm, Fri–Sat 11am–11pm. MBTA: Orange Line to Chinatown. VEGETARIAN/VIETNAMESE/CHINESE.

Yum, Yum, Dim Sum

Many restaurants in Chinatown offer dim sum, the traditional midday meal featuring a wide variety of appetizer-style dishes. You'll see steamed buns (*bao*) filled with pork or bean paste; dumplings filled with meats, shrimp, and vegetables; spareribs; eggplant stuffed with shrimp; sticky rice dotted with meat and vegetables and steamed in a lotus leaf; spring rolls; sweets such as coconut gelatin and sesame balls; and more. Waiters wheel carts laden with plates of tempting snack-sized morsels up to your table, and you order by pointing (unless you know Chinese). The waiter then stamps your check with the symbol of the dish, adding about $1 to $3 to your tab. Unless you're ravenous or you order à la carte items from the regular menu, the grand total won't be more than about $10 per person.

Dim sum varies from restaurant to restaurant and chef to chef; if something looks familiar, don't be surprised if it's different from what you're used to, and equally good. This is a great group activity, especially on weekends, when the variety is wider than on weekdays and you'll see two and three generations of families sharing dishes and calling for more. Even picky children can usually find something they enjoy. If you don't like or can't eat pork and shrimp, be aware that many, but not all, dishes include one or the other; calorie-counters should be aware that many dishes (again, not all) are fried.

Empire Garden Restaurant, 690–698 Washington St., second floor (☎ 617/482-8898), serves a dazzling variety of dim sum dishes in a cavernous, ornate former theater balcony. It opened in 1998 and instantly challenged the dim sum supremacy of the **Golden Palace Restaurant,** 14 Tyler St. (☎ 617/423-4565), and **China Pearl,** 9 Tyler St., second floor (☎ 617/426-4338). All three are excellent. Two other popular destinations are **Chau Chow City,** 83 Essex St. (☎ 617/338-8158) and **Dynasty Restaurant,** 33 Edinboro St. (☎617/350-7777).

This restaurant doesn't serve meat, poultry, fish, or dairy (some beverages have condensed milk), but through the wizardry of the chef, tofu and gluten are fried or barbecued to taste like chicken, pork, beef, and even lobster. Cuong Van Tran learned the secrets of vegetarian cooking from Buddhist monks in a temple outside Los Angeles. The results are delicious, healthy, and inexpensive. Try the Vietnamese fried spring rolls and "pizza" (similar to egg foo young, but without the egg). The house specialties are always good, as are soups, chow fun, and stir-fried noodles.

East Ocean City. 25–29 Beach St. ☎ 617/542-2504. Reservations accepted only for parties of 6 or more. Main courses $5–$22. MC, V. Sun–Thurs 11am–3am, Fri–Sat 11am–4am. MBTA: Orange Line to Chinatown. CANTONESE.

Don't get too attached to the inhabitants of the fish tanks at East Ocean City, because they might turn up on your plate. Tanks make up one wall of this high-ceilinged restaurant with lots of glass and other hard surfaces—it's modern-looking but rather noisy. The encyclopedic menu offers a huge range of dishes, but as the name indicates, seafood is the focus. It's fresh, delicious, and carefully prepared. One specialty is clams in black bean sauce, a spicy rendering of a messy, delectable dish. Just about anything that swims can be ordered steamed with ginger and scallions; for variety's sake, check out the chow foon section of the menu.

Grand Chau Chow. 45 Beach St. ☎ 617/292-5166. Reservations accepted only for parties of 10 or more. Main courses $5–$22. AE, DC, DISC, MC, V. Sun–Thurs 10am–3am, Fri–Sat 10am–4am. MBTA: Orange Line to Chinatown. CANTONESE.

This is one of the best and busiest restaurants in Chinatown, with niceties the smaller restaurants don't offer, such as tablecloths and tuxedoed waiters. In the large fish tanks, both salt- and freshwater, you can watch your dinner swimming around if you have the heart. Clams with black bean sauce is a signature dish, as is gray sole with fried fins and bones. Stick to seafood and you can't go wrong. Lunch specials are a great deal (but skip the chow fun, which quickly turns gelatinous). If you're in town during Chinese New Year celebrations, phone ahead and ask that a banquet be prepared for your group. For about $25 a person, you'll get so many courses that you'll lose track. It's a great way to start any year.

Across the street, **Chau Chow,** 52 Beach St. (☎ 617/426-6266), is Grand Chau Chow's bare-bones sibling. It's downright ugly, doesn't accept credit cards, and packs 'em in for the excellent food and reasonable prices, not the unyielding red plastic benches. The salt-and-pepper shrimp is the best around.

Penang. 685–691 Washington St. ☎ **617/451-6373.** Reservations accepted only for parties of 6 or more. Main courses $5–$17. MC, V. Sun–Thurs 11:30am–11:30pm, Fri–Sat 11:30am–midnight. MBTA: Orange Line to Chinatown. MALAYSIAN.

Funkier than the typical Chinatown destination, but with the customary reasonable prices, Penang (an offshoot of the popular New York restaurants) makes a nice contrast. It's an unusual room—on several levels, with lots of bamboo, glass, and noise—that suits the food well. Malaysian cuisine is a palate-pleasing combination of both unusual elements and others familiar from Asian and Indian cooking. *Satay,* skewers of grilled chicken or beef with an addictive peanut dipping sauce, makes a good appetizer, but one that's available at many restaurants—better to start with *roti cani,* an Indian-style rolled-up pancake you break apart with your hands and dip into flavorful chicken-and-potato curry. "Penang's favorite" main course, *prawn mee,* is savory shrimp broth brimming with shrimp, pork, and egg noodles, a good indication of the kitchen's facility with seafood—try any squid dish, or the splendid coconut shrimp. The frozen drink-desserts, with shaved ice and ingredients Westerners wouldn't automatically expect (red beans, tapioca, rice flour), make a refreshing conclusion on a hot night. If these seem to be pretty elaborate descriptions, that's because there's no guarantee your server will take the time to help the uninitiated through the menu—but the flip side of uneven service is the friendly, helpful staffers who sometimes ride to the rescue.

9 Theater District

EXPENSIVE

Galleria Italiana. 177 Tremont St. ☎ **617/423-2092.** Reservations recommended at dinner. Main courses $17–$24. AE, DC, DISC, MC, V. Mon-Fri 7am–3:30pm; Tues–Sat 5:30–10pm, Sun 4–9pm. MBTA: Green Line to Boylston. CENTRAL ITALIAN.

This slice of the Abruzzi region on a nondescript block opposite the Common is one of the best and most popular Italian restaurants in Boston. Co-owners Marisa Iocco and Rita D'Angelo hail from the small town of Orsogna, and they use their native region's strong flavors and hearty ingredients to exceptionally good effect. To start, put yourself in the chef's hands and order the antipasto sampler of vegetables, meats, and cheeses perfectly designed to leave you wanting more. The handmade pastas are invariably spectacular—you might try mustard-infused *pappardelle* with an earthy rabbit sauce, or feather-light open-face shrimp ravioli. Meats and fish are prepared equally well, from a huge pork chop grilled to perfection to pan-seared sea bass served with sautéed kale, clams, and sun-dried-tomato pesto. Creamy, crusty bread pudding with figs makes a luxurious finish, but a more authentic final course is the robust cheese plate.

Although it's centrally located, Galleria Italiana isn't on the beaten track—it's a cozy yet chic place popular with theater-goers and dedicated diners who have to seek it out (if they aren't lucky enough to work nearby and stop in for salads and sandwiches at lunch). The accommodating staff has the pretheater routine down, but the experience is far more enjoyable if you dine fashionably late (for Boston, not for Italy—after the 8pm curtain) and take your time.

Jae's. 212 Stuart St. ☎ **617/451-7788.** Reservations recommended at dinner. Main courses $8.25–$21; sushi from $5.25. AE, DC, MC, V. Mon–Sat 11:30am–4pm; Mon–Wed 5–10:30pm, Thurs–Sat 5pm–1am; Sun noon–10pm. MBTA: Green Line to Arlington, or Orange Line to New England Medical Center. KOREAN/SUSHI/PAN-ASIAN.

This free-standing restaurant is a three-story food festival, with sushi on the first floor, Korean and pan-Asian dishes on the second, and Korean barbecue on the third. Owner Jae Chung says it's his dream, and he must not get much rest if he's dreaming about a place as fun and frantic as this. It draws crowds of adventurous food fans, pretheater suburbanites, and hungry businesspeople to its dark spaces splashed with bright colors. The food is even more diverse; the encyclopedic menu ranges from pristine sushi to bountiful noodle dishes (lo mein with tiny clams is a great choice) to traditional Korean fare. A salad spring roll appetizer is an ethereal Vietnamese-style package of crispy vegetables with a spicy dipping sauce, and the crab cakes (not exactly pan-Asian, but so what?) are divine. The service is not, or at least not always—during the calmer times early in the week you'll get better attention. And desserts are delicious but, curiously, European in style, an unusual note on which to end. That didn't stop us from inhaling the white and dark chocolate mousse cake, though.

There are other branches of Jae's in the **South End,** 520 Columbus Ave. (☎ **617/421-9405**), and **Cambridge's Inman Square,** 1281 Cambridge St. (☎ **617/497-8380**), that are smaller but equally busy.

MODERATE

Jacob Wirth Company. 33–37 Stuart St. ☎ **617/338-8586.** Reservations recommended at dinner. Main courses $7–$17. AE, DC, DISC, MC, V. Mon 11:30am–8pm, Tues–Thurs 11:30am–11pm, Fri–Sat 11:30am–midnight, Sun noon–8pm. Validated parking available. MBTA: Green Line to Boylston, or Orange Line to New England Medical Center. GERMAN/AMERICAN.

In the heart of the Theater District, "Jake's" has been serving Bostonians for more than 130 years—since before there were theaters here. The wood floor and brass accents give the room the feeling of a saloon, or perhaps a beer garden. The hearty German meals are reasonably priced; dinner offerings include Wiener schnitzel, sauerbraten, mixed grills, bratwurst, and knockwurst, along with fish and prime rib. There are daily blackboard specials, a large selection of sandwiches and brews on tap, and, oddly enough, pasta specials. Service at lunchtime is snappy, but if you want to be on time for the theater, the suspense might be greater in the restaurant than at the show.

10 At the Public Garden/Beacon Hill

VERY EXPENSIVE

✪ **Aujourd'hui.** In the Four Seasons Hotel, 200 Boylston St. ☎ **617/451-1392.** Reservations recommended (imperative on holidays). Main courses $18–$23.50 at lunch, $35–$45 at dinner; Sun buffet brunch $44. AE, CB, DC, MC, V. Mon–Fri 6:30–11am, Sat 7am–noon, Sun

7–11am; Mon–Fri 11:30am–2:30pm; Sun brunch 11:30am–2:30pm; Mon–Sat 5:30–10:30pm, Sun 6–10:30pm. Valet parking available. MBTA: Green Line to Arlington. CONTEMPORARY AMERICAN.

On the second floor of the city's premier luxury hotel, the most beautiful restaurant in town has floor-to-ceiling windows overlooking the Public Garden. Even if it were under a pup tent, though, the incredible service and food would make Aujourd'hui a hit with its special-occasion and expense-account clientele. Yes, the cost is astronomical, but how often is it true that you get what you pay for? Here, it is.

The menu changes often, and it encompasses the basic offerings you'd expect in a hotel dining room and the creations that characterize an inventive kitchen. Executive chef Edward Gannon uses regional products and the freshest ingredients available, and the wine list is excellent. To start, you might try perfectly balanced squash-and-apple soup or a huge salad. Entrees include rack of lamb served with a timbale of layered potatoes, goat cheese, mushrooms and zucchini, and oven-roasted lobster with ginger sauce and a vegetable-filled nori roll. "Alternative Cuisine" offerings slash calories, cholesterol, sodium, and fat, but not flavor. The dessert menu also changes but always includes picture-perfect soufflés and homemade sorbets. A wonderful (to most) menu note asks that cellular phones not be used in the restaurant.

Biba. 272 Boylston St. ☎ **617/426-7878.** Reservations recommended. Main courses $13–$17 at lunch, $24–$39 at dinner; bar menu $3.50–$8.50. AE, CB, DC, DISC, JCB, MC, V. Mon–Fri 11:30am–2:30pm, Sun 11:30am–3pm; Sun–Thurs 5:30–10pm, Fri–Sat 5:30–11pm. Bar menu Mon–Thurs 5:15–11:30pm, Fri 5:15pm–midnight, Sat 11:30am–midnight, Sun 5:15–10:30pm. Valet parking available. MBTA: Green Line to Arlington. ECLECTIC.

The mastermind behind Biba is Lydia Shire, a legend in culinary circles. The menu here is well past the cutting edge, divided into six categories that include "offal" (organ meats) and "legumina" (vegetables), as well as fish and meat. The restaurant is in the sumptuous Heritage on the Garden complex across from the Public Garden, and the second-floor dining room attracts a chic crowd, especially at dinner. Expect to see lots of air-kissing and cellular phones.

The food, served à la carte, is as dynamic as the decor. The menu changes regularly and always includes the sublime lobster pizza. Sometimes that's the only dish you recognize, but exploring is half the fun. Try venison chop with shreds of oxtail, sweetbreads with crushed pistachios, or striped bass with fried green tomatoes. Desserts are luxurious and inventive, if a bit heavy.

Although Biba is popular with businesspeople, there is no dress code. The dining-room menu is on the pricey side, making the intimate ground-floor bar and its separate menu even more appealing for budget-conscious gourmets.

Around the corner and under the same management, **Pignoli,** 79 Park Plaza (☎ **617/338-7500**), offers a contemporary Italian menu that's a bit less expensive than Biba's but no less creative. It has a seasonal outdoor cafe and a bakery that's visible from the street.

The Ritz-Carlton Dining Room. 15 Arlington St. ☎ **617/536-5700.** Reservations required. Jacket and tie required for men. Main courses $28–$43. Sun buffet brunch $47. AE, CB, DC, DISC, JCB, MC, V. Sat noon–2:30pm, Sun brunch 10:45am–2:30pm; Sun–Thurs 5:30–10pm, Fri–Sat 5:30–11pm. Valet parking available. MBTA: Green Line to Arlington. FRENCH.

In "proper Bostonian" society, only one place will do when celebrating a special occasion: the magnificent second-floor restaurant at the elegant Ritz-Carlton, overlooking the Public Garden. Whether Sunday brunch or dinner under the crystal chandeliers with soft piano music in the background, a meal here is a memorable experience. The kitchen is noted for French classics, such as rack of lamb with thyme, broiled sirloin in shallot sauce, and lobster "au whiskey," in a cream and bourbon sauce. And it's hardly resting on its laurels. With the arrival of chef de cuisine Mark Allen, the only American to hold the job, the menu has advanced into more contemporary terrain—you might see tuna-wrapped oysters with apple-saffron *jus*, or rack of lamb with minted potato puree and caramelized onion-cabbage rolls. The lengthy appetizer menu ranges from smoked north Atlantic salmon to lobster bisque with Armagnac to beluga caviar with blini. The superb desserts include chocolate and Grand Marnier soufflés and baked Alaska. And the service is formal and correct, just what you'd expect in such a splendid setting.

MODERATE

Istanbul Café. 37 Bowdoin St. ☎ **617/227-3434.** Main courses $9–$15. AE, MC, V. Mon–Thurs 11am–10pm, Sat 11am–11pm, Sun noon–10pm. MBTA: Red or Green Line to Park, or Blue Line to Bowdoin. TURKISH.

Hidden away behind the State House, the Istanbul Café is worth seeking out. It's a small, crowded room, four steps down from the street, where the scent of Middle Eastern spices hits you when you open the door. This is a great place to go if you want to linger, because the always-helpful service sometimes grinds to a halt. Uncharacteristically, that's not a complaint—I go myself to catch up with long-lost friends and linger over the food, which ranges from familiar and unusually good to just unusual (and also good). The appetizer sampler makes a great introduction, especially if you ask for grape leaves, baba ghanoush, or falafel (or all three). *Adana kebab* appears several times in the main dish section of the menu, and the elongated meatballs of spiced ground lamb, threaded onto skewers and grilled, are a must if you like lamb. Turkish pizza, an odd but delicious item, comes in several versions; the plainest is the one any cheese lovers at the table will try to monopolize. And even in the dead of winter, the tomatoes in the chopped-vegetable salad that accompanies nearly every dish are juicy and flavorful. The baklava is a lovely rendition of the traditional sweet, crunchy and not overly cloying, and perfect with a Turkish coffee.

11 Back Bay

VERY EXPENSIVE

Ambrosia on Huntington. 116 Huntington Ave. ☎ **617/247-2400.** Reservations recommended. Main courses $6–$12 at lunch, $16–$29 at dinner. AE, CB, DC, MC, V. Mon–Fri 11:30am–2pm; Mon–Thurs 5:30–10pm, Fri 5:30–10:30pm, Sat 5–11pm, Sun 5–9pm. Valet parking available. MBTA: Orange Line to Back Bay, or Green Line E train to Prudential. FRENCH/ASIAN.

Felicitously named proprietors Anthony and Dorene Ambrose (he's the chef) have turned the ground floor of an office building into a dazzling glass-walled restaurant. This is a place to see and be seen, and you'll especially want to feast your eyes on the food, with its towering garnishes and accents of vegetables and pastry. Flavors are rich and unusual—the people planning a merger might not notice, but serious diners will. You might begin with Peruvian purple potato spring roll in crispy paper with Cabernet truffle oil, a plump pocket infused with winey flavor, or a green salad served with champagne mustard-seed vinaigrette. An entree of Gulf Stream swordfish in sage Provençal broth with potato galette is five huge chunks of fish, separated by upright fans of thinly sliced potato and resting on a mound of potatoes redolent of chives and garlic. "Very Traditional Pasta," simply dressed with olives and tomato broth, is as delicious as any of the more elaborate preparations. Some of the desserts are as intricate as the rest of the food, and quite sweet; you might prefer sorbet or fresh fruit. The service, by teams rather than individuals, is efficient, if a bit chilly, and your water glass will never be empty.

✪ **Anago.** In the Lenox Hotel, 710 Boylston St. ☎ **617/266-6222.** Reservations recommended at dinner. Main courses $12–$16 at lunch, $10-$32 at dinner. AE, DC, MC, V. Mon–Fri 11:30am–2pm, Sun brunch 11am–2pm; Mon-Thurs 5:30–10pm, Fri–Sat 5:30–11pm, Sun 5–9pm. MBTA: Green Line to Copley. CONTEMPORARY AMERICAN.

Anago opened in Boston in 1997 with a reputation for bold, inventive food (gained during its days as Anago Bistro in Cambridge) and quickly established itself as one of the city's top restaurants. In the open kitchen, chef Bob Calderone, co-owner with his wife, Susan Finegold, displays a creative style that never strays into hey-look-at-me territory. You can schedule a business lunch, romantic dinner, or family brunch here with equal confidence.

Calderone makes good use of the region's fresh produce, seafood, and meats. To start, winter-squash soup garnished with a risotto cake is impressive, as is the lush foie gras terrine with cranberry relish. Main dishes might include oven-roasted cod with shellfish minestrone (clams, mussels, and shrimp in flavorful broth), and toothsome seared lamb loin with fiddlehead ferns, garlic potato cake, and roasted golden beets. Desserts are more fanciful than you'd expect—try "chocolate, chocolate, chocolate" and be ready to swoon. Service is friendly but polite, and the tall, wide room is surprisingly quiet, thanks to the soundproofed ceiling, plush upholstery, and well-spaced tables and banquettes.

✪ **Grill 23 & Bar.** 161 Berkeley St. ☎ **617/542-2255.** Reservations recommended. Main courses $19–$30. AE, CB, DC, DISC, MC, V. Mon–Thurs 5:30–10:30pm, Fri–Sat 5:30–11pm, Sun 5:30–10pm. Valet parking available. MBTA: Green Line to Arlington. AMERICAN.

On the erstwhile trading floor of the Salada Tea Building, Grill 23 is a wood-paneled, glass-walled room with a businesslike air. It attracts a briefcase-toting clientele, but it's more than just a steak house—slabs of beef and chops ("Grill Classics") coexist with bolder entrees ("Signature Specials"). Steak au poivre and lamb chops are perfectly grilled, crusty, juicy, and tender. Pan-seared veal tenderloin comes with lentil ragout and cucumber-and-watercress salad, and the fish dishes rival those at any seafood restaurant. The bountiful à la carte side dishes include creamed spinach, roasted portobellas, and out-of-this-world garlic mashed potatoes. For dessert, try the deliriously good apple crisp or white chocolate cheesecake. Or risk being called a wimp and request a dish of berries (not on the menu, but available if you ask). The service is exactly right for the setting, helpful but not familiar.

Some caveats: Smoking is not only allowed but encouraged—a humidor makes the rounds—and despite the excellent ventilation, you can smell smoke in your clothes later. The wine list is pricey, even for a steak house. And the noise grows louder as the evening progresses, but you won't realize you're shouting until you're outside yelling about what a good time you had.

For holiday shoppers, there's a prix-fixe lunch on the last 8 to 10 weekdays before Christmas; call for reservations and the exact price ($35 or so).

✪ **L'Espalier.** 30 Gloucester St. ☎ **617/262-3023.** www.lespalier.com. Reservations required. Prix fixe dinner (4 courses) $62. Whole tables only: vegetable degustation menu (6 courses) $68; degustation menu (7 courses) $78. AE, DISC, MC, V. Mon–Sat 6–10pm. Valet parking available. MBTA: Green Line B, C, or D train to Hynes/ICA. NEW ENGLAND/FRENCH.

Dinner at L'Espalier is a unique experience, very much like spending the evening at the home of a dear friend who has only your pleasure in mind—and has a dozen helpers in the kitchen. Owners Frank and Catherine McClelland (he's the chef) preside over three dining rooms on the second floor of an 1886 townhouse. The space is formal yet inviting, and the service is beyond excellent, in that eerie realm where it seems possible that the waiter just read your mind. The food, an exploration of the freshest and most interesting ingredients available, is magnificent. A first course of roasted foie gras arrives on a quince, onion, and bacon tart tatin with pomegranate *jus,* and perfectly balanced fresh Cabernet grape vinaigrette dresses a salad of greens with wild rice, herbed polenta, and white asparagus. Main courses usually include a game offering, perhaps grilled venison with roasted shallots, fingerling potatoes, and sautéed spinach; salmon in a sesame crust over noodles in a ginger-and-sesame broth is equally impressive. The breads, sorbets, ice creams, and alarmingly good desserts (many adapted from the family's heirloom cookbooks) are made on the premises. Even if you have one of the superb soufflés, which are ordered with dinner, ask to see the desserts. Or order the celebrated cheese tray, which always includes two local cheeses.

Top of the Hub. 800 Boylston St., Prudential Center. ☎ **617/536-1775.** Reservations recommended. Jacket advised for men. Main courses $7–$16 at lunch, $18–$29 at dinner. Six-course tasting menu (2-person minimum) $65 per person. Sun brunch $29. AE, DC, DISC, MC, V. Mon–Sat 11:30am–2:30pm, Sun brunch 10am–2:30pm; Sun–Thurs 5:30–10pm, Fri–Sat 5:30–11pm. Discounted parking available in Prudential Center garage after 4pm Mon-Fri, all day Sat–Sun. MBTA: Green Line B, C, or D train to Hynes/ICA, or E train to Prudential. CONTEMPORARY AMERICAN.

For many years, the answer to the question "How's the food at Top of the Hub?" was, "The view is spectacular." Since a complete overhaul of the menu and the 52nd-floor space in 1995, the cuisine has improved dramatically—not to the point where it's a match for the panorama outside, but that would be nearly impossible. Still, if you can't reserve a table by the window, don't bother with the restaurant (you can always have a drink in the lounge). Check the weather forecast and aim to eat here when it's clear out, taking the best advantage of the space's three glass-walled sides. And consider coming before sunset and lingering until dark for a true spectacle.

The menu emphasizes the seafood that the tourist-intensive clientele expects, with the customary simple preparations and some that show off the kitchen's creative side, like an entree of roasted monkfish flavored with eleven spices and served with orzo and seasonal vegetables. Pan-roasted medallions of beef tenderloin is another good choice at dinner. Lunch offerings include pizzas and half a dozen tasty sandwiches. At either meal, the clam chowder is a standout, with more broth than cream. Salads are large and varied, but if you don't like vegetables drowning in dressing, ask for it on the side.

EXPENSIVE

Casa Romero. 30 Gloucester St. ☎ **617/536-4341.** Reservations recommended. Main courses $12–$21. DISC, MC, V. Sun-Thurs 5–10pm, Fri-Sat 5–11pm. MBTA: Green Line B, C, or D train to Hynes/ICA. MEXICAN.

There's something about restaurants in alleys—they feel like secret clubs or speakeasies, and if they're really worth seeking out, so much the better. Casa Romero is just such a place. The tiled floor, heavy wood furnishings, dim lighting, clay pots, and many other decorations give it a real Mexican feel—you're definitely not at the local Tex-Mex counter. The food is excellent, both authentic and accessible, with generous portions of spicy-hot and milder dishes; the friendly staff will help you negotiate the menu. If the soup of the day is garlic, don't miss it. Main-dish specialties include several kinds of enchiladas and fajitas, excellent stuffed deviled squid in tomato and chipotle sauce, chicken breast in *mole poblano* (spicy chocolate) sauce, and terrific pork tenderloin marinated with oranges and smoked peppers. In the summer, reserve a table in the walled garden.

Davio's. 269 Newbury St. ☎ **617/262-4810.** Reservations recommended downstairs, not accepted upstairs. Main courses $10–$25. Pizzas $7–$8.50. AE, CB, DC, DISC, MC, V. Mon–Sat 11:30am–3pm, Sun brunch 11:30am–3pm; Sun–Thurs 5–10pm, Fri–Sat 5–11pm. Valet parking available. MBTA: Green Line to Copley. CREATIVE NORTHERN ITALIAN.

While the rest of the Boston-area culinary community regularly plays musical chefs, owner-chef Steve DiFillipo has buckled down and turned Davio's into a local favorite. The restaurant's excellent reputation rests on its top-notch kitchen, dedicated staff, and pleasant atmosphere. In a Back Bay brownstone, you wouldn't expect to find typical Italian fare, and you won't. Start with excellent minestrone, beautifully balanced salad, or the day's homemade ravioli selection (also available as a main course). Move on to grilled veal chop in port wine sauce, salmon grilled to pink perfection, or any dish that involves homemade sausage. There are usually three special entrees daily, plus a house pâté. Desserts change regularly; try the ethereal tiramisu if it's available. Davio's has a well-edited wine selection, including some rare and expensive Italian vintages. The upstairs cafe (from 11:30am to 3pm and 5 to 11pm) has a terrace that's open in good weather.

There's a Davio's in Cambridge, at the Royal Sonesta Hotel, 5 Cambridge Pkwy. (☎ **617/661-4810**), open the same hours, except that dinner service ends at 10pm nightly.

✪ **Legal Sea Foods.** 800 Boylston St., in the Prudential Center. ☎ **617/266-6800.** Reservations recommended at lunch, not accepted at dinner. Main courses $7–$13 at lunch, $14–$24 at dinner. AE, CB, DC, DISC, MC, V. Mon–Thurs 11am–10:30pm, Fri–Sat 11am–11:30pm, Sun noon–10pm. MBTA: Green Line B, C, or D train to Hynes/ICA, or E train to Prudential. SEAFOOD.

The food at Legal Sea Foods ("Legal's," in Bostonian parlance) isn't the fanciest, the cheapest, or the trendiest. It's the freshest, and management's commitment to that policy has produced a thriving chain. The family-owned business has an international reputation for serving only top-quality fish and shellfish prepared in every imaginable way. The menu includes regular selections (scrod, haddock, bluefish, salmon, shrimp, calamari, and lobster, among others) plus whatever looked good at the market that morning, and it's all splendid. The clam chowder is a winner, and some consider the fish chowder even better. Or start with creamy smoked bluefish pâté. Entrees run the gamut from plain grilled fish to seafood fra'diavolo on fresh linguine to salmon baked in parchment with vegetables and white wine. The classic dessert is the ice cream bonbons, and the key lime pie is also worth the calories.

The Prudential Center branch is suggested because it takes reservations (at lunch only), a deviation from a long tradition. In 1996, New England legend Jasper White became the chain's executive chef. He's gradually leaving his innovative mark on the menu, which now includes such departures as red clam chowder, clam fritters, and fallen chocolate cake. He is also expected to individualize the restaurants—the first step was the opening of **Legal C Bar** (☎ **617/426-5566**) at 27 Columbus Ave., where the food and music are Caribbean. There are regular branches at the Boston Park Plaza Hotel, 35 Columbus Ave. (☎ **617/426-4444**); Copley Place (☎ **617/266-7775**); Kendall Square, 5 Cambridge Center (☎ **617/864-3400**); and eight other locations with the same blue-and-white-checked decor and menu.

The Original Sports Saloon. In the Copley Square Hotel, 47 Huntington Ave. ☎ **617/536-9000.** Main courses $6.50–$18. AE, DC, DISC, MC, V. Daily 11:30am–1:30am. Full menu until 10pm, appetizers until closing. MBTA: Green Line to Copley. AMERICAN/ BARBECUE.

This tiny saloon serves gigantic portions of award-winning barbecue in a pleasant, if loud, glass-walled room with 11 large-screen TVs, photographs of sports figures, and cartoons by the *Boston Globe's* Paul Szep. The specialty is barbecued baby back ribs, which take more than 30 hours to prepare. They're slow-cooked in an authentic Memphis smoker, over a secret blend of hickory, ash, cherry, and apple woods, and served with a constellation of side dishes. Other menu items include delectable barbecued chicken, the Bloomin' Saloon'ion (an addictive battered, deep-fried whole onion), and pulled-pork and other sandwiches.

Turner Fisheries of Boston. In the Westin Copley Place Boston, 10 Huntington Ave. ☎ **617/424-7425.** Reservations recommended. Main courses $8.50–$14.50 at lunch, $17–$28 at dinner. AE, CB, DC, DISC, MC, V. Mon–Sat 11am–11pm; Sun 10:30am–2:30pm (brunch) and 3–11pm. Valet parking available. MBTA: Orange Line to Back Bay, or Green Line to Copley. SEAFOOD.

This restaurant is best known for winning the Boston Harborfest Chowderfest contest so many times that its superb clam chowder was elevated to the Hall of Fame. It's also known as a place to go when you can't get into Legal Sea Foods, which does it a disservice—it also serves some of the freshest fish in town, in a calmer atmosphere than you'll usually find at Legal's. Packed with businesspeople at lunch and out-of-towners (and savvy locals who appreciate the more placid atmosphere) at dinner, Turner Fisheries is obviously doing something right. The menu features each day's special catch and suggested preparations—pan-fried, broiled, grilled, baked, steamed, or "spicy bronzed." Specials are more inventive, from the signature bouillabaisse to pan-seared scallops in miso broth to excellent pastas (with and without seafood). The raw bar is also a draw, and there are always a few nonseafood options. Ask for a booth if you want privacy or a table if you want to enjoy the atrium-like ambiance.

INEXPENSIVE

Café Jaffa. 48 Gloucester St. ☎ **617/536-0230.** Main courses $4.25–$9.75. AE, DC, DISC, MC, V. Mon–Thurs 11am–10:30pm, Fri–Sat 11am–11pm, Sun 1–10pm. MBTA: Green Line B, C, or D train to Hynes/ICA. MIDDLE EASTERN.

A long, narrow brick room with a glass front, Café Jaffa looks more like a snazzy pizza place than the wonderful Middle Eastern restaurant it is. Young people flock here, drawn by the low prices, high quality, and large portions of traditional Middle Eastern offerings such as falafel, baba ghanoush, and hummus, as well as burgers and steak tips. Lamb, beef, and chicken kabobs come with Greek salad, rice pilaf, and pita bread. For dessert, try the baklava if it's fresh (give it a pass if not). There is a short list of beer and wine and, somewhat incongruously, many fancy coffee offerings.

12 The South End

VERY EXPENSIVE

Hamersley's Bistro. 553 Tremont St. ☎ **617/423-2700.** Reservations recommended. Main courses $21–$30. Menu degustation varies. AE, DISC, MC, V. Mon–Fri 6–10pm, Sat 5:30–10pm, Sun 5:30–9:30pm. Valet parking available. MBTA: Orange Line to Back Bay. ECLECTIC.

This is the place that put the South End on Boston's culinary map, a pioneering restaurant that's both classic and contemporary. The husband-and-wife team of Gordon and Fiona Hamersley presides over a long, narrow dining room with lots of soft surfaces that absorb sound, so you can see but not quite hear what's going on at the tables around you. That means you'll have to quiz your server about the dish that just passed by—perhaps a marvelous appetizer of potato galette, smoked salmon, crème fraîche, and three caviars, or a grilled asparagus and pickled onion salad. The menu changes seasonally and offers about a dozen carefully considered entrees (always including vegetarian dishes) noted for their emphasis on taste and texture. The signature roast chicken, flavored with garlic, lemon, and parsley, comes with roast potato, roast onions, and whole cloves of sweet baked garlic. Salmon au poivre with sorrel, leeks, and fingerling potatoes is delicious, as is grilled fillet of beef with garlic mashed potatoes and a delectable red wine sauce. And the wine list is excellent.

✪ **Icarus.** 3 Appleton St. ☎ **617/426-1790.** Reservations recommended. Main courses $19.50–$29.50; "Square Meal" $38. Brunch dishes $5–$12.50. AE, CB, DC, DISC, MC, V. Sun–Thurs 6–10pm, Fri 6–11pm, Sat 5:30–11pm; Sun brunch 11am–3pm. Valet parking available at dinner. MBTA: Green Line to Arlington, or Orange Line to Back Bay. ECLECTIC.

This shamelessly romantic subterranean restaurant offers every element of a great dining experience. It's perfect for everything from helping a friend heal a broken heart to celebrating a milestone anniversary. Marble accents and dark wood trim lend an elegant air to the two-level dining room, and the service is efficient but not formal. Chef and co-owner Chris Douglass uses choice local seafood, poultry, meats, and produce to create imaginative dishes that seem more like alchemy than cooking. The menu changes regularly—you might start with a salad of seared foie gras, apples, endive, and cider hazelnut vinaigrette, or the daily "pasta whim." Move on to cod encased in a shredded potato cake and floating in grass-green herbal broth, or garlicky grilled chicken with balsamic vinegar glaze and toasted garlic mashed potatoes so good you'll want to ask for a plate of them. Don't—save room for one of the unbelievable desserts. Chocolate coconut cake with toasted coconut ice cream and cherry rum sauce was pronounced a favorite and instantly dethroned (in the estimation of an unregenerate chocoholic) by a trio of fruit sorbets. The restaurant's newest offering, the prix fixe "Square Meal," consists of three courses plus dessert and derives no more than 30 percent of its calories from fat.

MODERATE

Addis Red Sea. 544 Tremont St. ☎ **617/426-8727.** Main courses $9–$13. AE, MC, V. Mon–Fri 5–11pm, Sat 4–11pm, Sun 4–10:30pm. MBTA: Orange Line to Back Bay. ETHIOPIAN.

If you're in the mood to experiment, Addis Red Sea is a good place to start. Colorful carpets and wall hangings decorate the dimly lit, subterranean space, and you sit on stools at *mesobs,* traditional Ethiopian tables. Wash your hands! Ethiopian food is served family-style on a platter, without utensils. The waiter covers the platter with a layer of *injera,* a spongy, tangy bread, and spoons the food on top of it. Tear off a piece of *injera,* scoop up a mouthful of food, and dig in. Your waiter will bring more *injera* if you need it to finish off the stewlike main courses. Many are vegetarian, and the vegetable combination makes a good introduction to this cuisine, with a choice of dishes that might include lentils, split peas, cracked wheat, onions, potatoes, beans, carrots, and greens. The spice level varies, but even the mildest dishes are flavorful and filling. There are also tasty meat dishes—*doro wat* is lemon-marinated chicken, and *kifto* is the Ethiopian version of steak tartare.

13 Mass. Ave. to Brookline

Smoking is not allowed in bars and restaurants in Brookline. Coincidence or not, that 1994 law went into effect just before a batch of good restaurants opened.

MASS. AVE. & THE FENS
MODERATE

Bangkok Cuisine. 177A Massachusetts Ave. ☎ **617/262-5377.** Reservations not accepted. Main courses $5–$8 at lunch, $8–$15 at dinner. AE, DISC, MC, V. Mon–Sat 11:30am–3pm; Mon–Thurs 5–10:30pm, Fri 5–11pm, Sat 3–11pm, Sun 4–10pm. MBTA: Green Line B, C, or D train to Hynes/ICA. THAI.

Extremely popular with patrons of nearby Symphony Hall and the students who dominate this neighborhood, Bangkok Cuisine is a classic. It opened in 1979, the first Thai restaurant in Boston, and it has set (and maintained) high standards for the many others that followed. For the unadventurous, it serves fantastic pad Thai, and the rest of the menu runs the gamut from excellent chicken and basil to all sorts of curry offerings, pan-fried or deep-fried whole fish, and hot and sour salads. In this long, narrow room, there are no secrets—if, say, the person at the next table is eating something appealing or you want something especially hot, ask the waiter. The green curry in coconut milk and vegetables prepared with strong green Thai chili pepper are the most incendiary dishes.

Bob the Chef's. 604 Columbus Ave. ☎ **617/536-6204.** Main courses $9–$15; sandwiches $5–$8. AE, DC, MC, V. Tues–Wed 5–10pm, Thurs–Sat 5pm–midnight; Sun 11am–3:30pm and 5–9pm. MBTA: Orange Line to Mass. Ave. SOUTHERN/CAJUN.

Bob the Chef's resembles a yuppie fern bar, but it's a place where Bostonians of every color enjoy jazz as they linger over generous servings of Southern specialties. You'll find dishes such as "glorifried" chicken, served alone or with barbecued ribs; pork chops; liver and onions; or "soul fish" (two whole pan-fried porgies). Cajun specialties such as jambalaya and shrimp étoufée were introduced in 1996, at the same time as the renovated space, which has exposed-brick walls and a high ceiling. Dinners come with a corn muffin and your choice of two side dishes—including black-eyed peas, macaroni and cheese, collard greens, rice, and sweet potatoes. Frying is done in vegetable oil, not the customary lard, and everywhere you'd expect bacon for flavoring, smoked turkey is used instead. For dessert, try the sweet-potato pie, which will ruin pumpkin pie for you the moment you taste it. There's self-parking across the street for $4, and takeout is available starting at 11am.

KENMORE SQUARE TO BROOKLINE
EXPENSIVE

✪ **Providence.** 1223 Beacon St., Brookline. ☎ **617/232-0300.** Reservations recommended. Main courses $11–$25; brunch dishes $9–$15. AE, DC, MC, V. Tues–Thurs 5:30–10pm, Fri–Sat 5:30—11pm, Sun 5–9:30pm; Sun brunch 11am–2pm. Valet parking available Thurs–Sat. MBTA: Green Line C train to St. Paul St. AMERICAN/ECLECTIC.

If Providence were in downtown Boston, it would appear on any list of the city's top restaurants. Because it's not, you can feel as though you're making a discovery—your palate will certainly feel that way. In an apparently formal room softened with warm colors, quirky fixtures, and a courteous staff, you'll find apparently traditional food livened up with quirky flavors and textures. The list of specials, which is almost as long as the menu, might include an appetizer of fresh fried Ipswich clams—standard stuff, until you taste the garlic-and-chipotle mayonnaise dribbled on top. The flatbread with eggplant puree and olives could be from any menu with Middle Eastern influences, but the flatbread is made of chick peas, the eggplant exudes cardamom, and there's goat cheese on the plate. Pan-roasted salmon comes with garlic potatoes and a ragout of artichokes, tomato, and beans. There's even pastrami, but it's veal pastrami, cured and smoked at the restaurant and served with

Restaurants from Mass. Ave. to Brookline

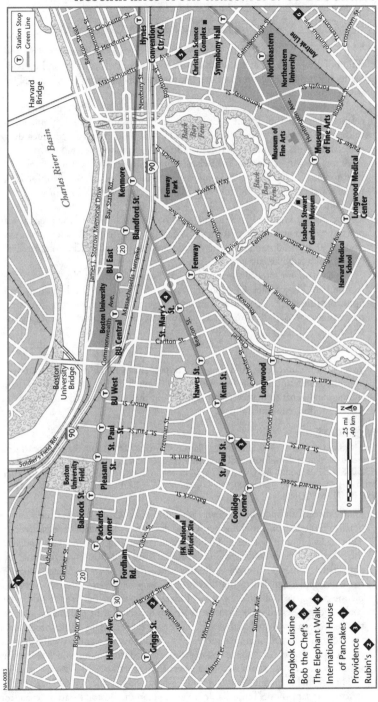

Station Stop Ⓣ
Green Line

Bangkok Cuisine 5
Bob the Chef's 6
The Elephant Walk 4
International House of Pancakes 1
Providence 3
Rubin's 2

NA-0083

117

Boston Tea Party, Part 2

This is Boston, the only city that has a whole tea party named after it, and the tradition of afternoon tea at a plush hotel is alive and well. Pots of tea and individual food items are available à la carte, but for the full effect, order light or full tea with all the trimmings.

The **Ritz-Carlton,** 15 Arlington St. (☎ **617/536-5700**), serves the city's most celebrated tea in the elegant Ritz Lounge every day from 3 to 5:30pm. Harp music plays as you're served a light tea ($12.50) of pastries and breads, including delectable scones, or full tea ($16), including finger sandwiches and pastries.

Across the Public Garden, the **Bristol Lounge** at the Four Seasons Hotel, 200 Boylston St. (☎ **617/351-2053**), offers a sensational view and wonderful scones, tea sandwiches, pastries, and nut bread ($17.50, or $24.50 with a kir royale) every day from 3 to 4:30pm.

The Boston Harbor Hotel, across the street from the site of the original tea party, serves tea at **Intrigue,** 70 Rowes Wharf (☎ **617/439-7000**), on weekdays from 2:30 to 4:30pm. Light tea ($6.25) makes a good snack; complete tea ($10.75) is a ladylike late lunch.

A player piano serenades tea partyers at **Swans Court,** in the lobby of the Boston Park Plaza Hotel, 64 Arlington St. (☎ **617/426-2000**), daily from 3 to 5pm. Because there's no view, the tea with finger sandwiches, pastries, strawberries, and cream ($8.50) isn't quite as elegant as at the other hotels, but it's a great deal.

sweet-potato dumplings. And desserts are spectacular, notably the signature warm chocolate fondant cake. Chef-owner Paul O'Connell is a wizard with flavors, combining ingredients so that everything brings out the best in everything else. Including the stuffed, contented diners.

MODERATE

The Elephant Walk. 900 Beacon St., Boston. ☎ **617/247-1500.** Reservations recommended at dinner Sun–Thurs, not accepted Fri–Sat. Main courses $6–$18.50 at lunch, $9.50–$18.50 at dinner. AE, DISC, MC, V. Mon–Sat 11:30am–2:30pm; Mon–Thurs 5–10pm, Fri 5–11pm, Sat 4:30–11pm, Sun 4:30–10pm. MBTA: Green Line C train to St. Mary's St. FRENCH/CAMBODIAN.

France meets Cambodia on the menu at the Elephant Walk, 4 blocks from Kenmore Square on the Boston-Brookline border and decorated with lots of little pachyderms. This madly popular spot has a two-part menu (French on one side, Cambodian on the other), but the boundary is quite porous. Many of the Cambodian dishes have part-French names, such as *poulet dhomrei* (chicken with Asian basil, bamboo shoots, fresh pineapple, and kaffir lime leaves) and *curry de crevettes* (shrimp curry with picture-perfect vegetables). The Asian influence shows on the French side, where you'll find pan-seared duck breast and leg confit served with scallion raviolis, and pan-seared tuna with red and green chile cream sauces. Many dishes are available with tofu substituted for animal protein. The pleasant staff members will help out if you need guidance. Ask to be seated in the plant-filled front room, which is less noisy than the main dining room and has a view of the street.

The original Elephant Walk is at 70 Union Sq., Somerville (☎ **617/623-9939**). It keeps the same hours but is harder to get to than the Boston location (even from most places in Cambridge).

Rubin's. 500 Harvard St., Brookline. ☎ **617/731-8787.** Reservations not accepted. Main courses $8–$18. No credit cards. Mon–Thurs 10am–8pm, Fri 9am to mid-afternoon, Sun 9am–8pm. MBTA: Green Line B train to Harvard St. KOSHER DELI.

The knock on this restaurant is that it's not a New York deli, and you shouldn't come expecting one. For what it is, though, it's quite good. Rubin's bills itself as the only full-service kosher deli and restaurant in greater Boston, and it has outlasted lots of competition in its 70-plus years. It maintains the highest standards of kashrut, and no dairy is served. You'll find omelettes, deli platters, and sandwiches in large and "overstuffed" sizes. The chopped liver is excellent, and the "Traditionals" section of the extensive menu includes tasty potato pancakes (a better choice than the potato knish). Entrees include roast brisket of beef; barbecued chicken; and broiled salmon, halibut, and scrod. The noodle pudding makes a good dessert in the unlikely event that you have room.

14 Cambridge

The dining scene in Cambridge, as in Boston, offers something for everyone, from penny-pinching students to the tycoons many of them aspire to become. The MBTA Red Line runs from downtown Boston to the heart of Harvard Square. Many of the restaurants listed here can easily be reached on foot from there; others (including a couple of real finds just over the Somerville border) are listed under the heading "Outside Harvard Square."

HARVARD SQUARE & VICINITY
VERY EXPENSIVE

✪   **Rialto.** 1 Bennett St., in the Charles Hotel. ☎ **617/661-5050.** Reservations recommended. Main courses $20–$29. AE, DC, MC, V. Sun–Thurs 5:30–10pm, Fri–Sat 5:30–11pm. Bar Sun–Thurs 5pm–1am, Fri–Sat 5pm–1:30am. MBTA: Red Line to Harvard. MEDITERRANEAN.

If Rialto isn't the best restaurant in the Boston area, it's close. It attracts a chic crowd, but it's not a "scene" in the sense that out-of-towners will feel left behind. Every element is carefully thought-out, from the architecture to the service to the extraordinary food. It's a dramatic but comfortable room, with floor-to-ceiling windows overlooking Harvard Square, cushy banquettes, and standing lamps that cast a golden glow. The staff is solicitous without being smothering, and chef Jody Adams's food speaks eloquently for itself.

The menu changes regularly. You might start with a blue-cheese tart in a flaky crust or Provençal fisherman's soup with rouille, Gruyère, and basil oil, the very essence of seafood. Main courses are so good that you might as well close your eyes and point. A plate of creamy potato slices and mushrooms is so juicy it's almost like eating meat. Seared duck breast with foie gras, squash raviolis, and quince is wonderful, and anything involving salmon is a guaranteed winner—even those who think they don't like it will fall for the perfectly flaky, orange-pink hunk, perhaps with sweet potatoes, dried cranberries, and pine nuts. For dessert, a trio of seasonal sorbets is a great choice, as is the popover served with tangerine cream.

Upstairs at the Pudding. 10 Holyoke St. ☎ **617/864-1933.** Reservations recommended. Main courses $9–$14 at lunch, $20–$30 at dinner, $9–$15 at brunch; tasting menu (dinner) $45. AE, CB, DC, MC, V. Mon–Sat 11:30am–2:30pm, Sun brunch 11:30am–2:30pm; daily 6–11pm. Validated parking available. MBTA: Red Line to Harvard. CONTINENTAL/NORTHERN ITALIAN.

Cambridge Dining

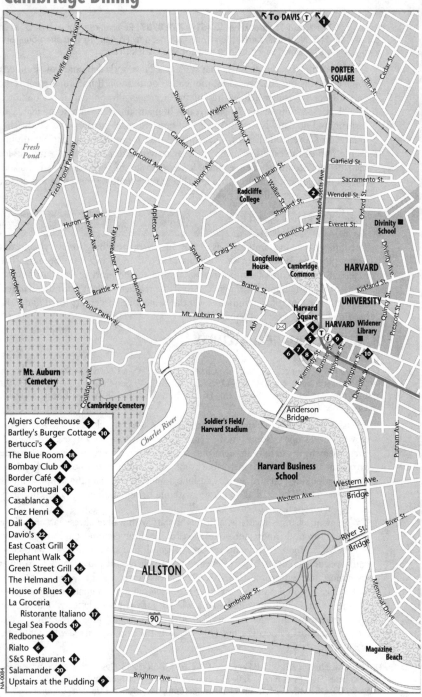

To DAVIS ①

PORTER SQUARE

Fresh Pond

Alewife Brook Parkway

Sherman St.

Walden St.

Raymond St.

Garden St.

Concord Ave.

Huron Ave.

Linnaean St.

Walker St.

Shepard St.

Garfield St.

Sacramento St.

Wendell St.

Massachusetts Ave.

Oxford St.

Elm St.

Cedar St.

Radcliffe College

Chauncey St.

Everett St.

Divinity School

Huron Ave.

Lakeview Ave.

Fayerweather St.

Appleton St.

Sparks St.

Craig St.

Longfellow House

Cambridge Common

HARVARD

Divinity Ave.

Aberdeen Ave.

Fresh Pond Parkway

Brattle St.

Channing St.

Brattle St.

Mt. Auburn St.

Ash St.

Kirkland St.

UNIVERSITY

Quincy St.

Prescott St.

Harvard Square ③ ④ ⑤

HARVARD ⑨

Widener Library

Mt. Auburn Cemetery

Coolidge Ave.

Cambridge Cemetery

Charles River

⑥ ⑦ ⑧

Dunster St.

Holyoke St.

Plympton St.

Dewolfe St.

⑩

Putnam Ave.

Soldier's Field/ Harvard Stadium

J.F. Kennedy St.

Anderson Bridge

Harvard Business School

Western Ave.
Bridge

Western Ave.

River St.
Bridge

River St.

ALLSTON

Cambridge St.

Memorial Drive

⑨0

Magazine Beach

Brighton Ave.

Algiers Coffeehouse ③
Bartley's Burger Cottage ⑩
Bertucci's ⑤
The Blue Room ⑱
Bombay Club ⑧
Border Café ④
Casa Portugal ⑮
Casablanca ③
Chez Henri ②
Dali ⑪
Davio's ㉒
East Coast Grill ⑫
Elephant Walk ⑬
Green Street Grill ⑯
The Helmand ㉑
House of Blues ⑦
La Groceria
 Ristorante Italiano ⑰
Legal Sea Foods ⑲
Redbones ①
Rialto ⑥
S&S Restaurant ⑭
Salamander ⑳
Upstairs at the Pudding ⑨

NA-0084

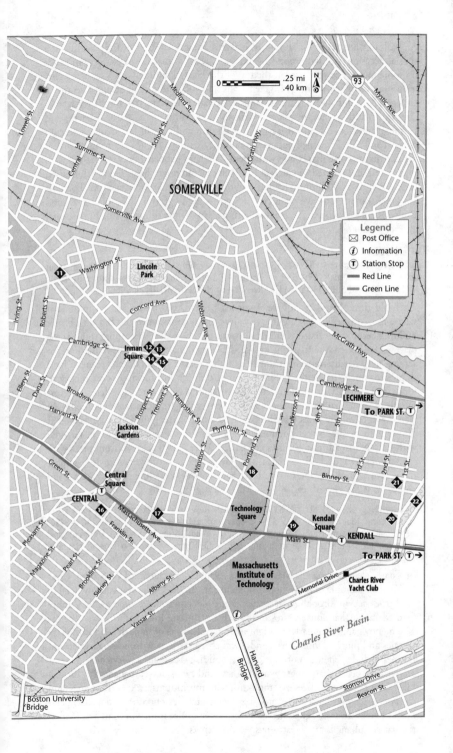

An oasis of calm above the tumult of Harvard Square, Upstairs at the Pudding is a special-occasion spot with food so good you'll want to make up a reason (and save up some money) to go there. At the top of the Hasty Pudding Club's creaky stairs, it's a high-ceilinged room with green walls and soft, indirect lighting. The menu changes daily and always features hand-rolled pasta. To start, you might try fettuccine with truffle cream, or pizzetta with tomato confit, olives, garlic, chèvre, and Parmesan. Entrees include at least one pasta dish and a small but choice selection of meat and fish. If mashed potatoes are on the menu, you can't go wrong by ordering any main course that comes with them—perhaps peppered beef tenderloin with blue cheese and charred tomato coulis. Rack of lamb might be offered with braised artichokes, roasted onions, creamer potatoes, and rosemary-mustard *jus*. Portions are large, but try to save room for dessert—anything with chocolate is a good choice. There is a lovely terrace and herb garden off the dining room for seasonal alfresco dining.

EXPENSIVE

Casablanca. 40 Brattle St. ☎ 617/876-0999. Reservations recommended at dinner. Main courses $7–$12 at lunch, $10–$19 at dinner. AE, MC, V. Daily 11:30am–3pm; Sun–Thurs 5:30–10pm, Fri–Sat 5:30–11pm. MBTA: Red Line to Harvard. MEDITERRANEAN.

This old-time Harvard Square favorite, better known for its hopping bar scene, moved (literally and figuratively) into the nineties when the Brattle Theater building became the Brattle Hall retail complex. These days the dining room is the place where you're sure to get lucky—Casablanca remains true to its reputation for serving tasty Mediterranean cuisine. The rather erratic service doesn't seem to have improved much (it's better at lunch than at dinner), but luckily there's plenty to look at. The walls of the long, skylighted dining room and crowded bar sport murals of scenes from the movie, and Humphrey Bogart looks as though he might lean down to ask for a taste of the skewered lamb or the grilled chicken, served at dinner with mashed sweet potatoes or as an hors d'oeuvre in wing form, flavored with fiery North African *harissa* spice paste. Other hors d'oeuvres, from pizza with sea scallops to Provençal chickpea fries, are so good you might want to assemble them into a meal. Just be sure to leave room for dessert—the cookies are a good choice, as is the gingerbread.

Chez Henri. 1 Shepard St. ☎ **617/354-8980.** Reservations accepted only for parties of 6 or more. Main courses $15–$19; 3-course prix fixe menu $28; bar food $5–$8. AE, DC, MC, V. Mon–Thurs 6-10pm, Fri–Sat 6–11pm, Sun 11am–2pm (brunch) and 6–9pm. Bar food Mon–Sat until midnight, Sun until 10pm. MBTA: Red Line to Harvard. FRENCH/CUBAN.

In a dark, elegant space off Massachusetts Avenue near Harvard Law School, Chez Henri is an example of how good fusion cuisine can be. Under the same ownership as Providence in Brookline, it draws academic types and foodies with a more focused menu that concentrates on French bistro-style food with Cuban accents. The menu changes regularly; it might include appetizers of spinach salad with duck tamales and mustard vinaigrette, and Swiss chard tartlette with horseradish cream. Entrees include generous portions of meat and fish—perhaps a juicy chicken breast served with black bean sauce, avocado slaw, and two spicy empanadas (turnovers) filled with potato and cheese; or monkfish with mushrooms, au gratin potatoes, and cinnamon-scented sauce. The prix fixe menu includes one of two appetizers and one of two entrees, as well as dessert—the crème brûlée is magnificent. The food at the bar is Cuban, as are the strong specialty drinks.

MODERATE

Bombay Club. 57 John F. Kennedy St., in the Galleria Mall. ☎ **617/661-8100.** Main courses $5–$9 at lunch, $9–$16 at dinner. Lunch buffet $7 Mon–Fri, $9 Sat–Sun. AE, DC, MC, V. Daily 11:30am–11pm. MBTA: Red Line to Harvard. INDIAN.

This third-floor restaurant overlooking Harvard Square is noted for not looking like a typical Indian restaurant and serving food that's a step up from what you'd find at one. True fame has come to this contemporary-looking spot through its lunch buffet, a generous assortment of some of the best items on the menu at a price that can't be beat. The chicken, lamb, seafood, and rice specialties are the best in town, and the breads are fantastic. The tandoori ovens deliver flavorful breads, including tandoori roti and tandoori nan, and dishes are baked to perfection in the traditional charcoal-fired clay oven. The house specials include *barra kebab* (lamb marinated in a spicy sauce for 3 days and then baked on skewers), chicken *korma* (in almond cream sauce), and "royal platters" with a selection of meat or vegetarian items. Portions aren't huge, but even your grandmother won't mind that you're filling up on bread when the bread is this good.

Border Café. 32 Church St. ☎ **617/864-6100.** Reservations not accepted. Main courses $7–$13. AE, MC, V. Mon–Thurs 11am–1am, Fri–Sat 11am–2am, Sun noon–11pm. MBTA: Red Line to Harvard. SOUTHWESTERN.

When you first see this restaurant, your thoughts might turn to, of all people, baseball Hall of Famer Yogi Berra. He supposedly said, "Nobody goes there anymore; it's too crowded." He was talking about a club in New York, but it's something people have been saying about this Harvard Square hangout for over 10 years. The festival atmosphere is only enhanced by the fact that patrons loiter at the bar for hours waiting to be seated for the generous portions of tasty, if not completely authentic, food. The menu features Cajun, Tex-Mex, and some Caribbean specialties, and the beleaguered wait staff keeps the chips and salsa coming. When you shout your order over the roar of the crowd, try the excellent enchiladas, any kind of tacos, Caribbean shrimp (dipped in coconut and spices before frying), or popcorn shrimp. The fajitas for one or two, served in the traditional way—sizzling noisily in a large iron frying pan—are also a popular choice. Set aside a couple of hours, be in a party mood, and ask to be seated downstairs if you want to be able to hear your companions.

House of Blues. 96 Winthrop St. ☎ **617/491-2583,** or 617/497-2229 for tickets. www.hob.com. Reservations (☎ 617/491-2100) accepted only for parties of 25 or more. Main courses $4–$9 at lunch, $6–$20 at dinner; Sun brunch tickets $25. AE, DC, DISC, MC, V. Mon–Wed 11:30am–1am, Thurs–Sat 11:30am–2am, Sun 4pm–1am. Sun brunch 10am, noon, 2pm. MBTA: Red Line to Harvard. AMERICAN.

This is the original House of Blues, a tourist magnet in a blue clapboard house near Harvard Square. Everything is blue at this noisy, crowded spot, and the walls and ceilings are dotted with folk art. On the ceiling near the bar area are plaster bas-reliefs of great blues musicians, and actual musicians play every night (usually at 9 or 10pm) and on Friday and Saturday afternoons. The menu ranges far and wide (farther and wider at dinner), from large salads to burgers to barbecue to sophisticated pasta dishes. There's also a selection of pizzas (try the one topped with feta cheese, sun-dried tomatoes, and garlic) baked in a wood-fired oven. Tickets must be purchased in advance for the Sunday Gospel buffet brunch.

INEXPENSIVE

Algiers Coffeehouse. 40 Brattle St. ☎ **617/492-1557.** Main courses $2.50–$12. AE, CB, DC, MC, V. Daily 8am–midnight. MBTA: Red Line to Harvard. MIDDLE EASTERN.

This is an excellent place to take a break from rushing around Harvard Square and have a snack or a drink (try the special Algiers mint coffee), but you might find yourself lingering. That's the nature of coffeehouses, after all, and this is a particularly nice one. Long known as a dark, smoke-filled literary hangout, Algiers is now upstairs in Brattle Hall, and still a favorite with Cambridge intellectuals and would-be intellectuals. Smoking is allowed only on the upper level. This a good spot to eavesdrop while you eat, and the soups, sandwiches, homemade sausages, falafel, and hummus are terrific. Or just order from the extensive beverage menu.

✪ **Bartley's Burger Cottage.** 1246 Massachusetts Ave. ☎ **617/354-6559.** Most items under $7. No credit cards. Mon–Sat 11am–10pm. MBTA: Red Line to Harvard. AMERICAN.

Great burgers and the best onion rings in the world make Bartley's a perennial favorite with a cross section of Cambridge, from Harvard students to regular folks. It's not a cottage, but a high-ceilinged, crowded room plastered with signs and posters, where the waitresses might call you "honey." Burgers bear the names of local and national celebrities; the names change, but the ingredients stay the same. Anything you can think of to put on ground beef is available here, from American cheese to béarnaise sauce. There are also some good dishes that don't involve meat, notably veggie burgers and creamy, garlicky hummus. Bartley's is one of the only places in the area where you can still get a real raspberry lime rickey (raspberry syrup, lime juice, lime wedges, and club soda—the taste of summer even in the winter).

OUTSIDE HARVARD SQUARE
VERY EXPENSIVE

Salamander. 1 Athenaeum St. (at First St.). ☎ **617/225-2121.** Reservations recommended. Main courses $20–$36; bar menu $5.50–$14. AE, DC, DISC, MC, V. Mon–Thurs 6–10pm, Fri–Sat 6–10:30pm; bar opens at 5pm. Validated parking available. MBTA: Red Line to Kendall; 10-minute walk. AMERICAN/ASIAN.

Celebrity chef-owner Stan Frankenthaler is a visionary, and this adventuresome restaurant is his vision. The dimly lit room centers around a wood-fired grill and draws diners who aren't afraid of unusual flavors and preparations. You might recognize Frankenthaler from the TV Food Network, and you'll certainly recognize the enthusiasm apparent in every lengthy description on the regularly changing menu. "Crispy whole bass with fiery hot dipping sauce and loads of cooling accompaniments, including sweet sticky rice, our own exotic pickles, and a tropical fruit-peanut salad" is practically a smorgasbord. The simplest entree (a relative term), almost always available, is lightly fried lobster with Asian flavors; you might also find Angus beef prepared three ways—spice-crusted fillet, smoked brisket filling for a steamed bun, short ribs—and served together. Tables are well spaced, and seating spills into the courtyard, where it's less warm and smoky (from the fire), but also less cozy. Considering the care that's apparent in the cooking, service could be more attentive while the necessarily lengthy preparation process is going on. After all this, a complicated dessert seems like overkill; if apple pie is on the menu, it makes an excellent contrasting finish.

EXPENSIVE

✪ **The Blue Room.** 1 Kendall Sq. ☎ **617/494-9034.** Reservations recommended. Main courses $16–$24. AE, CB, DC, DISC, MC, V. Sun–Thurs 5:30–10pm, Fri–Sat 5:30–11pm; Sun brunch 11am–2:30pm. Validated parking available. MBTA: Red Line to Kendall/MIT, 10-minute walk. ECLECTIC.

The Blue Room sits just below plaza level in an office-retail complex, a slice of foodie paradise in the midst of high-tech heaven. The cuisine is a rousing combination of top-notch ingredients and layers of aggressive flavors, the service is excellent, and the crowded dining room is not as noisy as you might fear when you first spy it through the glass front wall. Upholstered banquettes, carpeting, and draperies help soften the din, but this is still not a place for cooing lovers—it's a place for food lovers, who savor co-owner Steve Johnson's regularly changing menu. Appetizers range from salad with an assertive vinaigrette to grilled sardines to a selection of summer vegetables served with a lemony aioli. Entrees tend to be roasted, grilled, or braised, with at least two vegetarian choices. The roast chicken, served with garlic mashed potatoes, is world-class. Grilled tuna appears often, and pork loin with cider glaze will make you think twice the next time you skip over pork on a menu to get to the steak. In warm weather, there's seating on the brick patio.

✪ **Dalí.** 415 Washington St., Somerville. ☎ **617/661-3254.** www.tiac.net/users/dali. Reservations not accepted. Tapas $2.50–$7.50, main courses $17–$21. AE, DC, MC, V. Daily 5:30–11pm. MBTA: Red Line to Harvard; follow Kirkland St. to intersection of Washington and Beacon sts. SPANISH.

Dalí casts an irresistible spell—it is noisy and crowded, is not all that close to Harvard Square (though it's a short cab ride), doesn't take reservations, and still fills up with people cheerfully waiting an hour or more for a table. The bar offers plenty to look at while you wait, including a clothesline festooned with lingerie. The payoff is authentic Spanish food, notably tapas, little plates of hot or cold creations that burst with flavor. Entrees include excellent paella, but most people come in a group and cut a swath through the tapas offerings, 32 on the menu and 9 monthly specials, all perfect for sharing. They include delectable *patatas ali-oli* (garlic potatoes), crunchy-tender *gambas con gabardina* (saffron-battered shrimp), addictive *setas al ajillo* (sautéed mushrooms), and rich, light *queso de cabra montañes* (goat cheese baked with tomato and basil). The waiters seem a bit overwhelmed but never fail to supply bread for sopping up juices, and sangria for washing it all down. If you want to experiment and order in stages, that's fine. Finish up with excellent flan, or try the rich *tarta de chocolates* (order your own if you like chocolate).

The owners of Dalí also run **Tapéo** (☎ **617/267-4799**), at 266 Newbury St., between Fairfield and Dartmouth streets in Boston's Back Bay. It offers the same menu and similarly wacky decor.

East Coast Grill. 1271 Cambridge St. ☎ **617/491-6568.** Reservations accepted only for parties of 5 or more, Sun–Thurs. Main courses $12.50–$22. AE, DISC, MC, V. Sun–Thurs 5:30–10pm, Fri–Sat 5:30–10:30pm; Sun brunch 11am–2:30pm. MBTA: Red Line to Harvard, then no. 69 (Harvard-Lechmere) bus to Inman Square. SEAFOOD/SOUTHERN/BARBECUE.

This madly popular restaurant doubled in size in 1996, and it still fills with people and noise. Chef-owner Chris Schlesinger, a national authority on grilling and spicy food, presides over a rowdy spot where fresh seafood, barbecue, and grilled fish and meats are prepared with equal authority. The funky decor, country and rock music, huge portions, and dizzying menu combine for an all-around satisfying experience.

Among the appetizers are luscious crab cakes and (proceed with caution) "pasta from Hell." Specialties include an expanded variety of seafood—check out the raw bar offerings, or try shrimp with terrific sausage-cornbread stuffing or steelhead trout crusted with Asian spices. Southern barbecue comes in three forms: Texas beef, Missouri spareribs, and North Carolina pork. Barbecue platters come with cole slaw, beans, corn bread, and a slice of watermelon. Should you have room for dessert, know that a certifiable key lime pie fiend has pledged allegiance to the great slab served here. One quibble: service is friendly but more casual than you'd expect—not inattentive, exactly, but less helpful as the meal wears on. Considering how full you'll be, you might not care.

MODERATE

Casa Portugal. 1200 Cambridge St. ☎ **617/491-8880.** Reservations recommended on weekends. Main courses $8–$14. AE, DISC, MC, V. Daily 4:30–10pm. MBTA: Red Line to Harvard, then no. 69 (Harvard-Lechmere) bus to Inman Square. PORTUGUESE.

To evaluate this restaurant, we enlisted a friend of Portuguese descent, who kept glancing around and saying, "It looks like my grandmother's house." She apparently favored stucco, colorful decorations, and a low-ceilinged, cozy atmosphere, but we had to guess—after the food arrived, the conversation ran to "Wow, this is good," and "Are you going to finish that?" Generous portions of hearty, inexpensive Portuguese fare draw the locals to this noisy but comfortable spot, where soup of the day, rice, and traditional fried potatoes come with all entrees. Try a dish that includes the flavorful Portuguese sausages *linguiça* and *chouriço*. The tureens, which combine several types of shellfish, are excellent, as is the *bacalhau assado a cuca* (reconstituted salt cod baked with garlic, peppers, and potatoes). The only potential drawback here is that the food is prepared with *lots* of olive oil, but hey, it's good for you.

Green Street Grill. 280 Green St. ☎ **617/876-1655.** Reservations not accepted. Main courses $13–$18. AE, MC, V. Nightly 6–10pm. MBTA: Red Line to Central Square. CARIBBEAN.

This is a bar (and not a very promising-looking one, either) where the Caribbean food is among the tastiest and hottest in town. If you can take the heat, you'll be in heaven; if not, you might feel like a cartoon character with flames licking out of your head by the time you're through. Red-wine and squid-ink fettuccine with shrimp, scallops, and squid will clear that head cold right up, and some dishes have as many as five kinds of peppers. Not everything is completely incendiary—a special of lamb one night was tender and flavorful, oozing juices into a mountain of tasty sweet potatoes. The helpful staff can steer you in the right direction. Grilled seafood is also done well here, and there's a wide variety of beers to help put out the fire.

☯ The Helmand. 143 First St. ☎ **617/492-4646.** Reservations recommended. Main courses $9–$16. AE, MC, V. Sun–Thurs 5–10pm, Fri–Sat 5–11pm. MBTA: Green Line to Lechmere. AFGHAN.

Even in cosmopolitan Cambridge, Afghan food is a novelty, and if any competitors are setting their sights on the Helmand, they're contemplating a daunting task. The elegant setting belies the reasonable prices at this spacious spot near the CambridgeSide Galleria Mall. Knowing that the cuisine is probably unfamiliar to many diners, the courteous staff patiently answers questions about the food, which is distinctly Middle Eastern with Indian and Pakistani influences. Many vegetarian dishes are offered, and when meat appears it's often one element of a dish rather than the centerpiece. Every meal comes with delectable bread made while you watch in a wood-fired brick oven. To start, you might try the slightly sweet baked pumpkin topped with a spicy ground meat sauce—a great contrast of flavors and textures—or *aushak*, pasta pockets filled with leeks or potatoes and buried under a sauce of split peas and carrots. Aushak, also available as a main course, can be prepared with meat sauce as well. Other entrees include several versions of what Americans would call stew, including *deygee kabob*, an excellent mélange of lamb, yellow split peas, onion, and red peppers. For dessert, don't miss the Afghan version of baklava.

La Groceria Ristorante Italiano. 853 Main St. ☎ **617/497-4214** or 617/547-9258. Reservations recommended at dinner. Main courses $6–$9 at lunch, $10–$18 at dinner.

Pizzas $6–$9.50. Children's menu $5–$6. AE, CB, DC, DISC, MC, V. Mon–Fri 11:30am–4pm; Mon–Thurs 4–10pm, Fri–Sat 4–11pm; Sun 1–10pm. Valet parking available on weekends. MBTA: Red Line to Central Square. ITALIAN.

The Mastromauro family has dished up large portions of delicious Italian food at this colorful, welcoming restaurant since 1972. You'll see business meetings at lunch, family outings at dinner, and students and bargain-hunters at all times, and there's something for all of them. Cheery voices bounce off the stucco walls and tile floors, but it seldom gets terribly noisy, probably because everyone's mouth is full. You might start with the house garlic bread, which overflows with chopped tomato, red onion, fennel seed, and olive oil. The antipasto platter is crowded with the chef's choice of meats, cheeses, and roasted vegetables. Main dishes might include homemade pasta from the machine you see as you enter—the daily specials are always good bets. Lasagna (a vegetarian version) is an excellent choice, as are any of the veal dishes and the savory chicken marsala. Chicken also comes roasted, and 10 varieties of brick-oven pizza are available in individual and large sizes.

Redbones. 55 Chester St. (off Elm St.), Somerville. ☎ **617/628-2200.** Reservations accepted only for parties of 11 or more, Sun–Thurs. Main courses $7–$14. No credit cards. Daily 11am–4pm; Sun–Thurs 4:30–10pm, Fri–Sat 4:30–11pm. MBTA: Red Line to Davis. BARBECUE.

Geographically, Redbones is in Somerville, but it's *really* on a back road in Texas or Arkansas or someplace like that—where the sun is hot, the beer is cold, and a big slab of meat is done to a turn. The walls of the raucous dining room sport old photos, T-shirts, and hand-lettered signs to study while you wait for your authentic Southern food. Barbecued ribs (Memphis, Texas, and Arkansas style), smoked beef brisket, fried Louisiana catfish, and grilled chicken come with appropriate side dishes alone or in any combination you want. The chummy staff can help you choose sweet, hot, mild, or vinegar sauce. Portions are enormous, so pace yourself. You'll want to try the wonderful appetizers and sides—catfish "catfingers," buffalo shrimp served with blue cheese sauce, creamy corn pudding—and desserts, especially the pecan pie. There's a huge selection of beers, and valet parking for your bicycle in warm weather.

INEXPENSIVE

✪ **S&S Restaurant.** 1334 Cambridge St., Inman Sq. ☎ **617/354-0777.** Main courses $3–$11. No credit cards. Mon–Sat 7am–midnight, Sun 8am–midnight; Sat brunch 7am–4pm, Sun brunch 8am–4pm. MBTA: Red Line to Harvard, then no. 69 (Harvard-Lechmere) bus to Inman Square. DELI.

"Es" is Yiddish for "eat," and this Cambridge classic is as straightforward as its name ("eat and eat"). Founded in 1919 by the great-grandmother of the current owners, the wildly popular brunch spot draws what seems to be half of Cambridge at busy times on weekends. It's northeast of Harvard Square, west of MIT, and worth a visit during the week, too. With huge windows and lots of light wood and plants, it looks contemporary, but the brunch offerings run to the likes of traditional pancakes, waffles, fruit salad, and fantastic omelettes. Bagels were a tasty staple here long before they were available at every corner store, and you'll find other traditional deli items, such as corned beef, pastrami, tongue, and Reuben sandwiches, as well as potato pancakes, blintzes, knockwurst, lox, and whitefish. The S&S is also a full-service restaurant with beef, chicken, and fish entrees, plus quiche and croissants, and it serves breakfast anytime during restaurant hours. Be early for brunch, or plan to spend a good chunk of your Saturday or Sunday standing around people-watching and getting hungry.

7

What to See & Do in Boston

Whether you want to follow in the footsteps of Paul Revere or those of the crew from "The Real World," Boston offers something for everyone, and plenty of it. Throw out your preconceptions of the city as some sort of open-air history museum—although that's certainly one of the guises it can assume—and allow your interests to dictate where you go. It's possible to take in most major attractions in 2 or 3 days if you don't linger anywhere too long, but for a more enjoyable and less rushed visit, plan fewer activities and spend more time on them. (Incidentally, **"Real World"** fans can see the home of the 1997 MTV show's cast at the foot of Beacon Hill, on Mount Vernon Street near the corner of River Street.)

In 1998, one attraction expanded, another relocated, and a third temporarily closed. The new West Wing of the **New England Aquarium** opened, the first stage of an expansion project in which the Aquarium will more than double in size. The **Sports Museum of New England** moved to its third location, which likely will be the charm: it's in the FleetCenter. And March saw the temporary shuttering of the 30-foot glass **Mapparium** at the world headquarters of the First Church of Christ, Scientist. The hollow, walk-through globe was to be closed for building renovations for at least 18 months; call (☎ **617/450-3790**) to see whether it has reopened by the time of your visit.

SUGGESTED ITINERARIES

If You Have 1 Day

Sample some experiences unique to Boston—you won't have time to immerse yourself, but you can touch on several singular attractions. Follow part of the **Freedom Trail** (see chapter 8) on your own

---

A Special Exhibition

Visitors in the fall of 1998 have the opportunity to see the exhibition *Monet in the 20th Century* at its only U.S. venue, the Museum of Fine Arts (☎ **617/267-9300**). If you'll be in Boston between September 20 and December 27, call for ticket information while you're making plans.

Let's Make a Deal

As you plan your sightseeing, remember that visitors (and residents, for that matter) have access to valuable money-saving offers. If you'll be in town for more than a couple of days, make your first stop a **BosTix** (☎ **617/723-5181**) booth for a coupon book that offers discounts on admissions to many area museums and attractions. (See "Discount Tickets," in chapter 10, for locations.) It's not worth the money (currently $9) for single travelers, because many of the coupons offer two-for-one deals; couples and families can take good advantage of the reduced rates for—among many others—the Museum of Fine Arts, New England Aquarium, Kennedy Library, Beantown and Old Town trolleys, and Massachusetts Bay Lines cruises.

Even if you're visiting for only 1 day, the MBTA's **Boston Visitor Passport** (☎ **617/222-5218**) can be a good deal. See "Getting Around," in chapter 4.

---

from Boston Common to **Faneuil Hall Marketplace,** or take a 90-minute tour led by a National Park Service ranger from the Visitor Center, 15 State St. (☎ 617/242-5642). Pick up carry-out food at Faneuil Hall Marketplace or in the North End and head toward the water for a picnic lunch in Christopher Columbus Park (across Atlantic Avenue from the marketplace) or on Long Wharf (pass the Marriott and keep going to the end of the wharf).

If you'd rather eat indoors, stay at the marketplace and have lunch at **Durgin-Park** (see chapter 6). In the afternoon, complete your independent Freedom Trail foray in the **North End,** and take a **sightseeing cruise** from Long Wharf or Rowes Wharf. Or cruise, then explore the **New England Aquarium,** or head over to Museum Wharf and visit the **Computer Museum.** Or skip the sightseeing altogether and head to Downtown Crossing and **Filene's Basement.** Feast in a fine restaurant in Boston or Cambridge (see chapter 6 for suggestions), and then enjoy a panoramic view of Boston by night from the **John Hancock Observatory** or the **Prudential Center Skywalk** (see "On Top of the World," below).

If You Have 2 Days

On the first day, follow the suggestions for 1 day or pick and choose—you can spend more time along the Freedom Trail, on a longer harbor cruise, or perhaps at Filene's Basement (get there early, if possible). On the second day, branch out a little, again letting your preferences be your guide. Spend the morning at the **Museum of Fine Arts** and have lunch there or at the **Isabella Stewart Gardner Museum.** Start the afternoon at the Gardner Museum or, if it's a Friday during the season, at the **Boston Symphony Orchestra** (see chapter 10, "Boston After Dark"). If art isn't your passion, the **Museum of Science** or the **John F. Kennedy Library and Museum** might be a better choice, followed by lunch at the Prudential Center and a **Duck Tour.**

Then make a leisurely trek around the **Back Bay** (see chapter 8) or a high-intensity shopping trip to **Newbury Street** (see chapter 9). On summer weekdays, **Boston By Foot** (☎ 617/367-2345; www.bostonbyfoot.com) conducts a tour of **Beacon Hill** that starts at the State House at 5:30pm. Decompress with dinner in the North End, then coffee and dessert at a cafe. The **Comedy Connection** at Faneuil Hall is nearby if you want to cap off the day with some laughs. Or dress up for dinner and enjoy dessert and dancing at the **Custom House Lounge** at the Bay Tower, or a drink and a dance in the lounge at **Top of the Hub,** on the Prudential Center's 52nd floor.

Boston Attractions

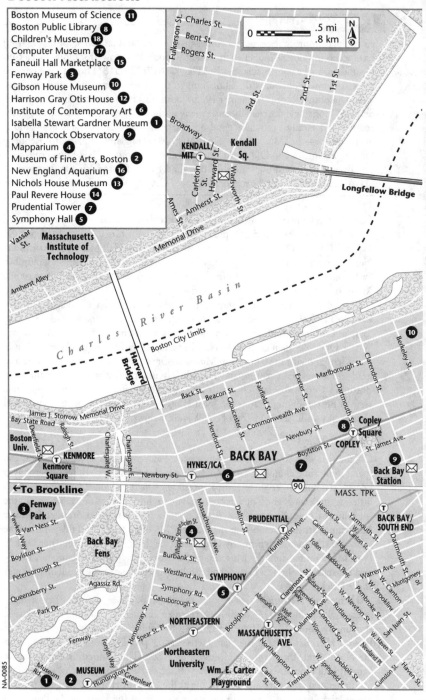

Boston Museum of Science **11**
Boston Public Library **8**
Children's Museum **18**
Computer Museum **17**
Faneuil Hall Marketplace **15**
Fenway Park **3**
Gibson House Museum **10**
Harrison Gray Otis House **12**
Institute of Contemporary Art **6**
Isabella Stewart Gardner Museum **1**
John Hancock Observatory **9**
Mapparium **4**
Museum of Fine Arts, Boston **2**
New England Aquarium **16**
Nichols House Museum **13**
Paul Revere House **14**
Prudential Tower **7**
Symphony Hall **5**

0 .5 mi
.8 km

N

Charles St.
Bent St.
Rogers St.
Fulkerson St.

3rd St.
2nd St.
1st St.

Broadway

KENDALL/ MIT 🚇   Kendall Sq.

Carleton St.
Amherst St.
Hayward St.
Wadsworth St.
Ames St.

Longfellow Bridge

Vassar St.

Massachusetts Institute of Technology

Memorial Drive

Amherst Alley

C h a r l e s   R i v e r   B a s i n

Harvard Bridge

Boston City Limits

Berkeley St.

Back St.
Beacon St.
Gloucester St.
Fairfield St.
Exeter St.
Marlborough St.
Clarendon St.
Dartmouth St.

Commonwealth Ave.

Hereford St.

Newbury St.   Copley Square

Boylston St.   COPLEY   St. James Ave.

8 🚇

James J. Storrow Memorial Drive
Bay State Road
Deerfield St.
Raleigh St.
Charlesgate W.
Charlesgate E.

Boston Univ. ✉

KENMORE 🚇
Kenmore Square

Newbury St.   HYNES/ICA 🚇   **BACK BAY**

7   6 ✉

9 ✉
Back Bay Station

←**To Brookline**

90   MASS. TPK.

3 **Fenway Park**
Yawkey Way
Van Ness St.
Boylston St.

Back Bay Fens

Msgr. Reynolds St.
Norway St.
Stoneholm St.
Dalton St.

4 ✉

Burbank St.

Westland Ave.

PRUDENTIAL
Huntington Ave.
Harcourt St.
Camden St.
Yarmouth St.
Clinton St.
Follen St.
Holyoke St.

🚇
BACK BAY/ SOUTH END
Dartmouth St.

Peterborough St.
Queensberry St.
Park Dr.

Agassiz Rd.

SYMPHONY

Symphony Rd.
Gainsborough St.

5 🚇

Massachusetts Ave.

Claremont St.
Rutland St.
W. Newton St.
Pembroke St.
W. Brookline St.
W. Canton St.

Warren Ave.
W. Canton St.
W. Brookline St.
Pembroke St.
W. Newton St.

Fenway
Forsyth Way
Hemenway St.
Spear St. Pl.

NORTHEASTERN 🚇

Botolph St.

Allerton St.
Wellington St.
Greenwich St.
Greenwich Ave.
Columbus Ave.
Concord Sq.
Rutland Sq.

W. Springfield St.
Worcester St.
Springfield St.
Deblois St.
Newland Pl.
Cunston St.
Haven St.

Museum Rd.

1

2 **MUSEUM** 🚇
Huntington Ave.
Greenleaf St.

Northeastern University

Wm. E. Carter Playground

Camden St.

MASSACHUSETTS AVE.
Northampton St.
Tremont St.
San Juan St.
W. Haven St.

NA-0085

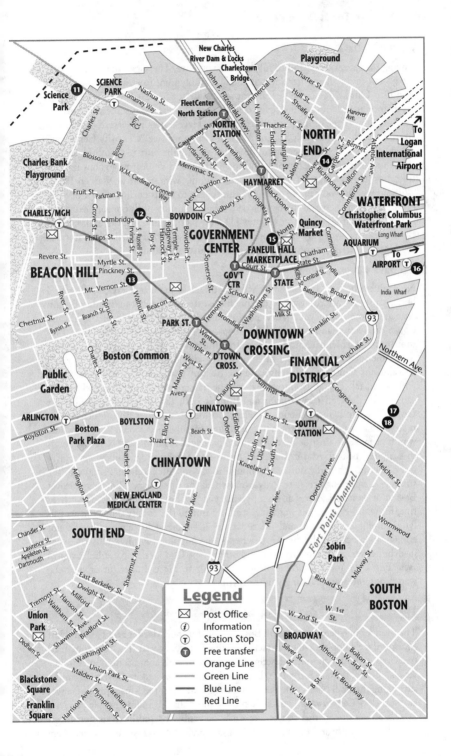

If You Have 3 Days

The options seem to expand to fill the time you have. The suggestions for the first 2 days can easily fill another day, but you'll probably want to explore farther afield. A visit to **Cambridge** is the logical next step. Ride the MBTA Red Line or the no. 1 bus to Harvard and see the sights (see chapter 8), squeeze in some shopping, or head straight to one of the museum complexes. Have lunch in Harvard Square and continue exploring, or visit **Mount Auburn Cemetery** (see "Celebrity Cemetery," below). Motorists have even more freedom. You might start in Cambridge, have lunch in **Lexington** or **Concord,** and spend the afternoon learning about the historical or literary legacy of the area, or communing with nature at **Walden Pond.** Without wheels, you can use public transportation to reach Lexington or Concord, but not to travel between them—forced to choose, history buffs opt for Lexington, literary types for Concord (see chapter 11). Have dinner in Cambridge (or back in Boston if that wasn't part of your itinerary on the first day), and enjoy live music at the **Hatch Shell,** a jazz or rock club, or the **House of Blues.**

If You Have 4 Days or More

Now you're cooking. Having scratched the surface in the first 3 days, you'll have a better sense of what you want to explore more extensively. Check out other Boston attractions that catch your fancy, perhaps including one or more of the historic **house museums,** and plan a full day trip—to Lexington and Concord, to **Plymouth,** to **Marblehead** and **Salem,** or to **Gloucester** and **Rockport.** If you didn't have time for the Computer Museum at first, visit Museum Wharf, where you'll also find the **Children's Museum** and the **Boston Tea Party Ship & Museum.** If you haven't taken a sightseeing cruise, try one that goes to Charlestown, where you can explore the **USS *Constitution*** and **Bunker Hill.** Take in a show at the **Mugar Omni Theater** at the Museum of Science, or decide whether Boston deserves its reputation as a great **sports** town by attending a pro or college event. Go on a **whale watch** or make an unstructured visit to a city **neighborhood** (see "Neighborhoods to Explore," below). And if you're just plain sick of sightseeing, don't worry, you're not alone (just the only one brave enough to say so). An excellent antidote in the summer is a daylong **cruise to Provincetown,** at the tip of Cape Cod. A boat leaves Boston at 9am and arrives at noon, giving you 3½ hours in P-Town. You'll have time for world-class people watching, strolling around the novelty shops and art galleries, dining on seafood, and—dare we say it—more sightseeing, although not enough to check out the famous beaches or the hopping gay nightlife scene. (For in-depth coverage of Provincetown and other Cape Cod locales, consult *Frommer's New England.*) You'll return to Boston at 6:30pm. Have dinner on or near the waterfront and start planning your next trip.

1 The Top Attractions

The number one people magnet in Boston is the **Quincy Market and Faneuil Hall Marketplace** complex, which attracts 14 million visitors a year. The **Freedom Trail** (see chapter 8 for a complete description) is second, with about 5 million visitors a year, a number the city is trying to boost with renovations and improvements of the sites along the trail. Next come the **Museum of Fine Arts,** the **Museum of Science,** and the **USS *Constitution,*** which each draw more than 1 million people per year.

The attractions in this section are easily accessible by **public transportation;** given the difficulty and expense of parking, it's preferable to take the T everywhere but the Kennedy Library, which has a large free parking lot (as well as a free shuttle bus from the Red Line). To maximize your enjoyment, try to go during relatively slow times. If possible, visit on weekdays, especially in the summer; if you're traveling without children, aim for times when school is in session. And if you're sightseeing on a weekend in July or August, relax and try to convince yourself that you love crowds.

Boston Tea Party Ship & Museum. Congress Street Bridge. ☎ **617/338-1773.** E-mail: bostps@historictours.com. Admission $7 adults, $5.50 students, $3.50 children 4-12, free for children under 4. Mar 1-Nov 30 daily 9am-dusk (about 6pm in summer, 5pm in winter). Closed Thanksgiving, Dec-Feb. MBTA: Red Line to South Station. Walk north on Atlantic Ave. 1 block, past the Federal Reserve Bank, turn right onto Congress St., and walk 1 block.

On December 16, 1773, a public meeting of independent-minded Bostonians led to the symbolic act of resistance commemorated here. The brig *Beaver II* is a full-size replica of one of the three merchant ships emptied by colonists poorly disguised as Indians on the night of the raid. It's anchored alongside a museum with exhibits on the "tea party." The audio and video displays (including a 15-minute film), dioramas, and information panels tell the story of the uprising. You can dump your own bale of tea into Boston Harbor (a museum staffer retrieves it), drink some complimentary tax-free tea (iced in summer, hot in winter), and buy some tea to take home at the museum store.

The Computer Museum. 300 Congress St. (Museum Wharf). ☎ **617/426-2800** or 617/423-6758 for the "Talking Computer." www.tcm.org. Admission $7 adults, $5 seniors, students, and children 3-18, free for children under 2. Tickets half-price Sun 3-5pm. Fall, winter, spring Tues-Sun and Mon during Boston school holidays and vacations 10am-5pm; summer daily 10am-6pm. MBTA: Red Line to South Station. Walk north on Atlantic Ave. 1 block, past the Federal Reserve Bank, turn right onto Congress St., and walk 1½ blocks.

As computer technology develops, the world's premier computer museum also changes and grows. The exhibits here tell the story of computers from their origins in the 1940s to the latest in PCs and virtual reality. The signature exhibit is the *Walk-Through Computer 2000*™, a networked multimedia machine 50 times larger than the real thing. When the computer is as large as a two-story house, the mouse is the size of a car, the CD-ROM drive is 8 feet long, the monitor is 12 feet high, and the humans enjoying the 30 hands-on activities are the equivalent of crayon-size. The exhibit even has a 7-foot-square Pentium processor, installed in 1995 during a million-dollar upgrade.

Computers don't exist in a vacuum, of course, and the *Networked Planet* exhibit allows visitors to explore the information superhighway and its offshoots by logging on to real and simulated networks and learning about weather forecasting, financial markets, and air-traffic control. There are also exhibits on robots, the history of the computer, and the practical and recreational uses of the PC—you might compose music or "drive" a race car. New offerings include the *Best Software for Kids* gallery, where the selections change regularly; a chance to experience *Virtual Worlds* of flight simulation and recumbent biking; and a "tank" where you can launch your own "virtual fish" and watch them interact with other visitors' creations. In all, you'll find more than 170 hands-on exhibits, two theaters, and countless ideas to try on your home computer.

Special activities, including Internet lessons, are offered on weekends. Call the Talking Computer for information about special programs and events. And check out the chocolate floppy disks and microchip jewelry at the Museum Store.

✪ **Faneuil Hall Marketplace.** Between North, Congress, and State sts. and I-93. ☎ **617/338-2323.** Marketplace Mon–Sat 10am–9pm, Sun noon–6pm. Colonnade food court opens earlier; some restaurants open early for Sun brunch and close at 2am daily. MBTA: Green Line to Government Center, Orange Line to State or Haymarket, or Blue Line to State or Aquarium.

It's impossible to overestimate the effect of Faneuil Hall Marketplace on Boston's economy and reputation. A daring idea when it opened in 1976, the festival market has been widely imitated, and each new complex of shops, food stands, restaurants, bars, and public spaces in urban centers around the country reflects its city. Faneuil Hall Marketplace, brimming with Boston flavor and regional goods and souvenirs, is no exception. Its success with tourists and suburbanites is so great, in fact, that you could be forgiven for thinking that the only Bostonians in the crowd are employees.

The marketplace includes five buildings—the central three-building complex is listed in the National Register of Historic Places—set on brick and stone plazas that teem with crowds shopping, eating, performing, watching performers, and just people watching. **Quincy Market** (you'll hear the whole complex called by that name as well) is the central three-level Greek revival-style building. It reopened after renovations turned it into a festival market on August 26, 1976, 150 years of hard use after Mayor Josiah Quincy opened the original market. The **South Market building** reopened on August 26, 1977, the **North Market building** on August 26, 1978.

The central corridor of Quincy Market, known as the **Colonnade,** is the food court, where you can find anything from a bagel to a full Greek dinner, a fruit smoothie to a hunk of fudge. On either side, under the glass canopies, are pushcarts bearing the full range of crafts created by New England artisans and hokey souvenirs hawked by enterprising merchants. In the plaza between the **South Canopy** and the South Market building is an **information kiosk,** and throughout the complex, you'll find an enticing mix of chain stores and unique shops (see chapter 9). On summer evenings, the tables that spill outdoors from the restaurants and bars fill with people. One constant since the year after the market opened—after the *original* market opened, that is—is **Durgin-Park,** a traditional New England restaurant with traditionally crabby waiters (see chapter 6).

✪ **Faneuil Hall** itself sometimes gets overlooked, but it's well worth a visit. Known as the "Cradle of Liberty" for its role as a center of inspirational (some might say inflammatory) speeches in the years leading to the Revolutionary War, the building opened in 1742 and was expanded using a Charles Bulfinch design in 1805. National Park Service rangers give **free 20-minute talks** every half-hour from 9am to 5pm in the second-floor auditorium, which, after a recent refurbishment, is in mint condition.

✪ **Isabella Stewart Gardner Museum.** 280 The Fenway. ☎ **617/566-1401.** www.boston.com/gardner. Admission $10 adults, $7 seniors, $5 college students with valid ID, $3 college students on Wed, free for children under 18. Tues–Sun 11am–5pm and some Mon holidays. Closed Mon, Jan 1, Thanksgiving, Dec 25. MBTA: Green Line E train to Museum.

Isabella Stewart Gardner (1840 to 1924) was an incorrigible individualist long before such behavior was acceptable for a woman in polite Boston society, and her iconoclasm has proven a great boon to art lovers. "Mrs. Jack" designed her exquisite home in the style of a 15th-century Venetian palace and filled it with European, American, and Asian painting and sculpture, much chosen with the help of her friend and protégé Bernard Berenson. You'll see works by Titian, Botticelli,

Raphael, Rembrandt, Matisse, and Mrs. Gardner's friends James McNeill Whistler and John Singer Sargent. Titian's magnificent *Europa,* which many scholars consider his finest work, is one of the most important Renaissance paintings in the United States.

The building, which was opened to the public after Mrs. Gardner's death, holds a hodgepodge of furniture and architectural details imported from European churches and palaces. The *pièce de résistance* is the magnificent skylighted courtyard, filled year-round with fresh flowers (lilies at Easter, chrysanthemums in the fall, poinsettias at Christmas) from the museum's own greenhouse. Although the terms of Mrs. Gardner's will forbid changing the arrangement of the museum's content, there has been some evolution: a special exhibition gallery, which opened in September 1992, features two or three changing shows a year. An exhibition scheduled for the summer of 1999 will highlight **Sargent's late landscapes.**

The Tapestry Room fills with music on weekends from September through April for the ✪ **concert series** (☎ **617/734-1359**), which showcases soloists, chamber groups, and local students. The tiled floor and gorgeous wall hangings make a lovely setting. Concerts begin at 1:30pm on Saturday and Sunday. Tickets, which include museum admission, are $15 for adults, $11 for seniors, $9 for college students with valid ID, $7 for ages 12 to 17, and $5 for ages 5 to 11.

Lunch and desserts are served in the museum cafe, and unique items are available at the gift shop.

✪ **John F. Kennedy Library and Museum.** Columbia Point. ☎ **617/929-4523.** Admission $8 adults, $6 seniors and students with ID, $4 children 13-17, free for children under 13. Daily 9am-5pm (last film begins at 3:55pm); June-Aug Wed until 8pm. Closed Jan 1, Thanksgiving, Dec 25. MBTA: Red Line to JFK/UMass, then take the free shuttle bus, which runs every 20 minutes. By car, take the Southeast Expressway (I-93/Rte. 3) south to Exit 15 (Morrissey Blvd./JFK Library), turn left onto Columbia Rd., and follow signs to free parking lot.

The Kennedy era springs to life at this dramatic library, museum, and educational research complex overlooking Dorchester Bay. It captures the 35th president's accomplishments and legacy in sound and video recordings and fascinating displays of memorabilia and photos.

Your visit begins with a 17-minute film narrated by John F. Kennedy himself— a detail that seems eerie for a moment, then perfectly natural. Through skillfully edited audio clips, he discusses his childhood, education, war experiences, and early political career. Then you're turned loose to spend as much time as you like on each exhibit. Starting with the 1960 presidential campaign, you're immersed in the era. In a series of connected galleries, you'll see campaign souvenirs, a film of Kennedy debating Richard Nixon and delivering his inaugural address, a replica of the Oval Office, gifts from foreign dignitaries, letters, documents, and keepsakes. There's a film about the Cuban Missile Crisis, and displays on the civil rights movement, the Peace Corps, the space program, and the Kennedy family. New expanded exhibits focus on First Lady Jacqueline Bouvier Kennedy and on Atty. Gen. Robert F. Kennedy's efforts in the civil rights movement. As the tour winds down, you pass through a darkened chamber where news reports of John Kennedy's assassination and funeral play in a continuous loop. In a room called simply "Legacy," books, archival documents, and video footage explain the programs the president initiated and how they affect the world today.

From the final room, the soaring glass-enclosed pavilion that is the heart of the I. M. Pei design, there's a glorious view of the water and the Boston skyline. In the summer, JFK's boyhood sailboat, *Victura,* sits on a strip of dune grass between the library and the harbor. The nine-story Archives Tower houses papers, books, films,

MFA FYI

The Huntington Avenue entrance to the Museum of Fine Arts is usually much less busy than the West Wing lobby—and farther from the parking garage, gift shop, restaurants, and access to special exhibits. If you're eager to get started on a lengthy visit (which generally involves lots of walking anyway), walk back along Huntington Avenue when you leave the T and enter from the curved driveway.

and oral histories of the Kennedys and many of their political contemporaries. Scholars and researchers can obtain access to the materials by appointment.

✪ **Museum of Fine Arts.** 465 Huntington Ave. ☎ **617/267-9300.** www.mfa.org. Adults $10 when entire museum is open, $8 when only West Wing is open. Students and senior citizens $8 when entire museum is open, $6 when only West Wing is open. Children under 18 free when accompanied by an adult. Voluntary contribution, Wed 4-9:45pm. No admission fee to visit only the Museum Shop, restaurants, library, or auditoriums. Entire museum, Mon-Tues 10am-4:45pm, Wed 10am-9:45pm, Thurs-Fri 10am-5pm, Sat-Sun 10am-5:45pm; West Wing only, Thurs-Fri 5-9:45pm. Closed Thanksgiving, Dec 25. MBTA: Green Line E train to Museum, or Orange Line to Ruggles.

Not content with the MFA's reputation as the second-best art museum in the country (after New York's Metropolitan Museum of Art), the museum's management team works nonstop to make the collections more accessible and interesting. In recent years the approach to raising the museum's profile has ranged from apparently little things, such as reopening the Huntington Avenue entrance, to mounting even more top-notch exhibitions, expanding educational programs, and opening new permanent galleries for the art of Africa, Oceania, and the ancient Americas.

The 129-year-old museum's not-so-secret weapon in its quest is a powerful one: its magnificent collections. Your visit is guided by a curatorial attitude that makes even those who go in with a sense of obligation leave with a sense of discovery and wonder. The MFA is especially noted for its Asian and Old Kingdom Egyptian collections, classical art, Buddhist temple, and medieval sculpture and tapestries, but the works you might find more familiar are American and European paintings and sculpture, notably the Impressionists. Some favorites: Childe Hassam's *Boston Common at Twilight,* Gilbert Stuart's 1796 portrait of George Washington, John Singleton Copley's 1768 portrait of Paul Revere, a bronze casting of Edgar Degas's sculpture *Little Dancer,* Paul Gauguin's *Where Do We Come From? What Are We? Where Are We Going?,* a wall of Fitz Hugh Lane's Luminist masterpieces, and all 43 Monets. There are also magnificent print and photography collections, and that's not even touching on the furnishings and decorative arts, including the finest collection of Paul Revere silver in the world.

Exhibitions planned for late 1998 and 1999 include **Monet in the 20th Century** (September 20 to December 27, 1998), whose only U.S. venue is the MFA, and **Mary Cassatt: A Retrospective** (February 14 to May 19, 1999).

I. M. Pei designed the West Wing (1981), the latest addition to the original 1909 structure. It contains the main entrance, climate-controlled galleries, an auditorium, and an atrium with a tree-lined "sidewalk" cafe. The excellent Museum Shop expanded in 1997, adding a huge selection of art books. The Fine Arts Restaurant is on the second floor, and there's also a cafeteria. Pick up a floor plan at the information desk, or take a free guided tour.

The museum is between Huntington Avenue and the Fenway. If you're driving, you can park in the garage or lot off Museum Road, but from anywhere downtown, the T is much faster.

On Top of the World

Two of Boston's top attractions are literally *top* attractions. From hundreds of feet in the air, you'll get an unbeatable look at the city and its surroundings. The nearest T stops to both are Copley on the Green Line and Back Bay on the Orange Line and commuter rail.

The **John Hancock Observatory,** 200 Clarendon St. (☎ **617/572-6429**), would be a good introduction to Boston even if it didn't have a sensational 60th-floor view. The multimedia exhibits include a light-and-sound show that chronicles the events leading to the Revolutionary War and demonstrates how Boston's land mass has changed. There are an illustrated time line; an interactive computer quiz about the city; and a display that generates walking, driving, and public transportation directions to points of interest of your choosing. Powerful binoculars (bring quarters) allow long-distance views, and facsimiles of newspapers give a look at headlines from the past. Admission is $4.25 for adults, $3.25 for seniors and children 5 to 15. Hours are from 9am to 11pm Monday through Saturday; Sunday from 10am to 11pm May to October, and from noon to 11pm November to April. The ticket office closes at 10pm.

The **Prudential Center Skywalk,** 800 Boylston St. (☎ **617/236-3318**), offers the only 360° view of Boston and beyond. From the enclosed observation deck on the 50th floor of the Prudential Tower, you can see for miles, even (when it's clear) as far as the mountains of southern New Hampshire to the north and the beaches of Cape Cod to the south. The limited exhibits are less interesting than those at the John Hancock Observatory, but the view is a little better, especially at sunset. Hours are 10am to 10pm daily. Admission is $4 for adults, $3 for seniors and children ages 2 to 10. On the 52nd floor you can enjoy the view with food and drink at the Top of the Hub restaurant and lounge (see chapter 6).

✪ **Museum of Science.** Science Park. ☎ **617/723-2500.** www.mos.org. Admission to exhibit halls $9 adults, $7 seniors and children ages 3-14, free for children under 3. To Mugar Omni Theater, Hayden Planetarium, or laser shows, $7.50 adults, $5.50 seniors and children ages 3-14, free for children under 3. Tickets to 2 or 3 parts of the complex available at discounted prices. Sat-Thurs 9am-5pm, Fri 9am-9pm. Closed Thanksgiving, Dec 25. MBTA: Green Line to Science Park. Or commuter rail to North Station, then 10-minute walk.

For the ultimate pain-free educational experience, head to the Museum of Science. The demonstrations, experiments, and interactive displays introduce facts and concepts so effortlessly that everyone winds up learning something. Take a couple of hours or a whole day to explore the permanent and temporary exhibits, which are dedicated to improving "science literacy."

Among the more than 450 exhibits, you might meet an iguana or a dinosaur, find out how much you'd weigh on the moon, or climb into a space module. In the activity center *Investigate!* visitors to learn to think like scientists, formulating questions, finding evidence, and drawing conclusions through activities such as strapping on a skin sensor to measure reactions to stimuli or sifting through an archaeological dig. In the *Seeing Is Deceiving* section, auditory and visual illusions challenge your belief in what is "real." The *Science in the Park* exhibit introduces the concepts of Newtonian physics—through familiar recreational tools such as playground equipment and skateboards. You can also visit the theater of electricity to see lightning manufactured indoors. And there's a *Discovery Center* especially for preschoolers.

The separate-admission theaters are worth planning for. Even if you're skipping the exhibits, try to see a show. If you're making a day of it, buy all your tickets at once, not only because it's cheaper but because shows sometimes sell out. Tickets for daytime shows must be purchased in person. Evening show tickets can be ordered over the phone using a credit card; there's a service charge for doing so.

The **Mugar Omni Theater,** one of only about 150 in the world, is an intense experience. You're bombarded with images on a four-story domed screen, and sounds from a 12-channel sound system with 84 speakers. Even though you know you're not moving, the engulfing sensations and steep pitch of the seating area will have you hanging on for dear life, whether the film you're watching is on whales, Mount Everest, or hurricanes and tornadoes. The films change every 4 to 6 months.

The **Charles Hayden Planetarium** takes you deep into space with daily star shows and shows on special topics that change several times a year. On weekends, rock-music laser shows take over—Pink Floyd fans, this is the place for you. At the entrance is a hands-on astronomy exhibit, *Welcome to the Universe.*

The museum has a terrific gift shop, where toys and games promote learning without lecturing, and the ground-floor Galaxy Cafés have spectacular views of the skyline and river. There's a parking garage on the premises; but it's on a busy street, and entering and exiting can be harrowing.

New England Aquarium. Central Wharf. ☎ 617/973-5200. www.neaq.org. Admission $11 adults, $10 seniors, $5.50 children 3-11, free for children under 3. $1 off all fees 4-8pm summer Wed and Thurs. No admission fee for those visiting only the outdoor exhibits, cafe, and gift shop. July 1-Labor Day Mon-Tues and Fri 9am-6pm, Wed-Thurs 9am-8pm, Sat-Sun and holidays 9am-7pm. Early Sept-June Mon-Fri 9am-5pm, Sat-Sun and holidays 9am-6pm. Closed Thanksgiving, Dec 25, and until noon Jan 1. MBTA: Blue Line to Aquarium.

Like a crab molting its outgrown shell, the New England Aquarium has expanded, into a new West Wing building that echoes the waves on adjacent Boston Harbor. The dramatic structure opened in 1998, with an enlarged exhibit space and gift shop, and a new cafe with views of the city and the harbor. The frolicking seals in outdoor enclosures have been joined by California sea otters that greet you as you approach, the perfect welcome to an entertaining complex that's home to more than 7,000 fish and aquatic mammals. When you head inside, buy an exhibit guide and plan your route as you commune with the penguin colony.

The focal point of the main building is the aptly named Giant Ocean Tank. A four-story spiral ramp encircles the cylindrical glass tank, which contains 187,000 gallons of saltwater, a replica of a Caribbean coral reef, and a conglomeration of sea creatures who seem to coexist amazingly well. Part of the reason for the peace might be that the sharks are fed five times a day by scuba divers who bring the food right to them. Other exhibits show off freshwater specimens, denizens of the Amazon, and the ecology of Boston Harbor. At the *Edge of the Sea* exhibit, you're encouraged to touch the sea stars, sea urchins, and horseshoe crabs in the tide pool. Be sure to leave time for a show at the floating marine mammal pavilion, *Discovery,* where sea lions perform every 90 minutes throughout the day.

The aquarium sponsors **whale-watching expeditions** (☎ 617/973-5281) daily from May through mid-October and on weekends in April and late October. You'll travel several miles out to sea to Stellwagen Bank, the feeding ground for the whales as they migrate from Newfoundland to Provincetown. Tickets (cash only) are $24 for adults, $19 for senior citizens and college students, $17.50 for children ages 12 to 18, and $16.50 for children ages 3 to 11. Children must be 3 years old and at least 30 inches tall. Reservations are recommended and can be held with a Master-Card or Visa.

2 More Museums

The **Sports Museum of New England** has announced plans to open at the Fleet-Center, but many details had not been worked out at press time. The museum's permanent collection of memorabilia and art highlights the region's storied professional sports legacy as well as its high school, college, and Olympic participants. The displays, in the 5th- and 6th-floor concourse areas of the FleetCenter, will highlight the Bruins and Celtics. For information, call the museum's administrative offices (☎ 617/787-7678) or the FleetCenter (☎ 617/624-1000).

Boston Public Library. 700 Boylston St., at Copley Sq. ☎ **617/536-5400.** www.bpl.org. Free admission. Mon-Thurs 9am-9pm, Fri-Sat 9am-5pm. Sun (Oct-May only) 1-5pm. Closed Sun June-Sept and legal holidays. MBTA: Green Line to Copley.

The central branch of the city's library system is an architectural and intellectual monument. The original 1895 building, a registered National Historic Landmark designed by Charles F. McKim, is an Italian Renaissance-style masterpiece that fairly drips with art. The lobby doors are the work of Daniel Chester French (who also designed the *Minute Man* statue in Concord, the statue of Abraham that's in his memorial in Washington, and the John Harvard statue in Cambridge). The newly restored murals are by John Singer Sargent and Pierre Puvis de Chavannes, among others, and you'll see notable frescoes, sculptures, and paintings. Visit the lovely courtyard or peek at it from a window on the stairs. The adjoining addition, of the same height and material (pink granite), was designed by Philip Johnson and opened in 1972. It's a utilitarian building with a dramatic skylighted atrium. Visitors are welcome to wander throughout both buildings—the lobby of the McKim building alone could take half an hour—but you must have a library card (available to Massachusetts residents) to check out materials. The library has more than 6 million books and more than 11 million other items, such as prints, photographs, films, and sound recordings.

Free **Art & Architecture Tours** are conducted Monday at 2:30pm, Tuesday and Wednesday at 6:30pm, Thursday and Saturday at 11am, and September through May on Sunday at 2pm. Call (☎ 617/536-5400, ext. 216) to arrange group tours.

The Institute of Contemporary Art. 955 Boylston St. ☎ **617/266-5152.** www.primalpub.com/ica. Admission $5.25 adults, $3.25 students, $2.25 seniors and children under 16; free to all Thurs 5-9pm. Wed and Fri-Sun noon-5pm, Thurs noon-9pm. Closed major holidays. MBTA: Green Line B, C, or D train to Hynes/ICA.

Across from the Hynes Convention Center, the ICA hosts rotating exhibits of 20th-century art, including painting, sculpture, photography, and video and performance art. The institute also offers films, lectures, music, video, poetry, and an educational program for children and adults. The 1886 building, originally a police station, is a showpiece in its own right. Plans for renovation and possible expansion were in the works at press time—call before setting out.

Massachusetts Archives. 220 Morrissey Blvd., Columbia Point. ☎ **617/727-2816.** Free admission. Mon-Fri 9am-5pm, Sat 9am-3:30pm. Closed legal holidays. MBTA: Red Line to JFK/UMass.

The history of one of Boston's most famous families is explored at the nearby Kennedy Library; the history of your family might be documented here. The state archives contain passenger lists for ships that arrived in Boston from 1848 to 1891; state census schedules that date to 1790; and documents, maps, and military and court records starting with the Massachusetts Bay Company (1628 to 1629).

Knowledgeable staff members are on hand to answer researchers' questions in person, by mail, or by phone.

In the same building, you'll find the **Commonwealth Museum** (☎ 617/727-9150), which has videos, slide shows, and other interactive exhibits on the people, places, and politics of Massachusetts. Topics covered recently in the regularly changing exhibits include war photography, the archaeology of a military fort, and the Quabbin Reservoir.

Museum of Transportation. 15 Newton St. (in Larz Anderson Park), Brookline. ☎ **617/522-6547.** Admission $5 adults, $3 seniors, students with valid ID, and children ages 6-16. April-Oct, Wed-Sun 10am-5pm; Nov-March, Wed-Sun 10am-4pm. Hours might vary when installations are changing; call for information. Closed Jan 1, Thanksgiving, Dec 25. MBTA: Green Line D train to Reservoir, then take bus 51 (Forest Hills); the museum is 5 blocks from the intersection of Newton and Clyde sts. Call for driving directions.

Automobile buffs will delight in this museum based in an 1888 carriage house modeled after a French château. Beginning in 1899, Larz and Isabel Anderson acquired the antique cars that form the core of the museum's collection, now the country's oldest private assemblage of antique autos. The cars boast what was then the latest equipment, from a two-cylinder engine (in a race car—a 1901 Winton) to a full lavatory (in a 1906 CGV). Autos and memorabilia from the collection and from other sources are on display. From May through October, cars are shown on the lawn on most weekends, with a different theme each time, such as Corvettes, Cadillacs, Triumphs, German cars, or Italian imports. Call to find out what's featured during your visit.

3 Historic Houses

The home in Boston imbued with the most history is the ✪ **Paul Revere House,** 19 North Sq. (☎ 617/523-2338), and not just because it's the oldest in downtown Boston, dating to about 1680. Many people know no more about Revere than the first few lines of Henry Wadsworth Longfellow's poem "Paul Revere's Ride"—many people don't even know that—but his house brings the legendary revolutionary to life. The tour is self-guided, allowing you to linger on the artifacts that hold your interest, and is particularly thought-provoking. Revere had eight children (he called them "my lambs") with each of his two wives, and he supported the family with his thriving silversmith's trade. At his home, you'll get a good sense of the risks he took with his role in the events that led to the Revolutionary War.

The house is open daily April 15 through October 9:30am to 5:15pm, and November through April 14 9:30am to 4:15pm. It's closed Mondays from January through March and on January 1, Thanksgiving, and December 25. Admission is $2.50 for adults, $2 for seniors and students, and $1 for children 5 to 17. Special programs and events are scheduled to coincide with Patriot's Day, Fourth of July, and Christmas; call for details.

The adjacent **Pierce/Hichborn House,** a suitably furnished Georgian structure built around 1711 and occupied by Revere's cousins, is shown by guided tour only. There are usually two tours a day at busy times; call the Paul Revere House for schedules.

Houses that are as interesting for their architecture as for their occupants can be found on **Beacon Hill.** The south slope, facing Boston Common, has been a fashionable address since the 1620s; excellent tours of two houses (one on the north slope) focus on the late 18th and early 19th centuries. The homes were designed by Charles Bulfinch, who was also the architect of the nearby Massachusetts State House.

❓ Did You Know?

- Robert Newman, who hung the lanterns in the steeple of the Old North Church to signal to Paul Revere, was a great-grandson of George Burroughs, one of the victims of the Salem witch trials of 1692.
- Martin Luther King, Jr., studied at Boston University and left it many of his important papers.
- The Boston subway system, which opened in 1897, was the first in the Western Hemisphere.
- Susan B. Anthony (now immortalized on the dollar coin) was arrested in Boston in 1872 for trying to vote in the presidential election.
- The wreaths that adorn the heads of the Boston Marathon winners are made from the leaves of olive trees in Olympia, Greece.
- Kahlil Gibran, the Lebanese-American poet who wrote *The Prophet,* grew up in Boston's South End.
- The French Protestants known as Huguenots were a small but important group in colonial Boston. Two Huguenot names you'll see today: Faneuil and Revere.
- The Marquis de Lafayette, a hero of the American and French revolutions, is buried in Paris under soil taken from Bunker Hill in Charlestown.
- The first public school in America, attended by John Hancock and Benjamin Franklin, among others, was on School Street in Boston. Other alumni include Charles Bulfinch, Ralph Waldo Emerson, George Santayana, Arthur Fiedler, and Leonard Bernstein.

The ✪ **Harrison Gray Otis House,** 141 Cambridge St. (☎ **617/227-3956**), was designed in 1796 for an up-and-coming young lawyer who later became mayor of Boston. The restoration was one of the first in the country to use computer analysis of paint, and the result was revolutionary, revealing that the colors on the walls were drab because the paint was faded, not because they started out dingy. Furnished in the style to which a wealthy family in the young United States would have been accustomed, the restored Federal-style mansion is a colorful, elegant treasure. It is at the foot of Beacon Hill, near the Government Center and Charles T stops.

Tours (the only way to see the house) discuss its architecture and post-Revolutionary social, business, and family life, and touch on the history of the neighborhood. They start on the hour Wednesday through Sunday from 11am to 4pm. Admission is $4 for adults, $3.50 for seniors, $2 for children 12 and under.

The **Society for the Preservation of New England Antiquities** (SPNEA) makes its headquarters at the Otis House, which is just the tip of the iceberg. SPNEA owns and operates 34 historic properties throughout New England, and the results of its restoration techniques can be seen at museums all over the area. Contact the society, 141 Cambridge St., Boston, MA 02114 (☎ **617/227-3956;** www.spnea.org), for brochures, visiting hours, and admission fees.

The **Nichols House Museum,** 55 Mount Vernon St. (☎ **617/227-6993**), is an 1804 Beacon Hill home with beautiful antique furnishings collected by several generations of the Nichols family. From May through October, it's open Tuesday through Saturday; November through April, Monday, Wednesday, and Saturday (open days might vary, so call ahead). Tours start at 12:15pm and continue every half-hour on the quarter-hour through 4:15pm. Admission is $5.

In the Back Bay, the **Gibson House Museum,** 137 Beacon St. (☎ **617/267-6338**), is an 1859 brownstone that embodies the word *Victorian*. You'll see dozens of family photos and portraits, petrified-wood hat racks, a sequined pink-velvet pagoda for the cat, a Victrola, and all manner of decorations. The museum is open for tours at 1, 2, and 3pm Wednesday through Sunday from May to October, and weekends only from November to April. It's closed on major holidays. Admission is $5.

At the **John F. Kennedy National Historic Site,** 83 Beals St., Brookline (☎ **617/566-7937**), the 35th president's birthplace is restored to its appearance in 1917, affording a fascinating look at domestic life of the period and the roots of the Kennedy family. A unit of the National Park Service, the house is shown only by guided ranger tour, at 10:45 and 11:45am and 1, 2, 3, and 4pm. Guided tours are $2 for adults and free for children under 16. The house is open from mid-May to October, Wednesday through Sunday from 10am to 4:30pm. Take the Green Line C train to Coolidge Corner, then walk 4 blocks north on Harvard Street.

4 Heritage Trails

THE BLACK HERITAGE TRAIL

Before you leave home, be sure to contact the **Greater Boston Convention & Visitors Bureau,** 2 Copley Place, Suite 105, Boston, MA 02116 (☎ **888/ SEE-BOSTON** or 617/536-4100; fax 617/424-7664; www.bostonusa.com; e-mail visitor@bostonusa.com), and ask for a copy of the 22-page "Boston African American Discovery Guide," which lists many cultural and historical activities and events.

The **Black Heritage Trail** covers sites on Beacon Hill that are part of the history of 19th-century Boston. You can take a 2-hour guided tour given by the rangers at the National Park Service's **Boston African American National Historic Site,** which starts at the Visitor Center, 46 Joy St. (☎ **617/742-5415**), or you can go on your own, using a brochure that includes a map and descriptions of the buildings. The sites include stations of the Underground Railroad, homes of famous citizens, and the first integrated public school.

One of the most interesting sites on the Black Heritage Trail is the 193-year-old **African Meeting House,** at 8 Smith Court, the oldest standing black church in the United States. It was there that William Lloyd Garrison founded the New England Anti-Slavery Society and Frederick Douglass made some of his great abolitionist speeches. The building once known as the "Black Faneuil Hall" offers an informative audiovisual presentation, lectures, concerts, and church meetings.

The meeting house is the chief artifact of the **Museum of Afro-American History,** 46 Joy St. (☎ **617/742-1854**), which has the most comprehensive information on the history and contributions of blacks in Boston and Massachusetts. It's open weekdays from 10am to 4pm. The suggested donation is $5 for adults, $3 for seniors, students, and children.

The **Museum of the National Center of Afro-American Artists,** 300 Walnut Ave., Roxbury (☎ **617/442-8614**), is dedicated to the cultural and visual arts heritage of African-Americans and others of African descent from all over the world. Admission is $4 for adults, $3 for children and seniors. The museum is open Tuesday through Sunday from 1 to 5pm. To get there, take the Orange Line or commuter rail to Ruggles, then bus 22 or 29 to Walnut Avenue and Seaver Street.

THE BOSTON WOMEN'S HERITAGE TRAIL

The **Boston Women's Heritage Trail** is a walking route with stops at the homes, churches, and social and political institutions where 20 women lived; made great contributions to society; or both. Subjects include Julia Ward Howe, Dorothea Dix, and other famous Bostonians, as well as the lesser known, such as Phillis Wheatley, a slave who became the first African-American published poet, and Lucy Stone, a feminist and abolitionist. Guides can be purchased at the National Park Service Visitor Center at 15 State St., at local bookstores, and at historic sites, such as the Paul Revere House and the Old South Meeting House. For more detailed information, call ☎ **617/522-2872.**

5 Parks & Gardens

Green space is an important part of Boston's appeal, and the public parks are hard to miss. The latest development on this front is City Hall Plaza, where flowers, trees, and plants are welcome invaders on the vast expanse of brick. It's not a park, but it's getting there.

The best-known park, for good reason, is the spectacular **Public Garden,** bordered by Arlington, Boylston, Charles, and Beacon streets. Although something lovely is in bloom at the country's first botanical garden at least half of the year, the spring flowers are particularly impressive, especially if your visit should happen to coincide with the first really warm day of the year. It's hard not to enjoy yourself when everyone around you seems ecstatic just to be seeing the sun. For many people, the official return of spring coincides with the return of the **swan boats** (☎ **617/522-1966** or 617/624-7020). The pedal-powered vessels plunge into the lagoon on the Saturday before Patriot's Day (the third Monday of April), and although they don't move fast, they'll transport you. They operate from 10am to 6pm in summer, 10am to 4pm in spring and fall. The cost is $1.75 for adults, 95¢ for children under 13.

Across Charles Street is **Boston Common,** the country's first public park. The property was purchased in 1634 and officially set aside as public land in 1640, so if it seems a bit run-down (especially compared to the Public Garden), it's no wonder. The Frog Pond, where there really were frogs at one time, has been completely overhauled, and it makes a pleasant spot to splash around in the summer and skate in the winter. There's also a bandstand where you might take in a free concert, and many beautiful shade trees.

The most spectacular garden of all is the ✪ **Arnold Arboretum,** 125 Arborway, Jamaica Plain (☎ **617/524-1718;** www.arboretum.harvard.edu). One of the oldest parks in the United States, founded in 1872, it is open daily from sunrise to sunset. Its 265 acres contain more than 15,000 ornamental trees, shrubs, and vines from all over the world. In the spring, the dizzying scent of dogwood, azaleas, rhododendrons, and hundreds of varieties of lilacs, for which the arboretum is especially famous, perfumes the air. Lilac Sunday is in May, and it's the only time picnicking is allowed in the arboretum. This is definitely a place to take a camera.

There is no admission fee for this National Historical Landmark, which Harvard University administers in cooperation with the Boston Department of Parks and Recreation. To get there, take the MBTA Orange Line to the Forest Hills stop and follow the signs to the entrance. The Visitor Center is open weekdays from 9am to 4pm, and weekends from noon to 4pm. Call for information about educational programs.

6 Diversions

ART GALLERIES

Everyone has to start somewhere, and the artists whose work you'll find in the big museums years from now might be showing at galleries in Boston today. You'll find the greatest concentration of galleries along Newbury Street (see chapter 9). The other main gallery area, the Leather District around South Street, is muddling through the Central Artery/Third Harbor Tunnel project. You'll still find galleries in that neighborhood, between South Station and Chinatown, but you're equally likely to see bulldozers.

One way to see artists at work is to check listings in the *Globe* and *Herald* for information about open studio days in a particular neighborhood. The artists' communities in the South End, the Fort Point Channel area, and Somerville stage weekend events once or twice a year that allow visitors to meet artists in their work spaces (which are often their homes) and see what they're concocting. You might be asked to make a contribution to charity in exchange for a map of the studios.

BREWERIES

Boston Beer Company. 30 Germania St., Jamaica Plain. ☎ **617/368-5080.** www.samadams.com. $1 requested for guided tour; proceeds go to charity. Tours Thurs-Fri 2pm, Sat noon, 1, and 2pm; July-Aug, Wed 2pm. MBTA: Orange Line to Stony Brook; go left onto Boylston St. Walk 2 blocks and turn right onto Bismark St. at the Samuel Adams sign. Call for driving directions.

The Boston Beer Company produces Samuel Adams beer, widely considered (especially by Boston-area beer snobs) the best in the country. The brew is named after the same Samuel Adams whose statue is next to Faneuil Hall, the patriot, revolutionary—and brewer. Samuel Adams Boston Lager has been served at the White House and was the first American beer allowed to be sold in Germany. The company also brews Samuel Adams Scotch Ale, Cream Stout, Honey Porter, and Lightship, and six seasonal brews. During the 30-minute guided tour, you'll learn about the history and process of brewing and have a chance to sample the results.

Mass. Bay Brewing Co. 306 Northern Ave. ☎ **617/574-9551.** Free admission. Tours Fri-Sat, 1pm. MBTA: Red Line to South Station, or Blue Line to Aquarium. Follow Atlantic Ave. to the Northern Avenue Bridge, cross over, and take Northern Ave. past the World Trade Center and the Fish Pier; the brewery is on the left.

This company brews and bottles Harpoon Ale and other Harpoon products in small batches without preservatives. Visitors can sample the wares and see the stages of processing from the tap room, on an enclosed platform above the brewery floor. You're not allowed on the floor, however, and the machinery might not be running—this is really just an excuse to drink a little free beer. Parking is available; leave time if you take the T, because the closest stations are about a mile away.

7 Neighborhoods to Explore

This section attempts to answer briefly the second-most-asked question visitors have for Boston residents: "Where do people who live here go?" (The most-asked question is "Why aren't there more public bathrooms?" We wish we knew.)

Boston is a city of neighborhoods, some of which are touched on in the walking tours described in chapter 8. Here are several other areas that are fun to explore. Bear in mind that many of the buildings you will see are private residences, not tourist attractions. See chapter 6 for dining suggestions and chapter 9 for shopping tips.

BEACON HILL

MBTA: Red Line to Charles/MGH, or Green Line to Park St.

The original Boston settlers, clustered around what are now the Old State House and the North End, considered Beacon Hill outlandishly distant. Today the distance is a matter of atmosphere; climbing "the Hill" is like traveling back in time. Lace up your walking shoes (the brick sidewalks gnaw at anything fancier, and driving is next to impossible), wander the narrow streets, and admire the brick and brownstone architecture.

At Beacon and Park streets is a figurative high point (literally it's *the* high point): Charles Bulfinch's magnificent **State House.** The 60-foot **monument** at the rear illustrates the hill's original height, before the top was shorn off to use in the landfill projects of the 19th century. **Beacon and Mount Vernon streets** run downhill to commercially dense **Charles Street,** but if ever there was an area where there's no need to head in a straight line, it's this one. Your travels might take you past where Louisa May Alcott lived at 10 Louisburg Sq., Henry Kissinger at 1 Chestnut St., Julia Ward Howe at 13 Chestnut St., Edwin Booth at 29A Chestnut St., or Robert Frost at 88 Mount Vernon St. One of the oldest black churches in the country, the **African Meeting House,** is at 8 Smith Court.

Alcott probably wouldn't even be able to afford the rent for a home on **Louisburg Square** (say "*Lew*-is-burg") today. The lovely private park is surrounded by 22 homes where a struggling writer would more likely be an employee than a resident. The iron-railed square is open only to tenants with keys.

Your wandering will probably land you on Charles Street sooner or later, and after you've had your fill of the shops and restaurants, you might want to investigate the architecture of the **"flats,"** between Charles Street and the Charles River. Built on landfill, the buildings are younger than those higher up, but often just as eye-catching. This is the area where you'd look for signs that MTV's **"The Real World"** passed through—you might recognize the converted firehouse used as a residence; it's at Mount Vernon and River streets.

CHINATOWN

MBTA: Orange Line to Chinatown, or Green Line to Boylston.

This close-knit residential and commercial community is constantly pushing its borders, expanding into the nearly defunct "Combat Zone" (red-light district) on Washington Street and crossing the Massachusetts Turnpike extension into the South End. It's also expanding to include more Vietnamese and Cambodian residents. The Expressway, the downtown shopping district, the Theater District, and the Tufts University medical complex border the heart of Chinatown. You'll know you're there when the phone booths suddenly sprout pagoda tops.

Start your visit at Beach Street and the Surface Artery. There aren't many street signs, but you can't miss the three-story **Chinatown Gateway.** The gate with four marble lions was a bicentennial gift from the government of Taiwan.

Beach Street is the closest thing Chinatown has to a main drag, and the streets that cross it and run parallel are nearly as congested and equally as interesting. You'll see fish tanks full of entrees-to-be, fresh produce stands, gift shops, and markets. After wandering around for a while and working up an appetite, stop for **dim sum** (see chapter 6 for pointers). If you have room for dessert, stop at a bakery—perhaps

Impressions

And this is good old Boston,
The home of the bean and the cod,
Where the Lowells talk to the Cabots,
And the Cabots talk only to God.
 —John Collins Bossidy, toast at the Holy Cross College alumni dinner, 1910

As a family, the Bradlees had been around for close to three hundred years, but well
down the totem pole from the Lowells and the Cabots. Proper enough as proper
Bostonians went, but not that rich, and not that smart.
 —Former *Washington Post* executive editor Ben Bradlee, *A Good Life,* 1995

Hing Shing Pastry, 67 Beach St. (☎ **617/451-1162**) or **Ho Yuen Bakery,** 54
Beach St. (☎ **617/426-8320**)—for giant walnut cookies, pastries in the shape of
animals, fried sesame balls, and moon cakes. The wares in the gift shops run from
classic to cartoonish, and prices tend to be quite reasonable.

During the celebration of **Chinese New Year** (January or February, depending
on the moon), masses of people turn out even in the harshest weather to watch the
parade. Dragons dance in the streets, and firecrackers punctuate the musical accompaniment. In August, you'll see the **Festival of the August Moon,** a local street fair.
Call the **Chinese Merchants Association,** 20 Hudson St. (☎ **617/482-3972**), for
information on special events. The building's bronze bas-reliefs represent the eight
immortals of Taoism, and there are mirrored plaques along Oxford Alley to ward
off evil spirits.

Before you leave, you might want to stop at a food store for supplies to take
home. One of the largest in size and selection, the **88 Supermarket,** 50 Herald St.,
at Washington Street (☎ **617/423-1688**), is across the Pike extension. It's not just
Chinese—every ingredient of every Asian cuisine seems to be on the shelves somewhere, and the fresh produce ranges from lemons to lemongrass. In Chinatown
proper, **See Sun Co.,** 25 Harrison Ave. (☎ **617/426-0954**), isn't as large, but the
selection and prices are good.

THE SOUTH END

MBTA: Orange Line to Back Bay, or Green Line to Copley.

One of the city's most diverse neighborhoods is also one of its largest, but fans of
Victorian architecture won't mind the sore feet they have after trekking around the
South End.

The South End was laid out in the mid-19th century, slightly earlier than the
Back Bay; while the layout of the Back Bay echoes the boulevards of Paris, the South
End tips its hat to London. The main streets are broad, the side streets dotted with
pocket parks. The gentrification movement of the 1970s saw many South End
brownstones reclaimed from squalor and converted into luxury condominiums, but
even on run-down buildings, you'll see wonderful details.

With Back Bay Station to your left, walk down **Dartmouth Street,** crossing
Columbus Avenue. Proceed on Dartmouth and explore some of the streets that
extend to the left, including **Chandler, Lawrence, and Appleton streets.** This area
is known as **Clarendon Park.** Find your way to **Clarendon Street,** parallel to Dartmouth. At Tremont Street is the part of the South End you're most likely to see if
you're not out exploring. This is the area where businesses and restaurants surround

the **Boston Center for the Arts** (☎ **617/426-7700** for events; 617/426-0320 for box office). The BCA's **Cyclorama** building (the interior is dome-shaped), at 539 Tremont St., is listed on the National Register of Historic Places. Here you can see a show, have a meal, or continue your expedition. This is not the greatest neighborhood to roam through at night, but in daylight you can feel comfortable taking **Tremont Street** or **Columbus Avenue** (and wandering down the streets that run between them) all the way to Mass. Ave. From there, you can take the no. 1 bus to the Back Bay or into Cambridge, or the Orange Line downtown.

JAMAICA PLAIN

MBTA: Orange Line to Forest Hills.

You can combine a visit to the Arnold Arboretum (see "Parks & Gardens," above) with a stroll around Jamaica Pond or along Centre Street. Culturally diverse Jamaica Plain is less gentrified than the South End, with plenty of interesting architecture and considerably more open space. The pond is especially pleasant in good weather, when you'll see people walking, running, skating, fishing, picnicking, and sunbathing. Many of the 19th-century mansions overlooking the pond date to the days when families fled the oppressive heat downtown and moved to the "country" for the summer.

After you've had your fill of nature (or before you set out), Centre Street makes a good destination for wandering and snacking. Our favorite target, black-and-white cow motif and all, is **JP Licks Homemade Ice Cream,** 674 Centre St. (☎ **617/524-6740**). You'll find excellent vegetarian food at the **Centre Street Café,** 597 Centre St. (☎ **617/524-9217**) and nouveau Italian at **Bella Luna,** 405 Centre St. (☎ **617/524-6060**).

8 Cambridge

Cambridge is so closely associated with Boston that many people believe they're the same city—a notion both cities' residents and politicians would be happy to dispel. Cantabrigians are often considered more liberal and better educated than Bostonians, which is another idea that's sure to get you involved in a heated discussion. Take the Red Line across the river and see for yourself.

For a good overview, begin at the main Harvard T entrance. Follow the walking tour described in chapter 8, or set out on your own. At the **information booth** (☎ **617/497-1630**) in the middle of Harvard Square at the intersection of Mass. Ave., John F. Kennedy Street, and Brattle Street, trained volunteers dispense maps and brochures and answer questions Monday through Saturday from 9am to 5pm and Sunday from 1 to 5pm. From mid-June through Labor Day there are guided tours that include the entire old Cambridge area. Check at the booth for rates, meeting places, and times, or call ahead. If you prefer to sightsee on your own, you can purchase an Old Cambridge or East Cambridge walking guide prepared by the Cambridge Historical Commission.

Whatever you do, spend some time in **Harvard Square.** It's a hodgepodge of college and high school students, instructors, commuters, street performers, and sightseers. Near the information booth are two well-stocked newsstands, **Nini's Corner** and **Out of Town News** (where you can find out what's happening at home from the extensive collection of newspapers and magazines), and the **Harvard Coop.** There are restaurants and stores along all three streets that spread out from the center of the square and the streets that intersect them. If you follow **Brattle**

Cambridge Attractions

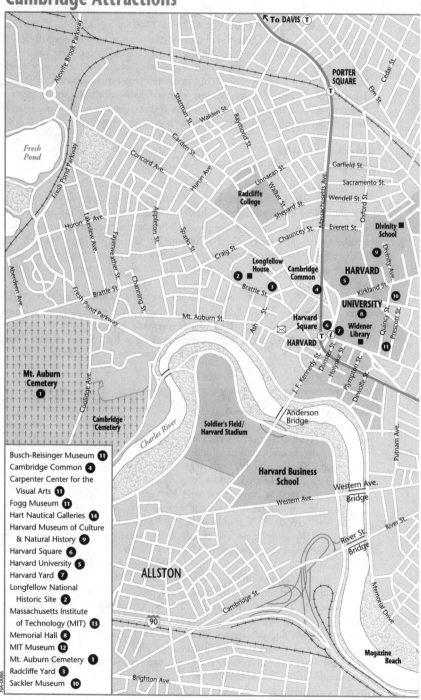

To DAVIS Ⓣ

PORTER
SQUARE
Ⓣ

Fresh
Pond

Alewife Brook Parkway

Sherman St.

Walden St.

Raymond St.

Garden St.

Concord Ave.

Fresh Pond Parkway

Huron Ave.

Linnean St.

Walker St.

Shepard St.

Garfield St.

Sacramento St.

Wendell St.

Massachusetts Ave.

Everett St.

Oxford St.

Cedar St.

Elm St.

Divinity
School ■

Huron Ave.

Lakeview Ave.

Fayerweather St.

Appleton St.

Sparks St.

Craig St.

Chauncey St.

Radcliffe
College

Longfellow
House

Cambridge
Common

Ⓨ

HARVARD

Divinity Ave.

Aberdeen Ave.

Brattle St.

Channing St.

Mt. Auburn St.

Ash St.

Brattle St.

②

③

④

⑤

⑥
Ⓣ ⓘ ⑦

UNIVERSITY

⑧

Harvard
Square

HARVARD

Kirkland St.

Widener
Library ■

Quincy St.

Prescott St.

⑩

⑪

J. F. Kennedy St.

Dunster St.

Holyoke St.

Plympton St.

Dewolfe St.

Putnam Ave.

Mt. Auburn
Cemetery
①

Coolidge Ave.

Cambridge
Cemetery

Charles River

Soldier's Field/
Harvard Stadium

Anderson
Bridge

Harvard Business
School

Western Ave.

Bridge

Western Ave.

River St.

River St.
Bridge

Memorial Drive

Busch-Reisinger Museum ⑪
Cambridge Common ④
Carpenter Center for the
  Visual Arts ⑪
Fogg Museum ⑪
Hart Nautical Galleries ⑭
Harvard Museum of Culture
  & Natural History ⑨
Harvard Square ⑥
Harvard University ⑤
Harvard Yard ⑦
Longfellow National
  Historic Site ②
Massachusetts Institute
  of Technology (MIT) ⑬
Memorial Hall ⑧
MIT Museum ⑫
Mt. Auburn Cemetery ①
Radcliffe Yard ③
Sackler Museum ⑩

ALLSTON

Cambridge St.

⑨0

Magazine
Beach

Brighton Ave.

NA-0086

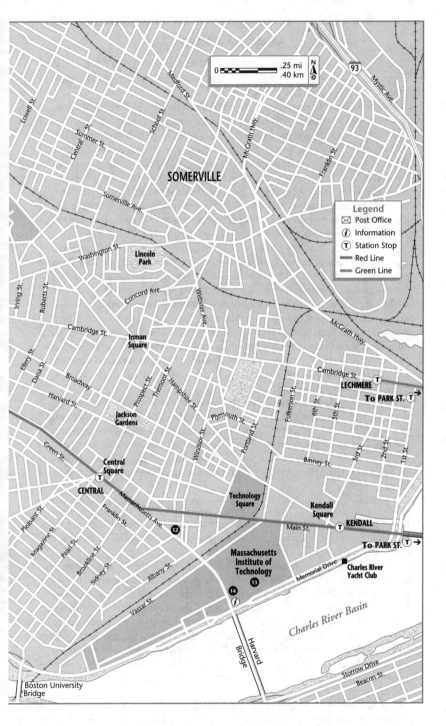

Celebrity Cemetery

Three important colonial burying grounds—Old Granary, King's Chapel, and Copp's Hill—are in Boston on the Freedom Trail (see chapter 8). The most famous cemetery in the area is in Cambridge.

Mount Auburn Cemetery, 580 Mount Auburn St. (☎ **617/547-7105**), the final resting place of many well-known people, is also famous simply for existing. Dedicated in 1831, it was the first of America's rural, or garden, cemeteries. The establishment of burying places removed from city and town centers reflected practical and philosophical concerns. Development was encroaching on urban graveyards, and the ideas associated with the Greek revival (the word "cemetery" derives from the Greek for "sleeping place") and Transcendentalism dictated that communing with nature take precedence over organized religion. Since the day it opened, Mount Auburn has been a popular place to retreat and reflect—in the 19th century, it was often the first place out-of-town visitors asked to go.

A modern visitor will find history and horticulture coexisting with celebrity. The graves of Henry Wadsworth Longfellow, Oliver Wendell Holmes, Julia Ward Howe, and Mary Baker Eddy are here, as are those of Charles Bulfinch, James Russell Lowell, Winslow Homer, Transcendentalist leader Margaret Fuller, and abolitionist Charles Sumner. In season, you'll see gorgeous flowering trees and shrubs (the Massachusetts Horticultural Society had a hand in the design). Stop at the office or front gate to pick up brochures and a map or to rent the 60-minute audiotape tour ($5; a $12 deposit is required), which you can listen to in your car or on a portable tape player. **The Friends of Mount Auburn Cemetery** (☎ **617/864-9646**) conduct workshops and lectures, and coordinate walking tours. Call for topics, schedules, and fees.

The cemetery is open daily from 8am to dusk; there is no admission charge. Animals and recreational activities such as jogging and picnicking are not allowed. MBTA bus routes no. 71 and 73 start at Harvard station and stop near the cemetery gates; they run frequently on weekdays, less often on weekends. By car (5 minutes) or on foot (30 minutes), take Mount Auburn Street or Brattle Street west from Harvard Square; just after the streets intersect, the gate is on the left.

Street to the residential area just outside the square, you'll come to a part of town known before and during the American Revolution as **"Tory Row"** because the residents were loyal to King George.

The ravishing yellow mansion at 105 Brattle Street is the ✪ **Longfellow National Historic Site** (☎ **617/876-4491**; www.nps.gov/long/index.htm), where the books and furniture have remained intact since the poet Henry Wadsworth Longfellow died there in 1882. Now a unit of the National Park Service, during the siege of Boston in 1775 to 1776 the house served as the headquarters of Gen. George Washington, with whom Longfellow was fascinated. The poet first lived there as a boarder in 1837, and when he and Fanny Appleton married in 1843, her father gave it to them as a wedding present. On a tour—the only way to see the house—you'll learn about the history of the building and its famous occupants.

The house is open from mid-March through mid-December. Tours are offered Wednesday through Sunday at 10:45 and 11:45am, and 1, 2, 3, and 4pm from June to October and on weekends from mid-March to May and November to mid-December; and Wednesday through Friday spring and fall at 12:30, 1:30, 2:30, and 3:30pm. Admission is $2 for adults, free for children under 17 and seniors.

Farther west, near where Brattle Street and Mount Auburn Street intersect, is **Mount Auburn Cemetery** (see "Celebrity Cemetery," above). It's a pleasant but long walk; you might prefer to drive or take the bus. Or you can return to the square and investigate Harvard.

HARVARD

Free, student-led tours leave from the **Events & Information Center** in Holyoke Center, 1350 Mass. Ave. (☎ **617/495-1573**), during the school year twice a day on weekdays and once on Saturday, except during vacations, and during the summer four times a day Monday through Saturday and twice on Sunday. Call for exact times; reservations aren't necessary. You're also free to wander on your own (see chapter 8). Note that Harvard buildings are integrated into the community as well as set apart from it—structures in use by the school typically have plaques or other identifying features on the front. The Events & Information Center has maps, illustrated booklets, and self-guided walking-tour directions, as well as a bulletin board where campus activities are publicized. You might want to check out the university's Web site (www.harvard.edu) before your trip.

The best-known part of the university is **Harvard Yard,** actually two large quadrangles. The **statue of John Harvard,** one of the school's original benefactors, is in the Old Yard, which dates to the college's founding in 1636. Most first-year students live in the dormitories here—even in the school's oldest building, **Massachusetts Hall** (1720), where the university president's office takes up the first floor. The other side of the Yard (sometimes called Tercentenary Theater because the college's 300th-anniversary celebration was held there) is home to the imposing **Widener Library,** named after a Harvard graduate who perished when the *Titanic* sank.

The architectural consistency at the center of the Yard frays at the edges and breaks up completely on the outside of the brick walls, often to good effect. On Quincy Street you'll find the curvilinear **Carpenter Center for the Visual Arts,** the only building in North America designed by the Swiss-French architect **Le Corbusier.** At the corner of Quincy and Cambridge streets is **Memorial Hall,** which, depending on your perspective, is either a monstrosity or a fitting monument to the Union soldiers who died in the Civil War. Behind the adjacent Science Center is the campus of **Harvard Law School;** on the far side of the Yard from the Law School, between Mass. Ave. and the river, are residential houses where many upperclassmen live (other dorms, formerly Radcliffe College residences, are northwest of the Yard).

Also on campus are two engaging museum complexes.

Harvard University Art Museums. 32 Quincy St. and 485 Broadway (at Quincy St.). ☎ **617/495-9400.** Admission to all 3 museums $5 adults, $4 seniors, $3 students, free for children under 18; free to all Sat 10am-noon. Mon-Sat 10am-5pm, Sun 1-5pm; closed major holidays. MBTA: Red Line to Harvard. Cross Harvard Yard diagonally from the T station and cross Quincy St., or turn your back on the Coop and follow Mass. Ave. to Quincy St., then turn left.

The Harvard art museums house a total of about 150,000 works of art in three collections, at the Fogg Art Museum, the Busch-Reisinger Museum, and the Arthur M. Sackler Museum. The exhibit spaces also serve as teaching and research facilities. You can take a 1-hour guided tour on weekdays September through June, and Wednesdays only in July and August.

Impressions

I should sooner live in a society governed by the first 2,000 names in the Boston
telephone directory than in a society governed by the 2,000 faculty members of Har-
vard University.
 —Yale alumnus William F. Buckley, Jr., *Rumbles Left and Right,* 1963

I won't say there aren't any Harvard graduates who have never asserted a superior
attitude. But they have done so to our great embarrassment and in no way represent
the Harvard I know.
 —Harvard president (and Stanford graduate) Derek C. Bok, 1984

The **Fogg Art Museum** (32 Quincy St., near Broadway) centers around an impressive 16th-century Italian stone courtyard, with two floors of galleries opening off it. You'll see something different in each of the 19 rooms—17th-century Dutch and Flemish landscapes, 19th-century British and American paintings and drawings, French paintings and drawings from the 18th century through the Impressionist period, contemporary sculpture, and changing exhibits. In the morning, you might also see bleary-eyed students heading to the classrooms on the third floor.

The **Busch-Reisinger Museum** in Werner Otto Hall (enter through the Fogg) opened in 1991 and is the only museum in North America devoted to the painting, sculpture, and decorative art of northern and central Europe—specifically Germany. Its encyclopedic collection also includes prints and illustrated books, and it is particularly noted for its early—20th-century collections, including works by Klee, Feininger, Kandinsky, and artists and designers associated with the Bauhaus.

The **Arthur M. Sackler Museum** (485 Broadway, at Quincy St.) houses the university's collections of Asian, ancient, and Islamic art. Included is an assemblage of Chinese jades and cave reliefs that's considered the best in the world, as well as Korean ceramics, Roman sculpture, Greek vases, and Persian miniature paintings and calligraphy.

Harvard University Museum of Cultural and Natural History. 26 Oxford St. ☎ **617/495-3045.** www.peabody.harvard.edu Admission $5 adults, $4 students and seniors, $3 children 3-13, free for children under 3; free to all Sat 9am-noon. Mon-Sat 9am-5pm, Sun 1-5pm; closed Jan 1, July 4, Thanksgiving, Dec 25. MBTA: Red Line to Harvard. Cross Harvard Yard, keeping the John Harvard statue on your right, and turn right at the Science Center. Take the first left onto Oxford St.

This fascinating museum is actually four institutions: the Botanical Museum, the Museum of Comparative Zoology, the Mineralogical & Geological Museum, and the Peabody Museum of Archaeology & Ethnology. The world-famous scholarly resource center offers interdisciplinary programs and exhibitions that tie in elements of all four collections. You'll certainly find something interesting here, be it a dinosaur skeleton, a hunk of meteorite, a Native American artifact, or the world-famous *Glass Flowers*.

The best-known of the four is the **Botanical Museum,** and the best-known display is the *Glass Flowers,* 3,000 models of more than 840 plant species devised between 1887 and 1936 by the German father-and-son team of Leopold and Rudolph Blaschka. You might have heard about them, and you might be skeptical, but it's true: they actually look real. Children love the **Museum of Comparative Zoology,** where the dinosaurs share space with preserved and stuffed insects and

In case you want to see the world.

At American Express, we're here to make your journey a smooth one. So we have over 1,700 travel service locations in over 120 countries ready to help. What else would you expect from the world's largest travel agency?

do more

Travel

http://www.americanexpress.com/travel

In case you want to be welcomed there.

We're here to see that you're always welcomed at establishments everywhere. That's why millions of people carry the American Express® Card — for peace of mind, confidence, and security, around the world or just around the corner.

do more®

In case you're running low.

We're here to help with more than 118,000 Express Cash locations around the world. In order to enroll, just call American Express before you start your vacation.

do more

Express Cash

And just in case.

We're here with American Express® Travelers Cheques and Cheques *for Two*.® They're the safest way to carry money on your vacation and the surest way to get a refund, practically anywhere, anytime.

Another way we help you…

do more

Travelers Cheques

animals that range in size from butterflies to giraffes. Young visitors also enjoy the dollhouse-like *Worlds in Miniature* display at the **Peabody Museum of Archaeology & Ethnology,** which represents people from all over the world in scaled-down homes. The Peabody also boasts the *Hall of the North American Indian,* where 500 Native American artifacts representing 10 cultures are on display. The **Mineralogical & Geological Museum** is the most specialized of the four—unless there's an interesting interdisciplinary display or you're really into rocks, your time can be more productively spent elsewhere.

The Peabody Museum has a terrific gift shop (☎ **617/495-2248**) packed with reasonably priced folk art and craftwork.

MASSACHUSETTS INSTITUTE OF TECHNOLOGY (MIT)

The public is also welcome at the Massachusetts Institute of Technology campus, a mile or so down Mass. Ave. from Harvard Square, across the Charles River from Beacon Hill and the Back Bay. Visit the **Information Center,** 77 Mass. Ave. (☎ **617/253-4795**), to take a free guided tour (weekdays, 10am and 2pm), or pick up a copy of the "Walk Around MIT" map and brochure. At the same address, the **Hart Nautical Galleries** (open weekdays, 9am to 5pm) contain ship and engine models that trace the development of marine engineering. The school has an excellent outdoor sculpture collection, which includes works by Picasso and Alexander Calder, and notable modern architecture by Eero Saarinen and I. M. Pei. Even more modern are the holography displays at the **MIT Museum,** 265 Mass. Ave. (☎ **617/253-4444**), where you'll also find works in more conventional media. The museum is open Tuesday through Friday from 10am to 5pm, weekends from noon to 5pm; it's closed on major holidays. Admission is $3 for adults, $1 for students, seniors, and children under 12.

To get to MIT, take the MBTA Red Line to Kendall/MIT. By car from Boston, cross the river at the Museum of Science, Cambridge Street, or Mass. Ave. and follow signs to Memorial Drive, where you'll usually be able to find parking during the day.

9 Especially for Kids

What can children do in Boston? A better question might be "What *can't* children do in Boston?" Just about every major destination in the city either is specifically designed to appeal to youngsters or can be easily adapted to do so. These attractions are covered extensively elsewhere in this chapter; here's the boiled-down version for busy parents.

Hands-on exhibits are a big draw at several institutions: The **New England Aquarium** (☎ **617/973-5200**), the **Computer Museum** (☎ **617/426-2800** or 617/423-6758), and the **Boston Tea Party Ship & Museum** (☎ **617/338-1773**). And you might get your hands on a baseball at a **Red Sox game** (see "Spectator Sports," below). The **Museum of Science** (☎ **617/723-2500**) not only is a hands-on paradise but also is home to the **Hayden Planetarium** and the **Mugar Omni Theater.**

For those in the mood to let other people do the work, take in the shows by the street performers at **Faneuil Hall Marketplace** (☎ **617/338-2323**).

Admission is free for those under 18 at the **Museum of Fine Arts** (☎ **617/267-9300**), which offers special weekend and after-school programs. Remember that what adults hear as "magnificent Egyptian collections," children hear as "mummies!"

The allure of seeing people the size of ants draws young visitors to the **John Hancock Observatory** (☎ 617/572-6429) and the **Prudential Center Skywalk** (☎ 617/236-3318). And they can see actual ants—though they might prefer dinosaurs—at the Museum of Comparative Zoology, part of the **Harvard University Museum of Cultural and Natural History** (☎ 617/495-3045).

Older children who have studied modern American history will enjoy a visit to the **John F. Kennedy Presidential Library and Museum** (☎ 617/929-4523). And kids interested in cars will like the **Museum of Transportation** (☎ 617/522-6547).

Young visitors who have read Robert McCloskey's children's classic, *Make Way for Ducklings*, will relish a visit to the **Public Garden,** as will fans of E. B. White's *The Trumpet of the Swan*, who certainly will want to ride on the **swan boats** (☎ 617/522-1966 or 617/624-7020).

Considerably less tame and much longer are **whale watches** (see "Organized Tours," below).

The walking-tour company **Boston By Foot,** 77 N. Washington St. (☎ 617/367-2345, or 617/367-3766 for recorded information; www. bostonbyfoot. com) has a special program, **Boston By Little Feet,** geared to children 6 to 12 years old. The 60-minute walk gives a child's-eye view of the architecture along the Freedom Trail and of Boston's role in the American Revolution. Children must be accompanied by an adult, and a map is provided. Tours run from May through October and meet at the statue of Samuel Adams on the Congress Street side of Faneuil Hall, Saturday at 10am, Sunday at 2pm, and Monday at 10am, rain or shine. The cost is $6 per person.

The **Historic Neighborhoods Foundation,** 99 Bedford St. (☎ 617/426-1885), offers a 90-minute "Make Way for Ducklings" tour ($7 adults, $5 children 5 and up, under 5 free). The tour, popular with children and adults, follows the path of the Mallard family described in Robert McCloskey's famous book and ends at the Public Garden. Every year on Mother's Day, the HNF organizes the Ducklings Day Parade.

Blue Hills Trailside Museum. 1904 Canton Ave., Milton. ☎ **617/333-0690.** Admission $3 adults, $2 seniors, $1.50 children ages 3-15, free for children under 3 and Massachusetts Audubon Society members with a valid membership card. Tues-Sun and Mon holidays 10am-5pm. Closed Jan 1, Thanksgiving, Dec 25.

An outdoor spot younger children will love is the Blue Hills Trailside Museum, at the 7,500-acre Blue Hills Reservation, a short drive south of Boston on Route 138 (I-93, exit 2B). There's room to hike, climb hills, and study replicas of the natural habitats of the Blue Hills. Visitors can climb the lookout tower, crawl through logs, experience a Native American wigwam, and see various native animals, including owls, honeybees, deer, otters, foxes, bobcats, snakes, and turtles. The big animals are in pens outside; the little ones are inside. Children can feed the ducks and deer. A wall of glass overlooks an outdoor pond. Weekend activities for children of all ages include story time (11am) and educational/instructional programs run by staff naturalists: a live "mystery animal" presentation (12:30pm), family hour (2pm), and the Naturalist's Choice (3:30pm). Special events change with the seasons and include maple sugaring in early spring, honey harvest in the fall, and owl prowls in January and February.

✪ **Children's Museum.** 300 Congress St. (Museum Wharf). ☎ **617/426-8855.** Admission $7 adults, $6 children ages 2-15 and seniors, $2 children age 1, free for children under 1; Fri 5-9pm, $1 for all. Sept-June Tues-Sun 10am-5pm, Fri until 9pm; June-Aug daily 10am-5pm, Fri until 9pm. Closed Jan 1, Thanksgiving, Dec 25, and Mon Sept-June, except Boston school vacations and holidays. MBTA: Red Line to South Station. Walk north on Atlantic Ave. 1 block, past the Federal Reserve Bank, and turn right onto Congress St. Call for information about discounted parking.

As you approach the Children's Museum, don't be surprised to see adults suddenly being dragged by the hand when their young companions realize how close they are and start running. You know the museum is near when you see the 40-foot-high red-and-white milk bottle out front. It makes both children and adults look small in comparison—which is probably part of the point. No matter how old, everyone behaves like a little kid at this delightful museum.

Not only is touching encouraged, it's practically a necessity. Children can stick with their parents or wander on their own, learning, doing, and role-playing. Some favorites: the **Dress-Up Shop,** a souped-up version of playing in Grandma's closet; **Under the Dock,** an environmental exhibit that teaches young people about the Boston waterfront and allows them to dress up in a crab suit; rooms where children can race golf balls on tracks through various structures and create soap bubbles in water tanks; and **Boats Afloat,** which has an 800-gallon play tank and a replica of the bridge of a working boat.

You'll also see **El Mercado,** a marketplace that immerses children in Hispanic culture, surrounding them with Spanish newspapers, ethnic food products, and salsa music. The **Climbing Sculpture** is a giant maze designed especially for children (adults might get stuck). Another oversize display is a desk with a phone so big it doubles as a slide. You can also explore a Japanese house and subway train from Kyoto (Boston's sister city) and learn about young adults in **Teen Tokyo.** Children under 4 and their caregivers have a special room, **Playspace,** that's packed with toys and activities.

Call ahead for information about special programs that can be scheduled during your visit. And be sure to check out the excellent gift shop (as if you have a choice).

Franklin Park Zoo. Northeast section of Franklin Park. ☎ **617/442-2002.** $6 adults, $5 seniors, $3 children 2-15, free for children under 2. Apr-Oct weekdays 10am-5pm, weekends and holidays 10am-6pm; Nov-Mar daily 10am-4pm. Closed Thanksgiving, Dec 25. MBTA: Orange Line to Forest Hills, then bus no. 16 to the main entrance.

Under the direction of new president Brian A. Rutledge, the Franklin Park Zoo has become more enjoyable for animals as well as people. New exhibits include homes for cheetahs, lions, and snow leopards, and **Bongo Congo,** which houses bongo antelopes, zebras, aoudad sheep, ibex, ostriches, warthogs, and vultures. The **African Tropical Forest** exhibit is a sprawling complex where you'll see more than 50 species of animals, including western lowland gorillas, who appear to be roaming free in an approximation of their natural habitat. If you're traveling with animal-mad youngsters, the Children's Zoo is both entertaining and educational; it's slated to undergo a major upgrade beginning in late 1998.

Note: It's a fairly long walk from the main gate and the parking area to the zoo itself, so leave plenty of time, especially for those with little legs.

Puppet Showplace Theatre. 32 Station St., Brookline. ☎ **617/731-6400.** E-mail: ShopPuppets@aol.com. Tickets $6. MBTA: Green line D train to Brookline Village.

The Puppet Showplace stages programs of favorite fables, ethnic legends, and folk and fairy tales from around the world. They are produced for children by professional puppeteers year-round in a lovely theater that seats 120. Historic puppets and puppet posters are on display, puppet-making workshops are offered, and toy puppets are for sale. Call for schedules and reservations.

10 Organized Tours

ORIENTATION TOURS
GUIDED WALKING TOURS

If you prefer not to explore on your own, **Boston By Foot,** 77 N. Washington St. (☎ **617/367-2345,** or 617/367-3766 for recorded information; www.bostonby-foot.com), offers excellent tours. From May through October, the nonprofit educational corporation conducts historical and architectural tours that focus on particular neighborhoods or themes. The rigorously trained guides are volunteers who encourage questions. All tours are $8 per person; reservations are not required. Tickets can be purchased from the guide. The 90-minute tours take place rain or shine; all excursions from Faneuil Hall start at the statue of Samuel Adams on Congress Street.

The **"Heart of the Freedom Trail"** tour starts at Faneuil Hall Tuesday through Saturday at 10am. Tours of **Beacon Hill** begin at the foot of the State House steps on Beacon Street weekdays at 5:30pm, Saturday at 10am, and Sunday at 2pm. **"Boston Underground"** looks at subterranean technology, including crypts, the subway, and the depression of the Central Artery. It starts at Faneuil Hall Sunday at 2pm. Other tours and meeting places are **Victorian Back Bay,** on the steps of Trinity Church, 10am Friday and Saturday; the **Waterfront,** at Faneuil Hall, Friday at 5:30pm and Sunday at 10am; and the **North End,** at Faneuil Hall, Saturday at 2pm.

Special theme tours can be arranged if there are enough requests. Included in the request tours are "Great Women of Boston," "Literary Landmarks," and a Chinatown tour.

The **Society for the Preservation of New England Antiquities** (☎ **617/ 227-3956;** www.spnea.org) offers a fascinating tour that describes and illustrates life in the mansions and garrets of Beacon Hill in 1800. "Magnificent and Modest," a 2-hour program, costs $10 and starts at the Harrison Gray Otis House, 141 Cambridge St., at 11am on Saturdays and Sundays from May through October. The price includes a tour of the Otis House, and reservations are recommended.

The **Historic Neighborhoods Foundation,** 99 Bedford St. (☎ **617/426-1885**) offers 90-minute walking tours in several neighborhoods, including Beacon Hill, the North End, Chinatown, the Waterfront, and the Financial District. Schedules change with the season, and the programs highlight points of interest to visitors while covering history, architecture, and topographical development. Tours usually cost about $6 per person; write or call for schedules and meeting places of tours during your visit.

The **Boston Park Rangers** (☎ **617/635-7383**) offer free guided walking tours of the Emerald Necklace, a loop of green spaces designed by pioneering American landscape architect Frederick Law Olmsted. You'll see and hear about the city's major parks and gardens, including Boston Common, the Public Garden, the Commonwealth Avenue Mall, the Muddy River in the Fenway, Olmsted Park, Jamaica Pond, the Arnold Arboretum, and Franklin Park. The full 6-hour walk includes a 1-hour tour of any of the sites. Call for schedules.

TROLLEY TOURS

A narrated trolley tour can give you an overview of the sights before you focus on specific attractions, or you can use the all-day pass to hit as many places as possible in 8 hours or so. Because Boston is so pedestrian friendly, this isn't the best choice

Duck, Duck, Loose

The most unusual way to see Boston is with ✪ **Boston Duck Tours** (☎ 617/ 723-DUCK). Sightseers board a "duck," a reconditioned World War II amphibious landing craft, on the Huntington Avenue side of the Prudential Center. The 80-minute narrated tour hits the high points, including Trinity Church, the Boston Public Library, the North End, Faneuil Hall, and the Old State House. The real high point comes when the duck lumbers down a ramp and splashes into the Charles River for a spin around the basin. The tours are pricey but great fun.

Tickets, available at the Prudential Center, are $19 for adults, $16 for seniors and students, $10 for children 4 to 12, and 25¢ for children under 4. Tours run every 30 minutes from 9am to 1 hour before sunset. Reservations are not accepted (except for groups of 16 or more), and tickets usually sell out, especially on weekends. Try to buy same-day tickets early in the day, or plan ahead and ask about the limited number of tickets available 2 days in advance. There are no tours from December through March.

for the able-bodied and unencumbered making a long visit, but if you are unable to walk long distances, traveling with children, or short on time, a trolley tour can be worth the money. The business is extremely busy and competitive, with various firms offering different stops in an effort to distinguish themselves from the rest. All cover the major attractions and offer informative narratives and anecdotes in their 90- to 120-minute tours; most offer free reboarding if you want to visit the sites.

Each tour is only as good as its guide, and quality varies widely—every few years one of the TV stations or newspapers runs an "exposé" of the wacky information a tour guide is passing off as fact. Have a grain of salt ready and be thankful you're not lugging the children.

Trolley tickets cost $17 to $20 for adults, less for children. Boarding spots are at hotels, historic sites, and tourist information centers. Each company paints its cars a different color. Orange-and-green **Old Town Trolleys** (☎ 617/269-7150 or 617/268-7010) are the most numerous, and Old Town is the only company that offers a tour of Cambridge. Minuteman Tours's **Boston Trolley Tours** (☎ 617/269-3626) are blue; **Beantown Trolleys** (☎ 617/236-2148) say "Gray Line" but are red; and **CityView Luxury Trolleys** (☎ 617/363-7899, or 800/ 525-2489 outside 617) are silver. The **Discover Boston Multilingual Trolley Tours** (73 Tremont St.; ☎ 617/742-0767) vehicle is white, and it conducts tours in Japanese, Spanish, French, German, and Italian.

SIGHTSEEING CRUISES

Take to the water for a taste of Boston's rich maritime history or a daylong break from walking and driving. You can cruise around the harbor or go all the way to Provincetown or Gloucester. The season runs from April through October, with spring and fall offerings often restricted to weekends. If you're traveling in a large group, call ahead for information about reservations and discounted tickets. And if you're prone to seasickness, check the size of the vessel for your tour before buying tickets; larger boats provide more cushioning and comfort than smaller ones.

Boston Harbor Cruises, 1 Long Wharf (☎ 617/227-4321 or 617/227-4320), offers narrated trips around the harbor. The 90-minute **historic sightseeing cruises,** which tour the Inner and Outer Harbor, depart at 11am and 1, 3, and 7pm (the sunset cruise). Tickets are $12 for adults, $10 for seniors, $8 for children under 12. The 45-minute *Constitution* **cruise** takes you around the Inner Harbor and docks at the Charlestown Navy Yard so that you can go ashore and visit the USS *Constitution.* Tours leave Long Wharf every hour on the half hour from 10:30am to 4:30pm, and on the hour from the navy yard from 11am to 5pm. The cruise is $7 for adults, $6 for seniors, and $5 for children. The same company offers service to **Georges Island,** where free water-taxi service to the rest of the Boston Harbor Islands is available (see the box "A Vacation in the Islands," later in the chapter).

Massachusetts Bay Lines (☎ 617/542-8000) offers 55-minute **harbor tours** from Memorial Day through Columbus Day. Cruises leave from Rowes Wharf on the hour from 10am to 6pm; the price is $8 for adults, $5 for children and seniors. The same company offers 3-hour **live-music cruises** (blues, Wednesday at 7pm; rock, Thursday at 7:30pm) for $12. You must be at least 21 and have a photo ID.

The **Charles Riverboat Company** (☎ 617/621-3001) offers 55-minute narrated cruises around the **lower Charles River basin.** Boats depart from the CambridgeSide Galleria on the hour from noon to 5pm. The company also conducts 55-minute tours that go in the opposite direction, through the **Charles River locks to Boston Harbor.** Boats depart from the CambridgeSide Galleria Mall; river tours leave on the hour from noon to 5pm, harbor tours once a day, at 10:30am. Tickets for either tour are $8 for adults, $6 for seniors, $5 for children 2 to 12.

For almost a full day at sea, Bay State Cruises's MV *Provincetown II* (☎ 617/457-1428) sails from Commonwealth Pier daily from mid-June to Labor Day, and on weekends in late May and September. Be at the pier by 9am (the water shuttle from Long Wharf leaves at 8:30 and costs $1) for the 3-hour trip to Provincetown, at the tip of Cape Cod. The return trip leaves at 3:30pm, giving you 3½ hours for shopping and sightseeing. Same-day round-trip fares are $30 for adults, $23 for senior citizens, and $21 for children. Bringing a bike costs $5 extra each way.

Bay State also offers cruises with **live entertainment** on Friday and Saturday at 8:30pm from late June through early September. Tickets are $15 to $20, depending on who's performing; you must be at least 21 and have a photo ID.

A.C. Cruise Line (☎ 800/422-8419 or 617/261-6633) offers a day trip to **Gloucester.** The *Virginia C II* leaves Pier 7 (290 Northern Ave.) daily from late June through Labor Day at 10am and returns at 5pm. You'll have about 2½ hours to explore Gloucester. Tickets are $18 for adults, $14 for senior citizens, $10 for children. A.C. Cruise Line also offers a 3-hour country-western dance cruise ($12) with live entertainment Thursdays at 8pm.

The elegant three-level *Odyssey* (☎ 617/654-9700; www.odyssey-cruises.com) serves weekday and Saturday lunch, Sunday brunch, dinner nightly, and hors d'oeuvres on the nightly "Midnight Prom Cruise." Cruises begin with an hour of dining on the 170-foot yacht, then last 2 to 3 hours; prices range from $27 for the prom cruise to $40 for Sunday brunch to $75 for Saturday dinner. The climate-controlled vessel leaves from Rowes Wharf. Reservations are recommended.

The *Spirit of Boston,* a sleek 192-foot harbor-cruise ship operated by Bay State Cruises (☎ 617/457-1450; www.spiritcruises.com), offers a New England lobster clambake luncheon cruise (daily from noon to 2:30pm) and a dinner dance cruise (nightly from 7 to 10pm). It sails from the World Trade Center. Call for prices and reservations.

WHALE WATCHING

The **New England Aquarium** (see "The Top Attractions," above) runs its own whale watches. For whale-watching trips based out of Cape Ann, see "A Whale of an Adventure," in chapter 11.

Boston Harbor Whale Watch (☎ **617/345-9866**) sends the 100-foot *Majestic* out to sea at speeds topping 20 knots and promises more time watching whales than trying to find them. Tours depart from Rowes Wharf beginning in mid-June and operate Friday, Saturday, and Sunday only through June. From July through early September, there's daily service. Departure times are 10am on weekdays, 9am and 2pm on weekends. Expect to spend about 4½ hours at sea. Tickets are $20 for adults, $18 for seniors and children under 13. Reservations are suggested, and discounted parking is available.

The following cruise companies also offer whale watches: **A.C. Cruise Line** (☎ **800/422-8419** or 617/261-6633), Tuesday through Sunday, leaving at 10:30am and returning at 5pm; adults $19, seniors $15, children under 12 $12. **Boston Harbor Cruises** (☎ **617/227-4321**), daily at 10am, returning at 3pm; adults $22, seniors $16, and children under 12 $19. **Massachusetts Bay Lines** (☎ **617/542-8000**), 5-hour cruises daily from late June through September 1; adults $24, children and seniors $18.

SPECIALTY TOURS
FOR KENNEDY BUFFS

Old Town Trolley (☎ **617/269-7150**) introduces visitors to "JFK's Boston" during a 3-hour tour that stops at John F. Kennedy's birthplace in Brookline and the presidential library in Dorchester (a co-presenter of the tour). The 3½-hour excursion starts at Atlantic Avenue and State Street and passes through the North End and Beacon Hill. Tickets are $22 for adults, $17 for seniors, and $12 for children, and they include admission to the John F. Kennedy National Historic Site (if space allows) and the Kennedy Library. Tours start at 9:30am on Friday, Saturday, and Sunday from Memorial Day through Labor Day.

FOR BEER NUTS

Old Town Trolley stages a tour of three brew pub/restaurants twice a month. The 3-hour journey includes stops at the Commonwealth Brewing Co. and Brew Moon Restaurant and Microbrewery in Boston, and John Harvard's Brew House in Cambridge. Food is served along with two 10-ounce beer samples at each location. Tickets are $38 and you must purchase them in advance by calling (☎ **617/269-7150**) for reservations.

11 Outdoor Activities

If you want to explore outdoors and you have Web access, while you're planning your trip, consult the incredibly helpful site maintained by the ✪ **Metropolitan District Commission** (www.magnet.state.ma.us/mdc/mdc_home.htm). It includes descriptions of properties and activities and has a planning area to help you make the most of your time.

BEACHES

The beaches in Boston proper (discussed below) are decent places to catch a cool breeze and splash around, but for real ocean surf, you'll need to head out of town.

NORTH SHORE BEACHES

North of Boston are sandy beaches that complement the rocky coastline. Two caveats: (1) it's not Florida, so don't expect 70° water (the operative word is "refreshing"), and (2) parking can be scarce, especially on weekends, and pricey—as much as $15 per car. If you can't set out early, wait till mid-afternoon and hope that the people who beat you to the beach in the morning have had enough. During the summer, lifeguards are on duty 9am to 5pm at larger public beaches. Surfing is generally permitted outside of those hours.

Probably the best-known North Shore beach is **Singing Beach,** off Masconomo Street in Manchester-by-the-Sea, named for the sound the sand makes under your feet. The legions of people walking six-tenths of a mile on Beach Street from the downtown commuter rail station attest to both the beach's reputation and the difficulty and expense of parking. Save some cash and aggravation by taking the MBTA (☎ 617/222-3200) from Boston's North Station.

Nearly as famous and equally popular is **Crane Beach,** off Argilla Road in Ipswich, part of a 1,400-acre barrier beach reservation. Expanses of white sand and fragile dunes lead down to Ipswich Bay, and the surf is calmer than that at less sheltered Singing Beach, but still quite chilly. Also on Ipswich Bay is Gloucester's **Wingaersheek Beach,** on Atlantic Street off Route 133. It has its own exit (number 13) off Route 128, about 15 minutes away. When you finally arrive, you'll find beautiful white sand, a glorious view, and more dunes.

Across the bay in Newburyport (follow signs from Route 1A or I-95) is **Plum Island.** The beach at the **Parker River National Wildlife Refuge** (☎ 508/465-5753) is *not* open all summer—it closes April 1 for piping plover nesting season. The areas not being used for nesting reopen July 1, and the rest of the beach opens in August when the birds are through with it. The currents are strong and can be dangerous, and there are no lifeguards—you might prefer to stick to surf fishing and exploring the trails that crisscross the gorgeous marshes and dunes and allow you to view the incredible variety of birds and wildlife.

Swimming or not, watch out for the **greenhead flies** at the North Shore beaches in late July and early August. They don't sting—they actually take little bites of flesh. Plan to bring or buy insect repellent.

Other good beaches in Gloucester are **Good Harbor Beach,** off Route 127A at Thatcher Road in East Gloucester, and **Half Moon Beach** and **Cressy's Beach,** at Stage Fort Park, off Route 127 near the intersection with Route 133. The park also contains a visitor information office (open only in summer), playgrounds, picnic and cookout areas, and the ruins of a Revolutionary War fortress.

Closer to Boston are **Nahant Beach** (follow the signs from the intersection of Route 1A and Route 129, near the Lynn-Swampscott border), which is large and extremely popular, and **Revere Beach.** Revere Beach is better known for its pickup scene than its narrow strip of sand; but the cruising crowds are friendly, and parking on the boulevard is free. The MBTA Blue Line has a Revere Beach stop; if you're driving, head north for smaller crowds at **Point of Pines,** which has its own exit off Route 1A. Across the street from the water is **Kelly's Roast Beef,** 410 Revere Beach Blvd. (☎ 617/284-9129), a local legend for its onion rings, fried clams, and roast beef sandwiches.

SOUTH SHORE BEACHES

Private beaches dominate the southern suburbs, but there are a couple of pleasant public options. In Hull (take Route 3 or 3A to Route 228), **Nantasket Beach** (☎ 617/925-4905) is right in town. It's popular with families for its fairly shallow water and the historic wooden carousel in a building across the street from the main parking lot. Nine-mile-long **Duxbury Beach** (take Route 3A to Route 139 north, and go right on Canal Street) makes an enjoyable stop on the way to Plymouth, if that's in your plans. **Plymouth Beach,** off Route 3A south of Plymouth at Warren Avenue, is smaller, with mild surf.

BOSTON BEACHES

The condition of Boston Harbor has improved considerably since its pollution was an issue in the 1988 presidential campaign. The **Metropolitan District Commission** (☎ 617/727-9547) is working to restore the run-down beaches under its purview, but it sometimes still has to fly red flags when swimming is not recommended (blue flags mean the water's fine). Be aware that these are very much neighborhood hangouts. In Dorchester, off Morrissey Boulevard, **Malibu Beach** and **Savin Hill Beach** are within walking distance of the Savin Hill stop on the MBTA Red Line. South Boston beaches are off Day Boulevard; you access them by taking the Red Line to Broadway or Green Line to Copley, then a bus marked "City Point" (routes 9, 10, and 11). Among them are **Castle Island, L Street,** and **Pleasure Bay.**

BIKING

Expert cyclists who feel comfortable with the layout of the city shouldn't have too much trouble navigating in traffic. If you don't fit that description, you're better off sticking to the many bike paths in the area and not tempting bloodthirsty drivers. State law requires that children under 12 wear helmets. Bicycles are forbidden on MBTA buses and the Green Line at all times and during rush hour on the other parts of the system. You must have a $5 permit (☎ 617/222-3302) to bring your bike on the Blue, Orange, and Red lines and commuter rail during non-rush hours.

The **Dr. Paul Dudley White Charles River Bike Path** is a 17.7-mile circuit that begins at Science Park (near the Museum of Science) and loops along both sides of the river to Watertown and back. You can enter and exit at many points along the way. Bikers share the path with lots of pedestrians, joggers, and in-line skaters, especially in Boston near the Esplanade and in Cambridge near Harvard Square. The path is maintained by the **Metropolitan District Commission,** or MDC (☎ 617/727-9547), as is the 5-mile **Pierre Lallement Bike Path,** in Southwest Corridor Park. It starts behind Copley Place and runs through the South End and Roxbury along the route of the MBTA Orange Line to Franklin Park. The 10½-mile **Minuteman Bikeway** starts at Alewife station at the end of the Red Line in Cambridge and runs through Arlington and Lexington to Bedford along an old railroad bed. It's a wonderful way to head out to the historic sites in Lexington, and it's popular with commuters and families. And on summer Sundays from 11am to 7pm, a 1½-mile stretch of **Memorial Drive** in Cambridge from Western Avenue to the Eliot Bridge (Central Square to west Cambridge) is closed to traffic. It's flat, it's not especially long, and it can get quite crowded.

Shops that rent require you to show a driver's license or passport and leave a deposit using a major credit card. Most charge around $5 an hour, with a minimum of at least 2 hours, or a flat daily rate of $20 to $25. In Boston, try **Earth Bikes 'n' Blades,** 35 Huntington Ave., near Copley Square (☎ 617/267-4733); **Back Bay Bikes & Boards,** 333 Newbury St., near Mass. Ave. (☎ 617/247-2336); and **Community Bicycle Supply,** 496 Tremont St., near East Berkeley Street (☎ 617/542-8623). At the Bedford end of the Minuteman Bikeway, **Pro Motion,** 1 Minuteman Bikeway, 111 South Rd., Bedford (☎ 781/275-1113), charges $5 per hour, with a 2-hour minimum.

For additional information, contact **MassBike** (☎ 617/491-7433; www. massbike.org), also known as the Bicycle Coalition of Massachusetts.

BOATING

Technically, riding a **swan boat** is boating. It's not exactly a transatlantic crossing, but it has been a classic Boston experience since 1877. The lagoon at the Public Garden (see "Parks & Gardens," above) turns into a fiberglass swan habitat every spring and summer and offers an excellent break in the midst of a busy day.

The pedal-powered swan boats (☎ 617/522-1966 or 617/624-7020) operate from the Saturday before Patriot's Day (the third Monday in April) through September, 10am to 6pm in summer, 10am to 4pm in spring and fall. The cost is $1.75 for adults, 95¢ for children.

There are also plenty of less-tame options (see "Sailing," below). The **Charles River Canoe and Kayak Center** (☎ 617/965-5110; www.charlesriv.com/~infor) has two locations, on Soldiers Field Road in Allston and at 2401 Commonwealth Ave. in Newton. Both centers rent canoes and kayaks (the Newton location also rents sculls), and lessons are available. From April through October, they open at 10am on weekdays and 9am on weekends and holidays, and close at dusk.

Non-inflatable water craft are allowed on the Charles River and in the Inner Harbor. If you plan to bring your own boat, call the Metropolitan District Commission **Harbor Master** (☎ 617/727-0537) for information about launches.

FISHING

Freshwater fishing is permitted at **Turtle Pond** in the Stony Brook Reservation in Hyde Park, at **Jamaica Pond** in Jamaica Plain, and on the banks of the **Charles River** (eating your catch is not recommended). For offshore saltwater fishing, the **Harbor Islands** are a good choice. You might also try fishing from the pier at **City Point** and the **John J. McCorkle Fishing Pier,** off Day Boulevard in South Boston.

For information on locations and regulations, call the Sport Fishing Information Line (☎ 800/ASK-FISH). Information is also available from the state **Division of Fisheries and Wildlife,** 100 Cambridge St., Room 1902, Boston, MA 02202 (☎ 617/727-3151), and in the fishing columns in the *Globe* and *Herald* on Fridays in the spring, summer, and fall.

GOLF

You won't get far in the suburbs without seeing a golf course, and with the recent explosion in the sport's popularity, you won't be the only one looking. Given a choice, opt for the lower prices and smaller crowds you'll find on weekdays.

At **Newton Commonwealth Golf Course,** 212 Kenrick St., Newton (☎ 617/630-1971), an excellent 18-hole layout designed by Donald Ross, par is 70 and greens fees are $21 on weekdays and $28 on weekends. At 9-hole, par-35 **Fresh Pond Golf Course,** 691 Huron Ave., Cambridge (☎ 617/349-6282), it's $15, or $22 to go around twice, on weekdays, and $18 and $28 on weekends. Within the city limits there are two 18-hole courses: the par-70 **William J. Devine Golf Course,** in Franklin Park, Dorchester (☎ 617/265-4084), where greens fees are $22 on weekdays and $25 on weekends; and **George Wright Golf Course,** 420 West St., Hyde Park (☎ 617/361-8313), where fees are $21 on weekdays and $24 on weekends.

The **Massachusetts Golf Association,** 175 Highland Ave., Needham, MA 02192 (☎ 781/449-3000; www.mga.org), represents more than 310 golf courses around the state and will send you a list of courses on request.

A Vacation in the Islands

Majestic ocean views, hiking trails, historic sites, rocky beaches, nature walks, campsites, and picnic areas abound in New England. To find them all together, take a 45-minute trip east (yes, *east*) of Boston. The **Boston Harbor Islands** (☎ 617/727-7676) were right under your nose if you arrived by plane, but until recently their accessibility wasn't widely known. They became a national park in 1997, and summer travelers can now take better advantage of their unspoiled beauty and easy access. For more information, stop at the **kiosk on Long Wharf** or consult the sources below.

There are 30 islands in the Outer Harbor, and at least a half-dozen are open for exploring, camping, or swimming. Bring a sweater or jacket. You can investigate on your own or take a ranger-led tour. Plan a day trip or even an overnight stay, but note that fresh water is not available on any of the islands.

Ferries run to the most popular, **Georges Island,** home of Fort Warren (1834), where Confederate prisoners were kept during the Civil War. Tours are offered periodically. The island has a visitor center, refreshment area, fishing pier, picnic area, and wonderful view of Boston's skyline. From there, free water taxis run to **Lovell, Gallops, Peddocks, Bumpkin,** and **Grape islands,** which have picnic areas and campsites. Lovell Island also has the remains of a fort (Fort Standish), as well as a sandy beach; it's the only harbor island with supervised swimming in the chilly water.

Newly included in the national park system and administered as a National Park Partnership, the Boston Harbor Islands National Recreation Area (www.nps.gov/boha/index.htm) is the focus of a public-private project designed to make the islands more interesting and accessible. **Boston Harbor Cruises** (☎ 617/227-4321) serves Georges Island from Long Wharf; the trip takes 45 minutes, and tickets are $7.50 for adults, $6.50 for seniors, $5.50 for children under 12. Cruises depart at 10am, noon, and 2pm in the spring and fall, and daily on the hour from 10am to 4pm in the summer. Water taxis and admission to the islands are free.

The **Metropolitan District Commission** (☎ 617/727-5290; www.magnet.state.ma.us/mdc/harbor.htm) administers Georges, Lovell, and Peddocks islands; the state **Department of Environmental Management** (☎ 617/740-1605) oversees Gallops, Grape, and Bumpkin islands. For more information, contact the Friends of the Boston Harbor Islands (☎ 617/740-4290; www.tiac.net/users/fbhi).

HIKING

The **Metropolitan District Commission** (☎ 617/727-0460) maintains hiking trails at several reservation parks throughout the state, some of which are within short driving distance of the city. They include the **Blue Hills Reservation** in Milton, **Beaverbrook Reservation** in Belmont, **Breakheart Reservation** in Saugus, **Hemlock Gorge** in Newton Upper Falls, the **Middlesex Fells Reservation** in five communities north of Boston, and **Belle Isle Marsh Reservation** in East Boston.

The **Boston Harbor Islands** also offer great hiking; it takes a half-day's hike to circle the largest island, Peddocks. See the box "A Vacation in the Islands," above.

ICE SKATING

The skating rink at the Boston Common **Frog Pond** (☎ 617/635-2197) underwent extensive renovations in 1997 and quickly became a popular cold-weather destination. It's an open surface with an ice-making system and a clubhouse where you can rent skates for $5; admission is $3 for adults, free for children under 14.

There's also skating at the lagoon at the **Public Garden** (see "Parks & Gardens," above), but the surface depends on New England's capricious weather.

IN-LINE SKATING

As with biking, unless you're very confident of your ability and your knowledge of Boston traffic, staying off the streets is a good idea.

A favorite spot for in-line skaters is the **Esplanade,** between the Back Bay and the Charles River. It continues onto the bike path that runs to Watertown and back, but be aware that after you leave the Esplanade the pavement isn't totally smooth, which can lead to mishaps. Your best bet is to wait for a Sunday in the summer, when **Memorial Drive** in Cambridge is closed to traffic. It's a perfect surface.

If you didn't bring your skates, you have several options for renting. A former Olympic cyclist and speed skater runs **Eric Flaim's Motion Sports,** 349 Newbury St. (☎ **617/247-3284**). Or try **Back Bay Bikes & Boards,** 333 Newbury St. (☎ **617/247-2336**); the **Beacon Hill Skate Shop,** 135 Charles St. South (☎ **617/482-7400**); **Earth Bikes 'n' Blades,** 35 Huntington Ave. (☎ **617/ 267-4733**); or **Ski Market,** 860 Commonwealth Ave. (☎ **617/731-6100**).

The **InLine Club of Boston's** Web site (www.sk8net.com/icb) offers up-to-date event and safety information and an extremely clever logo.

JOGGING

The concierge or desk staff at your hotel might be able to provide a map with suggested jogging routes. If you're staying close enough to the river, the bridges allow for circuits of various lengths. Other sources of information include the **Metropolitan District Commission** (☎ **617/727-1300**) and the **Bill Rodgers Running Center** in Faneuil Hall Marketplace (☎ **617/723-5612**). As in any large city, stay out of park areas (including the Esplanade) at night.

SAILING

You don't have to get wet to enjoy the glorious sight of sailboats filling up the Charles River basin or the Inner Harbor. If you want to take part, you have several options.

Community Boating, Inc., 21 Embankment Road, on the Esplanade (☎ **617/523-1038**), offers sailing lessons and boating programs for children and adults from April to November. It runs on a co-op system; a 30-day adult membership is $65. The **Courageous Sailing Center** (☎ **617/242-3821**) at Charlestown Navy Yard offers youth program lessons year-round. A five-lesson program (one in the classroom, four on the water) is $125. The **Boston Sailing Center,** 54 Lewis Wharf (☎ **617/227-4198**), offers lessons for sailors of all ability levels. The center is open all year (even for "frostbite" racing in the winter). Ten classes (five indoors, five outdoors) and a 35-day membership will run you $495. And the **Boston Harbor Sailing Club,** 200 High St., at Rowes Wharf (☎ **617/345-9202**), offers rentals and instruction. A package of four classes, 16 hours of on-water instruction, and a 30-day membership is $414. Private lessons (3-hour minimum) are $20 an hour plus the rental of the boat (from $25 an hour) plus tax.

SKIING

Generally speaking, "skiing" means Vermont or New Hampshire, but that doesn't rule out cross-country action in the Boston area. About 30 minutes from downtown, Charles River Recreation operates the **Weston Ski Track,** 200 Park Rd., on the Leo J. Martin Golf Course (☎ **781/891-6575;** www.charlesriv.com/~infor), from mid-December to mid-March. The 15 kilometers of groomed trails include a lighted 3-kilometer track, and rentals and instruction are available. The track is open weekdays from 10am to 10pm, Saturday from 9am to 8pm, and Sunday from 9am to 6pm.

Should you happen to have your cross-country skis with you after a monster snowstorm, head for **Commonwealth Avenue** in the Back Bay early in the morning and join the crowd.

Finally, if you insist on downhill skiing, be aware that Boston's official elevation is 20 feet. The closest downhill facility isn't pulling any punches—it has "hills" in its name. The **Blue Hills Ski Area,** 4001 Washington St., Canton (☎ **617/ 828-5090**), has a 350-foot vertical drop. Night skiing, rentals, and lessons are available. Lift tickets are $21 on weekends, $16 on weekdays. Canton is 40 minutes south of Boston on I-93.

TENNIS

Public courts are available throughout the city at no charge. They are maintained by the **Metropolitan District Commission** (☎ **617/727-1300**). To find the one nearest you, call the MDC or ask the concierge or desk staff at your hotel. Well-maintained courts near downtown that seldom get busy until after work are located at several spots on the **Southwest Corridor Park** in the South End (there's a nice one near West Newton Street) and off Commercial Street near the North Washington Street bridge in the **North End.** The courts in **Charlesbank Park,** overlooking the river next to the bridge to the Museum of Science, are more crowded during the day.

12 Spectator Sports

Boston's well-deserved reputation as a great sports town derives in part from the days when at least one of the professional teams was one of the world's best. With the exception of the Patriots, who play in suburban Foxboro, none of them has done much lately, but passions still run deep—insult the local teams and be ready to defend yourself. (And if the Red Sox win the 1998 World Series after this book goes to press, go ahead and call us on it—but pick Granddad off the floor first.) This enthusiasm applies to some college sports as well, particularly hockey, in which the Division I schools are fierce rivals.

In September 1995, the **FleetCenter** opened behind 67-year-old Boston Garden and the "*Gah*-den" shut down. The narrow, cramped seats and obstructed views in the incredibly steep Garden were replaced by cushy chairs in a wide-open bowl-shaped arena, and the feeling of being right on top of the action was replaced by the feeling of watching from a distance. Bring binoculars. One constant is the basketball floor, a collection of wood parquet tiles that made the trip to the new building.

The FleetCenter and the Garden History Center, 150 Causeway St. (☎ **617/624-1518;** www.fleetcenter.com), are open for tours; call for schedules during your visit. Tickets are $6 for adults, $5 for seniors and students, and $4.50 for children under 12.

BASEBALL

No experience in sports matches watching the **Boston Red Sox** play at **Fenway Park,** which they do from early April to early October, and later if they make the

Impressions

I never saw such enthusiastic fans as the ones in Boston.
                    —Pittsburgh Pirates shortstop Honus Wagner, 1903

play-offs. The quirkiness of the oldest park in the major leagues (1912) and the fact that (at press time) the team last won the World Series in 1918 only add to the mystique. A hand-operated scoreboard is built into the Green Monster, or left-field wall (watch carefully during a pitching change—the left fielder from either team might suddenly disappear into the darkness to cool off), and the wall itself is such a celebrity that it's often called simply The Wall. It's 37 feet tall, a mere 298 feet from home plate (don't believe the sign), and irresistibly tempting to batters who ought to know better. On two vertical white lines on the scoreboard you'll see Morse code for the initials of late owners Thomas A. and Jean R. Yawkey.

The crowds can be as interesting as the architecture. You'll see Cub Scouts on a field trip, positive that they're going to catch their first foul ball, and season-ticket holders in their eighties, positive that this is finally the year. Fans wedge themselves into narrow, uncomfortable seats close to the field, strike up conversations with total strangers, reminisce, and make bold predictions. A recent fan-relations campaign called "Friendly Fenway" has produced better-mannered employees, a greater variety of concession items (but not lower prices), and expanded family-seating sections, but for the most part the campaign is window dressing. You're in an intensely green place that's older than your grandparents, inhaling a Fenway Frank and wishing for a home run—what could be better?

Practical concerns: Compared with its modern brethren, Fenway is tiny. Tickets go on sale in early December for the following season, and the earlier you order, the better chance you'll have of landing seats during your visit. Forced to choose between tickets for a low-numbered grandstand section (say, 10 or below) and less-expensive bleacher seats, go for the bleachers. They can get rowdy during night games, but the view is better from there than from the deep right-field corner. If you plan to be in town around the same time as the Marathon, your chances of landing tickets for Patriot's Day aren't great (the game starts at 11am so that fans can, theoretically, be in Kenmore Square to watch the leading runners pass by), but don't despair. Throughout the season, a limited number of standing-room tickets go on sale the day of the game, and there's always the possibility that tickets will be returned. It can't hurt to check, especially if the team isn't playing well. The fans are incredibly loyal, but they're not all obsessed.

The **Fenway Park ticket office** (☎ **617/267-8661** for information, 617/267-1700 for tickets; www.redsox.com) is at 24 Yawkey Way, near the corner of Brookline Avenue. Tickets for people with disabilities and in no-alcohol sections are available. Smoking is not allowed in the park. Games usually begin at 7pm on weeknights and 1pm on weekends. Take the MBTA Green Line (B, C, or D train) to Kenmore, or D train to Fenway.

Fenway is the site of the 1999 Major League Baseball **All-Star Game.** See chapter 2 for more details.

BASKETBALL

The FleetCenter will play host to the opening rounds of the **NCAA Division I Men's Basketball Tournament** on March 12 and 14, 1999. See chapter 2 for more details.

Sixteen National Basketball Association championship banners hang from the ceiling of the FleetCenter, testimony to the glorious history of the **Boston Celtics.** Unfortunately, the most recent is from 1986. After a grim period following Larry Bird's retirement in 1992, however, the team seems to be back on track. Celebrity coach Rick Pitino has a young roster that might be making some noise by the time you visit.

The Celtics play from early October to April or May; when a top contender is visiting, you might have trouble buying tickets. Prices are as low as $10 for some games and top out at $70. For information, call the FleetCenter (☎ **617/ 624-1000;** www.bostonceltics.com); for tickets, call Ticketmaster (☎ **617/ 931-2000**). To reach the FleetCenter, take the MBTA Green or Orange Line or commuter rail to North Station.

The local college teams are competitive but not world-beaters. The schools and venues: **Boston College,** Conte Forum, Chestnut Hill (☎ **617/552-3000**); **Boston University,** Walter Brown Arena, 285 Babcock St. (☎ **617/353-3838**); **Harvard University,** Lavietes Pavilion, North Harvard Street, Allston (☎ **617/495-2211**); and **Northeastern University,** Matthews Arena, St. Botolph St. (☎ **617/373-4700**).

DOG RACING

Greyhounds race at **Wonderland Park** (☎ **617/284-1300**), and the day's entries appear in the *Globe* and *Herald*. The park is off Route 1A in Revere; the MBTA Blue Line has a Wonderland stop.

FOOTBALL

The **New England Patriots** (☎ **800/543-1776;** www.patriots.com) were playing to standing-room-only crowds even before they won the American Football Conference title in 1997 and went to the Super Bowl (they lost). They play from August through December (or January if they make the play-offs) at Foxboro Stadium on Route 1, about a 45-minute drive south of the city. You can drive (leave lots of extra time) or catch a bus from the entrance of South Station, the Riverside T station, or Shopper's World in Framingham, west of the city. Tickets ($23 to $60) almost always sell out. Plan as far in advance as you can.

Boston College, another tough ticket, is the only Division I-A college football team in New England. The Eagles play at Alumni Stadium in Chestnut Hill (☎ **617/552-3000**). The area's Division I-AA teams are **Harvard University,** Harvard Stadium, North Harvard Street, Allston (☎ **617/495-2211**); and **Northeastern University,** Parsons Field, Kent Street, Brookline (☎ **617/373-4700**).

GOLF TOURNAMENTS

The **Ryder Cup** will take place September 21 through 26, 1999, at The Country Club in Brookline. See chapter 2 for more details.

Two of the three major tours get within about an hour of downtown Boston. The tournaments have changed their schedules several times in recent years; call ahead for dates and other information. The **Welch's Championship,** an LPGA Tour event, is at Blue Hill Country Club in Canton (☎ **617/828-2000**). The **Bank of Boston Senior Classic** (☎ **508/371-0116**), a Senior PGA Tour event, takes place at Nashawtuc Country Club in Concord. The numerous amateur events for fun and charity are listed regularly in the *Globe* and *Herald*.

HOCKEY

The **Boston Bruins** are in roughly the same condition as the Celtics—burdened by history and looking to the future. In 1997, for the first time in 3 decades, the Bruins failed to make the play-offs. Their games are exciting, especially if you happen to be in town at the same time as the archrival Montreal Canadians, but incredibly expensive ($43 to $70). Tickets for many games sell out early despite being among the priciest in the league. For information, call the FleetCenter (☎ **617/624-1000;** www.bostonbruins.com); for tickets, call Ticketmaster (☎ **617/931-2000**). To reach the FleetCenter, take the MBTA Green or Orange Line or commuter rail to North Station.

Economical fans who don't have their hearts set on seeing a pro game will be pleasantly surprised by the quality of local **college hockey.** Even for sold-out games, standing-room tickets are usually available the night of the game. Local teams regularly hit the national rankings; they include **Boston College,** Conte Forum, Chestnut Hill (☎ **617/552-3000**); **Boston University,** Walter Brown Arena, 285 Babcock St. (☎ **617/353-3838**); **Harvard University,** Bright Hockey Center, North Harvard Street, Allston (☎ **617/495-2211**); and **Northeastern University,** Matthews Arena, St. Botolph Street (☎ **617/373-4700**). These four are the Beanpot schools, who play a tradition-steeped tournament on the first two Mondays of February at the FleetCenter.

HORSE RACING

✪ **Suffolk Downs,** 111 Waldemar Ave., East Boston (☎ **617/567-3900;** www.suffolkdowns.com), reopened under new management in 1992 after being closed for several years and being ghastly for years before that. Today it's one of the best-run smaller tracks in the country, an excellent family destination (really), sparkling clean, and the home of the Massachusetts Handicap, run in early June. Horse of the Year Cigar won the MassCap in 1995 and 1996, conferring instant cachet on the event and the facility. The season runs from early October to mid-June, and there are extensive simulcasting options during and after the live racing season. The day's entries appear in the *Globe* and the *Herald.* The track is off Route 1A, about a half-mile from Logan Airport; the MBTA Blue Line has a Suffolk Downs station.

MARATHON

Every year on Patriot's Day (the third Monday in April), the ✪**Boston Marathon** rules the roads from Hopkinton to Copley Square in Boston. Cheering fans line the entire route. An especially nice place to watch is tree-shaded Commonwealth Avenue between Kenmore Square and Mass. Ave., but you'll be in a crowd wherever you stand, particularly near the finish line in front of the Boston Public Library. For information about qualifying, contact the **Boston Athletic Association** (☎ **617/236-1652;** www.bostonmarathon.org).

ROWING

In late October, the **Head of the Charles Regatta** (☎ **617/864-8415**) attracts more rowers than any other crew event in the country to Boston and Cambridge. Some 4,000 oarsmen and oarswomen race against the clock for 4 miles from the Charles River basin to the Eliot Bridge in west Cambridge. Tens of thousands of spectators socialize and occasionally deign to watch the action, which runs nonstop on Saturday afternoon and all day Sunday.

Spring crew racing is far more exciting than the "head" format; the course is 2,000 meters and races last just 5 to 7 minutes. Men's and women's collegiate events take place on Saturday mornings in April and early May in the Charles River basin. You'll have a perfect view of the finish line from Memorial Drive between the MIT boathouse and the Hyatt Regency. To find out who's racing, check the Friday *Globe* sports section.

SOCCER

The **New England Revolution** (☎ 508/543-0350) of Major League Soccer plays at Foxboro Stadium on Route 1 from April through July. Tickets are available through Ticketmaster (☎ 617/931-2000), which charges a service fee. Unless the team or its opponent is doing incredibly well, buying tickets the day of the match shouldn't be too difficult. Be sure to leave extra time to negotiate the congested roads near the stadium.

TENNIS TOURNAMENT

The **U.S. Tennis Championship at Longwood** takes place in August at the Longwood Cricket Club, 564 Hammond St., Brookline (☎ 617/731-4500). Call for tickets and information about the weeklong event, sometimes used as a tune-up for the U.S. Open. The finals often sell out early, but demand isn't as high for preliminary matches.

8 Boston Strolls

Boston calls itself "America's Walking City," and it lives up to the name. The narrow, twisting streets that make driving such a headache are a treat for pedestrians, who are never far from something worth seeing. The central city is compact—walking east to west quickly from one end to the other takes about an hour—and dotted with historically and architecturally interesting buildings and neighborhoods.

In this chapter you'll find three tours of **Boston** and one of **Harvard Square** in Cambridge. The **Freedom Trail,** which links 16 historical sights with a 3-mile red line on the sidewalk first painted in 1958, is included (with some detours) in tours 1 and 2.

Remember to wear comfortable walking shoes, and if you're not inclined to pay designer prices for designer water, bring your own bottle and fill it with ice at the hotel. By the time it's ready for you, you'll be ready for it.

WALKING TOUR 1
Downtown Boston & Beacon Hill

Start: Boston Common (MBTA Green or Red Line to Park Street station).

Finish: Faneuil Hall (Congress and North streets).

Time: At least 2 hours, and possibly 3, depending on how long you spend at the attractions. If you elect to continue to Museum Wharf, add at least an hour.

Best Times: Early morning to early afternoon.

Worst Times: Mid-afternoon, when you will be rushed to see the sights before closing time.

From Park Street station, exit at the corner of Park and Tremont streets, the easternmost corner of:

1. **Boston Common.** In 1634, when their settlement was just 4 years old, the town fathers paid the Rev. William Blackstone £30 for this property. In 1640 it was set aside as common land. In the years since, the 50 or so acres of the country's oldest public park have fed cows; housed soldiers; and witnessed hangings, protest marches, and visits by dignitaries. Today it's a bit run-down, especially compared with the adjacent Public Garden, but it buzzes with activity all day. You might see a demonstration, a musical

Walking Tour 1—Downtown Boston & Beacon Hill

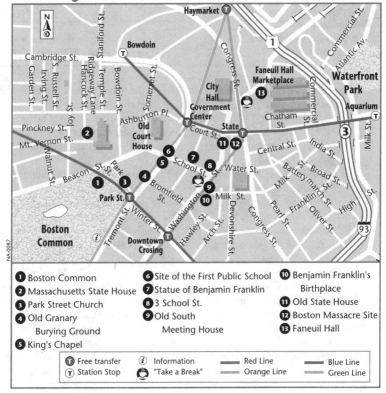

1 Boston Common
2 Massachusetts State House
3 Park Street Church
4 Old Granary
    Burying Ground
5 King's Chapel
6 Site of the First Public School
7 Statue of Benjamin Franklin
8 3 School St.
9 Old South
    Meeting House
10 Benjamin Franklin's
    Birthplace
11 Old State House
12 Boston Massacre Site
13 Faneuil Hall

T Free transfer   *(i)* Information   ━━━ Red Line   ━━━ Blue Line
(T) Station Stop   "Take a Break"   ━━━ Orange Line   ━━━ Green Line

performance, a picnic lunch, or a game of tag, but you won't see a cow (except during the Boston Dairy Festival in early June). Cows have been banned since 1830, which seems to be one of the few events related to the Common that isn't commemorated with a plaque. One of the loveliest markers is on our route; head up the hill from the train station inside the fence, not on the sidewalk. At Beacon Street is a memorial designed by **Augustus Saint-Gaudens** to celebrate the deeds (indeed, the very existence) of Col. Robert Gould Shaw and the Union Army's **54th Massachusetts Colored Regiment,** who fought in the Civil War. You might remember the story of the first American army unit made up of free black soldiers from the movie *Glory.*

Across Beacon Street is the:

2. Massachusetts State House (☎ **617/727-3676**). Boston is one of the only American cities where a building whose cornerstone was laid in 1795 (by Gov. **Samuel Adams**) would be called the "new" anything. Nevertheless, this is the new State House, to distinguish it from the Old State House, which you'll read about shortly. The great Federal-era architect **Charles Bulfinch** designed the central building of the state capitol, and the copper sheathing that replaced shingles on the dome in 1802 was manufactured by **Paul Revere.** The dome is now covered in golf leaf; during the blackouts of World War II, it was painted black. The state legislature, formally named the Massachusetts General Court, meets here. The House of Representatives congregates under a wooden fish, the **Sacred Cod.** John Rowe, known as "Merchant" Rowe (Rowes Wharf bears his name),

Just walking around Boston is amazing.
—*Good Will Hunting* star Robin Williams, 1998

donated the carving in 1784 as a reminder of the importance of fishing to the local economy. Tours (free, both guided and self-guided) leave from the second floor. Whether or not you decide to go inside, be sure to study some of the many statues outside the building. Subjects range from **Mary Dyer,** a Quaker hanged on the Common in 1660 for refusing to abandon her religious beliefs, to President **John F. Kennedy.**

Leaving the State House, walk down **Park Street**—laid out by Bulfinch in 1804—and look back at the second-floor balcony, where the governor sometimes steps outside for a breath of air. At the foot of the hill at Tremont Street is:

3. **Park Street Church,** 1 Park St. (☎ **617/523-3383**). Henry James described this 1809 structure as "the most interesting mass of bricks and mortar in America." Under its 217-foot steeple, this church has accumulated an impressive number of firsts: the first missionaries to Hawaii left from here in 1819; **William Lloyd Garrison** gave his first antislavery speech here on July 4, 1829; **"America"** ("My Country 'Tis of Thee") was first sung here on July 4, 1831. You're standing on **"Brimstone Corner,"** named either for the passion of the Congregational ministers who have declaimed from the pulpit or for the fact that during the War of 1812, gunpowder (made from brimstone) was stored in the basement. This was part of the site of a huge granary that became a public building after the Revolutionary War, when it was no longer needed for the storage of grain. In the 1790s the sails for the USS *Constitution* were manufactured in that building.

From late June to August, the church is open from 9:30am to 4pm Tuesday through Saturday. Sunday services are at 9 and 10:45am and 5:30pm year-round.

Walk away from the Common on Tremont Street. On your left is the:

4. **Old Granary Burying Ground.** This cemetery, established in 1660, was once part of Boston Common. You'll see the graves of patriots **Samuel Adams, Paul Revere, John Hancock,** and **James Otis;** merchant **Peter Faneuil** (spelled "Funal"); Benjamin Franklin's parents; the victims of the **Boston Massacre** (five colonists shot during a skirmish with British troops on March 5, 1770); and the wife of Isaac Vergoose, otherwise known as **"Mother Goose"** from the nursery rhymes of the same name. Note that gravestone rubbing, however tempting, is illegal in Boston's historic cemeteries. Open daily from 8am to 4pm.

Turn left as you leave the cemetery, and continue 1½ blocks on Tremont Street, crossing it at some point. At the corner of School Street is:

5. **King's Chapel,** 58 Tremont St. (☎ **617/523-1749**). Architect **Peter Harrison** sent the plans for this building from Newport, Rhode Island, in 1749. Rather than replacing the existing wooden chapel, the granite edifice was constructed around it. Completed in 1754, it was the **first Anglican church in Boston.** George III sent gifts, as did Queen Anne and William and Mary, who presented the communion table and chancel tablets (still in use today) before the church was even built. The Puritan colonists had little use for the royal religion; after the Revolution, this became the **first Unitarian church in America.** Unitarian Universalist services are conducted here, using the Anglican *Book of Common Prayer.* The chapel is open Tuesday through Saturday from 10am to 2pm. The **burying ground,** on Tremont Street, is the oldest in the city; it dates to 1630. Among the scary colonial headstones (winged skulls are a popular

decoration) are the graves of **John Winthrop,** the first governor of the Massachusetts Bay Colony; **William Dawes,** who rode with Paul Revere; **Elizabeth Pain,** the model for Hester Prynne in Nathaniel Hawthorne's novel *The Scarlet Letter;* and **Mary Chilton,** the first female colonist to step ashore on Plymouth Rock.

Now follow the red-brick line along School Street next to King's Chapel. On the sidewalk is a colorful folk-art mosaic marking the:

6. Site of the First Public School, where **Samuel Adams, Benjamin Franklin, John Hancock,** and **Cotton Mather** were students. It was founded in 1634, 2 years before Harvard College. The original building (1645) was demolished to make way for the expansion of King's Chapel, and the school was moved across the street. Now called Boston Latin School, the institution survives and is located in the Fenway.

The fence to your left encloses a courtyard where you'll see a:

7. Statue of Benjamin Franklin. This was the first portrait statue erected in Boston, in 1856. Franklin was born in Boston in 1706 and apprenticed to his half-brother James, a printer, but they got along so poorly that in 1723 Benjamin ran away to Philadelphia. It was a productive move for everyone but James. The lovely granite building behind the statue is **Old City Hall,** designed in Second Empire style by Arthur Gilman (who laid out the Back Bay) and Gridley J. F. Bryant, and opened in 1865. The administration moved to Government Center in 1969, and the building now houses offices and an excellent French restaurant, **Maison Robert.**

 TAKE A BREAK   At the corner of School and Washington streets, stop into the second-floor cafe at **Borders Books & Music,** 24 School St. (☎ **617/557-7188**) for a snack or light meal and a cup of coffee. Order tea if you're feeling rebellious—at stop number 9, you'll be reminded that in Boston, drinking tea was once considered unpatriotic. The store and cafe are open Monday through Saturday from 7am to 8pm, Sunday from 10am to 8pm.

School Street ends at Washington Street. On the left is:

8. 3 School St. This is the former Old Corner Bookstore, which also held the publishing house of Ticknor & Fields. Built in 1712, it's on a plot of land that was once home to the religious reformer **Anne Hutchinson,** who was excommunicated and expelled from Boston in 1638 for heresy. In the middle of the 19th century, the little brick building was the literary center of America. Publisher James Fields, known as "Jamie," counted among his friends such giants as Henry Wadsworth Longfellow, James Russell Lowell, Henry David Thoreau, Ralph Waldo Emerson, Nathaniel Hawthorne, and Harriet Beecher Stowe.

Across Washington Street near this intersection is what appears to be an alleyway but is actually one of the first streets in Boston, **Spring Lane.** For the first 2 centuries of the settlement, it was home to a real spring.

Facing Spring Lane, turn right and walk 1 block. On your left at the corner of Milk Street is the:

9. Old South Meeting House, 310 Washington St. (☎ **617/482-6439**). Originally built in 1670 and replaced by the current structure in 1729, the building reopened in the fall of 1997 after nearly 2 years and $7.2 million of renovations.

The Old South, as it's known, was a religious and political gathering place, and it is best known today as the site of one of the events leading to the Revolution. On December 16, 1773, a crowd of several thousand, too big to fit into Faneuil Hall, gathered here for word from the governor about whether the three ships full

Impressions

From John Adams to George Apley, Bostonians are smugly apt to like their own town best.

— Esther Forbes, *Paul Revere and the World He Lived In,* 1942

of tea in the harbor would be sent back to England. They were not, and the tea, priced to undercut the cost of smuggled tea and force the colonists to trade with merchants approved by the Crown, was cast into the harbor by revolutionaries poorly disguised as Mohawks. That uprising, the **Boston Tea Party,** is commemorated here, and you can even see a vial of the tea. In 1872 the devastating fire that destroyed most of downtown stopped at the Old South, a phenomenon considered to be a testament to the building's power. The building's storied history is told in an interactive multimedia exhibit, **"Voices of Protest."** The Old South is open daily, April to October from 9am to 5:30pm, November through March weekdays from 10am to 4pm, weekends from 10am to 5pm. Admission is $3 for adults, $2.50 for seniors, $1 for children 6 to 12, free for children under 6.

Around the corner on Milk Street, opposite the exit from the gift shop, is:

10. **Benjamin Franklin's Birthplace.** In a little house at 17 Milk St., Franklin was born in 1706, the 15th child of Josiah Franklin. The house is long gone, but step to the edge of the curb across the street, and look at the second floor of the office building that's in its place. When the building went up after the fire of 1872, the architect guaranteed that the Founding Father wouldn't be forgotten: a bust and the words **"Birthplace of Franklin"** are worked into the facade.

Backtrack on Washington Street for 2 blocks and you'll come to the:

11. **Old State House,** 206 Washington St. (☎ **617/720-3290**). Built in 1713, it served as the seat of **colonial government** of Massachusetts before the Revolution and as the state's capitol until 1797. For many years, it was considered a tall building. From its balcony the **Declaration of Independence** was first read to Bostonians on July 18, 1776. In 1789 President **George Washington** reviewed a parade from the building. The exterior decorations are particularly interesting— the clock was installed in place of a sundial, and the gilded lion and unicorn are reproductions of the original symbols of British rule that were ripped from the facade and burned the day the Declaration of Independence was read. Inside you'll find the Bostonian Society's museum of the city's history. There are an introductory video on the history of the building and regularly changing exhibits. The Old State House is open daily from 9:30am to 5pm. Admission is $3 for adults, $2 for seniors and students, $1 for children 6 to 18, and free for children under 6. Discounted combination tickets are available if you plan to visit the USS *Constitution* Museum during your stay.

On a traffic island in State Street, across from the T station under the Old State House, a ring of cobblestones marks the:

12. **Boston Massacre Site.** This skirmish on March 5, 1770, helped consolidate the spirit of rebellion in the colonies. Angered at the presence of royal troops in Boston, colonists threw snowballs, garbage, rocks, and other debris at a group of redcoats, who panicked and fired into the crowd, killing five men (their graves are in the Old Granary Burying Ground).

Continue on the trail by turning left onto Congress Street and walking toward Faneuil Hall, or detour from past to present by walking to the Washington Street side of the Old State House and crossing State Street to Washington Mall.

Follow it 1 block (its entire length) to **Boston City Hall.** The 8-acre red-brick plaza that curves around to the left is in the process of being improved with renovations and the addition of plants and flowers, but it's still quite windy. That doesn't stop people from congregating here for celebrations, protests, and farmer's markets. The building itself is an architectural masterpiece and/or a civic disgrace, depending on whether you're talking to an architect or a citizen who actually has to use it. Free guided tours are given weekdays from 10am to 4pm. The building is open weekdays from 9am to 5pm.

If you detoured, backtrack to Washington Mall and take the steps down to Congress Street. Near the corner of Congress and North streets is:

13. Faneuil Hall. Built in 1742 (and enlarged using a Charles Bulfinch design in 1805), it was given to the city by the merchant **Peter Faneuil.** The "Cradle of Liberty" rang with speeches by orators such as **Samuel Adams**—whose statue is on the Congress Street side—in the years leading to the Revolution, and with speeches by abolitionists, temperance advocates, and women's suffragists in the years after. The upstairs is still a public meeting (and sometimes concert) hall, and the downstairs area is a market, all according to Faneuil's will. The grasshopper **weather vane,** the sole remaining detail from the original building, is modeled after the weather vane on London's Royal Exchange.

A recent renovation restored the entire building and upgraded the wiring in the second-floor auditorium so that it's suitable for television production; it's sometimes used for televised debates and other political events. National Park Service rangers give **free 20-minute talks** every half-hour from 9am to 5pm in the second-floor auditorium and operate a visitor center on the first floor. On the top floor is a small museum that houses the weapons collection and historical exhibits of the **Ancient and Honorable Artillery Company of Massachusetts.** Admission is free.

☕ **WINDING DOWN**   **Faneuil Hall Marketplace** spreads out before you, and the **Quincy Market Colonnade** overflows with carry-away foodstuffs. Cross the street and head down **Long Wharf,** Boston's principal wharf since 1710 and a busy sightseeing-cruise dock, past the Marriott to the ❂ **brick plaza** at the very end of the wharf. The granite building dates to 1846, and the whole plaza affords a great view of the harbor and the airport. Or stay at **Christopher Columbus Park,** on the other side of the hotel, watch the action at the marina, and play in the playground.

If you prefer a sit-down restaurant, **Durgin-Park** is here, and **Ye Olde Union Oyster House** is a block away.

DETOUR DETAILS   If you want to continue to the **Waterfront** and **Museum Wharf,** set out from here and be ready to negotiate many construction-clogged areas. See chapter 7 for descriptions of the **New England Aquarium,** the **Children's Museum,** the **Computer Museum,** and the **Boston Tea Party Ship & Museum.**

WALKING TOUR 2
The North End & Charlestown

Start: Faneuil Hall Marketplace (MBTA Green Line to Government Center, Orange Line to State Street, or Blue Line to Aquarium).
Finish: Bunker Hill Monument, Charlestown.

Time: 2 to 3 hours.

Best Time: Morning and early afternoon. Aim for Friday or Saturday if you want to see Haymarket.

Worst Time: Late afternoon, when you'll be in the midst of rush-hour gridlock.

Facing the statue of **Samuel Adams** on the Congress Street side of Faneuil Hall, turn left and cross North Street. Walk up Union Street past the two statues of **James Michael Curley.** Looming above are the six glass columns that make up:

1. **The New England Holocaust Memorial.** Erected in 1995, the towers spring up in the midst of attractions that celebrate freedom, reminding visitors of the consequences of a world without it. The apparently decorative pattern on the glass is actually 6 million random numbers, one for each Jew who died during the Holocaust.

Across the street is:

2. **Ye Olde Union Oyster House,** 41 Union St. (☎ 617/227-2750). First opened in 1826, the Union Oyster House is the oldest restaurant in Boston that's still in operation.

Continue following Union Street, and then turn right onto Hanover Street. If it's Friday or Saturday, you'll soon be in the midst of:

3. **Haymarket.** The open-air market consists of stalls piled high with fruit, vegetables, and seafood, but shoppers aren't allowed to touch anything they haven't bought. It's a great scene, and a favorite of photographers. Two blocks up, you can turn right onto Blackstone Street and explore the merchandise further (the market runs to North Street), or cross Blackstone Street and take the **pedestrian passage** beneath the Central Artery (Fitzgerald Expressway). You'll probably walk near, over, or around indications that the Central Artery project is in the works; if construction appears to block your way, look for signs pointing to the North End.

You'll emerge at Cross and Salem streets, one of several gateways to:

4. **The North End.** This is Boston's Little Italy (although it's never called that), home to natives of Italy and their assimilated children, numerous Italian restaurants and private social clubs, and many historically significant sights. This is one of the oldest neighborhoods in the city, and it was home in the 17th century to the **Mather family** of Puritan ministers, who certainly would be shocked to see the merry goings-on at the festivals and street fairs that take over a different section of the North End each weekend in July and August.

The Italians (and their yuppie neighbors who have made inroads since the 1980s) are only the latest immigrant group to dominate the North End. In the mid–19th century, this was an eastern European Jewish enclave, and later an Irish stronghold. In 1894 **Rose Fitzgerald,** mother of President John F. Kennedy, was born on Garden Court Street and baptized at St. Stephen's Church.

Follow the Freedom Trail and turn right onto Cross Street. Walk 1 block to Hanover Street, where you must turn left. At the first traffic light, turn right onto Richmond Street, still following the Freedom Trail. Walk 1 block and turn left onto North Street. Wharves ran up almost this far in colonial days; in the 19th century, this was a notorious red-light district. Half a block up on the left is:

5. **The Paul Revere House,** 19 North Sq. (☎ 617/523-2338). One of the most pleasant stops on the Freedom Trail, it presents history on a human scale. Revere set out for Lexington from here on the evening of April 18, 1775, a feat immortalized in **Henry Wadsworth Longfellow's poem "Paul Revere's Ride"** (*Listen my children and you shall hear / Of the midnight ride of Paul Revere*). The

Walking Tour 2—The North End & Charlestown

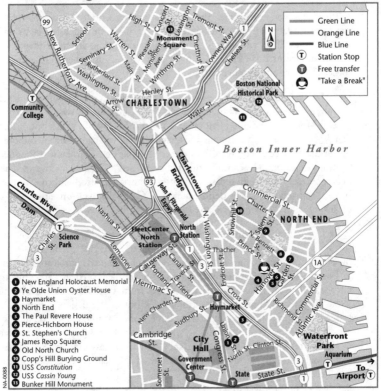

Legend:
- Green Line
- Orange Line
- Blue Line
- ⓣ Station Stop
- ⓣ Free transfer
- 👆 "Take a Break"

1. New England Holocaust Memorial
2. Ye Olde Union Oyster House
3. Haymarket
4. North End
5. The Paul Revere House
6. Pierce-Hichborn House
7. St. Stephen's Church
8. James Rego Square
9. Old North Church
10. Copp's Hill Burying Ground
11. USS *Constitution*
12. USS *Cassin Young*
13. Bunker Hill Monument

oldest house in downtown Boston, it was built around 1680, purchased by Revere in 1770, and put to a number of uses before being turned into a museum in the early 20th century. The 2½-story wood structure is filled with neatly arranged and identified 17th- and 18th-century furnishings and artifacts, including the famous Revere silver, considered some of the finest anywhere. The self-guided tour allows you to linger over the objects that particularly interest you.

The house is open April 15 through October from 9:30am to 5:15pm, and November through April 14 from 9:30am to 4:15pm; it's closed Mondays in January, February, and March, as well as January 1, Thanksgiving Day, and December 25. Admission is $2.50 for adults, $2 for seniors and students, and $1 for children 5 to 17.

Across the cobblestone courtyard from Revere's house is the home of his Hichborn cousins, the:

6. Pierce/Hichborn House. The 1711 Georgian-style home is a rare example of 18th-century middle-class architecture. It's suitably furnished and is shown only by guided tour (usually twice a day at busy times). Call the Paul Revere House for schedules.

Before you leave North Square, look across the cobblestone plaza at **Sacred Heart Church.** It was established in 1833 as the Seamen's Bethel, a church devoted to the needs of the mariners who frequented the area. Today it's Roman Catholic and has a large, active Italian-American congregation; one Mass every Sunday is said in Italian.

Turn left as you exit the Paul Revere House and walk up to Prince Street. Here you can turn left and walk 1 block to Hanover Street, or take a few steps onto Garden Court Street and look for no. 4, on the right. The private residence was the **birthplace of Rose Fitzgerald** (later Kennedy). Pause when you get to the corner of Prince and Hanover streets.

☕ **TAKE A BREAK**   You're in the heart of North End cafe country, the perfect place to have a cup of coffee or a soft drink and feast on sweets. Across the street is **Mike's Pastry,** 300 Hanover St. (☎ **617/742-3050**), which does a frantic take-out business and also has a few tables where you can sit down and order one of the confections on display in the cases. Mike's claim to fame is President Clinton's devotion to its **cannoli** (tubes of crisp-fried pastry filled with sweetened ricotta cheese); the cookies, cakes, and other pastries are excellent, too. You can also sit and relax at **Caffè dello Sport** and **Caffè Vittoria,** on either side of Mike's, or across the street at **Caffè Graffiti.**

Back at Prince and Hanover streets, with North Square behind you, turn right and walk 2 blocks on Hanover Street to Clark Street. At the corner is:

7. St. Stephen's Church, the only **Charles Bulfinch**-designed church still standing in Boston. The church was Unitarian when it was dedicated in 1804, and the next year the congregation purchased a **bell from Paul Revere's foundry** for $800. Architecture buffs will get a huge kick out of the design, a paragon of Federal-style symmetry. St. Stephen's became Roman Catholic in 1862 and was moved back when Hanover Street was widened in 1870. During refurbishment in 1965, it regained its original appearance, with clear glass windows, red carpets, white walls, and gilded organ pipes. It's one of the plainest Catholic churches you'll ever see.

Cross Hanover Street to reach:

8. James Rego Square (Paul Revere Mall), a pleasant little brick-paved park known as the Prado, with an equestrian statue of Paul Revere. Take time to read some of the **tablets** on the left-hand wall that describe famous people and places in the history of the North End.

Walk across the mall, past the fountain, and emerge at the side of the:

9. Old North Church, 193 Salem St. (☎ 617/523-6676; www.oldnorth.com). Officially known as Christ Church, this is the oldest church building in Boston; it dates to 1723. The building is in the style of Sir Christopher Wren, and the original steeple was the one where sexton **Robert Newman** hung two lanterns on the night of April 18, 1775, to indicate to **Paul Revere** that British troops were setting out for Lexington and Concord in boats across the Charles River, not on foot (**"One if by land, two if by sea"**). The steeple fell victim to hurricanes in 1804 and 1954; the current version is an exact copy of the original. The 175-foot spire, long a reference point for sailors, appears on navigational charts to this day. Members of the Revere family attended this church (their plaque is on Pew 54); famous visitors have included **Presidents James Monroe, Theodore Roosevelt, Franklin D. Roosevelt,** and **Gerald R. Ford,** and Her Majesty **Queen Elizabeth II.** There are markers and plaques throughout; note the bust of **George Washington,** reputedly the first memorial to the first president. The **gardens** on the north side of the church (dotted with more plaques) are open to the public. On the south side of the church, volunteers are re-creating an 18th-century garden. The church is open daily from 9am to 5pm; Sunday services (Episcopal) are at 9 and 11am and 4pm. The quirky **gift shop** and museum (☎ 617/523-4848), in a former chapel, is open daily from 9am to 5pm, and all proceeds go to support the church. Donations are appreciated.

As you leave the church, bear left and cross Salem Street onto **Hull Street.** Turn right and walk uphill past no. 44, the narrowest house in Boston (it's 10 feet wide). Across the street is the entrance to:

10. **Copp's Hill Burying Ground,** the second-oldest cemetery (1659) in the city. No gravestone rubbing is allowed. This is the burial place of **Cotton Mather** and his family, **Robert Newman,** and **Prince Hall.** Hall, a prominent member of the free black community that occupied the north slope of the hill in colonial times, fought at Bunker Hill and established the first black Masonic lodge. The highest point in the North End, Copp's Hill was the site of a windmill and of the British batteries that destroyed the village of Charlestown during the Battle of Bunker Hill, June 17, 1775. Charlestown is clearly visible (look for the masts of the USS *Constitution*) across the Inner Harbor. The burying ground is open daily from 9am to 5pm.

Many people, especially those traveling with fidgety children, opt to skip the next part of the tour. If your party's not too close to the breaking point, it's a worthwhile excursion.

From the burying ground, it's about a mile to **Charlestown.** Continue on Hull Street and follow it down the hill to Commercial Street (note that there's no crosswalk on Commercial at Hull). Turn left and walk 2 blocks to North Washington Street. Being very careful, cross Commercial Street. Walk across the bridge, and at the end, turn right and follow the signs and the Freedom Trail to the **Charlestown Navy Yard,** home of the:

11. USS *Constitution* (☎ **617/242-5670**). Active-duty sailors in 1812 dress uniforms give **free tours** daily from 9:30am to 3:50pm.

"**Old Ironsides,**" one of the U.S. Navy's six original frigates, never lost a battle. The ship was constructed in the North End from 1794 to 1797 at a cost of $302,718, using bolts, spikes, and other fittings from **Paul Revere's foundry.** As the new nation made its naval and military reputation, the *Constitution* played a key role, battling French privateers and Barbary pirates, repelling the British fleet during the **War of 1812,** participating in 40 engagements, and capturing 20 vessels. The frigate earned its nickname during an engagement on August 19, 1812, with the French warship *Guerriere,* whose shots bounced off its thick oak hull as if it were iron. Retired from combat in 1815, the *Constitution* was rescued from destruction when **Oliver Wendell Holmes's poem "Old Ironsides"** launched a preservation movement in 1830.

"Old Ironsides" was completely overhauled in 1995 through 1996 in preparation for its bicentennial. It sailed under its own power in 1997 for the first time since 1881, drawing international attention. Tugs tow the *Constitution* into the harbor every **Fourth of July** and turn it to ensure that the ship weathers evenly.

The **USS *Constitution* Museum** (☎ **617/426-1812**), just inland from the vessel, has several **participatory exhibits** that allow visitors to **hoist a flag, fire a cannon,** and learn more about the ship. The museum is open daily June 1 to Labor Day from 9am to 6pm; March to May and the day after Labor Day through November from 10am to 5pm; December to February from 10am to 3pm. It's closed January 1, Thanksgiving, and December 25. Admission is $4 for adults, $3 for seniors, $2 for children 6 to 16, and free for children 5 and under. Discounted combination tickets are available if you plan to visit the Old State House.

Turn left as you leave the museum (or right as you leave the ship), and follow the big-band music to the:

12. USS *Cassin Young* (☎ **617/242-5601**), a refurbished World War II destroyer. National Park Service rangers give **45-minute tours,** and unescorted visitors can also look around on the deck. Admission is free. Call for tour times.

Leave the Navy Yard, cross Chelsea Street, and climb the hill, following the Freedom Trail along Tremont Street. Your guidepost is also your destination, the:

13. Bunker Hill Monument (☎ **617/242-5644**), a 221-foot granite obelisk built in honor of the men who died in the **Battle of Bunker Hill** on June 17, 1775. The colonists lost the battle, but nearly half of the British troops were killed or wounded, a circumstance that contributed to Britain's decision to abandon Boston 9 months later. The **Marquis de Lafayette,** the celebrated hero of the American and French revolutions, helped lay the monument's cornerstone in 1825. The top is at the end of a flight of 295 stairs—a long climb for a decent view that prominently features I-93.

In the lodge at the base of the monument, there are dioramas and exhibits. It's staffed by National Park Service rangers and is open from 9am to 5pm. The monument is open daily from 9am to 4:30pm. Admission is free.

If you don't feel like retracing your steps, you have two public transportation options. At the foot of the hill on Main Street, take **bus no. 92 or 93** to Haymarket (where you can catch the MBTA Green and Orange lines). Or return to the Navy Yard for the **MBTA water shuttle to Long Wharf.** The 10-minute trip costs $1 and leaves every hour on the quarter hour from 6:45am to 7:45pm on weekdays and from 10:15am to 6:15pm on weekends. A shuttle bus from the USS *Constitution* will take you to the pier.

WALKING TOUR 3
The Back Bay

Start: The Public Garden (MBTA Green Line to Arlington).
Finish: Copley Square.
Time: 2 hours if you make good time, 3 if you detour to the Fiedler statue and the Esplanade, and longer if you take your time while shopping.
Best Time: Any time before late afternoon.
Worst Time: Late afternoon, when the streets are packed with people and cars. And don't attempt the detour on the Fourth of July. This is mostly an outdoor walk, so if the weather is bad you might find yourself in lots of shops. Decide for yourself whether that makes an overcast day a "best" or "worst" time.

The Back Bay is the youngest neighborhood in central Boston, the product of a massive landfill project that took place from 1835 to 1882. It's flat, symmetrical, logically designed—the names of the cross streets go in alphabetical order—and altogether anomalous in Boston's crazy-quilt geography.

Begin your walk in the:

1. Public Garden, bounded by Arlington, Beacon, Charles, and Boylston streets. Before the Back Bay was filled in, the **Charles River** flowed right up to Charles Street, which separates the Public Garden from Boston Common. On the night of April 18, 1775, the **British troops** bound for Lexington and Concord boarded boats to Cambridge (**"two if by sea"**) at the foot of the Common and set off across what's now the Public Garden.

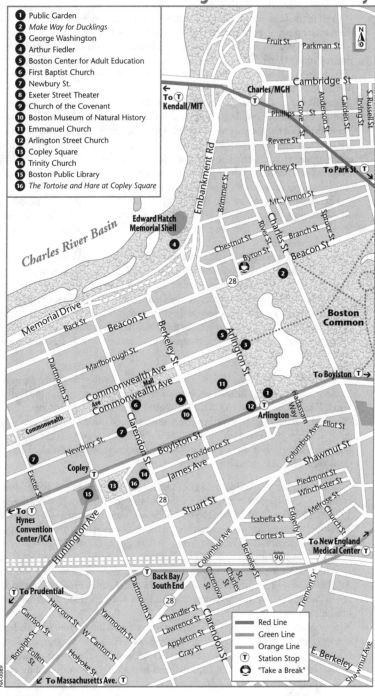

1. Public Garden
2. *Make Way for Ducklings*
3. George Washington
4. Arthur Fiedler
5. Boston Center for Adult Education
6. First Baptist Church
7. Newbury St.
8. Exeter Street Theater
9. Church of the Covenant
10. Boston Museum of Natural History
11. Emmanuel Church
12. Arlington Street Church
13. Copley Square
14. Trinity Church
15. Boston Public Library
16. *The Tortoise and Hare at Copley Square*

Explore the lagoon, the trees and other flora, and the statuary. Take a ride on the **swan boats,** if you like, and then make your way toward the corner of Charles and Beacon streets. A short distance away, within the confines of the Public Garden (listen for the cries of delighted children), you'll see a 35-foot strip of cobblestones topped with the bronze figures that immortalize Robert McCloskey's book:

2. *Make Way for Ducklings.* Installed in 1987 and wildly popular since the moment they were unveiled, **Nancy Schön's** renderings of **Mrs. Mallard and her eight babies** are irresistible. Mrs. Mallard is 38 inches tall, making her back a bit higher than a tricycle seat, but that doesn't keep people of all ages from climbing on. If you don't know the whole story of the Mallards' perilous trip across town to meet Mr. Mallard at the lagoon, ask one of the parents or children you'll certainly find here.

The city purchased the site of the Public Garden from private interests in 1824. Planting began in 1837, but it wasn't until the late 1850s that Arlington Street was built and the land permanently set aside. George F. Meacham executed the design.

Cross the lagoon using the little **suspension bridge** and look for the statue of:

3. George Washington. Unveiled in 1875, this was Boston's first equestrian statue. It stands 38 feet tall and is considered an excellent likeness of the first president of the United States, an outstanding horseman. The artist, **Thomas Ball,** was a Charlestown native who worked in Italy and numbered among his students noted sculptor and artist Daniel Chester French. Pass through the gate onto Arlington Street. Before you begin exploring in earnest, this is a good place to detour and:

☕ **TAKE A BREAK** Turn right and walk up Arlington Street, passing Marlborough Street, to Beacon Street. Across the busy intersection is the **Bull & Finch Pub,** 84 Beacon St. (☎ 617/227-9605), also known as the **"Cheers" bar.** The food is actually quite tasty, but two points must be made (not that anything's going to keep you from visiting if you have your heart set on it): the bar looks nothing like the set of the TV show, and the patrons generally consist of people from everywhere in the universe except Boston.

If you'd rather stay outdoors, turn right on Beacon and walk 1 block to the corner of Charles Street. Diagonally across the intersection is a **Starbucks,** 1 Charles Street (☎ 617/742-2664). And if you want to wander down Charles Street looking for a less generic snack, well, nobody's stopping you. You can pick up something tasty at **Cafe Bella Vita,** 30 Charles St. (☎ 617/720-4505), or **Panificio,** 144 Charles St. (☎ 617/227-4340).

When you've found something to eat, backtrack along Beacon Street just past Arlington Street to Embankment Road. Take the **Arthur Fiedler Footbridge** across Storrow Drive to the Esplanade, and unpack your food near the giant head of:

4. Arthur Fiedler. Installed in 1985, this sculpture by **Ralph Helmick** is made up of sheets of aluminum that eerily capture the countenance of the legendary conductor of the **Boston Pops,** who died in 1979. The amphitheater off to the right is the **Hatch Shell,** where the Pops perform free during the week leading up to and including the Fourth of July.

When you're ready, retrace your steps to the corner of Arlington Street and Commonwealth Avenue. This is the home of the:

5. Boston Center for Adult Education, 5 Commonwealth Ave. (☎ **617/ 267-4430**). Constructed in 1904 as a private residence, the building gained a huge ballroom in 1912. If it's not being used for a class or a function (it's extremely popular for weddings), you're welcome to have a look at the ballroom. The Boston Center was established in 1933 and is the oldest continuing-education institution in the country.

You're at the foot of the 8-block **Commonwealth Avenue Mall.** This graceful public promenade is the centerpiece of architect **Arthur Gilman's** design of the Back Bay. The mall is 100 feet wide (the entire street is 240) and stretches to Kenmore Square. The elegant Victorian mansions on either side—almost all divided into apartments or in commercial or educational use—are generally considered a great asset, but the attitude toward the apparently random collection of statues along the mall is hardly unanimous. Judge for yourself as you inspect the statues, starting with **Alexander Hamilton** across Arlington Street from **George Washington.** You could easily spend hours inspecting the monuments and wondering what in the world **William Lloyd Garrison,** Boston Mayor **Patrick Andrew Collins,** Revolutionary War Gen. **John Glover,** and **Leif Eriksson** have in common.

Two blocks from the Public Garden at the corner of Clarendon Street is the:

6. First Baptist Church, 110 Commonwealth Ave. Built in 1870 to 1872 of Roxbury pudding stone, it originally housed the congregation of the Brattle Street Church (Unitarian), which had been downtown, near Faneuil Hall. The design is notable mainly because its creators went on to work on much more famous projects. The architect, **H. H. Richardson,** is best known for nearby Trinity Church, which you'll read about shortly. The artist who created the frieze, which represents the sacraments, was **Frederic Auguste Bartholdi,** who designed the Statue of Liberty.

At Clarendon Street or Dartmouth Street, turn left and walk 1 block to:

7. Newbury Street. Commonwealth Avenue is the architectural heart of the Back Bay, and Newbury Street is the commercial center. Take some time to roam around here (see chapter 9 for pointers), browsing in the galleries, window-shopping at the expensive clothing stores, and watching the chic shoppers, artists, and students. On Exeter Street you'll see the building that was once the:

8. Exeter Street Theater, 26 Exeter St. Designed in 1884 as the First Spiritualist Temple, it was a movie house from 1914 to 1984. Once known for the crowds flocking to the *Rocky Horror Picture Show,* it's now the home of Waterstone's Booksellers and a Friday's restaurant.

When you're ready to continue your stroll (or when your credit cards cry for mercy), head back toward the Public Garden and seek out three of Newbury Street's oldest buildings, starting with the:

9. Church of the Covenant, 67 Newbury St., a Gothic revival edifice built in 1866 through 1867 and designed by **Richard Upjohn.** The stained-glass windows are the work of **Louis Comfort Tiffany.**

Across the street, set back from the sidewalk at 234 Berkeley St., is an opulent store in an equally opulent setting. The luxury clothing store Louis, Boston is housed in the original home of the:

10. Boston Museum of Natural History, a forerunner of the Museum of Science. Built in 1861 through 1864 using **William Preston's** French Academic design, it was originally only two stories, but it still has the original roof, preserved when the third floor was added.

Cross Newbury Street again and continue walking toward the Public Garden. On your left is:

11. **Emmanuel Church,** 15 Newbury St. (☎ **617/536-3355**), the first building completed on Newbury Street. The Episcopal church often ministers through the arts, so there might be a concert (classical to jazz, solo to orchestral) going on during your visit.

Now you're almost back at the Public Garden. On your left is the original **Ritz-Carlton** (1927), the pride and joy of the chain. Turn right onto Arlington Street and walk 1 block to Boylston Street. On your right is the:

12. **Arlington Street Church,** 351 Boylston St. It's the oldest church in the Back Bay, completed in 1861. An interesting blend of Georgian and Italianate details, it's the work of architect **Arthur Gilman,** who laid out the neighborhood. Here you'll see more Tiffany stained glass. Step inside to see the pulpit that was in use in 1788, when the congregation worshipped downtown on Federal Street, in a church that also served as an additional meeting place for Massachusetts delegates to the Constitutional Convention when the Old State House was full.

Follow Boylston Street away from the Public Garden. You'll pass the famous **FAO Schwarz** toy store, with the huge **bronze bear** out front at the corner of Berkeley Street. At the end of the block is:

13. **Copley Square.** Freshen up at the fountain, visit the farmer's market (Tuesday and Friday from July through November), but whatever you do, don't miss:

14. **Trinity Church** (to your left), **H. H. Richardson's** Romanesque masterpiece, completed in 1877. It's built on 4,502 pilings driven into the mud that was once the Back Bay. Should you happen to visit on a Friday at lunchtime, organ recitals are given at 12:15pm. Otherwise, brochures and guides are available to help you find your way around a building considered one of the finest examples of church architecture in the country. It's open daily from 8am to 6pm.

Across Dartmouth Street is the:

15. **Boston Public Library.** The work of architect **Charles Follen McKim** and many others, the Renaissance revival building was completed in 1895 after 10 years of construction. Its design reflects the significant influence of the Bibliothéque Nationale in Paris. Wander up the steps to check out the building's impressive interior (see chapter 7 for more details).

Leave through the **Daniel Chester French**–designed doors facing Dartmouth Street, and head across the street into the little Copley Square park. In a sense, you've come full circle; as at the Public Garden, you'll be greeted by a playful and compelling sculpture:

16. *The Tortoise and Hare at Copley Square,* also by **Nancy Schön.** Designed to signify the end of the **Boston Marathon** (the finish line is on Boylston Street between Exeter and Dartmouth streets), it was unveiled for the 100th anniversary of the event in 1996 and immediately became another shutterbug magnet.

From here you're in a good position to set out for any other part of town, or just walk a little way in any direction and continue exploring. **Copley Place** and the **Shops at Prudential Center** are nearby, **Newbury Street** is 1 block over, and there's an MBTA Green Line station at Boylston and Dartmouth streets. Or just hang around Copley Square, imagine yourself sitting in this spot 150 or so years ago, and be glad there's such a thing as landfill.

WALKING TOUR 4
Harvard Square

Start: Harvard Square (MBTA Red Line to Harvard).
Finish: John F. Kennedy Park.
Time: 2 to 4 hours, depending on how much time you spend in shops and museums.
Best Time: Almost any time during the day (see below); the Harvard museums are free on Saturday mornings.
Worst Time: The first full week of June. You might have trouble gaining admission to Harvard Yard during commencement festivities. The ceremony is Thursday morning, and without a ticket, you won't be allowed in.

Popular impressions to the contrary, Cambridge is not exclusively Harvard. In fact, Harvard Square isn't even exclusively Harvard, and during a walk around the Harvard Square area, you'll see historic buildings and sights, interesting museums, and notable architecture, on and off the university's main campus.

Ride the Red Line to Harvard Square. Leave the station by the **main entrance** (take the ramp to the turnstiles and the escalators to the outside) and emerge in the heart of:

1. **Harvard Square.** Town and gown meet at this lively intersection, where you'll get a taste of the improbable mix of people drawn to the crossroads of Cambridge. To your right is the landmark **Out of Town News** kiosk, which stocks newspapers and magazines from all over the world. At the booth in front of you, you can request information about the area. Step close to it so that you're out of the flow of pedestrian traffic, and look around.

The store across Massachusetts Avenue is the **Harvard Coop.** The name rhymes with "hoop"—say "*co*-op" and risk being taken for a Yale student. On the far side of the intersection at the corner of John F. Kennedy Street and Brattle Street, look up at the third floor of the brick building and find the sign for **"Dewey Cheetham & Howe"** (say it out loud). National Public Radio's hilarious show **"Car Talk"** originates here.

Turn around so that the Coop is at your back, and walk half a block, crossing Dunster Street. Across Massachusetts Avenue you'll see:

2. **Wadsworth House,** 1341 Massachusetts Ave. Most of the people waiting for the bus in front of this yellow wood building probably don't know it was built in 1726 as a residence for Harvard's fourth president—but then, neither do most Harvard students. Now the headquarters of the alumni association, its biggest claim to fame is a classic: **George Washington** slept here.

Cross the street and go left. Follow the outside of the red-brick wall past one gate until you see another T exit. Turn right and use Johnston Gate to enter:

3. **Harvard Yard.** This is the oldest part of "the Yard," which was just a patch of grass with animals grazing on it when Harvard College was **established in 1636** to train young men for the ministry. It wasn't much more when the **Continental Army** spent the winter here in 1775 through 1776. Harvard is the oldest college in the United States, with the most competitive admissions process, and if you suggest aloud that it's not the best, you might run up against the attitude that inspired the saying "You can always tell a Harvard man, but you can't tell him much."

Harvard, a private institution since 1865, includes the college and 10 graduate and professional schools located in more than 400 buildings scattered around

Boston and Cambridge. Some of the most interesting are around the perimeter of this quadrangle, the classroom and administration buildings and dormitories that make up the:

4. Old Yard. To your right is **Massachusetts Hall.** Built in 1720, this National Historic Landmark is the university's oldest surviving building. First-year students live upstairs, sharing the building with the first-floor office of the university president (or perhaps it's the other way around), who is traditionally invited upstairs for tea once a year. To your left, across from Massachusetts Hall, is **Harvard Hall,** a classroom building constructed in 1765. Turn left and walk down the side of Harvard Hall. The matching side-by-side buildings here are **Hollis** and **Stoughton halls.** Hollis dates to 1763 (Stoughton "only" to 1805), and it has been home to many students who went on to great fame, among them **Ralph Waldo Emerson, Henry David Thoreau,** and **Charles Bulfinch.** Almost hidden across the tiny lawn between these two buildings is **Holden Chapel,** a Georgian-style gem built in 1745. It has been an anatomy lab, a classroom building, and, of course, a chapel, and it is now home to the Harvard Glee Club.

Cross the Yard to the building opposite the gate where you entered. This is:

5. University Hall. Designed by **Charles Bulfinch** and constructed in 1812 through 1813 of granite quarried in nearby Chelmsford, it's the college's main administration building. In 1969 it was occupied by students protesting the Vietnam War, but it's best known as the backdrop of the:

6. John Harvard Statue, one of the most photographed objects in the Boston area. Designed by **Daniel Chester French** in 1884, it's known as the **"Statue of Three Lies"** because the inscription reads "John Harvard—Founder—1638." In fact, the college was founded in 1636; Harvard (one of many involved in its formation) didn't really establish the university, but donated money and his library; and this isn't John Harvard, anyway. No portraits of him survive, so the model for this benevolent-looking bronze gentleman was, according to various accounts, either his nephew or a student.

Walk around University Hall into the adjoining quadrangle. This is still the Yard, but it's the **"New Yard,"** sometimes called **Tercentenary Theater** because the college's 300th-anniversary celebration was held here. This is where commencement and other university-wide ceremonies (most recently, the 350th-birthday party in 1986) are held. On your right is:

7. Widener Library. The centerpiece of the world's largest university library system was built in 1913 as a memorial to **Harry Elkins Widener,** a 1907 Harvard graduate. Legend has it that he died when the *Titanic* sank in 1912 because he was unable to swim 50 yards to a lifeboat, and his mother donated $2 million for the library on the condition that every undergraduate prove his ability to swim 50 yards. Today the library holds more than 3 million volumes, including 3,500 rare volumes collected by Harry Elkins Widener. Don't even think about trying to swipe Harry's **Gutenberg Bible.** The last person to try, in 1969, gained access from above but couldn't climb back out. With the 70-pound bible in his knapsack, he fell six stories to the courtyard below. The library was designed by **Horace Trumbauer** of Philadelphia, whose primary design assistant was **Julian Francis Abele,** a student of architecture at the University of Pennsylvania and the first black graduate of L'Ecole des Beaux Arts in Paris. Climb the steps to enter and see the **dioramas of Cambridge** on the main level and the locked-up **memorial room** with Widener's collection behind the glass door overlooking the lobby. Or stop at the top of the outside staircase and enjoy the view. Facing the library is:

Walking Tour 4—Harvard Square

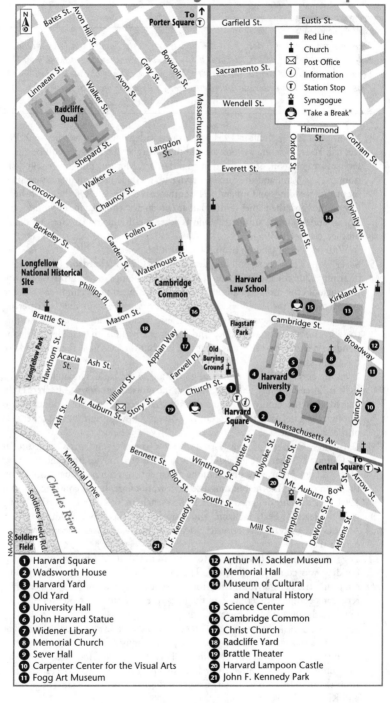

Legend:
- Red Line
- ✝ Church
- ✉ Post Office
- ⓘ Information
- Ⓣ Station Stop
- ✡ Synagogue
- ☕ "Take a Break"

1. Harvard Square
2. Wadsworth House
3. Harvard Yard
4. Old Yard
5. University Hall
6. John Harvard Statue
7. Widener Library
8. Memorial Church
9. Sever Hall
10. Carpenter Center for the Visual Arts
11. Fogg Art Museum
12. Arthur M. Sackler Museum
13. Memorial Hall
14. Museum of Cultural and Natural History
15. Science Center
16. Cambridge Common
17. Christ Church
18. Radcliffe Yard
19. Brattle Theater
20. Harvard Lampoon Castle
21. John F. Kennedy Park

One emerged, as one still does, from the subway exit in the Square and faced an old red-brick wall behind which stretched, to my fond eye, what remains still the most beautiful campus in America, the Harvard Yard. If there is any one place in all America that mirrors better all American history, I do not know of it.
—Theodore H. White, *In Search of History*, 1978

8. **Memorial Church,** built in 1931 and topped with a tower and weather vane 197 feet tall. You're welcome to look around this Georgian Revival-style edifice unless services are going on, or to attend them if they are. Morning prayers are said daily from 8:45 to 9am, and the Sunday service is at 11am. The building is also used for private weddings and funerals. The entrance is on the left. On the **south wall,** toward the Yard, the names of the Harvard graduates who died in the world wars, Korea, and Vietnam are listed. One is Joseph P. Kennedy, Jr., the president's brother, class of 1938.

   With Memorial Church behind you, turn left toward:

9. **Sever Hall,** a classroom building designed by **H. H. Richardson** (the architect of Trinity Church) and built from 1878 to 1880. Notice the gorgeous brickwork that includes roll moldings around the doors, the fluted brick chimneys, and the arrangement of the windows. The front door is set back in the **"whispering gallery."** Stand on one side of the entrance arch, station a friend or willing passerby on the opposite side, and speak softly into the facade. Someone standing next to you can't hear what you say, but the person at the other side of the arch can.

   Facing Sever Hall, turn right and go around to the back. The building to the right is **Emerson Hall,** which appeared in the movie *Love Story* as **Barrett Hall,** named after the family of Ryan O'Neal's character. Cross this quadrangle, go through the gate, and step onto **Quincy Street.** On your right on the other side of the street is the:

10. **Carpenter Center for the Visual Arts,** a concrete and glass structure at 24 Quincy St. There are art exhibitions in the lobby, movies from the extensive Harvard Film Archive are shown in the basement (you can pick up a schedule on the main floor), and the building itself is a work of art. It was constructed from 1961 to 1963 and designed by the Swiss-French architect **Le Corbusier,** along with the team of **Sert, Jackson, and Gourley.** It's the only building in North America designed by Le Corbusier. Facing the gate where you emerged from the Yard is the:

11. **Fogg Art Museum,** founded in 1895 and located at 32 Quincy St. since the building was completed in 1927. The Fogg's excellent collection of painting, sculpture, and decorative art runs from the Middle Ages to the present. See chapter 7 for a complete description of the Fogg, the adjacent Busch-Reisinger Museum, and the next stop on our walk, the:

12. **Arthur M. Sackler Museum,** 485 Broadway, to the left as you face the Fogg. The university's spectacular collection of Asian art is housed here.

   Continue on Quincy Street with the Fogg behind you and cross Broadway, then cross Cambridge Street, watching out for the confused drivers emerging from the underpass to your left. Covering the block between Cambridge Street and Kirkland Street is:

13. Memorial Hall, a Victorian structure built from 1870 to 1874. The entrance on Cambridge Street puts you in the actual **hall of memorials,** a transept where you can read the names of the Harvard men who died fighting for the Union during the Civil War—but not their Confederate counterparts. To the right is **Sanders Theatre,** prized as a performance space and lecture hall for its excellent acoustics and clear views. To the left is **Annenberg Hall,** originally Alumni Hall, which underwent a massive renovation in 1995 and was turned into a dining hall after 70 years as an open space used for class registration, blood drives, and final exams by the thousands. It has gorgeous stained-glass windows that you might be able to peek at. Harvard graduates **William Ware** and **Henry Van Brunt** won a design competition for Memorial Hall, which was constructed for a total cost of $390,000 (most of it donated by alumni). If it seems that the building should be taller, that might be because it once was. In 1956 a devastating fire tore through the tower, and it was never rebuilt.

Facing in the same direction you were when you entered, walk through the transept and exit onto Kirkland Street. Turn left and take the first right, onto Oxford Street. One block up on the right you'll see an entrance to the:

14. Museum of Cultural and Natural History, 26 Oxford St. This complex consists of the **Botanical Museum,** the **Museum of Comparative Zoology,** the **Mineralogical & Geological Museum,** and the **Peabody Museum of Archaeology & Ethnology.** Best known for the **Glass Flowers** on display at the Botanical Museum, the entire institution is becoming more interdisciplinary and accessible. See chapter 7 for a full description.

Leave through the back door at 11 Divinity Ave. and look around. Across the street at 6 Divinity Ave. is the **Semitic Museum** (☎ **617/495-4631**), where the second- and third-floor galleries hold displays of archaeological artifacts and photographs from the Near and Middle East. You might want to detour here. The building next door, **Two Divinity Ave.,** was designed by **Horace Trumbauer,** the architect of Widener Library, and it is the home of the Harvard-Yenching Institute, which promotes East Asian studies and facilitates scholar exchange programs. For every person who can tell you that, there are several thousand who know this building only for the pair of **Chinese stone lions** flanking the front door.

Turn right and return to Kirkland Street. At the intersection of Kirkland and Oxford streets is the university's:

15. Science Center, Zero Oxford St. A 10-story monolith said to resemble a **Polaroid camera** (Edwin H. Land, founder of the Cambridge-based Polaroid Corporation, was one of its main benefactors), the Science Center was designed by the Spanish architect **Josep Luis Sert** and built from 1970 to 1972. Sert, the dean of the university's Graduate School of Design from 1953 to 1969, was a disciple of Le Corbusier, whose Carpenter Center for the Visual Arts you've already seen. On the plaza between the Science Center and the Yard is the **Tanner Rock Fountain,** a group of 159 New England field boulders artfully arranged around a small fountain. Since 1985 this has been a favorite spot for students to relax and watch unsuspecting passersby get wet; the fountain sprays a fine mist, which begins slowly and gradually intensifies.

🅣 **TAKE A BREAK** The main level of the Science Center is open to the public and has several options if you want a soft drink, gourmet coffee, or chicken sandwich. Go easy on the sweets, though, in anticipation of your next break.

Leave the Science Center near the fountain and turn right. Keeping the under-pass on your left, follow the walkway for the equivalent of 1½ blocks as it curves around to the right. The **Harvard Law School** campus is on your right. You're back at Massachusetts Avenue, which, when you saw it last, took a right at the Coop and turned north. Cross carefully to:

16. **Cambridge Common.** Memorials and plaques dot this well-used plot of green-ery and bare earth. Follow the sidewalk along Massachusetts Avenue to the left, and after a block or so you'll walk near or over **horseshoes** embedded in the con-crete. This is the path **William Dawes,** Paul Revere's fellow alarm-sounder, took from Boston to Lexington on April 18, 1775. Turn right onto Garden Street and continue following the Common for 1 block. On your right you'll see a monu-ment marking the place where Gen. **George Washington** took control of the Continental Army on July 3, 1775. The elm under which he assumed command is no longer standing.

Cross Garden Street and backtrack to:

17. **Christ Church,** Zero Garden Street, the oldest church in Cambridge. **Peter Harrison** of Newport, Rhode Island (also the architect of King's Chapel in Boston), designed the church, which opened in 1761. Note the square wooden tower. Inside the vestibule you can still see **bullet holes** made by British muskets. At one time the church was used as the barracks for Connecticut troops, who melted down the organ pipes to make ammunition.

Facing the church, turn right and proceed on Garden Street to the first inter-section. This is Appian Way. Turn left and take the first right into:

18. **Radcliffe Yard.** Radcliffe College was founded in 1879 as the "Harvard Annex" and named for **Ann Radcliffe, Lady Mowlson,** Harvard's first female benefactor. Undergraduate classes merged with Harvard's in 1943, Radcliffe graduates first received Harvard degrees in 1963, and in 1977 Harvard officially assumed responsibility for educating undergraduate women. Today, Radcliffe remains an independent corporation within the university and has its own pres-ident, though its degrees, classes, and facilities are shared with Harvard. After you've strolled around, return to Appian Way and turn right. You'll emerge on Brattle Street. Turn right to take an interesting detour (and add about an hour to your walk) by visiting the **Longfellow National Historic Site,** 105 Brattle St. (see chapter 7). Otherwise, turn left and continue walking along Brattle Street (there are excellent shops on both sides of the street).

🙂 **TAKE A BREAK**   Yes, **Billings & Stover Apothecaries,** 41A Brattle St. (☎ 617/547-0502), on your left, is a drugstore. Look harder—the front of the store is an old-fashioned soda fountain.

Across the street is the:

19. **Brattle Theater,** 40 Brattle St. Opened in 1890 as Brattle Hall, it was founded by the Cambridge Social Union and used as a venue for cultural entertainment. In 1953, it was converted to a movie hall and quickly became known as Cam-bridge's center for art films. The Brattle Theater, one of the oldest independent movie houses in the country, started the *Casablanca* revival craze, which explains the name of the restaurant in the basement.

You're now in the **Brattle Square** part of Harvard Square. You might see street musicians or performers, a protest, a speech, or just more stores to explore. Cross Brattle Street at **WordsWorth Books,** turn right, and follow the curve of the building around the corner to Mount Auburn Street. Stay on the left-hand side of the street as you cross John F. Kennedy Street, Dunster Street, Holyoke Street, and Linden Street. On your left between Dunster and Holyoke streets is **Holyoke Center,** an administration building designed by **Josep Luis Sert** with commercial space on the ground floor. The corner of Mount Auburn and Linden streets is a good vantage point for viewing the:

20. Harvard Lampoon Castle, designed by **Wheelwright & Haven** in 1909. Listed on the National Register of Historic Places, this is the home of Harvard's undergraduate humor magazine, the *Lampoon.* The main tower looks like a face, with windows as the eyes, nose, and mouth, topped by what looks like a miner's hat. The *Lampoon* and the daily student newspaper, the *Crimson,* share a long history of reciprocal pranks and harmless vandalism. Elaborate security measures notwithstanding, *Crimson* editors occasionally make off with the bird that might be atop the castle (it looks like a crane but is actually an ibis), and *Lampoon* staffers have absconded with the huge wood president's chair from the Crimson.

You'll pass the *Crimson* building on your right if you decide to detour for a visit to the **Harvard Book Store** (turn left onto Plympton Street and follow it back to Mass. Ave.; the store is at the corner). Otherwise, follow Mount Auburn Street back to John F. Kennedy Street. Alternatively, cross Mount Auburn Street and walk away from Holyoke Center on Holyoke Street or Dunster Street to get a sense of some of the rest of the campus. Turn right on Winthrop Street or South Street, and proceed to John F. Kennedy Street.

Turn left onto John F. Kennedy Street, cross it at some point, and follow it toward the Charles River, almost to Memorial Drive. On your right is:

21. John F. Kennedy Park. This lovely parcel of land was an empty plot near the MBTA train yard in the 1970s (at that time the Red Line ended at Harvard), when the search was on for a site for the Kennedy Library. Traffic concerns led to the library's being built in Dorchester, but the **Graduate School of Government** and this adjacent park bear the president's name. Walk away from the street to enjoy the **fountain,** which is engraved with excerpts from the president's speeches. This is an excellent place to take a break and plan the rest of your day.

9

Shopping

Like many other elements of the Boston area, the shopping scene is a harmonious blend of the classic and the contemporary. You'll find intimate boutiques and sprawling malls, esoteric book shops and national chain stores, classy galleries and snazzy secondhand-clothing outlets, and the most famous discount store in the country, if not the world—Filene's Basement. It embodies a quality that Bostonians have always prized: Yankee thrift.

1 The Shopping Scene

The other major shopping areas in Boston and Cambridge have been overshadowed recently by the Back Bay, which seems only fitting—the Prudential Center casts a long shadow over the neighborhood, and the **Shops at Prudential Center** are the hot new retail destination in town. You could easily spend a day browsing the stores in the **Back Bay,** at the "Pru," upscale **Copley Place** (linked by a weatherproof walkway across Huntington Avenue), **Neiman Marcus, Lord & Taylor, Saks Fifth Avenue,** and the dozens of galleries, shops, and boutiques along **Newbury Street.**

Another popular destination is **Faneuil Hall Marketplace,** the busiest attraction in Boston not only because of its smorgasbord of food outlets, but also for its shops, boutiques, and pushcarts, which sell everything from rubber stamps to costume jewelry, flowers to souvenirs.

If the prospect of the hubbub at Faneuil Hall is too much for you, stroll over to **Charles Street,** at the foot of Beacon Hill. It's a short but commercially dense (and picturesque) street noted for its antique and gift shops.

One of Boston's oldest shopping areas is **Downtown Crossing.** Now a traffic-free pedestrian mall along Washington, Winter, and Summer streets near Boston Common, it's home to two major department stores (**Filene's** and **Macy's**), tons of smaller clothing and shoe stores, food and merchandise pushcarts, outlets of two major bookstore chains (**Barnes & Noble** and **Borders**), and the original **Filene's Basement.** A city project aimed at refurbishing Washington Street from Downtown Crossing to Chinatown is currently under way—note the elegant streetlights. Most stores are open weeknights and Saturday until 7pm, and Sunday until 5 or 6pm.

Taxes & Times

Massachusetts charges no sales tax on clothing priced below $175 or on food. All other items are taxed at 5%, as are restaurant meals and take-out food. The state no longer prohibits stores from opening before noon on Sunday, but many still wait until noon or don't open at all—call ahead before setting out.

Harvard Square in Cambridge, with its bookstores, boutiques, and T-shirt shops, is about 15 minutes from downtown Boston by subway. An aggressive neighborhood association has kept the area from being consumed by chain stores, and although the bohemian days of "the Square" are long gone, you'll find a mix of national and regional outlets as well as independent retailers. A walk along **Massachusetts Avenue** in either direction to the next T stop (**Porter Square** to the north, **Central Square** to the southeast) will take an hour or so, time well-spent for dedicated consumers—Mass. Ave., as it's known, is lined with shops.

2 Shopping A to Z

Here we've singled out establishments we especially like and indicated neighborhoods that suit shoppers interested in particular types of merchandise. Unless otherwise indicated, addresses are in Boston.

ANTIQUES

No antique hound worthy of the name will leave Boston without an expedition along both sides of **Charles Street** from Cambridge Street to Beacon Street.

Boston Antique Center. 54 Canal St., fourth floor. ☎ **617/742-1400.** MBTA: Green or Orange Line to North Station or Haymarket.

A stone's throw from North Station and Faneuil Hall, you'll find about 50 dealers; many concentrate on British goods.

✪ **Boston Antique Cooperative I & II.** 119 Charles St. ☎ **617/227-9810** and 617/227-9811. MBTA: Red Line to Charles/MGH.

These cooperatives are filled with merchandise from Europe, Asia, and the United States. They specialize in furniture, vintage clothing and photographs, jewelry, and porcelain, but you might come across just about anything. The traffic is heavy and the turnover rapid, so if you see something you like, buy it immediately or risk losing out.

Bromfield Pen Shop. 5 Bromfield St. ☎ **617/482-9053.** MBTA: Red or Orange Line to Downtown Crossing.

This shop's selection of antique pens will thrill any collector. It also sells new pens, including Mont Blanc, Pelikan, Waterman, and Omas.

Danish Country Antique Furniture. 138 Charles St. ☎ **617/227-1804.** MBTA: Red Line to Charles/MGH.

Owner James Kilroy specializes in Scandinavian antique furnishings dating from the 1700s onward. You'll also see folk art, crafts, Royal Copenhagen porcelain, and 19th-century Chinese furniture and home accessories.

✪ **Shreve, Crump & Low.** 330 Boylston St. ☎ **617/267-9100.** MBTA: Green Line to Arlington.

This Boston institution, founded in 1796, is best known for new jewelry, china, silver, crystal, and watches. But Shreve's, as it's widely known, also has an antiques department on the second floor. It specializes in 18th- and 19th-century American and English furnishings, British and American silver, and Chinese porcelain.

ART

If you're passionate or just curious about art, try to set aside a couple of hours for strolling along **Newbury Street.** You'll find an infinite variety of styles and media in the dozens of galleries at street level and on the higher floors (remember to look up). Browsers and questions are welcome. Most galleries are open Tuesday through Sunday from 10 or 11am to 5:30 or 6pm.

Once a year, in late June, the street from the Public Garden to Massachusetts Avenue is closed to traffic for a day, and more than 30 galleries are open for **Art Newbury Street.** The celebration of the area's galleries features work by regional and international artists, with special exhibits and outdoor entertainment. For information, contact the **Newbury Street League,** 158 Newbury St. (☎ 617/267-7961; www.newbury-st.tne.com).

Alpha Gallery. 14 Newbury St., second floor. ☎ **617/536-4465.** E-mail: alphagall@aol.com. MBTA: Green Line to Arlington.

Directed by Joanna E. Fink, daughter of founder Alan Fink, Alpha Gallery specializes in contemporary American paintings, sculpture, and works on paper, as well as modern master paintings and prints.

Barbara Krakow Gallery. 10 Newbury St., fifth floor. ☎ **617/262-4490.** MBTA: Green Line to Arlington.

This prestigious gallery, established more than 30 years ago, specializes in paintings, sculpture, drawings, and prints created after 1945.

Copley Society of Boston. 158 Newbury St. ☎ **617/536-5049.** MBTA: Green Line to Copley.

America's oldest art association (founded in 1879), the Copley Society counted James McNeill Whistler and John Singer Sargent among its exhibitors. Today most members come from the New England area, and shows are held regularly.

Gallery NAGA. 67 Newbury St. ☎ **617/267-9060.** MBTA: Green Line to Arlington.

In the neo-Gothic Church of the Covenant, Gallery NAGA exhibits contemporary painting, sculpture, prints, furniture, and works in glass. A stop here is a must if you want to see holography (trust me, you do).

✪ **Gargoyles, Grotesques & Chimeras.** 262 Newbury St. ☎ **617/536-2362.** MBTA: Green Line B, C, or D train to Hynes/ICA.

This intentionally gloomy space is decorated with gargoyles of all sizes. You'll also see plaster reproductions of details on the facades of famous cathedrals and other buildings, nongargoyle home decorations, and haunting photographs that set the Gothic mood.

Haley & Steele. 91 Newbury St. ☎ **617/536-6339.** MBTA: Green Line to Arlington.

If you prefer traditional to contemporary, this is the place. You'll find maritime, military, botanical, and historical prints, and 19th-century oil paintings and British sporting prints.

Koo De Kir. 34 Charles St. ☎ **617/723-8111.** MBTA: Red Line to Charles/MGH.

Back Bay & Beacon Hill Shopping

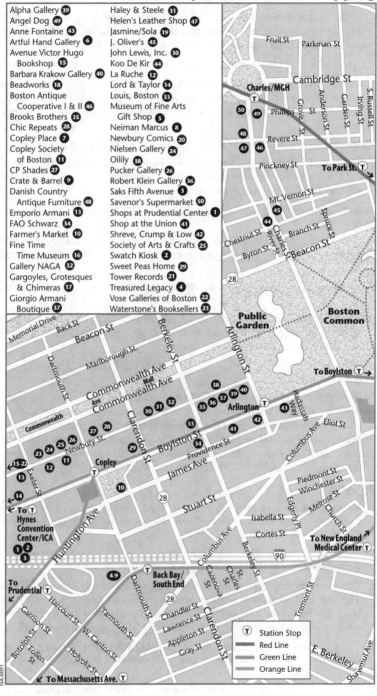

Alpha Gallery ❸❾
Angel Dog ❹❾
Anne Fontaine ❹❸
Artful Hand Gallery ❻
Avenue Victor Hugo
 Bookshop ❶❺
Barbara Krakow Gallery ❹⓿
Beadworks ❶❽
Boston Antique
 Cooperative I & II ❹❻
Brooks Brothers ❸❺
Chic Repeats ❷❽
Copley Place ❼
Copley Society
 of Boston ❶❶
CP Shades ❷❼
Crate & Barrel ❾
Danish Country
 Antique Furniture ❹❽
Emporio Armani ❶❸
FAO Schwarz ❸❹
Farmer's Market ❶⓿
Fine Time
 Time Museum ❶❻
Gallery NAGA ❸❷
Gargoyles, Grotesques
 & Chimeras ❶❼
Giorgio Armani
 Boutique ❸❼

Haley & Steele ❸❶
Helen's Leather Shop ❹❼
Jasmine/Sola ❶❾
J. Oliver's ❹❺
John Lewis, Inc. ❸⓿
Koo De Kir ❹❹
La Ruche ❶❷
Lord & Taylor ❶❹
Louis, Boston ❸❸
Museum of Fine Arts
 Gift Shop ❺
Neiman Marcus ❽
Newbury Comics ❷⓿
Nielsen Gallery ❷❹
Oilily ❸❽
Pucker Gallery ❷❻
Robert Klein Gallery ❸❻
Saks Fifth Avenue ❸
Savenor's Supermarket ❺⓿
Shops at Prudential Center ❶
Shop at the Union ❹❶
Shreve, Crump & Low ❹❷
Society of Arts & Crafts ❷❺
Swatch Kiosk ❷
Sweet Peas Home ❷❾
Tower Records ❷❶
Treasured Legacy ❹
Vose Galleries of Boston ❷❷
Waterstone's Booksellers ❷❸

195

In the heart of Beacon Hill's antiques wonderland, Koo De Kir is a splash of the 21st century. Its selection of contemporary home accessories, furniture, lighting, and sculpture ranges from classics-to-be to downright whimsical.

✪ **Nielsen Gallery.** 179 Newbury St. ☎ **617/266-4835.** MBTA: Green Line to Copley.

Owner Nina Nielsen personally selects the artists who exhibit in her gallery (which has been here for more than 30 years), and she has great taste. You might come across the work of a young, newly discovered talent or that of a more established artist.

✪ **Pucker Gallery.** 171 Newbury St. ☎ **617/267-9473.** MBTA: Green Line to Copley.

Spread over four floors, Pucker Gallery's eclectic offerings include Inuit, African, and Israeli art; contemporary paintings, prints, and drawings by regional and international artists; and excellent photographs.

Robert Klein Gallery. 38 Newbury St., fourth floor. ☎ **617/267-7997.** MBTA: Green Line to Arlington.

For 19th- and 20th-century photography, head to Robert Klein Gallery. Among the artists represented are Diane Arbus, Robert Mapplethorpe, Man Ray, and Ansel Adams.

Treasured Legacy. 100 Huntington Ave. ☎ **617/424-8717.** MBTA: Orange Line to Back Bay.

This small store is packed with African-American art, African sculpture and textiles, art books and general-interest titles. It's across Dartmouth Street from Back Bay Station, on the ground level of Copley Place.

Vose Galleries of Boston. 238 Newbury St. ☎ **617/536-6176.** MBTA: Green Line B, C, or D train to Hynes/ICA.

It seems fitting that one of Vose Galleries's specialties is paintings of the Hudson River School—the business and the mid-19th-century movement are about the same age. Vose Galleries, the oldest continuously operating gallery in the United States, opened in 1841 and is still run by the Vose family (now in its fifth generation). You'll see works of the Boston School and American Impressionists among the 18th-, 19th-, and early-20th-century American paintings.

BOOKS

Harvard Square is to books as Newbury Street is to art. Bibliophiles will relish wandering around the Square's used and new bookstores (as on Newbury Street, don't forget to look above street level).

Avenue Victor Hugo Bookshop. 339 Newbury St. ☎ **617/266-7746.** E-mail: avhbooks@world.std.com. MBTA: Green Line B, C, or D train to Hynes/ICA.

This two-story shop buys, sells, and trades new and used books and estate libraries. The stock of 150,000 books is comprehensive; the primary specialty is science fiction. You'll also find periodicals, with back issues of magazines that date to 1850, and a selection of general fiction titles that's billed as the largest north of New York City.

✪ **Brattle Book Store.** 9 West St. ☎ **800/447-9595** or 617/542-0210. E-mail: brattle@tiac.net. MBTA: Red or Orange Line to Downtown Crossing, or Green Line to Boylston.

This marvelous store near Downtown Crossing buys and sells used, rare, and out-of-print titles, and owner Kenneth Gloss does free appraisals. Be sure to check out the carts out front (in all but the nastiest weather) for good deals on books of all ages. *Warning:* Book lovers and collectors who make this the first stop on their visit to Downtown Crossing might not get any other shopping done.

Buck A Book. Various locations.

This discount chain sells a wild variety of books for adults and children for just $1 apiece. You'll also see gifts, greeting cards, wrapping paper, and office supplies, all deeply discounted. Books designated "just a bit more" top the dollar mark but seldom exceed $10. Be careful not to buy more than you can carry comfortably. There are stores in Boston at 125 Tremont St. (☎ **617/357-1919**), near the Park Street T; at 38 Court St. (☎ **617/367-9419**), near Government Center; and in Cambridge at 30 John F. Kennedy St. (☎ **617/492-5500**).

Globe Corner Bookstore. 500 Boylston St. ☎ **617/859-8008.** www.globecorner.com. MBTA: Green Line to Copley 28 Church St., Cambridge. ☎ **617/497-6277.** MBTA: Red Line to Harvard.

These overstuffed stores (offspring of the dear departed original on the Freedom Trail) carry huge selections of travel guides and essays, atlases, globes, maps, and nautical charts.

✪ **Harvard Book Store.** 1256 Massachusetts Ave., Cambridge. ☎ **800/542-READ** outside 617, or 617/661-1515. www.harvard.com. E-mail: hbs-info@harvard.com. MBTA: Red Line to Harvard.

The excellent scholarly selection and discounted best-sellers attract shoppers to the main level of this independent bookstore, and the basement is the draw for those in the know. Prices on remainders are good, and used paperbacks (many bought for classes and hardly opened) are 50% off their original price.

The Harvard Coop. 1400 Massachusetts Ave., Cambridge. ☎ **617/499-2000.** MBTA: Red Line to Harvard.

The Coop (rhymes with "hoop"), or Harvard Cooperative Society, is student-oriented but not a run-of-the-mill college bookstore. You'll find Harvard insignia merchandise, stationery, prints and posters, music, and books—including the required texts for Harvard classes, a good department for browsing. As at Boston University, Barnes & Noble runs the book operation.

Schoenhof's Foreign Books. 76A Mt. Auburn St., Cambridge. ☎ **617/547-8855.** www.schoenhofs.com. E-mail: info@schoenhofs.com. MBTA: Red Line to Harvard.

Schoenhof's stocks adult literature and children's books in more than two dozen languages, as well as dictionaries and language-learning materials for more than 300 languages and dialects. The multilingual staff arranges special orders at no extra charge.

Waterstone's Booksellers. 26 Exeter St. ☎ **617/859-7300.** MBTA: Green Line to Copley. Quincy Market, Upper Rotunda. ☎ **617/589-0930.** MBTA: Green or Blue Line to Government Center.

In the old Exeter Street Theater near the corner of Newbury Street, the Back Bay branch of this British import has three spacious floors that hold more than 160,000 titles. The Faneuil Hall Marketplace store is smaller but also great for browsing; both have good remainders and children's books, and discounted best-sellers. The Back Bay location schedules weekly author readings.

✪ **WordsWorth Books.** 30 Brattle St., Cambridge. ☎ **800/899-2202** or 617/354-5201. www.wordsworth.com. E-mail: info@wordsworth.com. MBTA: Red Line to Harvard.

This sprawling store stocks more than 100,000 volumes, all (except textbooks) discounted at least 10%. It's a great place for browsing; if you prefer, the information desk staff will brainstorm with you until the database generates the title you want. The online service lets you search for books by title, author, and keyword. The excellent children's selection is up the street at ✪ **Curious George Goes to WordsWorth** (1 John F. Kennedy St.; ☎ 617/498-0062).

CRAFTS

The Artful Hand Gallery. Copley Place. ☎ **617/262-9601.** MBTA: Orange Line to Back Bay, or Green Line to Copley.

The Artful Hand specializes, as you might guess, in handcrafted items. It shows and sells wonderful jewelry, ceramics, blown glass, wooden boxes, and sculpture exclusively by American artisans.

Pearl Art & Craft Supplies. 579 Massachusetts Ave., Cambridge. ☎ **617/547-6600.** E-mail: cambridge@pearlart.com. MBTA: Red Line to Central.

The Central Square branch of this national discount chain boasts three floors of everything you need to do it yourself, from pens and pencils to stamps and stencils to beads and fittings.

✪ **Society of Arts and Crafts.** 175 Newbury St. ☎ **617/266-1810.** E-mail: societycraft@earthlink.net. MBTA: Green Line to Copley.

Contemporary American work, much created by New Englanders, is the focus here, at the oldest nonprofit craft organization in the country. You'll find jewelry, furniture and home accessories, glass, and ceramics that range from the practical to the purely decorative. The **Downtown Crossing** branch, open on weekdays only, is on the second floor of 101 Arch St. (☎ 617/345-0033), off Summer Street.

DEPARTMENT STORES

There's so much else going on in the Back Bay that you might forget it's home to branches of three elegant chains. We particularly like **Lord & Taylor,** 760 Boylston St. (☎ 617/262-6000) for its great sales and costume jewelry. The high-end **Saks Fifth Avenue,** Prudential Plaza (☎ 617/262-8500), would be the classiest department store in town if not for **Neiman Marcus,** 5 Copley Place (☎ 617/536-3660), which charges Texas-size prices for the trappings of true luxury.

Filene's. 426 Washington St. ☎ **617/357-2100.** MBTA: Red or Orange Line to Downtown Crossing.

Now that Jordan Marsh has become Macy's, Downtown Crossing's remaining fine old New England name is Filene's (say "Fie-*leens*"). The full-service department store has all the usual amenities, including a good cosmetics department. Filene's is no longer affiliated with Filene's Basement (which is, yes, in the basement).

Macy's. 450 Washington St. ☎ **617/357-3000.** MBTA: Red or Orange Line to Downtown Crossing.

Across Summer Street from Filene's is New England's largest store. It was Jordan Marsh until Macy's subsumed that operation in 1996, and it bears the hallmarks of the New York–based chain, including excellent selections of housewares, china, and silver.

DISCOUNT SHOPPING

Eddie Bauer Outlet. 252 Washington St. ☎ **617/227-4840.** MBTA: Blue Line to State.

Less Is More

Follow the crowds to ✪ **Filene's Basement,** 426 Washington St. (☎ **617/542-2011**), a Downtown Crossing institution that has spoiled New Englanders for paying retail since 1908. Far from passing off their finds as pricey indulgences, true devotees boast about their bargains. Here's how it works: After 2 weeks on the selling floor, merchandise is automatically marked down 25% from its already discounted price. Check the boards hanging from the ceiling for the crucial dates; the original sale date is on the back of every price tag. Prices fall until, after 35 days, anything that hasn't sold (for 75% off) goes to charity. Filene's Basement split off from Filene's, the department store upstairs from which it leases space, in 1988. The independent discount chain has branches throughout the Northeast and Midwest, but the automatic markdown policy is in force only at the original store, which attracts 15,000 to 20,000 shoppers a day.

The crowds swell for special sales, scheduled when a store is going out of business or when a classy designer, retailer, or catalog house (say, Neiman Marcus, Barneys, or Saks Fifth Avenue) finds itself overstocked. You'll see the unpredictable particulars, sometimes including an early opening time, advertised in the newspapers. Four times a year, the legendary $249-wedding-dress sale sparks a truly alarming display of bridal bargain hunting; days are also set aside for dresses, men's and women's suits, raincoats, dress shirts, children's clothing, evening gowns, lingerie, cosmetics, leather goods, designer shoes, and anything else that looks promising to the store's eagle-eyed buyers. Two weeks later, leftovers wind up on the automatic-markdown racks, and the real hunting begins. Try to beat the lunchtime crowds, but if you can't, don't despair—just be patient. *Tip:* If you're not wild about trying on clothes in the open dressing rooms, slip them on over what you're wearing, an acceptable throwback to the days before there were dressing rooms. Or make like the natives and return what doesn't suit you, in person or even by mail.

If this is the sort of activity that gets your juices flowing, you haven't lived until you've clipped the original $225 price tag off a dress and responded to the first person who offers a compliment by saying, "Oh, do you like it? It was $17."

For reduced (albeit not spectacular) prices on men's and women's sportswear and outerwear, camping equipment, and luggage, check the regularly changing selection here.

Loehmann's. 387 Washington St. ☎ **617/338-7177.** MBTA: Red or Orange Line to Downtown Crossing.

The tradition of Bostonians explaining Filene's Basement to New Yorkers by comparing it to Loehmann's went out the window in 1997, when Downtown Crossing got a Loehmann's of its own. Costly women's fashions, accessories, and shoes at drastically reduced prices are the drawing card here.

FASHION
ADULTS

Anne Fontaine. 318 Boylston St. ☎ **617/423-0366.** MBTA: Green Line to Arlington.

This Heritage on the Garden boutique is the first U.S. outlet for the designer's "perfect white blouse collection from Paris." We wanted to laugh, but then we saw for ourselves—almost every item *is* a perfect (for one reason or another) white blouse. A few darker tops have sneaked in, too. Prices start at $80.

Brooks Brothers. 46 Newbury St. ☎ **617/267-2600.** MBTA: Green Line to Arlington. 75 State St. ☎ **617/261-9990.** MBTA: Blue or Orange Line to State.

Blue blazers, gray flannels, and seersucker suits are widely available, but only at Brooks Brothers will you find the business and casual styles that mark you as a "proper Bostonian." Brooks is also the only place for exactly the right preppy shade of pink button-down oxford shirts. The store stocks women's clothes and sportswear too.

CP Shades. 139B Newbury St. ☎ **617/421-0846.** MBTA: Green Line to Copley.

No, not sunglasses—comfortable knits and natural fabrics of every description that women can wear for everything from board meetings to baby-sitting.

Geoffrey B. Small/Edge. 115 Kingston St., second floor. ☎ **617/482-0459.** www.gbs.net. MBTA: Red Line to Downtown Crossing.

Pioneering designer Geoffrey B. Small's boutique is in his factory, near Downtown Crossing and Chinatown. A native of the Boston area, Small is a sensation in Japan and well-known in Europe for his reconditioned vintage clothing, assembled with couture-quality precision. Prices start at $30.

Giorgio Armani Boutique. 22 Newbury St. ☎ **617/267-3200.** MBTA: Green Line to Arlington.

Here you'll find Armani's sleek, sophisticated men's and women's clothing—in addition to ski, golf, and bridal collections—at true Armani prices. If your taste (and budget) is less grand, head down the street to **Emporio Armani** at 210–214 Newbury St. (☎ **617/262-7300**) for sportswear, jeans, and accessories.

Louis, Boston. 234 Berkeley St. ☎ **800/225-5135** or 617/262-6100. MBTA: Green Line to Arlington.

This ultraprestigious store (with prices to match) sells designer men's suits that can be coordinated with handmade shirts, silk ties, and Italian shoes. Louis, Woman, at the same address—a building that was once the Museum of Natural History—caters to an elegant female clientele. Also on the premises are a full-service hair salon and Café Louis, which serves lunch and dinner.

CHILDREN

Calliope. 33 Brattle St., Cambridge. ☎ **617/876-4149.** MBTA: Red Line to Harvard.

The must-see window displays at this Harvard Square shop use clothes, toys, and stuffed animals to illustrate sayings and proverbs, often twisted into hilarious puns. The merchandise inside—clothing, shoes, and a huge selection of plush animals—is equally delightful.

Oilily. 31 Newbury St. ☎ **617/247-9299.** MBTA: Green Line to Arlington.

At this end of Newbury Street, even kids must be *au courant*. Lend a hand with a visit to the Boston branch of the chi-chi international chain, which specializes in brightly colored fashions and accessories.

Saturday's Child. 1762 Massachusetts Ave., Cambridge. ☎ **617/661-6402.** MBTA: Red Line to Porter.

Never mind the nursery rhyme—"Saturday's child works hard for a living," my foot. You won't want your little angel lifting a finger in these precious (in both senses of the word) outfits. You'll also find top-quality shoes, accessories, and toys.

SECONDHAND CLOTHING

Boomerangs. 60 Canal St. ☎ **617/450-1500.** MBTA: Green or Orange Line to North Station or Haymarket.

It's not all used, and it's not all clothing, but the austere store and the designer duds are so classy, you'll forget you're in a warehouse building near North Station. Proceeds benefit the AIDS Action Committee.

Chic Repeats. 117 Newbury St. ☎ **617/536-8580.** MBTA: Green Line to Arlington.

High-rent attire goes for low-rent prices at these nonprofit consignment boutiques sponsored by the Junior League of Boston. They carry fancy women's (upstairs) and children's (downstairs) clothing.

The Garment District. 200 Broadway, Cambridge. ☎ **617/876-5230.** MBTA: Red Line to Kendall.

You're hitting the clubs and you want to look cool, but you have almost no money. You'll be right at home among the shoppers here, paying great prices for a huge selection of contemporary and vintage clothing.

VINTAGE CLOTHING

Keezer's. 140 River St., Cambridge. ☎ **617/547-2455.** MBTA: Red Line to Central.

Generations of local college students have bought their first (and often only) tuxedo at this institution just south of Central Square. The terrific prices also extend to excellent nonformal designer menswear and a decent women's section.

✪ **Oona's.** 1210 Massachusetts Ave., Cambridge. ☎ **617/491-2654.** MBTA: Red Line to Harvard.

From funky accessories and costume jewelry to vintage dresses nice enough to get married in, Oona's, just outside Harvard Square, has an extensive selection of "experienced clothing" and good prices.

FOOD

Cardullo's Gourmet Shoppe. 6 Brattle St., Cambridge. ☎ **617/491-8888.** E-mail: cardullo@tiac.net. MBTA: Red Line to Harvard.

A veritable United Nations of fancy food, Cardullo's carries specialties (including a huge variety of candy) from just about everywhere. If you can't afford the big-ticket items, order a tasty sandwich to go.

✪ **Dairy Fresh Candies.** 57 Salem St. ☎ **800/336-5536** or 617/742-2639. MBTA: Green or Orange Line to Haymarket.

This North End hole-in-the-wall is crammed with sweets and other delectables, from bagged nuts and dried fruit to imported Italian specialties. It's too small to turn the children loose, but they'll be happy they waited outside when you return with confections to fortify them along the Freedom Trail.

Le Saucier. Quincy Market, North Canopy. ☎ **617/227-9649.** MBTA: Green or Blue Line to Government Center.

The sauces collected in this little space might bring tears to your eyes. The variety verges on infinite, and the hot sauces (check the front counter for free samples) are concocted from positively diabolical ingredients.

J. Pace & Son. 42 Cross St. ☎ **617/227-9673.** MBTA: Green or Orange Line to Haymarket.

Imported Italian food items, from fine meats and cheeses to pasta and cookies, over-flow the shelves and cases at this bustling market on the threshold of the North End. Prices are good, especially for olive oil, and there's never a dull moment at the front counter. Order a sandwich if you don't feel like hauling groceries around.

Savenor's Supermarket. 160 Charles St. ☎ **617/723-6328.** MBTA: Red Line to Charles/MGH.

Long a Cambridge institution (and a Julia Child favorite), Savenor's moved to Bea-con Hill after a fire in 1993. It's the perfect place to load up on cheese and crack-ers on the way to a concert or movie on the nearby Esplanade. And it's still *the* local purveyor of exotic meats—if you crave buffalo or rattlesnake meat, this is the place.

✪ **Trader Joe's.** 727 Memorial Dr., Cambridge. ☎ **617/491-8582.** 1317 Beacon St., Brookline. ☎ **617/278-9997.** MBTA: Green Line C train to Coolidge Corner.

This celebrated California-based retailer stocks a great selection of natural and organic products, wine, cheese, nuts, baked goods, and other edibles, all at great prices. The Cambridge location is a good place to stop for picnic provisions if you're driving. Get a preview from the Web site (www.traderjoes.com), or just ask devotees—they can't shut up about it.

GIFTS/SOUVENIRS

Boston has dozens of shops and pushcarts that sell T-shirts, hats, and other sou-venirs. At the stores listed below, you'll find gifts that say Boston without actually *saying* "Boston" all over them. Remember to check out shops at museums, which offer unique items, including crafts and games, that will serve as reminders of your trip. Particularly good retail outlets can be found at the **Museum of Fine Arts,** the **Museum of Science,** Harvard's **Peabody Museum,** the **Isabella Stewart Gardner Museum,** the **Concord Museum,** and the **Peabody Essex Museum** in Salem.

Angel Dog. 131 Charles St. ☎ **617/742-6435.** MBTA: Red Line to Charles/MGH.

If it can be on a dog or a dog can be on it, you'll find it here.

✪ **Joie de Vivre.** 1792 Massachusetts Ave., Cambridge. ☎ **617/864-8188.** MBTA: Red Line to Porter.

Joie de Vivre's selection of toys for adults and sophisticated children is beyond com-pare. The kaleidoscope collection alone is worth the trip to this little shop outside Porter Square, and you'll also find salt and pepper shakers, jewelry, note cards, and puzzles.

Museum of Fine Arts Gift Shop. Copley Place. ☎ **617/536-8818.** MBTA: Orange Line to Back Bay, or Green Line to Copley. South Market Building, Faneuil Hall Marketplace. ☎ **617/720-1266.** MBTA: Green or Blue Line to Government Center.

For those without the time or inclination to visit the museum, these delightful branches carry posters, prints, cards and stationery, books, educational toys, scarves, mugs, T-shirts, and reproductions of jewelry in the museum's collections. You might even be inspired to make the trip to see the real thing.

J. Oliver's. 38 Charles St. ☎ **617/723-3388.** MBTA: Red Line to Charles/MGH.

You'll want to invent occasions to justify buying the greeting cards, postcards, pic-ture frames, jewelry, wrapping paper, gardening ornaments, and other funky gift items at this Beacon Hill boutique.

The Shop at the Union. 356 Boylston St. ☎ **617/536-5651.** MBTA: Green Line to Arlington.

This large, crowded store has a wide selection of high-quality home, garden, and personal accessories. You'll see jewelry, greeting cards, antiques, needlework, hand-made children's clothes, toys, and confections. Most of the merchandise is manufactured by women or woman-owned firms. Proceeds benefit the human services programs of the Women's Educational and Industrial Union, a nonprofit educational and social-service organization founded in 1877.

HOME & GARDEN

Crate & Barrel. South Market Building, Faneuil Hall Marketplace. ☎ **617/742-6025.** MBTA: Green or Blue Line to Government Center. Copley Place. ☎ **617/536-9400.** MBTA: Orange Line to Back Bay, or Green Line to Copley. 48 Brattle St., Cambridge. ☎ **617/876-6300.** MBTA: Red Line to Harvard.

This is wedding-present heaven, packed with contemporary and classic housewares. The sleek merchandise, from juice glasses and linen napkins to top-of-the-line knives and roasting pans, suits every budget. The four-floor Harvard Square location is the largest in the immediate Boston area (there are 5 others in the suburbs and 50 or so nationwide), and it is a 15-minute stroll from a branch that carries only furniture and home accessories (1045 Massachusetts Ave.; ☎ 617/547-3994).

La Ruche. 168 Newbury St. ☎ **617/536-6366.** MBTA: Green Line to Copley.

If you've never dreamed of living in a birdhouse, that might be because you've never been to this boutique. It stocks European and American glassware and pottery (including the complete line of Mackenzie-Childs majolica ware), unusual home and garden accessories, hand-painted furnishings, and dazzling architectural bird-houses.

Stoddard's. 50 Temple Place. ☎ **617/426-4187.** MBTA: Red or Orange Line to Downtown Crossing.

The oldest cutlery shop in the country, dating from 1800, Stoddard's is full of items you don't know you need until you see them. You'll find sewing scissors, nail scissors (as well as scissors for any other use you can think of), knives of all descriptions (including a spectacular selection of Swiss army knives), shaving brushes, binoculars, fishing tackle, and fly rods. There's also a branch at Copley Place (☎ 617/536-8688).

Sweet Peas Home. 216 Clarendon St. ☎ **617/247-2828.** MBTA: Green Line to Copley.

Just off Newbury Street, this jam-packed little shop carries engagingly funky home and bath accessories, picture frames, lamps, candles, and the like. You'll see a lot of faux rustic items, many made or painted by hand, at unrustic prices.

INSIGNIA MERCHANDISE

Boston University Bookstore. 660 Beacon St. ☎ **617/267-8484.** MBTA: Green Line B, C, or D train to Kenmore.

The BU crest, mascot (a terrier), or name appears somewhere on at least a floor's worth of clothing and just about any other item with room for a logo. The bookstore operation is run by Barnes & Noble.

✪ **The Harvard Shop.** 52 John F. Kennedy St., Cambridge. ☎ **617/864-3000.** MBTA: Red Line to Harvard.

Kids in shopping malls from Jacksonville to Juneau wear Harvard shirts in every color of the rainbow and every outlandish pattern under the sun. Visit the Harvard Shop for authentic paraphernalia in the shadow of the school.

JEWELRY & WATCHES

Beadworks. 349 Newbury St. ☎ **617/247-7227.** MBTA: Green Line B, C, or D train to Hynes/ICA. 23 Church St., Cambridge. ☎ **617/868-9777.** MBTA: Red Line to Harvard.

The jewelry at these shops will suit you exactly—you make it yourself. Prices for the dazzling variety of raw materials start at 5¢ a bead, fittings (hardware) are available, and you can assemble your finery at the in-store worktable.

Fine Time Time Museum. 279 Newbury St. ☎ **617/536-5858.** MBTA: Green Line B, C, or D train to Hynes/ICA.

Watch collectors won't want to miss the unique selection of vintage timepieces assembled by proprietor William Zeitler, who offers a 1-year guarantee on his merchandise. Through the material, workmanship, mechanical workings, or engraving, every piece tells a story.

High Gear. 139 Richmond St. ☎ **617/523-5804.** MBTA: Green or Orange Line to Haymarket.

Don't be put off by the sign that says this little shop around the corner from the Paul Revere House (and right on the Freedom Trail) is a wholesale outlet. Retail shoppers are welcome to peruse the impressive selection of costume jewelry.

✪ **John Lewis, Inc.** 97 Newbury St. ☎ **617/266-6665.** MBTA: Green Line to Arlington.

The imaginative women's and men's jewelry at this museum-like shop suits both traditional and trendy tastes, and the staff is cordial and helpful. The pieces that mark you as a savvy Bostonian are the earrings, necklaces, and bracelets made of hammered silver or gold circles.

Swatch Store. 57 John F. Kennedy St. (in the Galleria Mall), Cambridge. ☎ **617/864-1227.** MBTA: Red Line to Harvard.

Swatch watch fiends will revel in the largest Swatch store in the world, also the home of the Swatch Museum (a collection of every design since 1983). There are also Swatch kiosks at the Shops at Prudential Center and Faneuil Hall Marketplace.

LOBSTER

If you relished the fresh seafood in Boston and want to share some with a friend, these businesses will ship a top-quality live lobster overnight and make someone at home very happy: **Bay State Lobster,** 379–395 Commercial St. (☎ **617/523-7960;** MBTA: Green or Orange Line to Haymarket); **James Hook & Co.,** 15 Northern Ave. at Atlantic Ave. (☎ **617/423-5500;** MBTA: Blue Line to Aquarium, or Red Line to South Station); and **Legal Seafoods Fresh by Mail,** Logan Airport Terminal C. (☎ **800/477-5342** or 617/569-4622; MBTA: Blue Line to Airport).

MALLS/SHOPPING CENTERS

CambridgeSide Galleria. 100 CambridgeSide Place, Cambridge. ☎ **617/621-8666.** MBTA: Green Line to Lechmere, or Red Line to Kendall and free shuttle bus.

This three-level mall has two large department stores—**Filene's** (☎ 617/621-3800) and **Sears** (☎ 617/252-3500)—and more than 100 specialty stores. In addition to the usual suspects, you'll find traditional sportswear at **Abercrombie & Fitch** (☎ 617/494-1338), tea as well as coffee at **Gloria Jean's Coffee Beans** (☎ 617/577-1424), and casual clothing at **J. Crew** (☎ 617/225-2739). There are also three restaurants and a food court that opens onto an outdoor plaza. The mall's business center provides office services such as fax machines and typing. Strollers and complimentary wheelchairs are available.

A free shuttle bus runs between the mall and the Red Line stop at Kendall Square every 10 to 20 minutes Monday through Saturday from 10am to 9:30pm and Sunday from 11am to 7pm. There's plenty of garage parking.

✪ **Copley Place.** 100 Huntington Ave. ☎ **617/375-4400.** MBTA: Orange Line to Back Bay, or Green Line to Copley.

Since it opened in 1985, Copley Place has set the standard for upscale shopping in Boston, and its convenient location near the Westin and Marriott hotels and the Prudential Center makes it a crossroads for office workers, film fans, out-of-towners, and enthusiastic consumers. You can while away a couple of hours or a whole day shopping and dining here and at the adjacent Shops at Prudential Center (see below) without ever going outdoors.

Some of Copley Place's 100-plus shops will be familiar from the mall at home, but this is emphatically not a suburban shopping complex that happens to be in the city. You'll see famous stores that don't have another branch in Boston: **Caswell-Massey** (☎ 617/437-9292), **Gucci** (☎ 617/247-3000), **Joan & David** (☎ 617/536-0600), **Liz Claiborne** (☎ 617/859-3787), **Louis Vuitton** (☎ 617/437-6519), **Polo Ralph Lauren** (☎ 617/266-4121), **Tiffany & Co.** (☎ 617/353-0222), and a suitably classy "anchor" department store, **Neiman Marcus** (☎ 617/536-3660).

Even if you plan to head straight to the 11-screen movie theater (warning: some of the screens are unbelievably tiny), leave time to walk around and examine the design. The 6-block, $500 million complex is on the border between the Back Bay and the South End. There's pink marble everywhere, incorporated into the exterior and paving the floors, and a 60-foot-high waterfall sculpture in the skylighted atrium.

Copley Place is open Monday through Saturday from 10am to 8pm, and Sunday from noon to 6pm. Some stores have extended hours, and the theaters and some restaurants are open through late evening. By car, the Massachusetts Turnpike eastbound has a Copley exit. Park in the **Copley Place Garage** (☎ 617/375-4488), off Huntington Avenue at Exeter Street. To pay a reduced rate, have your ticket validated when you make a purchase. Time limits might apply during the day.

Faneuil Hall Marketplace. Between North, Congress, and State sts. and I-93. ☎ 617/338-2323. MBTA: Green or Blue Line to Government Center, or Orange Line to Haymarket.

The original festival market is both wildly popular and widely imitated, and as Faneuil Hall Marketplace moves into its third decade, the complex changes constantly to appeal to visitors as well as natives wary of its touristy reputation. **Faneuil Hall** itself has been refurbished, and the lower floors take it back to its retail roots. The **Quincy Market Colonnade,** in the central building, houses a gargantuan selection of food and confections. The bars and restaurants always seem to be crowded, and the shopping is terrific, if a tad generic.

In and around the five buildings surrounded by brick-and-stone plazas, the shops combine "only in Boston" with "only at every mall in the country." **Marketplace Center** and the ground floors of the **North Market** and **South Market buildings** have lots of chain outlets—a magnet for many, a distraction to some. Most of the unique offerings are under **Quincy Market's canopies** on the pushcarts piled high with crafts and gifts, and upstairs or downstairs in the market buildings. The only way to find what suits you is to explore. Just a few of the shops you'll find are the **Boston Pewter Company** (☎ 617/523-1776), **Celtic Weavers** (☎ 617/720-0750), **Kites of Boston** (☎ 617/742-1455), **Purple Pizazz** (☎ 617/742-6500), and **Whippoorwill Crafts** (☎ 617/523-5149).

Shop hours are Monday through Saturday from 10am to 9pm and Sunday from noon to 6pm. The Colonnade opens earlier, and most bars and restaurants close later. Take the Green or Blue Line to Government Center, or the Orange Line to Haymarket, and just follow the crowds. If you must drive, there's parking in the Government Center garage off Congress Street and the marketplace's own crowded garage off Atlantic Avenue.

The Garage. 36 John F. Kennedy St., Cambridge. No phone. MBTA: Red Line to Harvard.

Wander up the corkscrew ramp to the boutiques and shops (a record store, a clothing store, a jewelry store, and two stores carrying sci-fi paraphernalia) on the upper levels of this little mall, or stay on the main floor and have a light or filling meal at **Formaggio's Deli** (☎ 617/547-4795) or **Bruegger's Bagel Bakery** (☎ 617/661-4664).

The Shops at Prudential Center. 800 Boylston St. ☎ **800/SHOP-PRU** or 617/267-1002. www.prudentialcenter.com. MBTA: Green Line all trains to Copley; E train to Prudential; or B, C, or D train to Hynes/ICA.

In the early 1990s, the poorly lit, windswept plaza level of the "Pru" was completely renovated, enclosed, and reopened as The Shops at Prudential Center, an instant hit. In addition to **Lord & Taylor** (☎ 617/262-6000) and **Saks Fifth Avenue** (☎ 617/262-8500), there are a food court, a "fashion court," a post office, more than 40 shops and boutiques, and five restaurants. Alongside the most famous of the restaurants, Legal Sea Foods, is **Legal Sea Foods Marketplace** (☎ 617/267-5566), where you can pick up chowder or a meal to go. The arcades are dotted with vendors selling gifts, souvenirs, and novelty items off pushcarts, and there's outdoor space in front and back if you need some fresh air. If you're planning a picnic, at ground level on Boylston Street is a **Star Market** supermarket (☎ 617/267-9721). Complimentary strollers and wheelchairs are available.

Hours are Monday through Saturday from 10am to 8pm, Sunday from 11am to 6pm. The restaurants and food court stay open later.

MARKETS

Farmers' Markets. City Hall Plaza, Monday and Wednesday. MBTA: Green or Blue Line to Government Center. Copley Square, Tuesday and Friday. MBTA: Green Line to Copley, or Orange Line to Back Bay.

Massachusetts farmers and growers under the auspices of the state **Department of Food and Agriculture** (☎ 617/227-3018) dispatch trucks filled with whatever's in season to the heart of the city from July through November. Depending on the time of year, you'll have your pick of berries, herbs, tomatoes, squash, pumpkins, apples, corn, and more, all fresh and reasonably priced.

Haymarket. Blackstone Street between North and Hanover sts. No phone. MBTA: Green or Orange Line to Haymarket.

Adjacent to Faneuil Hall Marketplace and the North End, Haymarket is a produce market, open Friday and Saturday only, where prices are great but shoppers are forbidden to touch the merchandise. Trust your eyes—a stall with beautiful peppers might have tired-looking bok choy, or vice versa—or skip shopping altogether and just watch the boisterous scene as vendors hawk their wares and elderly women slug it out with weekend chefs for the freshest items. In addition to produce from the stalls, you'll find meats and cheeses at the shops on Blackstone Street.

MEMORABILIA

✪ **Boston City Store.** Faneuil Hall, lower level. ☎ **617/635-2911.** MBTA: Green or Blue Line to Government Center.

A great, wacky idea, the Boston City Store sells the equivalent of the contents of the municipal attic and basement, from old street signs (look for your name) to used office equipment and furniture. The selection changes regularly according to what has outlived its usefulness or been declared surplus, but you'll always find lucky horseshoes from the mounted police for $5 apiece. Closed Sunday.

✪ **Nostalgia Factory.** 51 North Margin St. ☎ **800/479-8754** or 617/720-2211. www. nostalgia.com. MBTA: Green or Orange Line to Haymarket.

The Nostalgia Factory has gained national attention for its million-piece collection of old advertising, all for sale and arranged in monthly theme exhibits (breakfast foods, cigar boxes, cars, and so on). Long a Newbury Street fixture, the store moved to the North End in 1997 and now has even more room for its enormous collections, which also include original movie posters of all ages and in many languages, vintage war and travel posters, and political memorabilia.

MUSIC

Looney Tunes. 1106 Boylston St. ☎ **617/247-2238.** MBTA: Green Line B, C, or D train to Hynes/ICA. 1001 Massachusetts Ave., Cambridge. ☎ **617/786-5624.** MBTA: Red Line to Harvard.

Where there are college students, there are pizza places, copy shops, and used-record (and CD) stores. These two specialize in jazz and classical, and they have tons of other tunes at excellent prices.

Newbury Comics. 332 Newbury St. ☎ **617/236-4930.** MBTA: Green Line B, C, or D train to Hynes/ICA.

You'll find a wide selection of CDs, tapes, posters, T-shirts, and, of course, comics at the branches of this funky chain. The music is particularly cutting-edge, with lot of independent labels and imports. There are also stores at 1 Washington Mall, near City Hall (☎ **617/248-9992**), and in Harvard Square at 36 John F. Kennedy St., in the Garage mall (☎ **617/491-0337**).

Tower Records. 360 Newbury St. (at Massachusets Ave.). ☎ **617/247-5900.** MBTA: Green Line B, C, or D train to Hynes/ICA.

One of the largest record stores in the country, Tower boasts three floors of records, tapes, CDs, videos, periodicals, and books. The Harvard Square branch, 95 Mount Auburn St. (☎ **617/876-3377**), is smaller but still quite impressive.

PERFUME

✪ **Colonial Drug.** 49 Brattle St., Cambridge. ☎ **617/864-2222.** MBTA: Red Line to Harvard.

The perfume counter at Colonial Drug is a perfect example of what happens when a store decides to do one thing exactly right. You can choose from more than 1,000 fragrances with the help of the gracious staff members, who remain unflappable even during Harvard Square's equivalent of rush hour, Saturday afternoon.

SHOES

Berk's. 50 John F. Kennedy St. ☎ **617/492-9511.** MBTA: Red Line to Harvard.

"Trendy" only scratches the surface in describing the wares at this Harvard Square institution. Come here for Doc Martens (the largest selection in New England), outrageous platforms, and whatever else is fashionable right this red-hot minute.

Helen's Leather Shop. 110 Charles St. ☎ **617/742-2077.** MBTA: Red Line to Charles/MGH.

Homesick Texans visit Helen's just to gaze upon the boots. Many are handmade from exotic leathers, including ostrich, buffalo, and snakeskin (of many varieties). Name brands such as Tony Lama and Dan Post are also available, along with a large selection of other leather goods.

Jasmine/Sola. 37A and 35 Brattle St., Cambridge. ☎ **617/354-6043.** MBTA: Red Line to Harvard.

These Harvard Square boutiques sell men's and women's fashions that are as chic as the spectacular shoe collections. There's also a store in Boston at 329 Newbury St. (☎ **617/437-8466**).

TOYS

FAO Schwarz. 440 Boylston St. ☎ **617/262-5900.** MBTA: Green Line to Copley.

The giant teddy bear at the corner of Berkeley Street is the first indication that you're in for a rollicking good time, and a teddy bear wouldn't steer you wrong. A branch of the famed New York emporium, FAO Schwarz stocks top-quality toys, dolls, stuffed animals, games, books, and vehicles (motorized and not). Children can happily spend hours here, and should you happen to find yourself out shopping without a child, go in anyway—the store is on the first floor of an office building, and nobody has to know you're buying that Barbie for yourself.

Learningsmith. 25 Brattle St., Cambridge. ☎ **617/661-6008.** MBTA: Red Line to Harvard.

Children and parents alike will be delighted with Learningsmith. It offers an excellent selection of toys, games, and other activities that are fun and (shh!) educational.

The Magic Hat. Marketplace Center, Faneuil Hall Marketplace. ☎ **617/439-8840.** MBTA: Green or Blue Line to Government Center, or Orange Line to Haymarket.

Bring your Houdini fantasies along to this small shop with a big "wow" factor. At least one staff member practices sleight-of-hand at the counter, and the stock of props, tricks, gifts, and other fun merchandise is (literally) incredible.

Boston After Dark

10

Countless musicians, actors, and comedians went to college or otherwise got their start in the Boston area, and it's a good place to check out rising stars and promising unknowns. You might get the first look at the next Tracy Chapman, Jack Lemmon, Billy Joel, or Rosie O'Donnell, and you'll certainly be able to enjoy the work of established artists. They perform with one of the world's best symphony orchestras, with a prestigious ballet company, at top-of-the-line jazz and rock clubs, and in shows bound for Broadway or out on tour, just to name a few.

The nightlife scene isn't quite world-class—you can be back from a night of club-hopping when your friends in New York are still deciding what to wear. It isn't all that backward, though—**Planet Hollywood** is coming. It should be open in the Back Bay at Boylston and Fairfield streets by the time you read this. The address and phone number weren't set at press time, but don't let that stop you. Just follow the crowds.

For up-to-date entertainment listings, consult the "Calendar" section of the Thursday *Boston Globe,* the "Scene" section of the Friday *Boston Herald,* and the Sunday arts sections of both papers. The weekly *Boston Phoenix* (published on Thursday) has especially good club listings, and the biweekly *Improper Bostonian* (free at newspaper boxes around town) offers extensive live music listings.

GETTING TICKETS **Ticketmaster** (☎ 617/931-2000; www.ticketmaster.com) and **Next Ticketing** (☎ 617/423-NEXT; www.boston.com/next), the major agencies that serve Boston, calculate service charges per ticket, not per order. To avoid the charge, visit the venue in person. If you wait until the day before or the day of a performance, you'll sometimes have access to tickets that were held back for one reason or another and have just gone on sale.

DISCOUNT TICKETS Yankee thrift is artistically expressed at the ✪ **BosTix** booths at Faneuil Hall Marketplace (on the south side of Faneuil Hall), in Copley Square (at the corner of Boylston and Dartmouth streets), and in Harvard Square (in the Holyoke Center arcade at 1350 Massachusetts Ave.). Same-day tickets to musical and theatrical performances are on sale for half price, subject to availability. A coupon book offering discounted and two-for-one admission to many area museums is available, too. Credit cards are not accepted, and there are no refunds or exchanges. Check the board for the day's offerings.

Boston After Dark

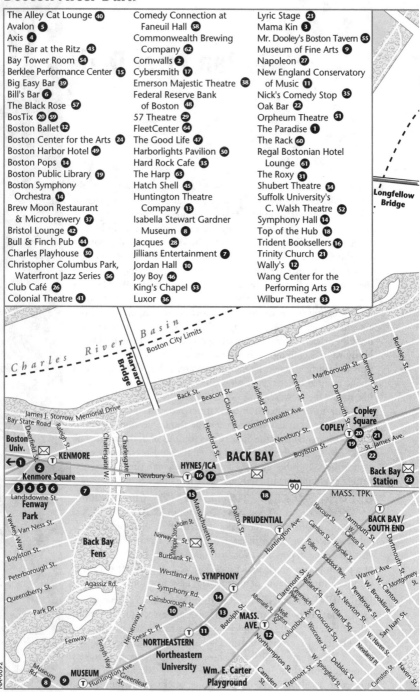

The Alley Cat Lounge **40**
Avalon **5**
Axis **4**
The Bar at the Ritz **43**
Bay Tower Room **54**
Berklee Performance Center **15**
Big Easy Bar **39**
Bill's Bar **6**
The Black Rose **57**
BosTix **20** **59**
Boston Ballet **32**
Boston Center for the Arts **24**
Boston Harbor Hotel **49**
Boston Pops **14**
Boston Public Library **19**
Boston Symphony
  Orchestra **14**
Brew Moon Restaurant
  & Microbrewery **37**
Bristol Lounge **42**
Bull & Finch Pub **44**
Charles Playhouse **30**
Christopher Columbus Park,
  Waterfront Jazz Series **56**
Club Café **26**
Colonial Theatre **41**

Comedy Connection at
  Faneuil Hall **58**
Commonwealth Brewing
  Company **62**
Cornwalls **2**
Cybersmith **17**
Emerson Majestic Theatre **38**
Federal Reserve Bank
  of Boston **48**
57 Theatre **29**
FleetCenter **64**
The Good Life **47**
Harborlights Pavilion **50**
Hard Rock Cafe **35**
The Harp **63**
Hatch Shell **45**
Huntington Theatre
  Company **13**
Isabella Stewart Gardner
  Museum **8**
Jacques **28**
Jillians Entertainment **7**
Jordan Hall **10**
Joy Boy **46**
King's Chapel **53**
Luxor **36**

Lyric Stage **23**
Mama Kin **3**
Mr. Dooley's Boston Tavern **55**
Museum of Fine Arts **9**
Napoleon **27**
New England Conservatory
  of Music **11**
Nick's Comedy Stop **35**
Oak Bar **22**
Orpheum Theatre **51**
The Paradise **1**
The Rack **60**
Regal Bostonian Hotel
  Lounge **61**
The Roxy **31**
Shubert Theatre **34**
Suffolk University's
  C. Walsh Theatre **52**
Symphony Hall **14**
Top of the Hub **18**
Trident Booksellers **16**
Trinity Church **21**
Wally's **12**
Wang Center for the
  Performing Arts **32**
Wilbur Theater **33**

NA-0092

210

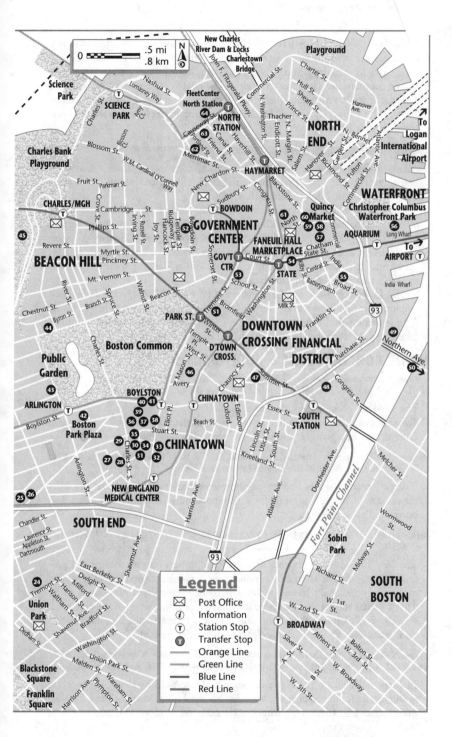

BosTix (☎ 617/723-5181; www.boston.com/artsboston) also offers full-price advance ticket sales; discounts on more than 100 theater, music, and dance events; and tickets to museums, historic sites, and attractions in and around town. The Boston locations are Ticketmaster outlets. The booths are open Tuesday through Saturday from 10am to 6pm (half-price tickets go on sale at 11am), and Sunday from 11am to 4pm. The Copley Square and Harvard Square locations are also open Monday from 10am to 6pm.

1 The Performing Arts

Year-round, you can find a performance that fits your taste and budget, be it a touring theater company or a children's chorus.

The biggest names in classical music, dance, theater, jazz, and world music often appear as part of the **BankBoston Celebrity Series,** 20 Park Plaza, Boston, MA 02116 (☎ **617/482-2595,** or 617/482-6661 for Celebrity Charge; www.celebrityseries.org). It's a subscription series that also offers tickets to individual events, which take place at Symphony Hall, Jordan Hall, the Wang Center, and the DeCordova Museum in suburban Lincoln.

The ✪ **Hatch Shell** on the Esplanade (☎ **617/727-9547,** ext. 555) is an amphitheater best known as the home of the Boston Pops's Fourth of July concerts. Almost every night in the summer, free music and dance performances and films take over the Hatch Shell stage to the delight of crowds on the lawn.

MAJOR CONCERT HALLS & AUDITORIUMS

Berklee Performance Center. 136 Massachusetts Ave. ☎ **617/266-7455** (concert line), or 617/266-1400, ext. 261. MBTA: Green Line B, C, or D trains to Hynes/ICA.

The Berklee College of Music's theater features the work of faculty members, students, and professional recording artists (many of them former Berklee students). Offerings are heavy on jazz and folk, with plenty of other options.

Boston Center for the Arts. 539 Tremont St. ☎ **617/426-7700** (events line), or 617/426-0320 (box office). MBTA: Orange Line to Back Bay.

Five performance spaces and an anything-goes booking policy make the BCA the place to go in the South End for contemporary theater, music, and dance, and poetry and prose readings.

Jordan Hall. 30 Gainsborough St. ☎ **617/536-2412,** or 617/262-1120, ext. 700 (concert line). MBTA: Green Line E train to Symphony.

The New England Conservatory of Music's auditorium features student and professional productions of instrumental and vocal classical, baroque, and chamber music, and occasionally contemporary artists. After a complete renovation in 1995, a lively debate ensued about whether the excellent acoustics were ruined, enhanced, or unchanged. Because the refurbishment greatly improved the building's condition, even those who were appalled at first are coming around.

Sanders Theatre. 45 Quincy St. (corner of Cambridge St.), Cambridge. ☎ **617/496-2222.** www.fas.harvard.edu/~memhall. Closed June–July. MBTA: Red Line to Harvard.

In Memorial Hall on the Harvard campus, 113-year-old Sanders Theatre was a multipurpose facility before there was such a thing—it's a lecture hall and a performance space that features big names in classical, folk, and world music, as well as student performances.

Impressions

Tonight I appear for the first time before a Boston audience—4,000 critics.
—Mark Twain, 1869

The New England conscience . . . does not stop you from doing what you shouldn't—it just stops you from enjoying it.
—Cleveland Amory, 1980

Symphony Hall. 301 Massachusetts Ave. (at Huntington Ave.). ☎ **617/266-1492,** 617/CONCERT (program information), or 617/266-1200 (SymphonyCharge). MBTA: Green Line E train to Symphony.

Home to one of the world's best orchestras, Symphony Hall is a world-class performance venue. When the Boston Symphony Orchestra and the Boston Pops are away, top-notch classical and chamber music ensembles from elsewhere take over.

Wang Center for the Performing Arts. 270 Tremont St. ☎ **617/482-9393,** or 617/931-2787 (Ticketmaster). MBTA: Green Line to Boylston.

Also known as the Wang Theatre, this Art Deco palace is home to Boston Ballet and numerous national dramatic, dance, and music companies. On some Monday evenings in the winter, it reverts to its roots as a movie theater and shows classic films on its enormous screen.

CLASSICAL MUSIC

J Boston Pops. Performing at Symphony Hall, 301 Massachusetts Ave. (at Huntington Ave.). ☎ **617/266-1492,** 617/CONCERT (program information), or 617/266-1200 (Symphony-Charge). www.bso.org. Tickets $33–$45 for tables, $12.50–$28 for balcony seats. MBTA: Green Line E train to Symphony.

From early May to early July, members of the Boston Symphony Orchestra lighten up. Tables and chairs replace the floor seats at Symphony Hall, waiters serve drinks and light refreshments, and the Pops play a range of music from light classical to show tunes to popular music (hence the name), sometimes with celebrity guest stars. Conductor Keith Lockhart is so popular that he could almost give the orchestra its name all by himself. Performances are Tuesday through Sunday evenings. The season ends with a week of free outdoor concerts at the Hatch Shell on the Charles River Esplanade, including the traditional Fourth of July concert, which features fireworks.

✪ Boston Symphony Orchestra. Performing at Symphony Hall, 301 Massachusetts Ave. (at Huntington Ave.). ☎ **617/266-1492,** 617/CONCERT (program information), or 617/266-1200 (SymphonyCharge). www.bso.org. Tickets $23–$71. Rush tickets $8 (on sale 9am Fri; 5pm Tues, Thurs). Rehearsal tickets $13.50. MBTA: Green Line E train to Symphony.

The Boston Symphony Orchestra, one of the world's greatest, was founded in 1881 and has performed at acoustically perfect Symphony Hall since 1900. Music director Seiji Ozawa is the latest in a line of distinguished conductors of an institution known for contemporary as well as classical music; the 1996 Pulitzer Prize in music was awarded to *Lilacs,* composed for voice and orchestra by George Walker and commissioned by the BSO.

The season runs from October through April, with performances most Tuesday, Thursday, and Saturday evenings; Friday afternoons; and some Friday evenings. Check at the box office 2 hours before show time if you weren't able to buy tickets in advance—returns from subscribers go on sale at full price at that time.

A limited number of rush tickets (one per person) are available on the day of the performance for Tuesday and Thursday evening and Friday afternoon programs. Wednesday evening and Thursday morning rehearsals are sometimes open to the public.

Handel & Haydn Society. 300 Massachusetts Ave. ☎ **617/266-3605.** www. handelandhaydn.org. Tickets $21–$51. MBTA: Green Line E train to Symphony.

The Handel & Haydn Society uses period instruments and techniques in its orchestral and choral performances, and it still is as cutting-edge as any ensemble in town. Established in 1815, it's the oldest continuously performing arts organization in the country. Under the direction of Christopher Hogwood, the society prides itself on its creative programming of "historically informed" concerts. The season runs year-round with performances at Symphony Hall, Jordan Hall, and Sanders Theatre.

ADDITIONAL OFFERINGS

Students and faculty members at two prestigious institutions perform frequently during the academic year; admission is usually free. For information, contact the **New England Conservatory of Music,** 290 Huntington Ave. (☎ **617/262-1120,** ext. 700), and Cambridge's **Longy School of Music,** 1 Follen St. (☎ **617/ 876-0956,** ext. 120).

The repertoire of the **Boston Lyric Opera,** 45 Franklin St. (☎ **617/542-6772**), includes classical and contemporary works. The season runs from October through March. Performances are at the Emerson Majestic Theatre, 219 Tremont St. (☎ **617/824-8000**).

CONCERT SERIES
FREE LUNCHTIME CONCERTS

Federal Reserve Bank of Boston. 600 Atlantic Ave. ☎ **617/973-3453.** MBTA: Red Line to South Station.

Local groups perform jazz, classical, and contemporary music in the bank's ground-floor auditorium on Thursdays and some Fridays at 12:30pm.

King's Chapel Noon Hour Recitals. 58 Tremont St. ☎ **617/227-2155.** Donation requested. MBTA: Red or Green Line to Park St.

Organ, instrumental, and vocal solos fill this historic building with music and make for a pleasant break along the Freedom Trail. Concerts are at 12:15pm on Tuesdays.

Fridays at Trinity. Trinity Church, Copley Sq. ☎ **617/536-0944.** Donations accepted. MBTA: Green Line to Copley, or Orange Line to Back Bay.

This landmark church features organ recitals by local and visiting artists on Fridays at 12:15pm. Take advantage of the chance to look around this architectural showpiece.

MUSIC IN THE MUSEUMS

A treat for the eyes and the ears, live music at a museum could be the offering that helps you plan your visit. If you're on a sojourn to Lexington or Concord, see whether your trip coincides with one of the occasional concerts at the **DeCordova Museum and Sculpture Park** (☎ 617/259-8355), on Sandy Pond Road in nearby Lincoln.

✪ **Isabella Stewart Gardner Museum.** 280 The Fenway. ☎ **617/734-1359.** Concert fees (including museum admission) $15 adults, $11 seniors, $9 students with ID, $7 ages 12–17, $5 ages 5–11. MBTA: Green Line E train to Museum.

This gorgeous museum, originally a home modeled after a 15th-century Venetian palace, features soloists, local students, and chamber music in the Tapestry Room Saturday and Sunday at 1:30pm, from September through April.

Museum of Fine Arts. 465 Huntington Ave. ☎ **617/267-9300** or 617/369-3300. Tickets $13, $11 seniors and students, $4 under 12. MBTA: Green Line E train to Museum.

The "Concerts in the Courtyard" series brings folk and jazz artists to the MFA on Wednesday evenings from June through September at 7:30pm. The courtyard opens to picnickers at 6pm; bring dinner, or buy it there. Chair seating is limited, and you're encouraged to bring a blanket or lawn chair.

CONCERT VENUES

FleetCenter. 150 Causeway St. ☎ **617/624-1000** (events line), or 617/931-2000 (Ticket-master). www.fleetcenter.com. MBTA: Orange or Green Line to North Station.

The state-of-the-art FleetCenter opened in September 1995, replacing legendary (but woefully outdated) Boston Garden. It's the home of the Bruins (hockey), the Celtics (basketball), and touring rock and pop artists of all stripes, as well as the circus (in October) and touring ice shows. Concerts are in the round or in the arena stage format.

Great Woods Center for the Performing Arts. Rte. 140, Mansfield. ☎ **508/339-2333,** or 617/423-NEXT to order tickets. www.greatwoods.com.

For major mainstream and alternative rock acts out on summer tours, with a smattering of folk, pop, country, reggae, and light classical, head about an hour south of Boston. Great Woods is a sheltered (it has a roof but no sides) auditorium surrounded by a lawn, and shows are held rain or shine.

✪ **Harborlights Pavilion.** Fan Pier, Northern Ave. ☎ **617/374-9000,** or 617/423-NEXT to order tickets. www.harborlights.com.

Harborlights's lease is up—be sure to call before setting out in 1999, when the venue probably will have relocated. It's a giant white tent on the waterfront that holds single-level seating for soft rock, pop, folk, and jazz performers on evenings from June through September.

Orpheum Theater. 1 Hamilton Place ☎ **617/679-0810,** or 617/423-NEXT for tickets. MBTA: Red or Green Line to Park St.

Although it's old (the building went up in 1852) and cramped, the Orpheum offers an intimate setting for megastars—Bruce Springsteen and John Mellencamp, for example—taking a break from the arena circuit. Most of the time, it books top local acts and national artists such as Fiona Apple, Third Eye Blind and Smashmouth, and Blues Traveler. Hamilton Place is the alleyway off Tremont Street across from the Park Street Church.

The Paradise. 967 Commonwealth Ave. ☎ **617/562-8804,** or 617/423-NEXT for tickets. www.tparty.com/tpc/paradise.html. MBTA: Green Line B train to Pleasant St.

Hard by the Boston University campus, the medium-sized Paradise draws enthusiastic, student-intensive crowds for top local rock and alternative performers. You might also see national names (lately, Jewel, Everclear, and the Wallflowers) who want a relatively small venue, and others who aren't quite ready to headline a big show on their own—Son Volt, BR5-49, and Paula Cole have played recently. Most shows are 18-plus (you must be 21 to drink alcohol).

DANCE

Boston Ballet. 19 Clarendon St. ☎ **617/695-6955,** or 617/931-ARTS (Ticketmaster). Performing at the Wang Theatre (box office, 270 Tremont St., Mon–Sat 10am-6pm). Tickets $21–$69. Student rush tickets (1 hour before curtain) $12.50, except for *The Nutcracker.* MBTA: Green Line to Boylston.

Boston Ballet's reputation seems to jump a notch every time someone says, "So it's not just *The Nutcracker.*" The country's fourth-largest dance company is a holiday staple, and during the rest of the season (October through May), it presents an eclectic mix of classic story ballets and contemporary works.

Dance Umbrella. 515 Washington St., 5th floor. ☎ **617/482-7570.** www.danceumbrella.org.

Contemporary dance aficionados will want to check out the latest offerings sponsored by Dance Umbrella. It commissions and presents international, culturally diverse works—a broad definition that covers everything from acrobats and jazz tap dancers to well-known groups such as the Mark Morris and Bill T. Jones/Arnie Zane companies. Performances take place at venues in Boston and Cambridge, most often at the **Emerson Majestic Theatre,** 219 Tremont St., Boston (☎ **617/824-8000**).

THEATER

Local and national companies, professional and amateur actors, classic and experimental drama combine to make the theater scene in Boston and Cambridge a lively one, and in the past few years it has positively exploded. Call ahead or check the papers or BosTix (see "Discount Tickets," above) after you arrive—you're sure to find something of interest.

Boston is one of the last cities where pre-Broadway tryouts are held, allowing an early look at a classic (or classic flop) in the making. It's also a popular destination for touring companies of established Broadway hits. You'll find most of the shows headed to or coming from Broadway in the Theater District, at the **Colonial Theatre** (106 Boylston St.; ☎ **617/426-9366**), the **Shubert Theatre** (265 Tremont St.; ☎ **617/482-9393**), the **Wang Center for the Performing Arts** (270 Tremont St.; ☎ **617/482-9393**), and the **Wilbur Theater** (246 Tremont St.; ☎ **617/423-4008**).

The excellent local theater scene boasts the **Huntington Theatre Company,** which performs at the Boston University Theatre, 264 Huntington Ave. (☎ **617/266-0800**), and the **American Repertory Theatre** (ART), which makes its home at Harvard University's Loeb Drama Center, 64 Brattle St., Cambridge (☎ **617/547-8300;** www.amrep.org).

The **Lyric Stage,** 140 Clarendon St. (☎ **617/437-7172**), mounts contemporary and modern works in an intimate second-floor setting. The **Emerson Majestic Theatre,** 219 Tremont St. (☎ **617/824-8000**), offers dance and music performances and Emerson College student productions. The **57 Theatre,** 200 Stuart St., in the Radisson Hotel Boston (☎ **800/233-3123**), often books one-person shows. Some ART projects and independent productions are at the **Hasty Pudding Theatre,** 12 Holyoke St., Cambridge (☎ **617/496-8400**).

The Loeb and the Hasty Pudding also feature student productions. Other college venues include Suffolk University's **C. Walsh Theatre,** 55 Temple St., Boston (☎ **617/573-8680**), various performance spaces at **MIT** (☎ **617/253-4720,** Theater Arts Hotline), the **Tufts Arena Theater** (☎ **617/627-3493**) in Medford, and the **Spingold Theatre** (☎ **617/736-3400**) at Brandeis University in Waltham.

Blue Like Me

The off-Broadway sensation *Blue Man Group* branched out from New York to Boston in 1995 and immediately began selling out the Charles Playhouse. Famous for reducing even the most eloquent theatergoer to one-syllable sputtering, the troupe of three cobalt-colored entertainers backed by a rock band uses music, percussion, food, and audience participants in its overwhelming performance art. Props include social commentary, Twinkies, marshmallows, breakfast cereal, toilet paper, and lots of blue paint. Older children and teenagers enjoy the mayhem as much as adults.

The Charles Playhouse (☎ 617/426-6912), which is also home to *Shear Madness*, is at 74 Warrenton St. in the Theater District. Performances are at 8pm Tuesday through Thursday, 7 and 10pm Friday and Saturday, and 4pm Sunday. Tickets ($35 and $45) are available at the box office and through Ticketmaster.

Two other local institutions offer entertaining, long-running theatrical productions that appeal to adults and children.

Le Grand David and His Own Spectacular Magic Company. Cabot Street Cinema Theater, 286 Cabot St., Beverly, and Larcom Theatre, 13 Wallis St., Beverly. ☎ **978/927-3677.** E-mail: lgdmagic@nii.net. Tickets $10–$15.

Three generations of magicians make up this company, a nationally acclaimed troupe of illusionists. They stage 2-hour shows at two theaters in Beverly, about 40 minutes from Boston by car. Le Grand David has received national attention for his sleight-of-hand and has performed at Easter parties at the White House.

Shear Madness. Charles Playhouse, Stage II. 74 Warrenton St. ☎ **617/426-5225.** Tickets $28–$32. www.shearmadness.com MBTA: Green Line to Boylston.

This "comic murder mystery" has turned the Charles Playhouse stage into a unisex hairdressing salon since 1980, and the show's never the same twice. One of the original audience-participation productions, the play changes at each performance as the spectator-investigators question suspects, reconstruct events, and then name the murderer. *Shear Madness* is the longest-running nonmusical play in theater history. Performances are Tuesday through Friday at 8pm, Saturday at 6:30 and 9:30pm, and Sunday at 3 and 7:30pm.

OUTSIDE BOSTON
A MAJOR MUSIC FESTIVAL

Tanglewood. Lenox. ☎ **413/637-5165,** or 617/266-1492 out of season. Music Shed $14–$74, lawn $12–$14; open rehearsals $13. To order tickets call SymphonyCharge (☎ 800/274-8499) or Ticketmaster (☎ 800/347-0808).

The Berkshires of western Massachusetts are a favorite summer destination for many Bostonians, including the Boston Symphony Orchestra. Tanglewood concerts, from the end of June through the end of August, also feature guest conductors and artists and run the gamut from classical to popular music, from chamber music to jazz.

Acoustically, the best seats are in the Koussevitzky Music Shed and Seiji Ozawa Hall. A picnic on the lawn can be even more enjoyable if you don't mind small children running wild. Performances are Friday and Saturday evenings and Sunday afternoons, open rehearsals are on Saturday mornings, and student concerts take place on some evenings. Daytime tickets usually aren't difficult to get, but plan in advance if you hope to take in an evening show and especially if you want to stay overnight. (Consult *Frommer's New England* for in-depth coverage of western Massachusetts.) From Boston, Lenox is a 2½- to 3-hour drive on the Massachusetts Turnpike.

2 The Club & Music Scene

The club scene in Boston and Cambridge is multifaceted and constantly changing, and somewhere out there is a good time for everyone, regardless of age, clothing style, musical taste, or budget. Check the "Calendar" section of the Thursday *Globe,* the *Phoenix,* the *Improper Bostonian,* or the "Scene" section of the Friday *Herald* while you're making plans.

A night on the town in Boston is relatively brief: most bars close by 1am, clubs close at 2am, and the T shuts down between 12:30 and 1am. The drinking age is 21; a valid driver's license or passport is required as proof of age, and the law is strictly enforced, especially near college campuses (in other words, practically everywhere). Be prepared to show ID if you appear to be younger than 35 or so, and try to be patient while the amazed 30-year-old ahead of you fishes out a license.

Head for the corner of Boylston and Fairfield streets in the Back Bay if you want to check out the newest **Planet Hollywood,** which was well along in the planning process as we went to press.

COMEDY CLUBS

The days when every motel and truck stop had a "laff lounge" are, mercifully, behind us. Boston was one of the first cities with a hopping comedy-club scene, and as the fad fades, the quality clubs are hanging in there and skimming off the cream. The goal is to emulate Jay Leno, Steven Wright, Paula Poundstone, Rosie O'Donnell, Denis Leary, Anthony Clark, and others who parlayed success in Boston into careers in film and TV (or at least TV commercials).

✪ **Comedy Connection at Faneuil Hall.** Quincy Market, Upper Rotunda. ☎ **617/ 248-9700.** Cover $8-$30. MBTA: Green or Blue Line to Government Center; Green or Orange Line to Haymarket.

A large room with a clear view from every seat, the oldest original comedy club in town, established in 1978, draws top-notch talent from near and far. Big-name national acts lure enthusiastic crowds, and the openers are often just as funny but not as famous—yet. Shows are nightly at 8pm with late shows on Friday and Saturday at 10:15pm. The cover charge seldom tops $12 during the week but jumps for a big name appearing on a weekend.

Nick's Comedy Stop. 100 Warrenton St. ☎ **617/482-0930.** Cover $8-$15. MBTA: Green Line to Boylston.

This old reliable in the Theater District doesn't have the cachet of the Comedy Connection, but it's still a good time. On Thursday and Sunday, there's usually one show at 8:30; weekend slates add another show or two. Wednesday is open-mike night.

DANCE CLUBS

Boston's clubs cater to a wide range of musical tastes. Many are in the areas surrounding Boston's **Kenmore Square** (there's a particularly impressive strip along Lansdowne Street) and Cambridge's **Central Square.** That makes club-hopping easy, but it also means that on Friday and Saturday nights students overrun the neighborhoods (Kenmore Square in particular). If you don't feel like dealing with huge crowds of loud teenagers and recent college graduates, stick to slightly more upscale and isolated nightspots.

Axis. 13 Lansdowne St. ☎ **617/262-2437.** Cover $7–$10. MBTA: Green Line B, C, or D train to Kenmore.

Progressive rock at bone-rattling volume and "creative dress"—break out the leather—attract a young crowd to Axis. There are special nights for alternative rock, house, techno, soul, and funk music, and for international DJs. The private room upstairs is called "DV8" (say it out loud). Open Tuesday through Sunday (gay night with adjoining Avalon) 10pm to 2am.

✪ **Avalon.** 15 Lansdowne St. ☎ **617/262-2424.** Cover $5–$10. MBTA: Green Line B, C, or D train to Kenmore.

A cavernous space divided into several levels, with a full concert stage, private booths and lounges, large dance floors, and a spectacular light show, Avalon is either great fun or sensory overload. A recent push to book more concerts has landed, among others, Chumbawamba, Sneaker Pimps, and Fiona Apple. When the stage is not in use, DJs take over for international music and—particularly on Saturday (suburbanites' night out)—mainstream dance hits. The dress code calls for jackets, shirts with collars, and no jeans or athletic wear. The crowd is slightly older than at Axis; for special events, the connecting doors open to make the two clubs one enormous space. Open Thursday (international night) to Sunday (gay night) 10pm to 2am.

The Roxy. 279 Tremont St., in the Tremont House. ☎ **617/338-7699.** Cover $8–$10. MBTA: Green Line to Boylston.

A hotel ballroom–turned–dance club, the Roxy boasts excellent DJs and live music, a huge dance floor, a concert stage, and a balcony (perfect for checking out the action down below). The occasional concert offerings take good advantage of the acoustics and sight lines. Open 10:30pm to 2am on Thursday (African-American professional night), Friday (international night), Saturday (Top-40 night), and some Sundays for special events. No jeans or athletic shoes.

ECLECTIC

✪ **Johnny D's.** 17 Holland St., Davis Sq., Somerville. ☎ **617/776-2004,** or 617/776-9667 (concert line). www.johnnyds.com. Cover $2–$16, usually $5–$10. MBTA: Red Line to Davis.

This family-owned and -operated restaurant and music club is one of the best in the area. It draws a congenial crowd for acts on national and international tours, and acts that haven't been out of the 617 area code. The music ranges from zydeco to rock, rockabilly to jazz, blues to ska. The food's even good (try the terrific weekend brunch). Johnny D's is worth a long trip, but it's only two stops past Harvard Square on the Red Line, about a 15-minute ride at night. Open daily from 11:30am to 1am; dinner Tuesday through Saturday from 4:30 to 9:30pm, with lighter fare until 11pm.

Kendall Café. 233 Cardinal Medeiros Way, Cambridge. ☎ **617/661-0993.** Cover $5–$10. MBTA: Red Line to Kendall.

This friendly neighborhood bar near the 1 Kendall Sq. office-retail complex show-cases three up-and-coming artists each night. Folk predominates, and you might also hear rock, country, or blues in the tiny back room, where waiters weave through the crowds to serve burgers and such. Or just stay at the bar—you won't be able to see, but it's such a small place that you'll have no trouble hearing. Shows are Monday through Saturday at 8pm, Sunday at 4pm.

The Western Front. 343 Western Ave., Cambridge. ☎ **617/492-7772.** Cover $3–$10. MBTA: Red Line to Central.

A 30-ish friend swears by the Western Front for one reason: "You're never the oldest one there." This casual spot on a nondescript street south of Central Square attracts an integrated crowd for world-beat music, blues, and especially reggae. Sunday is dance-hall reggae night, and the infectious music makes every night dancing night. Open Tuesday through Sunday from 5pm to 1:30am; live entertainment begins at 9pm.

FOLK

Platform shoes are back, punk rock is back, and you might say folk is back. In Harvard Square, where folk musicians flock (Tracy Chapman is just one famous "graduate" of the street performance scene), you'd say it never left. Check the papers to see whether the **Nameless Coffee House** is open during your visit. A local legend for 30 years, the Nameless pops up periodically from September to June at the First Parish in Cambridge, 3 Church St.

✪ **Club Passim.** 47 Palmer St., Cambridge. ☎ **617/492-7679.** Cover $5–$22; most shows $12 or less. MBTA: Red Line to Harvard.

Passim has launched more careers than the mass production of acoustic guitars—Joan Baez, Suzanne Vega, and Tom Rush started out here. In a basement on the street between buildings of the Harvard Coop, this coffeehouse is still building on a reputation of more than 30 years of nurturing new talent and showcasing established musicians. Patrons who have been regulars since day one mix with college students. There's live music 4 to 6 nights a week and Sunday afternoons, and coffee and light meals are available all the time. Open Sunday through Thursday from 11am to 11pm, Friday and Saturday from 11am to 4am.

JAZZ & BLUES

If you're partial to these genres, consider timing your visit to coincide with the ***Boston Globe* Jazz & Blues Festival** (☎ **617/929-2000**), usually scheduled for the third week of June. Constellations of jazz and blues stars (large and small) appear at lunchtime, after-work, evening, and weekend events, some of them free, many of them outdoors. The festival wraps up with a free Sunday-afternoon program at the Hatch Shell.

On summer Fridays at 6:30pm, the ✪ **Waterfront Jazz Series** (☎ **617/635-3911**) brings amateurs and professionals to Christopher Columbus Park, on the waterfront, for a refreshing interlude of music and cool breezes.

Cantab Lounge. 738 Massachusetts Ave., Cambridge. ☎ **617/354-2685.** Cover $3–$6. MBTA: Red Line to Central.

Follow your ears to this friendly neighborhood bar in Central Square, which attracts a three-generation crowd. Whenever the door swings open at night, deafening music (usually R&B or rock, sometimes jazz) spills out. The source on weekends often is Little Joe Cook and the Thrillers, headliners since the early '80s whose catchy tunes you'll dance to all night and hum all the next day—because your ears will still be ringing.

✪ **House of Blues.** 96 Winthrop St., Cambridge. ☎ **617/491-BLUE,** or 617/497-2229 for tickets. www.hob.com. Cover $7–$30; $3 Saturday matinees. MBTA: Red Line to Harvard.

The original House of Blues packs 'em in for evening and weekend matinee shows, attracting big names—Junior Brown, Maceo Parker, Koko Taylor, and the Fabulous Thunderbirds have played recently—and hordes of fans. And there's no telling when one of the legions of out-of-towners in the audience will turn out to be someone famous who winds up on stage jamming. Advance tickets are highly recommended. Open until 1am Sunday through Wednesday, 2am Thursday through Saturday. (See chapter 6 for a full listing.)

Regattabar. In the Charles Hotel, 1 Bennett St., Cambridge. ☎ **617/661-5000,** or 617/876-7777 (Concertix). Tickets $6–$25. MBTA: Red Line to Harvard.

The Regattabar's selection of local and international artists is considered the best in the area—a title that Scullers (see below) is happy to dispute. Shirley Horn, Betty Carter, Tito Puente, the Count Basie Orchestra, and Karen Akers have appeared within the past 2 years. The large third-floor room holds about 200 and has a 21-foot picture window overlooking Harvard Square; unfortunately, it sometimes gets a little noisy. Buy tickets in advance from Concertix (there's a $2 per ticket service charge), or try your luck at the door 1 hour before the performance is scheduled to start. Open Tuesday through Saturday and some Sundays with one or two performances per night.

Ryles Jazz Club. 212 Hampshire St., Inman Sq., Cambridge. ☎ **617/876-9330.** www.rylesjazz.com. Cover $5 weeknights, $7–$15 weekends.

Ryles recently expanded and announced plans to start booking more national acts, which should only make it more popular. Hard-core music buffs of every stripe turn out for a wide variety of first-rate jazz, R&B, world beat, and Latin performances in two rooms. Both levels offer top-notch music and a friendly atmosphere. The Sunday jazz brunch runs from 10am to 3pm. Open Tuesday through Sunday; shows start at 9pm.

Scullers Jazz Club. In the Doubletree Guest Suites hotel, 400 Soldiers Field Rd. ☎ **617/562-4111.** www.scullersjazz.com. Tickets $10–$25.

Overlooking the Charles River, Scullers is a lovely, comfortable room that books top singers and instrumentalists—recent notables include Eartha Kitt, Branford Marsalis, Dave Brubeck, and (quite a coup) Bobby Short. Patrons tend to be more hard-core and quieter than the crowds at the Regattabar, but it really depends on who's performing. Shows are usually at 8 and 10pm Tuesday through Saturday; the box office is open those days from 11am to 6:30pm. Ask about dinner packages, which include preferred seating.

Wally's. 427 Massachusetts Ave. ☎ **617/424-1408.** No cover. MBTA: Orange Line to Massachusetts Ave.

Wally's recently expanded, which should only increase the fame of this Boston institution, near a busy corner in the South End. It draws a notably diverse crowd—gay, straight, black, white, affluent, indigent—for free performances by students and instructors from the Berklee College of Music, local ensembles, and, infrequently, internationally renowned musicians. Although there is no cover, patrons are expected to buy at least one drink (alcoholic or non).

ROCK

Bill's Bar. 5½ Lansdowne St. ☎ **617/421-9678.** Cover $5–$7. MBTA: Green Line B, C, or D train to Kenmore.

Long known as the only real hangout on Lansdowne Street, Bill's has transformed itself into a live-music destination and kept its friendly atmosphere. There are a

Log On, Tune In, Drop Out

Cutting-edge computer technology contributes to the local economy in many ways, most entertainingly at the area's two **Cybersmith** locations, where you can check out a selection of more than 50 hot CD-ROMs, surf the World Wide Web, videoconference, and take a crack at virtual reality. From businesspeople dropping in to check their e-mail to whole families "skiing," from novices to expert programmers, a wide range of people are amused and even educated at the cutting-edge business's two area locations.

Here's how it works: You're issued a "Cybercard," which works like a debit card, and the various stations deduct the appropriate amount for the activity you've chosen. The cost for working or playing on a computer terminal (in a restaurant-like booth rather than at a desk) ranges from $9.95 an hour to as little as $1.99 per hour if you purchase 50 hours at once. Virtual reality is $3.75 per "experience," and skiing, snowboarding, or skateboarding is $1.50 per run.

Cybersmith has a branch in Harvard Square at 42 Church St. (☎ 617/492-5857); its new location at 326 Newbury St. in Boston's Back Bay was in the works at press time. Each has different CD-ROMs and other features. The Cambridge location is open Monday through Thursday from 10am to 11pm, Friday and Saturday until midnight, and Sunday from 11am to 9pm; the Boston branch is expected to keep roughly the same hours.

great beer menu and performances—by up-and-comers such as the Verve Pipe, Dishwalla, and Jen Trynin—or DJs most nights at 9:30pm. Sunday is reggae night; Wednesday, lounge night. Open nightly 8pm to 2am.

Lizard Lounge. 1667 Massachusetts Ave., Cambridge. ☎ **617/547-0759.** Cover $2–$7. MBTA: Red Line to Harvard.

In the basement of the Cambridge Common restaurant, the Lizard Lounge features well-known local rock and folk musicians who draw a postcollegiate-and-up crowd (Harvard Law School is next door), with a smattering of people who look like extras from *Swingers*. Shows Wednesday through Saturday at 10pm; Sunday is open-mike poetry jam night.

Mama Kin and Lansdowne Playhouse. 36 Lansdowne St. ☎ **617/536-2100.** Cover $2–$25. MBTA: Green Line B, C, or D train to Kenmore.

Members of the Boston-based band Aerosmith co-own Mama Kin and the adjacent concert space, which opened in December 1994 to wide acclaim and instant popularity. You probably won't see Steven Tyler, but you will see up-and-comers early in the week (when the cover charge is lower), and more established artists toward the weekend. Doors open at 8 or 9pm every night. Some shows are 19-plus (you must be 21 to drink alcohol).

✪ **Middle East.** 472–480 Massachusetts Ave., Central Sq., Cambridge. ☎ **617/492-9181.** Cover $3–$16. MBTA: Red Line to Central.

The Middle East books an impressive variety of progressive and alternative rock in two rooms (upstairs and downstairs) 7 nights a week. Showcasing top local talent as well as bands with international reputations, it's a popular hangout that gets crowded, hot, and *loud*. The bakery next door, under the same management, features acoustic artists most of the time and belly dancers on Wednesdays. Most shows are 18-plus (you must be 21 to drink alcohol); some are all ages, but the age of the crowd varies with the performer.

T.T. the Bear's Place. 10 Brookline St., Cambridge. ☎ **617/492-0082,** or 617/492-BEAR (concert line). www.tiac.net/users/ttbears. Cover $3–$15, usually less than $10. MBTA: Red Line to Central.

This no-frills spot admits people 18 and older (you must be 21 to drink alcohol), so the crowd is on the young side, but 30-somethings will feel comfortable, too. Bookings range from cutting-edge alternative rock and roots music to ska and funk shows to up-and-coming pop acts. Monday is Stone Soup Poetry open-mike night. Open Monday from 7pm to midnight, Tuesday through Sunday from 6pm to 1am.

3 The Bar Scene

Bostonians had some quibbles with the TV show "Cheers," but no one ever complained that the concept of a neighborhood bar where the regulars practically lived was implausible. From the Littlest Bar (a closet-sized downtown watering hole) to the Bull & Finch (on which "Cheers" is based), the neighborhood bar occupies a vital niche. It tends to be a fairly insular scene—as a stranger, you probably won't be confronted, but don't expect to be welcomed with open arms, either. This is one area where you can and probably should judge a book by its cover. If you poke your head in the door and see people who look like you and your friends, give it a whirl. The patrons will tend to reflect the neighborhood. You'll find wrung-out lawyers drinking $8 martinis all over downtown, yuppies quaffing chardonnay in the Back Bay, beeper-wearing doctors having a quick Guinness on Beacon Hill, middle-aged ex-hippies and artists drinking ale in Cambridge taverns, and locals drinking Bud from the bottle in the college areas. And, of course, there are students everywhere. Have your ID ready.

BARS, PUBS & LOUNGES

The Alley Cat. 1 Boylston Place. ☎ **617/351-2510.** Cover $3. MBTA: Green Line to Boylston.

In an alley off Boylston Street near the Common, this unpretentious lounge caters to a collegiate and postcollegiate crowd—think beer commercial, but noisier— more interested in dancing and mingling than in seeing and being seen. The DJs are the cream of the local crop. Open Thursday through Saturday from 8pm to 2am.

The Big Easy Bar. Boylston Place. ☎ **617/351-7000.** Cover $5. MBTA: Green Line to Boylston.

Buttoned-up Boston meets let-it-all-hang-out New Orleans—it could get ugly. Not so here, in a large, inviting space with a balcony (great for people watching), a billiard room, a dance floor, and music that runs from soul to alternative rock. No ripped jeans or athletic shoes.

Bull & Finch Pub. 84 Beacon St. ☎ **617/227-9605.** www.cheersbos.com. MBTA: Green Line to Arlington.

If you're out to impersonate a native, try not to be completely shocked when you walk into "the 'Cheers' bar" and realize that it looks nothing like the bar on "Cheers" (the outside does, though). The Bull & Finch really is a neighborhood bar, but today it's far better known for attracting legions of out-of-towners, who find good pub grub, drinks, and plenty of souvenirs. Food is served from 11am to 1:15am.

Casablanca. 40 Brattle St., Cambridge. ☎ **617/876-0999.** MBTA: Red Line to Harvard.

Students and professors jam this legendary Harvard Square watering hole, especially on weekends. You'll find excellent food (see chapter 6), an excellent jukebox, and excellent eavesdropping.

Cornwalls. 510 Commonwealth Ave. ☎ **617/262-3749.** MBTA: Green Line B, C, or D train to Kenmore.

This subterranean spot is an entertaining dash of England in a city noted for its Irish bars. It's known for expertly dispensed brews, authentic pub fare, and its habit of requesting ID from everyone under, oh, 50 or so (Boston University is a stone's throw away).

Bay Tower Room. 60 State St. ☎ **617/723-1666.** $12 minimum Friday and Saturday after 9:30pm. MBTA: Green or Orange Line to State, or Blue Line to Aquarium.

The view from the 33rd floor of any building is bound to be amazing; sitting atop 60 State St., you'll be mesmerized by the harbor, the airport, and Faneuil Hall Marketplace directly below. There's dancing to live music Monday through Saturday (piano on weeknights, jazz quartet Friday and Saturday). No jeans or athletic shoes.

The Good Life. 28 Kingston St. ☎ **617/451-2622.** MBTA: Red or Orange Line to Downtown Crossing.

The city's premier retro hot spot, the Good Life is a 1950s-style lounge and restaurant, where the roar of the crowd often drowns out the Sinatra music playing in the background. Two blocks from Downtown Crossing, it's also popular with office workers who flock here for the burgers.

Green Street Grill. 280 Green St., Cambridge. ☎ **617/876-1655.** MBTA: Red Line to Central.

This atmospheric Central Square hangout draws a congenial crowd for live blues, rock, and jazz on weekends and, on Tuesdays (we kid you not), magicians. You enter through Charlie's Tap, where blues and jazz aficionados will find perhaps the best jukebox on the planet. There's also excellent food (see chapter 6). Open nightly until 1am.

Hard Rock Cafe. 131 Clarendon St. ☎ **617/424-ROCK.** www.bostondine.com. No cover. MBTA: Orange Line to Back Bay, or Green Line to Copley.

This link in the 28-year-old Hard Rock chain is a fun one—just ask the other tourists in line with you. The bar is shaped like a guitar; taped music plays at a dull roar; stained-glass windows glorify rock stars; and the room is decorated with memorabilia of Jimi Hendrix, Elvis Presley, Madonna, local heroes Aerosmith, and others. The restaurant menu favors salads, burgers, and sandwiches (including the legendary "pig sandwich"). There's live acoustic music downstairs on weekends, and T-shirts and other goods are for sale. Open daily from 11am to 1am (until 2am Friday and Saturday).

Top of the Hub. Prudential Center. ☎ **617/536-1775.** No cover. MBTA: Green Line E train to Prudential.

Boasting a panoramic view of greater Boston, Top of the Hub is 52 stories above the city; the view is especially beautiful at sunset. There is music and dancing nightly. Dress is casual but neat. (See chapter 6 for restaurant listing.)

The Burren, 247 Elm St., Somerville. ☎ 617/776-6896. *"There is an Irish bar called the Burren near the Davis stop on the Red Line which plays live contemporary Irish music, especially on Thursday nights. The band I saw were called Ruby Horse and pretty good—they're regulars, apparently."*
—K. Authrie, Rouen, France

Author's Note: There's traditional Irish music in the front room of the Burren (no cover), and acoustic rock in the large back room (cover $5 to $10). Ruby Horse was the regular Thursday night entertainment at press time, and it was attracting interest from some big-time recording labels.

HOTEL BARS

Many popular nightspots are associated with hotels and restaurants (see chapters 5 and 6); the following are particularly agreeable, albeit pricey, places to while away an hour or three.

The Bar at the Ritz. 15 Arlington St. (in the Ritz-Carlton). ☎ **617/536-5700.** MBTA: Green Line to Arlington.

Famous for its martinis, The Bar at the Ritz is an elegant room with walnut paneling, a fireplace, live piano music, and a magnificent view of the Public Garden. The spectacular setting and service make it an excellent place for a celebration. Open Monday through Saturday from 11:30am to 1am, Sunday from noon to midnight. No jeans or athletic shoes.

Boston Harbor Hotel. 70 Rowes Wharf (entrance on Atlantic Ave.). ☎ **617/439-7000.**

You have two appealing options on the ground floor: **Intrigue,** which looks like a comfortable living room and boasts a harbor view, and the **Rowes Wharf Bar,** with a serious businesslike atmosphere and serious martinis.

✪ **Bristol Lounge.** 200 Boylston St. (in the Four Seasons Hotel). ☎ **617/351-2000.** MBTA: Green Line to Arlington.

This is a perfect choice after the theater, after work, or any time at all. An elegant room with soft lounge chairs, a fireplace, and fresh floral arrangements, it features a fabulous "Viennese Dessert Buffet" on weekends. There's live piano music every night. An eclectic menu is available until 11:30pm (12:30am on Friday and Saturday).

Oak Bar. In the Fairmont Copley Plaza Hotel, Copley Sq. ☎ **617/267-5300.** MBTA: Green Line to Copley, or Orange Line to Back Bay.

The paneled, high-ceilinged Oak Bar is a haven for cigar smokers. The lighting is muted, the leather chairs and couches are soft and welcoming, and there are an oyster bar and nightly live entertainment. Proper dress is required. Open Monday through Saturday from 5pm to midnight.

Regal Bostonian Hotel lounge. At Faneuil Hall Marketplace. ☎ **617/523-3600.** MBTA: Green or Blue Line to Government Center, or Orange Line to Haymarket.

The floor-to-ceiling windows of this ground-floor room across the street from Faneuil Hall Marketplace allow for great people watching. There are champagne by the glass, live piano music on weeknights, and cushy furnishings that encourage lingering. Open daily until midnight.

IRISH BARS

The Black Rose. 160 State St. ☎ **617/742-2286.** www.irishconnection.com. Cover $3–$5. MBTA: Orange or Blue Line to State.

Purists might sneer at the Black Rose's touristy location, but performers don't. Sing along with the authentic entertainment—you might be able to make out the tune on a fiddle over the din—at this jam-packed tavern at the edge of Faneuil Hall Marketplace. Open daily from 11am to 2am.

The Harp. 85 Causeway St. ☎ **617/742-1010.** Cover $5. MBTA: Green or Orange Line to North Station.

Live music on Thursday, Friday, and Saturday nights draws a young crowd that mills about in long lines along Causeway Street, across from Boston Garden and the FleetCenter. Open Monday through Saturday from 11am to 2am, Sunday from noon to midnight.

✪ **Matt Murphy's Pub.** 14 Harvard St., Brookline. ☎ **617/232-0188.** MBTA: Green Line D train to Brookline Village.

A long, narrow room that draws a friendly, brogue-intensive crowd, Matt Murphy's has great bartenders, excellent food, live music on weekend nights, and even a traditional pub quiz every other Wednesday. A big plus: no smoking.

Mr. Dooley's Boston Tavern. 77 Broad St. ☎ **617/338-5656.** Cover $3. MBTA: Blue Line to Aquarium.

The selection of imported beers on tap might be more of a draw than the live music at this Financial District spot, but sometimes an expertly poured Guinness is all you need. Open daily from 11am to 2am.

The Snug. 2067 Massachusetts Ave., Cambridge. ☎ **617/576-2240.** No cover to $3 cover. MBTA: Red Line to Porter.

Homesick Hibernians mingle with students and locals at the bar at Finnegan's Wake, an Irish restaurant just north of Porter Square, and especially at The Snug, in the basement. There are live music on weekends, a pub quiz on Monday, a pool and dart room, and incredible fries (called "chips," of course). Open Sunday through Wednesday from 5:30pm to 1am, Thursday through Saturday from 11:30am to 1am.

GAY/LESBIAN CLUBS & BARS

In addition to the clubs listed below, 1 night a week is gay night at some mainstream clubs. On Sunday, **Avalon** and **Axis** play host to the largest gathering of gay men in town; Sunday is "Convent" night for women at **The Snug;** and on Fridays Joy turns into **Joy Boy,** 533 Washington St. (☎ 617/338-6999). For listings, check *Bay Windows* and the monthly *Phoenix* supplement "One in 10."

Club Café. 209 Columbus Ave. ☎ **617/536-0966.** MBTA: Green Line to Arlington, or Orange Line to Back Bay.

This trendy South End spot draws men and women for conversation (the noise level is reasonable), dining, live music in the front room, and video entertainment in the back room, called Moonshine. Open daily from 2pm to 1am; lunch is served weekdays from 11:30am to 2:30pm, dinner 5:30 to 10pm Sunday through Wednesday, and until 11pm Thursday through Saturday. Sunday brunch starts at 11:30am.

Luxor. 69 Church St., Park Sq. ☎ **617/423-6969.** MBTA: Green Line to Arlington.

A diverse crowd frequents this 13-year-old video bar to see the latest music clips and compilations of snippets from movies and old TV shows concocted by the VJs. Downstairs is Jox, a small sports bar. Open daily 4pm to 1am.

Jacques. 79 Broadway, Bay Village. ☎ **617/426-8902.** MBTA: Green Line to Arlington.

The only drag venue in town, Jacques draws a friendly crowd of gay and straight patrons who mix with the "girls" and sometimes engage in a shocking activity— that's right, disco dancing. The eclectic entertainment includes live bands, performance artists, and, of course, drag shows. Open daily from noon to midnight.

Napoleon Club. 52 Piedmont St., Park Sq. ☎ **617/338-7547.** MBTA: Green Line to Arlington.

There's dancing upstairs on weekends, but what draws an exuberant all-ages crowd to sing along emanates from the pair of baby grand pianos downstairs. Two words: *show tunes.* Open daily 5pm to 2am.

4 More Entertainment

BREW PUBS

One of the first cities to develop microbrewery overload was Boston, where hanging copper tubing on a brick wall and proclaiming yourself a master brewer is practically an industry. If you're secretly harboring such aspirations, check out these places first. Most don't charge a cover, but beer will set you back at least $3 a mug, more if something fancy is involved. These are also popular dining destinations— all serve full meals, some as good as the brews, and all a step up from burgers and nachos.

Boston Beer Works. 61 Brookline Ave. ☎ **617/536-2337.** MBTA: Green Line B, C, or D train to Kenmore.

Across the street from Fenway Park, this cavernous, cacophonous microbrewery is chaotic anyway, and before and after Red Sox games it's a madhouse. It has a full food menu and 14 brews on tap, including excellent bitters and ales, seasonal concoctions such as Red Oktoberfest, lager with blueberries floating in it (not as dreadful as it sounds), and especially good cask-conditioned offerings, seasoned in wood till they're as smooth as fine wine. Sweet-potato fries make a terrific snack, but don't plan to be able to hear anything your friends are saying. Open daily from 11:30am to 1am.

Brew Moon Restaurant & Microbrewery. 115 Stuart St. ☎ **617/523-6467.** MBTA: Green Line to Boylston.

Hand-crafted beer meets tasty edibles at this popular Theater District spot, where bar food, sandwiches, and salads accompany freshly made brews. The Munich Gold won a gold medal at the 1996 Great American Beer Festival; if you're looking for something lighter, try the Grasshopper IPA or the out-of-this-world house-brewed root beer. Open daily from 11:30am to 2am. There's an equally busy branch in Harvard Square at 50 Church St. (☎ **617/499-2739**) that stays open till 1am (midnight on Sunday). Both have live music at the ✪ **Sunday jazz brunch,** 11am to 3pm.

Commonwealth Brewing Company. 138 Portland St. ☎ **617/523-8383.** MBTA: Green or Orange Line to North Station.

Boston's first brew pub is still going strong 13 years after it started the trend. It doesn't hurt that the "Commonwealth Brewery," as you'll often hear it called, is a block from North Station and madly popular with the crowds heading to the Fleet-Center. The top-notch English-style brews are served alone and in traditional combinations such as the snakebite (lager and hard cider) and shandy (ale and lemon soda). Here, too, the food is good—try the hummus plate. Open from 11:30am to midnight Sunday through Thursday, till 1am Friday and Saturday. There are live music and dancing downstairs Thursday through Saturday nights; the $3 cover is waived if you've been eating upstairs.

John Harvard's Brew House. 33 Dunster St., Cambridge. ☎ **617/868-3585.** No cover. MBTA: Red Line to Harvard.

This subterranean Harvard Square hangout pumps out English-style brews in a clublike setting (see whether you can make out the sports figures in the stained-glass windows) and prides itself on its food. The selection of beers changes regularly, and aficionados will have fun sampling John Harvard's Pale Ale, Nut Brown Ale, Pilgrim's Porter, and head brewer Gwen Lloyd's other concoctions. Open daily from 11:30am to 12:30am; food is served until 11:30pm.

COFFEEHOUSES

As in most other American cities, you can't get far in Boston or Cambridge without seeing a **Starbucks.** We'll submit to the passive-aggressive counter routine if it ends in a frozen drink, but for coffee, tea, and hanging out, there are plenty of less generic options. Many are in the North End (see chapter 6), and some more favorites are listed here. At all of them, loitering is encouraged—these are good places to bring your journal.

1369 Coffeehouse. 757 Massachusetts Ave., Cambridge. ☎ **617/576-4600.**

A long, narrow room that often attracts an (ahem) eccentric clientele, the 1369 offers excellent baked goods and a Crayola-like range of coffee flavors.

Algiers Coffeehouse. 40 Brattle St. ☎ **617/492-1557.**

Middle Eastern food and music, plain and flavored coffees, and a legendary atmosphere make this a classic Harvard Square hangout. (See chapter 6 for a full listing.)

BeanTowne Coffee House. 1 Kendall Sq., Cambridge. ☎ **617/621-7900.**

This splash of the bohemian in a buttoned-up office-retail complex is perfect for before or after a film at the Kendall Square Cinema. There's only one problem—it's too popular. If a table empties, make your move *fast.*

✪ **Someday Café.** 51 Davis Sq., Somerville. ☎ **617/623-3323.**

If "Friends" featured real people of all ages, they might hang out here, up the street from the Somerville Theater. The coffee and tea selections are impressive, and there are great lemonade in summer, cider in winter, and brownies all the time.

Trident Booksellers & Café. 338 Newbury St. ☎ **617/267-8688.**

This Back Bay institution has a view of the funkier end of Newbury Street, a browsing-friendly book selection, and a soothing, New Age-y atmosphere.

LECTURES

The Thursday *Globe* "Calendar" section is the best place to check for listings of lectures, readings, and talks on a wide variety of subjects, often at local colleges. Many are free or charge a small fee.

The **Ford Hall Forum** runs the longest-running public lecture series in the country. Tickets are sold by subscription; but there are usually extra seats in the large lecture halls, and the public is admitted free of charge 15 minutes before the program begins. The range of topics is what you might find in a good civics class—politics, the American justice system, civil rights—all discussed by experts who range from high-ranking government officials to celebrated professors. For advance program information, write to Ford Hall Forum, 271 Huntington Ave., Suite 240, Boston, MA 02115 (☎ 617/373-5800).

The **John F. Kennedy Library Public Forums** (☎ 617/929-4554) offer discussions of political and social issues. They're free, but reservations are suggested.

The **Arco Forum of Public Affairs,** at Harvard's Kennedy School of Government, 79 John F. Kennedy St., Cambridge (☎ 617/495-1380), draws big names for free discussions of domestic and foreign affairs during the school year. Arrive early for celebrity speakers or risk getting shut out.

The **Old South Meeting House,** 310 Washington St. (☎ 617/482-6439), on the Freedom Trail, presents lectures and concerts that explore American history and culture on Thursdays at 12:15pm from October through April. Admission to **"Middays at the Meeting House"** events is $4 for adults, $3 for seniors and students with ID.

MOVIES

In the age of the suburban megaplex, the number of first-run theaters downtown shrinks by the year—but you can see the latest blockbuster at home. The Boston area has some excellent outlets for classic, independent, and art films.

✪ **Free Friday Flicks at the Hatch Shell** (☎ 617/727-9547, ext. 550) are family films shown on a large screen in the amphitheater on the Esplanade usually used for concerts. The lawn in front of the Hatch Shell turns into a giant car-less drive-in as hundreds of people picnic while the sky grows dark, then watch a classic crowd pleaser (*The Wizard of Oz* and *Raiders of the Lost Ark* are favorites). Bring sweaters in case the breeze off the river grows chilly.

Classic films are shown in series at the Boston Public Library (☎ 617/536-5400; www.bpl.org) and the Museum of Fine Arts (☎ 617/267-9300; www.mfa.org). The BPL's free films are usually organized by theme (say, all Audrey Hepburn or all sports). There is a charge for films at the MFA, which also features premieres of independent and avant-garde films. Ticket prices (usually less than $10) vary according to the film-maker's reputation and whether the showing is a premiere.

For first-run independent and foreign films, head straight to the ✪ **Kendall Square Cinema,** 1 Kendall Sq., Cambridge (☎ 617/494-9800). The best movie theater in the Boston area offers five excellent screening rooms and discounted parking in the adjoining garage.

The area theaters closest to true revival houses—they feature lectures and live performances in addition to foreign and classic films—are the **Brattle Theater,** 40 Brattle St., Cambridge (☎ 617/876-6837; www.beaconcinema.com/brattle), and the **Coolidge Corner Theater,** 290 Harvard St., Brookline (☎ 617/734-2500; www.coolidge.org/Coolidge). Classic and foreign films are the tip of the iceberg at the quirky **Harvard Film Archive,** 24 Quincy St., Cambridge (☎ 617/495-4700), which also shows student films.

For inexpensive second- and third-run movies, ride the Red Line to the newly renovated **Somerville Theater,** 55 Davis Sq. (☎ 617/925-5700), which also stages live music performances on some weekend nights. Or take the MBTA no. 77 bus from Harvard station to Arlington, home of the **Capitol Theater,** 204 Massachusetts Ave. (☎ **617/648-4340**).

POOL PLUS

Plenty of bars have pool tables, but at the new, relatively upscale pool palaces that have invaded Boston, drinking is what you do while you're playing pool, not the other way around.

Boston Billiard Club. 126 Brookline Ave. ☎ **617/536-POOL.** Weekend evenings $11 an hour for 2 players. Each additional person $2 an hour. Prices lower during the day and on weeknights. MBTA: Green Line B, C, or D train to Kenmore.

The Boston Billiard Club, decorated with hunting prints, brass wall sconces, and a mahogany bar, has 42 tables and has been rated the top club in the country by *Billiard Digest Magazine.* There is full liquor service at the tables. If you don't want to wait for a table, ask about taking a back room (they can't be reserved) for $16 an hour. Open Monday through Saturday from 11am to 2am, Sunday from noon to 2am.

Flat Top Johnny's. 1 Kendall Sq., Cambridge. ☎ **617/494-9565.** Weekend evenings $12 an hour for 2 or more players. Prices lower during the day and on weeknights. MBTA: Red Line to Kendall.

A spacious but loud room with a bar and 12 red-topped tables, Flat Top Johnny's has a neighborhood feel despite being in a rather sterile office-retail complex. Open weekdays from 3pm to 1am, weekends at noon.

Jillians Entertainment. 145 Ipswich St. (corner of Lansdowne St.). ☎ **617/437-0300.** Evenings $11 an hour for 1 or 2 people, $13 for 3 or more. Prices lower during the day. MBTA: Green Line B, C, or D train to Kenmore.

Jillians's owners revived an interest in pool in Boston and continue expanding their horizons as entertainment technology becomes more sophisticated. The 70,000-square-foot complex contains a 50-table pool parlor, a virtual reality "ride," an interactive aviation game, a 200-game video midway, dart boards, a table tennis area, and more. There are five full bars and a restaurant. Jillians is open Monday through Saturday from 11am to 2am and Sunday from noon to 2am. Children under 18 accompanied by an adult are admitted before 7pm.

The Rack. 20 Clinton St. (at North St.). ☎ **617/725-1051.** $12 an hour after 4:30pm, $6 an hour before 4:30pm. MBTA: Green Line to Government Center, Blue Line to Aquarium, or Orange Line to Haymarket.

Across the street from Faneuil Hall Marketplace and the Regal Bostonian Hotel, The Rack is an enormous space. It encloses 22 tournament-size tables, two bars, and a lounge, and the action spills onto the patio out front in good weather.

11

Side Trips from Boston

Sights and attractions of great beauty and historical significance surround Boston. The destinations described here—Lexington and Concord, the North Shore and Cape Ann, and Plymouth—all make fascinating, manageable day trips and also offer enough diversions to fill several days.

1 Lexington & Concord

The shooting stage of the Revolutionary War began here, and parts of the towns still look much as they did in April 1775, when the fight for independence began. Start your visit in **Lexington,** where colonists and British troops first clashed. On the border with **Concord,** spend some time at **Minute Man National Historical Park,** investigating the battle that raged there more than 200 years ago. Decide for yourself where the "shot heard round the world" was fired—bearing in mind that Ralph Waldo Emerson, who wrote the words, lived in Concord. Emerson's house and Louisa May Alcott's family home (also in Concord) are just two of the fascinating destinations in this area.

Some attractions are closed from November through March or mid-April, opening after **Patriot's Day,** which is celebrated on the Monday closest to April 19.

LEXINGTON

6 miles NW of Cambridge; 9 miles NW of Boston

Lexington, a country village turned Boston suburb, takes great pride in its history. The **Battle Green,** next to a bustling business district, is an open common where you can see the famous **Minuteman Statue** and several other memorials.

British troops marched from Boston to Lexington late on April 18, 1775 (no need to memorize the date; you'll hear it everywhere), preceded by patriots Paul Revere and William Dawes, who sounded the warning. Members of the local militia, called "Minutemen" for their ability to prepare for battle quickly, were waiting at the **Buckman Tavern.** John Hancock and Samuel Adams, leaders of the revolutionary movement, were sleeping (or trying to) at the nearby **Hancock-Clarke House.** The warning came around midnight, followed about 5 hours later by some 700 British troops, headed to Concord to destroy the rebels' military supplies. Ordered to

Around Boston

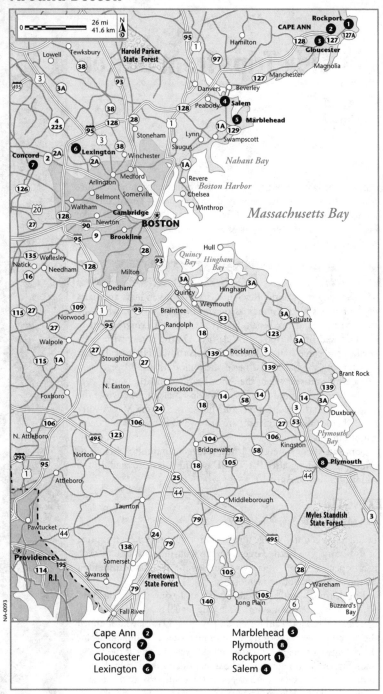

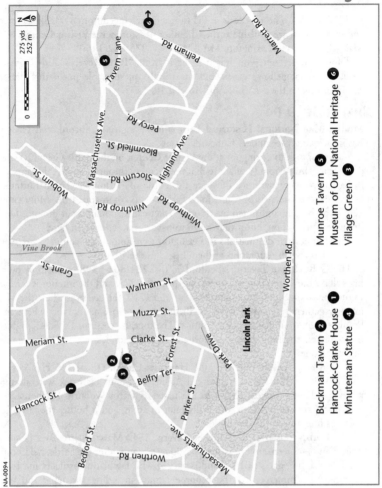

Buckman Tavern ❷ Munroe Tavern ❺
Hancock-Clarke House ❶ Museum of Our National Heritage ❻
Minuteman Statue ❹ Village Green ❸

NA-0094

disperse, the patriots—fewer than 100, and some accounts say 77—stood their ground. Nobody knows who started the shooting, but when it was over, 8 militia members were dead, including a drummer boy, and 10 were wounded.

GETTING THERE   Modern-day Route 2A approximates Paul Revere's path, but if you attempt to follow it during rush hour, you'll wish you had a horse of your own. Instead, take Route 2 from Cambridge through Belmont, and follow the signs for Route 4/225 into the center of Lexington. Or take Route 128 (I-95) to Exit 31, and proceed to the center of town. Massachusetts Avenue (the same street you might have seen in Boston and Cambridge) runs through Lexington.

The **MBTA** (☎ 617/222-3200; www.mbta.com) runs bus routes no. 62, "Bedford," and no. 76, "Hanscom," from Alewife Station (the last stop on the Red Line) to Lexington. Buses operate every hour during the day and every half hour during rush periods, Monday through Saturday. There is no service on Sundays, and no public transportation between Lexington and Concord.

ESSENTIALS The **area code** is 781 (it recently changed from 617). Sketch maps and information are available at the **Chamber of Commerce Visitor Center,** 1875 Massachusetts Ave., Lexington, MA 02473 (☎ **978/862-1450**).

Before you set out, you might want to read **"Paul Revere's Ride,"** Henry Wadsworth Longfellow's classic but historically questionable poem that dramatically chronicles the events of April 18 and 19, 1775.

WHAT TO SEE & DO

Minute Man National Historical Park is in Lexington, Concord, and Lincoln. For information, see under "Concord," below.

Start your visit to Lexington at the **Visitor Center,** on the Battle Green. It's open daily from 9am to 5pm (9:30am to 3:30pm October through June). A diorama and the accompanying narrative illustrate the Battle of Lexington. The **Minuteman Statue** on the Green is of Capt. John Parker, who commanded the Minutemen. When the British confronted his troops, Parker called: "Stand your ground. Don't fire unless fired upon, but if they mean to have a war, let it begin here!"

Three important destinations in Lexington were among the country's first "historic houses" when restoration of them began in the 1920s.

The ✪ **Buckman Tavern,** 1 Bedford St. (☎ **781/862-5598**), is the only building still on the Green that was there on April 19, 1775, and the interior is restored to the appearance it had that day. Built around 1710, the tavern is where the Minutemen gathered to await word of British troop movements, and where they brought their wounded after the conflict. The tour, by costumed guides, is educational and entertaining. If time is short and you have to pick just one house to visit, this is the one.

Within easy walking distance, the **Hancock-Clarke House,** 36 Hancock St. (☎ **781/861-0928**), is where Samuel Adams and John Hancock were sleeping when Paul Revere arrived. They were evacuated to nearby Woburn. The house, furnished in Colonial style, was originally built in 1698, and it houses the Historical Society's museum of the Revolution.

The British took over the **Munroe Tavern,** 1332 Massachusetts Ave. (about 1 mile from the Green), to use as their headquarters and, after the battle, field hospital. The building dates to 1690 and is packed with fascinating artifacts and furniture carefully preserved by the Munroe family, including the table and chair President George Washington used when he dined here in 1789. The gardens in the rear are beautifully planted and maintained.

All three houses are open for guided tours Monday through Saturday from 10am to 5pm and Sunday from 1 to 5pm, April through October. Admission for adults is $4 per house, $10 for all three; for ages 6 to 16, $1 per house, $2 for all three. The last tour starts at 4:30pm; tours take 30 to 45 minutes. Call for information about group tours, which are offered by appointment. The Munroe Tavern houses the **Lexington Historical Society** (☎ 781/862-1703; link.ci.lexington.ma.us/LexHistSoc/lhspage.htm), which operates all three.

The fascinating exhibits at the **Museum of Our National Heritage,** 33 Marrett Rd., Route 2A, at Massachusetts Avenue (☎ **781/861-6559** or 781/861-9638; www.mnh.org), explore history through popular culture. The installations in the six exhibition spaces change regularly; you can start with another dose of the Revolution, the exhibit "Lexington Alarm'd." Other topics have ranged from gravestones to jigsaw puzzles, American circus posters to quilting. Lectures, concerts, and family programs are also offered. Admission is free. The museum is open Monday through Saturday from 10am to 5pm and Sunday from noon to 5pm, and closed

January 1, Thanksgiving, and December 25. The museum is sponsored by the Scottish Rite of Freemasonry.

DINING

Bertucci's, 1777 Massachusetts Ave. (☎ **781/860-9000**), is a branch of the family-friendly pizzeria chain. **Aesop's Bagels,** 1666 Massachusetts Ave. (☎ **781/ 674-2990**), is a good place to pick up a light meal.

Lemon Grass. 1710 Massachusetts Ave. ☎ **781/862-3530.** Main courses $5.50–$8.25 at lunch, $7–$15.50 at dinner. AE, DISC, MC, V. Mon–Fri 11:30am–3pm; Mon-Thurs 5–9:30pm, Fri-Sat 5–10pm, Sun 4–9pm. THAI.

A welcome break: The only revolution going on here is in Americans' culinary habits. The space is a former coffee shop disguised with plenty of white paint, bamboo decorations, and the aromas of Asian spices. You might start with *satay* (skewers of meat served with a delectable peanut sauce), or chicken coconut soup, with a kick of pepper and plenty of chicken. Entrees range from a tasty rendition of traditional pad Thai to excellent curry dishes, and the accommodating staff will adjust the heat and spice to suit your taste.

CONCORD

18 miles NW of Boston, 15 miles NW of Cambridge, 6 miles W of Lexington

Concord (say "conquered") revels in its legacy as a center of groundbreaking thought and its role in the country's political and intellectual history. The first official battle of the Revolutionary War took place at the **North Bridge** (now part of **Minute Man National Historical Park**), and Concord later became an important literary and intellectual center.

After just a little time in this charming town, you might find yourself adopting the local attitudes toward two of its most famous residents: **Ralph Waldo Emerson,** who comes across as a well-respected uncle figure, and **Henry David Thoreau,** everyone's favorite eccentric cousin. The contemplative writers wandered the countryside nearby and did much of their writing and reflecting in Concord, forming the nucleus of a group of important writers who settled in the town. By the middle of the 19th century, Concord was the center of the Transcendentalist movement; sightseers can visit the former homes of **Emerson, Thoreau, Nathaniel Hawthorne,** and **Louisa May Alcott.** Lovers of literature can also visit **Sleepy Hollow Cemetery,** the authors' final resting place. Consider starting your visit at the **Concord Museum,** which offers an excellent overview.

GETTING THERE From Lexington, take Route 2A west from Route 4/225 at the Museum of Our National Heritage; follow signs reading BATTLE ROAD along the route the British took between the towns. From Boston and Cambridge, take Route 2 into Lincoln and stay in the right lane. Where the road makes a sharp left, go straight onto Cambridge Turnpike, and follow signs reading HISTORIC CONCORD.

MBTA (☎ **617/222-3200;** www.mbta.com) commuter trains take about 45 minutes from North Station in Boston, with a stop at Porter Square in Cambridge. There is no bus transportation from Boston to Concord, and no public transportation between Lexington and Concord. The station is about three-quarters of a mile from the town center.

ESSENTIALS The **area code** is 978 (it recently changed from 508). The **Chamber of Commerce,** 2 Lexington Rd., Concord, MA 01742 (☎ **978/ 369-3120**), maintains an information booth on Heywood Street, 1 block southeast

Impressions

Listen, my children, and you shall hear
Of the midnight ride of Paul Revere,
On the eighteenth of April, in Seventy-five;
Hardly a man is now alive
Who remembers that famous day and year. . . .

—Henry Wadsworth Longfellow, "Paul Revere's Ride," 1863

of Monument Square. It's open weekends in April and daily May through October, 9:30am to 4:30pm. One-hour tours are available starting in May on Saturday, Sunday, and Monday holidays, or on weekdays by appointment. Group tours are available by appointment. Concord also has a **Web site** (www.concordma.com), which has an area with visitor information.

MINUTE MAN NATIONAL HISTORICAL PARK   This 900-acre national park preserves the scene of the first Revolutionary War battle at Concord on (all together now) April 19, 1775. After the skirmish at Lexington, the British moved on to Concord in search of stockpiled arms, which had already been moved by the militiamen. Warned of the advance of the British troops, the colonists were preparing to confront them. The Minutemen crossed the North Bridge, evading the "regulars" who were standing guard, and waited for reinforcements on a nearby hilltop. In Concord, the British searched homes and burned any guns they found. The Minutemen saw the smoke and, mistakenly thinking the troops were torching the town, attacked the soldiers standing guard at the bridge. The gunfire that ensued is remembered as "the shot heard round the world," the opening salvo of the Revolution.

The park is open daily, year-round. To reach the **North Bridge,** follow Monument Street out of Concord Center until you see the parking lot on the right. Park and walk a short distance to the bridge (a reproduction), stopping along the unpaved path to read the narratives and hear the audio presentations. On one side of the bridge is a plaque commemorating the British soldiers who died in the Revolutionary War; on the other is Daniel Chester French's *Minute Man* statue.

You can also start your visit at the **North Bridge Visitor Center,** 174 Liberty St., off Monument Street (☎ **978/369-6993;** www.nps.gov/mima), which overlooks the Concord River and the bridge from a hilltop. A diorama and video program illustrate the battle, and exhibits include uniforms, weapons, and tools of colonial and British soldiers. Park rangers are on duty if you have questions. Outside, picnicking is allowed, and the scenery (especially the fall foliage) is lovely. The center is open daily in summer from 9am to 5:30pm and in winter from 9:30am to 4pm, and closed January 1 and December 25.

At the Lexington end of the park, the **Battle Road Visitor Center,** off Route 2A, one-half mile west of I-95 Exit 33B (☎ **781/862-7753**), is open mid-April through October from 9am to 5pm daily. The park includes the first 4 miles of the Battle Road, the route the defeated British troops took as they left Concord. At the visitor center, you'll see informational displays, a new multimedia program about the Revolution, and a new 40-foot mural illustrating the battle. On summer weekends, rangers lead tours of the park—call ahead for specific times. The new **Battle Road Interpretive Trail,** a 5½-mile path, permits pedestrian, wheelchair, and bicycle traffic. Exhibit panels and granite markers bear information about the military, social, and natural history of the area and point the way along the trail.

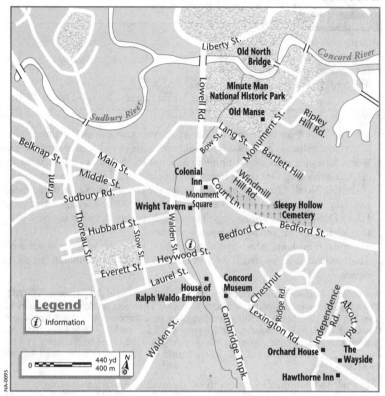

WHAT TO SEE & DO

At the **Walden Pond State Reservation,** Route 126 (☎ **978/369-3254**), a pile of stones marks the site of the cabin where Thoreau lived from 1845 to 1847. Today the picturesque park is an extremely popular destination for hiking (a path circles the pond), swimming, and fishing. Call for the schedule of interpretive programs. Take Walden Street (Route 126) south, away from Concord Center, cross Route 2, and look for signs directing you to the parking lot. From Memorial Day through Labor Day, a daily parking fee is charged, and the lot fills early every day—call before setting out.

✪ **Concord Museum.** Lexington Rd. and Cambridge Tpk. ☎ **978/369-9763.** www.concordmuseum.org. Admission $6 adults, $5 seniors, $4 students, $3 children under 16, $12 families. Apr–Dec, Mon–Sat 9am–5pm, Sun noon–5pm; Jan–Mar, Mon–Sat 11am–4pm, Sun 1–4pm. Parking on road is allowed. Follow Lexington Rd. out of Concord Center and bear right at museum onto Cambridge Tpk.; entrance is on left.

Just when you're (understandably) suspecting that everything interesting in this area started on April 18, 1775, and ended the next day, a visit to this superb museum sets you straight. It's a great way to start your visit to the town.

In the History Galleries, you'll explore answers to the question "Why Concord?" Artifacts, murals, films, maps, documents, and other presentations illustrate the town's role as a Native American settlement, Revolutionary War battleground, 19th-century intellectual center, and focal point of the 20th-century historic

Impressions

By the rude bridge that arched the flood.
Their flag to April's breeze unfurled.
Here once the embattled farmers stood,
And fired the shot heard round the world.

—Ralph Waldo Emerson, *Concord Hymn,* 1836

preservation movement. Items on display include archaeological artifacts, silver pieces from colonial churches, a fascinating collection of embroidery samplers, and rooms furnished with period furniture and textiles. Explanatory text places the exhibits in context. One of the lanterns that signaled Paul Revere from the steeple of the Old North Church is on display, as are the contents of Ralph Waldo Emerson's study, arranged the way it was at his death in 1882, and a large collection of Henry David Thoreau's belongings. There are changing exhibits in the New Wing throughout the year and an outstanding gift shop.

On the front lawn, what appears to be a shed is actually a replica of the cabin Thoreau lived in at Walden Pond from 1845 to 1847 (the furnishings are in the museum).

DeCordova Museum and Sculpture Park. 51 Sandy Pond Rd., Lincoln. ☎ **781/ 259-8355.** www.decordova.org. Museum $6 adults, $4 seniors, students, and ages 6–12. Tues–Sun and Mon holidays 11am–5pm. Sculpture park admission free. Daily 8am–10pm. Closed Jan 1, July 4, Thanksgiving, Dec 25. From Rte. 2 E., take Rte. 126 to Baker Bridge Rd. (first left after Walden Pond). When it ends, go right onto Sandy Pond Rd.; museum is on left. From Rte. 2 W., take I-95 to exit 28B, follow Trapelo Rd. 2½ miles to Sandy Pond Rd., and then follow signs.

Indoors and out, the DeCordova shows the work of American contemporary and modern artists, with an emphasis on living New England residents. The main building, on a leafy hilltop, overlooks a pond and the area's only outdoor public sculpture park. Recent renovations have added several galleries, room for interactive exhibits, a video space for regular exhibitions, a roof garden, and a sculpture terrace, which displays the work of one sculptor per year. Picnicking is allowed in the sculpture park; bring lunch, or buy it at the cafe.

The **Store @ DeCordova** (☎ 617/259-8692) has an excellent selection of prints, jewelry, clothing, and other work by local artists, including instructors at the Museum School.

The Old Manse. 269 Monument St. (at North Bridge). ☎ **978/369-3909.** Guided tour $5 adults, $4 students and seniors, $3.50 ages 6–12, $13 families (3–5 people). Mid-Apr to Oct, Mon–Sat 10am–5pm, and Sun and holidays noon–5pm. Closed Nov to mid-Apr. From Concord Center, follow Monument St. until you see North Bridge parking lot on right; the Old Manse is on left.

The Reverend William Emerson built the Old Manse in 1770 and watched the Battle of Concord from the yard. He died during the Revolutionary War, and the house was occupied for almost 170 years by his widow, her second husband, their descendants, and two friends: Nathaniel Hawthorne and his bride, Sophia Peabody, moved in after their marriage in 1842 and stayed for 3 years. As a wedding present, Henry David Thoreau sowed the vegetable garden for them; in 1997 cultivation began again after a 49-year absence. This is also where William's grandson Ralph Waldo Emerson wrote the essay "Nature." Today you'll see mementos and memorabilia of the Emerson and Ripley families and of the Hawthornes, who scratched notes on two windows with Sophia's diamond ring.

Orchard House. 399 Lexington Rd. ☎ **978/369-4118.** Guided tours $6 adults, $5 seniors and students, $4 ages 6–17, $16.50 families (up to 2 adults and 4 children). Apr–Oct, Mon–Sat 10am–4:30pm, Sun 1–4:30pm. Nov–Mar, Mon–Fri 11am–3pm, Sat 10am–4:30pm, Sun 1–4:30pm. Closed Jan 1–15, Easter, Thanksgiving, Dec 25. Follow Lexington Rd. out of Concord Center past Concord Museum; house is on left. Overflow parking lot is across street.

With the theatrical and video release of the 1994 movie *Little Women* (which was filmed elsewhere), Louisa May Alcott's best-known and most popular work moved from the world of preadolescent girls back into the mainstream. The book, published in 1868, was written and set at Orchard House, though most of the actual events took place earlier—Louisa was in her mid-30s when *Little Women* appeared. Seeing the Alcotts' home brings the family to life. Fans won't want to miss the excellent tour, copiously illustrated with family heirlooms.

Louisa's father, Amos Bronson Alcott, was a writer, educator, philosopher, and leader of the Transcendentalist movement. He created Orchard House by joining and restoring two early-18th-century homes already on the 12 acres of land he purchased in 1857. The family lived here from 1858 to 1877, socializing in the same circles as Emerson, Thoreau, and Hawthorne. Bronson Alcott's passion for educational reform eventually led to his being named superintendent of schools, and he ran the Concord School of Philosophy in Orchard House's backyard.

The rest of the Alcott family is known for artistic and cultural contributions, and for being the models for the characters in *Little Women.* Anna ("Meg"), the eldest, was an amateur actress, and May ("Amy") was a talented artist. Elizabeth ("Beth"), a gifted musician, died before the family moved to Orchard House. Bronson's wife, Abigail May Alcott, was a social activist and frequently assumed the role of family breadwinner—Bronson, as Louisa wrote in her journal, had "no gift for money making."

Ralph Waldo Emerson House. 28 Cambridge Tpk. ☎ **978/369-2236.** Guided tours $4.50 adults, $3 seniors and ages 7–17. Call to arrange group tours (10 people or more). Mid-April to Oct, Thurs–Sat 10am–4:30pm, Sun 2–4:30pm. Follow Cambridge Tpk. out of Concord Center; just before Concord Museum, house is on right.

Emerson, the philosopher, essayist, and poet, moved here in 1835 and remained until his death in 1882. He had just married his second wife, Lydia Jackson, whom he called "Lydian"; she called him "Mr. Emerson," as the staff still do. The tour gives a good look at the personal side of the great man and at the fashionably ornate interior decoration of the time. You'll see original furnishings and some of Emerson's personal effects (the contents of his study at the time of his death are in the Concord Museum).

Sleepy Hollow Cemetery. Entrance on Rte. 62 W.

Follow the signs for AUTHOR'S RIDGE, and climb the hill to the graves of some of the town's literary lights, including the Alcotts, Emerson, Hawthorne, and Thoreau. Emerson's grave, fittingly, bears no religious symbols but is marked by an uncarved quartz boulder. Thoreau's grave is nearby; at his funeral in 1862, his old friend Emerson concluded his eulogy with these words: "Wherever there is knowledge, wherever there is virtue, wherever there is beauty, he will find a home."

The Wayside. 455 Lexington Rd. ☎ **978/369-6975.** www.nps.gov/mima. Guided tours $4 adults, free for children under 17. Mid–Apr to Oct, Thurs–Tues 10:30am–4:30pm. Closed Nov to mid–Apr. Follow Lexington Rd. out of Concord Center past Concord Museum and Orchard House; The Wayside is on left.

Part of Minute Man National Historical Park, the Wayside was Nathaniel Hawthorne's home from 1852 until his death in 1864. The Alcott family lived here (the girls called it "the yellow house"), as did Harriett Lothrop, who wrote the *Five Little Peppers* books under the pen name Margaret Sidney and owned most of the current furnishings. The fascinating tour illuminates the lives of the occupants and the house's crazy-quilt architecture. The newest exhibit, housed in the barn, consists of audio presentations and figures of Louisa May and Bronson Alcott, Hawthorne, and Sidney.

ACCOMMODATIONS & DINING

Colonial Inn. 48 Monument Sq., Concord, MA 01742. ☎ **800/370-9200** or 978/ 369-9200. Fax 978/369-2170. 45 units (some with shower only). A/C TV TEL. Apr–Oct $169–$175 main inn; $109–$169 Prescott wing; $230–$275 cottage. Nov–Mar $139–$145 main inn; $105–$139 Prescott wing; $200–$235 cottage. AE, CB, DC, DISC, MC, V.

The Colonial Inn has overlooked Monument Square since 1716, when the main building went up. Additions since it became a hotel in 1889 have left the inn large enough to offer modern conveniences and small enough to feel friendly. The 12 original colonial-era guest rooms—one of which supposedly is haunted—are in great demand, so reserve early if you have your heart set on staying in the main inn. Rooms in the three-story Prescott wing are a bit larger and have country-style decor. The public areas, including a sitting room and front porch, are decorated in Colonial style. Dry cleaning and laundry service are available, as are conference rooms.

In addition to overnight accommodations, the Colonial Inn has two **lounges** that serve drinks and bar food, and a lovely **restaurant** that offers salads, sandwiches, and pasta at lunch, and traditional American fare at dinner. Afternoon tea is served Wednesday through Sunday; reservations (☎ **978/369-2373**) are required.

✪ **Aïgo Bistro.** 84 Thoreau St. (Rte. 126), at Concord Depot. ☎ **978/371-1333.** Reservations recommended. Main courses $7–$10 at lunch, $15–$25 at dinner; 3-course prix fixe Mon–Wed before 6:30pm $19. AE, DC, DISC, MC, V. Daily 11:30am–2:30pm, 5–10pm. MEDITERRANEAN.

"Aïgo" is Provençal patois for "garlic," which perfumes the air half a block away from this delightful spot. It's pronounced "I go," and you'll want to, for scrumptious food and top-notch service in a sophisticated setting. Settle in on a tapestry banquette, play with the brightly colored salt and pepper shakers, and prepare for hearty food, with an emphasis on garlic and grilling. This is a great place to fortify yourself in the middle of a day of sightseeing, or to wind down at the end. At either meal, you might start with the house special soup, *aïgo bouido*, a puree of roasted garlic thickened with almonds and bread. The lunch menu runs to generous portions of salads and sandwiches (grilled portobello is a good choice), served on focaccia. At dinner, meats, fresh fish, and at least one vegetarian option are skillfully prepared. Salmon in roasted tomato broth is a winner, as is grilled beef fillet with roasted red pepper, fennel, and black olive tapenade. Desserts are few but delectable—try the fresh fruit tart.

2 The North Shore & Cape Ann

The areas north of Boston abound with historic sights and attractions and with gorgeous ocean vistas. Cape Ann is a rocky peninsula so enchantingly beautiful that when you hear the slogan "Massachusetts's *other* Cape," you might forget what the first one was. Cape Ann and Cape Cod do share some attributes—scenery, shopping, seafood, traffic—but the smaller cape's proximity to Boston and manageable scale make it a wonderful day trip, as well as a good choice for a longer stay.

The **North of Boston Convention & Visitors Bureau,** 17 Peabody Sq., Peabody, MA 01960 (☎ **800/742-5306** or 978/977-7760), publishes a visitor guide. The **Cape Ann Chamber of Commerce** information center (see the section "Gloucester," below) can also be helpful.

MARBLEHEAD

15 miles NE of Boston

Like an attractive person with a great personality, Marblehead has it all. Scenery, history, architecture, and shopping combine to make it one of the area's most popular day trips, for residents and visitors alike. It's also a good place to spend a night or more. One of the most picturesque neighborhoods in New England is **"Old Town" Marblehead,** where the narrow, twisting streets lead down to the magnificent harbor that helps make this the self-proclaimed "Yachting Capital of America." There is sailboat racing in the outer harbor all summer, and "Race Week" in July attracts enthusiasts from all over the country.

Marblehead celebrates its history without wallowing in it. As you walk around Old Town, you'll see plaques on the houses bearing the date of construction, as well as the names of the builder and original occupant—a history lesson without studying. Many of the houses have stood since before the Revolutionary War, when Marblehead was a center of merchant shipping. Two historic homes are open for tours.

GETTING THERE   By car, take Route 1A north through Revere and Lynn; pick up Route 129 where you see signs for Swampscott and Marblehead, and follow it into town. Or take I-93 or Route 1 to Route 128, then Route 114 through Salem into Marblehead.

MBTA (☎ **617/222-3200;** www.mbta.com) bus route no. 441/442 runs from Haymarket (Orange or Green Line) in Boston to downtown Marblehead. During rush periods on weekdays, the no. 448/449 connects Marblehead to Downtown Crossing. The trip takes about an hour. The 441 and 448 buses detour to Vinnin Square shopping center in Swampscott; otherwise, the routes are the same.

ESSENTIALS   The **area code** is 781 (it recently changed from 617). The **Marblehead Chamber of Commerce,** 62 Pleasant St., P.O. Box 76, Marblehead, MA 01945 (☎ **781/631-2868;** www.marbleheadchamber.org), publishes a visitor's guide; individual pamphlets that list dining, shopping, and accommodations options and marine services; and a map of the historic district with two well-plotted walking tours. It also operates an **information booth** (daily in season, 10am to 5:30pm) on Pleasant Street near Spring Street. Marblehead also has a community Web site (www.marblehead.com).

WHAT TO SEE & DO

Marblehead is a wonderful place for aimless wandering; to add some structure, consult the Chamber of Commerce's walking tour pamphlet.

North of Boston: Road Trips

The trip from Boston to Cape Ann on I-93 and Route 128 takes about an hour. A more leisurely drive on Routes 1A and 129 allows you to explore the North Shore towns of Swampscott, Marblehead, and Salem on your way to Gloucester and Rockport. You can also follow Route 1 to I-95 and 128, but during rush hour the traffic is unbearable.

You'll probably want to travel by car even if your plans include visiting only one town. Although public transportation in this area is good, it doesn't go everywhere, so scheduling might prove difficult; and in many towns, the commuter rail station is some distance from the attractions.

Try to visit on a spring, summer, or fall weekday; many areas are ghost towns from November through March, and traffic is brutal on warm weekends. To go straight to Gloucester and Rockport—or to start there and work your way back—take I-93 north; where it turns into I-95 (signs point to New Hampshire and Maine), stay left and take Route 128 to the end. The last exit, number 9, puts you in East Gloucester. To take Route 1A, check a map or ask at the front desk of your hotel for directions to the Callahan Tunnel, which is at the heart of a huge construction site. East Boston is at the other end of the tunnel; ignore signs for the airport and continue on Route 1A north. If you miss the tunnel and wind up on I-93, follow signs to Route 1 and pick up Route 1A in Revere.

Whatever else you do, be sure to spend some time in **Crocker Park,** on the harbor off Front Street. Especially in the warmer months, when boats jam the water nearly as far as the eye can see, the view is breathtaking. There are benches and a swing, and picnicking is allowed. You might not want to leave, but snap out of it— the view from **Fort Sewall,** at the other end of Front Street, is equally mesmerizing.

Just inland, the **Lafayette House** is at the corner of Hooper and Union streets. The missing corner of the private residence was chopped off to make room for the passage of the Marquis de Lafayette's carriage when he visited the town in 1824. In Market Square on Washington Street, near the corner of State Street, is the **Old Town House,** in use for meetings and gatherings since 1727.

Marblehead is a legendary (or notorious, if you're on a budget) **shopping** destination. All along Washington and Front streets, and scattered on Atlantic Avenue, shops and boutiques will call your name.

Abbot Hall. Washington Sq. ☎ **781/631-0528.** Free admission. Year-round, Mon, Tues, Thurs 8am–5pm, Wed 7:30am–7:30pm, Fri 8am–1pm; May–Oct, Fri 1–5pm, Sat 11am–6pm, Sun 9am–6pm. From the historic district, follow Washington St. up the hill.

The town offices and Historical Commission share Abbot Hall with Archibald M. Willard's famous painting *The Spirit of '76,* which is on display in the Selectmen's Meeting Room. The thrill of recognizing the ubiquitous drummer, drummer boy, and fife player is the main reason to stop here. The deed that records the sale of the land by the Native Americans to the Europeans in 1684 is also on view. In the cases in the halls are objects and artifacts from the collections of the Historical Society. The building's clock tower is visible from all over Old Town.

✪ **Jeremiah Lee Mansion.** 161 Washington St. ☎ **781/631-1069.** Guided tours $4 adults, $3.50 students, free for children under 11. Mid–May to Oct, Mon–Sat 10am–4pm, Sun 1–4pm. Closed Nov to mid–May. Follow Washington St. until it curves right and heads uphill toward Abbot Hall; house is on right.

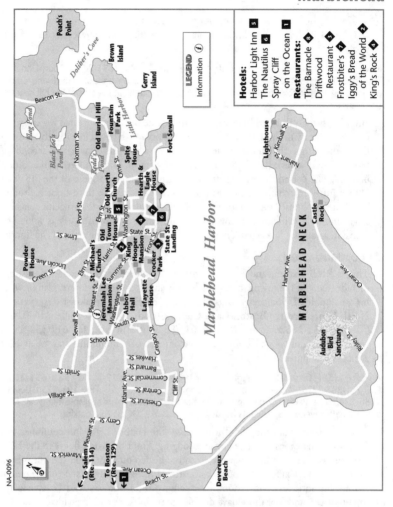

The prospect of seeing original hand-painted wallpaper in an 18th-century home is reason enough to visit this house, built in 1768 for a wealthy merchant and considered an outstanding example of pre-Revolutionary Georgian architecture. Original rococo carving and other details complement historically accurate room arrangements, and ongoing restoration and interpretation by the Marblehead Historical Society place the 18th- and 19th-century furnishings and artifacts in context. The friendly guides are well versed in the history of both the home and the renovations, including the restoration of the exterior, completed in 1997. Displays on the third floor draw on the society's collections of children's furniture, toys, nautical and military artifacts, and work by primitivist painter J. O. J. Frost. The lawn and gardens are open to the public.

The Historical Society, which makes its headquarters in the mansion, occasionally offers walking tours of Marblehead and candlelight tours of the house. Call ahead to see whether your schedules match.

Tip: On the hill between the mansion and Abbot Hall, the private homes at 185, 181, and 175 Washington St. are other good examples of the architecture of this period.

King Hooper Mansion. 8 Hooper St., Marblehead. ☎ **781/631-2608.** Tour: Donation requested. Mon–Sat 10am–4pm, Sun 1–5pm. Call ahead; tours are not held during private parties. Look for the colorful sign where Washington St. curves at the foot of the hill near the Lee Mansion.

Shipping tycoon Robert Hooper got his nickname because he treated his sailors so well, but it's easy to think he was called "King" because he lived like royalty. Around the corner from the home of Jeremiah Lee (whose sister was the second of Hooper's four wives), the 1728 King Hooper Mansion gained a Georgian addition in 1747. The period furnishings, though not original, give a sense of the life of an 18th-century merchant prince, from the wine cellar to the third-floor ballroom. The building houses the headquarters of the Marblehead Arts Association, which stages monthly exhibits and runs a gift shop where members' work is sold. The mansion also has a lovely garden; enter through the gate at the right of the house.

ACCOMMODATIONS

This is B&B heaven, and the Chamber of Commerce accommodations listings include many of the town's innumerable inns and bed-and-breakfasts. Call or write for a pamphlet. If you prefer to use an agency, try **Bed & Breakfast Reservations North Shore/Greater Boston/Cape Cod,** P.O. Box 35, Newtonville, MA 02460 (☎ **800/832-2632** outside MA, or 617/964-1606 in MA; fax 617/332-8572; www.bnbinc.com; e-mail bnbinc@ix.netcom.com). A minimum stay of at least 2 nights is required.

Harbor Light Inn. 58 Washington St., Marblehead, MA 01945. ☎ **781/631-2186.** Fax 781/631-2216. 21 units (some with shower only). A/C TV TEL. $95–$150 double; $160–$245 suite. Rates include continental breakfast. Corporate rate available mid-week. Minimum 2 nights weekends, 3 nights holiday weekends. AE, MC, V. Free parking.

A stone's throw from the Old Town House, the Harbor Light Inn combines two Federal-era mansions into one gracious lodging. From the wood floors to the 1729 beams in one of the third-floor rooms to the heated outdoor pool, the inn is both historical and relaxing, with rooms comfortably furnished in the style of the period (with some antiques). Most rooms have canopy or four-poster beds; 11 have working fireplaces, and 5 of those have double Jacuzzis. VCRs and free video rentals are available. Rooms at the back overlook the lawn, sundeck, and pool (open seasonally). There are gorgeous harbor views from some rooms and from the rooftop observation deck, which is open to all guests. There is also a conference room.

The Nautilus. 68 Front St., Marblehead, MA 01945. ☎ **781/631-1703.** 4 units (none with private bathroom). $65–$70 double. No credit cards. Ask for parking suggestions when you call for reservations.

This little guest house is as close to the harbor as you can get without being drenched. Rooms are on the second floor of a plain but comfortable private home and have semiprivate bathroom facilities. Make your reservations well in advance, because the combination of location and cheerful, homey service makes the Nautilus a popular destination.

Spray Cliff on the Ocean. 25 Spray Ave., Marblehead, MA 01945. ☎ **800/626-1530** or 781/631-6789. Fax 781/639-4563. www.marbleheadchamber.org/spraycliff. E-mail: spraycliff@aol.com. 7 units (some with shower only). May–Oct $175–$215 double. Off-season discounts available. Extra person $25. Rates include continental breakfast, evening refreshments, and use of bicycles. Minimum 2 nights on weekends, 3 nights on busy holiday weekends. AE, MC, V. Free parking. Take Atlantic Ave. (Rte. 129) to traffic light at Clifton Ave. and turn east (right driving north, left driving south); parking area is at end of street. No children accepted.

Spray Cliff, a three-story Victorian Tudor built in 1910 on a cliff overlooking the ocean, is 5 minutes from town and a world away. Five of the large, sunny rooms face the water, three have fireplaces, and all are luxuriously decorated in contemporary style with bright accents. Roger and Sally Plauché have run their romantic inn on a quiet residential street 1 minute from the beach since 1994.

DINING

At a number of places in Old Town, you can provision yourself for a picnic along the water. **Iggy's Bread of the World,** 5 Pleasant St. (☎ 781/639-4717), offers fabulous gourmet baked goods and coffee. **Frostbiter's,** 78 Front St. (☎ 781/631-6222), sells deli sandwiches, soups, and ice cream. Both also have small seating areas, but really, go outside.

The Barnacle. 141 Front St. ☎ 781/631-4236. Reservations not accepted. Main courses $4–$13 at lunch, $11–$16 at dinner. No credit cards. Daily 11:30am–4pm and 5–10pm. SEAFOOD.

This unassuming spot doesn't look like much from the street, but at the end of the gangplank-like entrance hall is a front-row seat for the action on the water. Even if you don't land a seat on the deck or along the counter facing the windows, you'll still have a shorebird's-eye view of the mouth of the harbor and the ocean from the jam-packed dining room. The food won't provide much of a distraction, but it's tasty, plentiful, and fresh—the restaurant's own lobster boat delivers daily. The chowder and fried seafood, especially the clams, are terrific. This is an ideal place to quaff a beer and watch the boats sail by.

Driftwood Restaurant. 63 Front St., Marblehead. ☎ 781/631-1145. Main courses $2–$9.50. No credit cards. Summer, daily 5:30am–5pm; winter, daily 5:30am–2pm. DINER/SEAFOOD.

At the foot of State Street next to Clark Landing (the town pier) is an honest-to-goodness local hangout. Whether you're in the mood for pancakes and hash, or chowder and a seafood "roll" (a hot dog bun filled with, say, fried clams or lobster salad), join the crowd. The house specialty, served on weekends and holidays, is fried dough, which is exactly as delicious and indigestible as it sounds.

King's Rook. 12 State St. ☎ 781/631-9838. Reservations not accepted. Main courses $4.50–$8. MC, V. Mon–Fri noon–2:30pm; Tues–Fri 5:30–11:30pm; Sat–Sun noon–11:30pm. CAFE/WINE BAR.

There's no better place to complete the sentence "I'm thirsty and I'd like . . ." than this cozy spot, a favorite long before coffeehouses ruled prime-time television. Coffees, teas, hot chocolates, soft drinks, and more than 2 dozen wines by the glass are available, and the food has a sophisticated flair. The intimate side-street atmosphere and racks of newspapers and magazines make this a great place to linger over a pesto pizza, a salad, or a sinfully rich dessert—and, of course, a beverage.

SALEM

17 miles NE of Boston, 4 miles NW of Marblehead

Settled in 1626 (4 years before Boston) and later known around the world as a center of merchant shipping, Salem is internationally famous today for a 7-month episode in 1692. The witchcraft trial hysteria led to 20 deaths, 3 centuries of notoriety, countless lessons on the evils of prejudice, and countless bad puns ("Stop by for a spell" is a favorite slogan).

Unable to live down its association with witches, Salem has embraced it. The high-school sports teams are called the Witches, and the logo of the *Salem Evening News* is a silhouette of a witch. Today you'll see plenty of witch-associated attractions, as well as reminders of Salem's rich maritime history. The newest is the replica of the 1797 East Indiaman tall ship *Friendship* anchored near the Salem Maritime National Historic Site.

GETTING THERE By car from Marblehead, follow Route 114 west. From Boston, take Route 1A north into downtown Salem, being careful in Lynn, where the road turns left and immediately right. Or take I-93 or Route 1 to Route 128, then Route 114 into downtown Salem. Once there, follow the color-coded signs— brown for the Visitor Center, blue for parking, and green for museums and historic sights. There's a reasonably priced municipal garage across the street from the Visitor Center.

From Boston, the **MBTA** (☎ 617/222-3200; www.mbta.com) operates bus route no. 450 from Haymarket (Orange or Green Line) and commuter trains from North Station. The bus takes an hour, the train 30 to 35 minutes.

ESSENTIALS The **area code** is 978 (it recently changed from 508). An excellent place to start your visit is the **National Park Service Visitor Center,** 2 New Liberty St. (☎ 978/740-1650; www.nps.gov/sama), where exhibits highlight early settlement, maritime history, and the leather and textiles industries. The center (open daily 9am to 5pm) distributes brochures and pamphlets, including one that describes a walking tour of the historic district, and has an auditorium where a free film on Essex County provides a good overview. The **Salem Chamber of Commerce** in Old Town Hall, 32 Derby Sq., Salem, MA 01970 (☎ 978/744-0004), maintains an information booth (weekdays 9am to 5pm). The chamber also collaborates with the **Salem Office of Tourism & Cultural Affairs,** 93 Washington St., Salem, MA 01970 (☎ 800/777-6848; e-mail SalemMA@cove.com), to publish a free visitor's guide. Salem has an excellent community Web site (www.salemweb.com).

WHAT TO SEE & DO

Downtown Salem is spread out but flat, and the historic district extends well inland from the waterfront. Many 18th-century houses still stand, some with original furnishings. Ship captains lived near the water at the east end of downtown, in relatively small houses crowded close together. The captains' employers, the shipping company owners, built their homes away from the water (and the accompanying aromas). Many of them lived on **Chestnut Street,** which is preserved as a registered National Historic Landmark. Residents along the grand thoroughfare must, by legal agreement, adhere to colonial style in their decorating and furnishings.

In the immediate downtown area, walking is the way to go, but you might not want to hoof it to all of the sights, especially in the summer. At the Essex Street side of the Visitor Center, you can board the **Salem Trolley** (☎ 978/744-5469; daily 10am to 5pm, April through October, weekends March and November) for a 1-hour narrated tour. Tickets ($8 adults, $7 students, $4 children 5 to 12; family of 2 adults and 2 or more children $20) are good all day, and you can reboard as many times as you like at any of the 15 stops. It's a great deal if you're spending the day and don't want to keep moving the car or carrying leg-weary children.

Salem

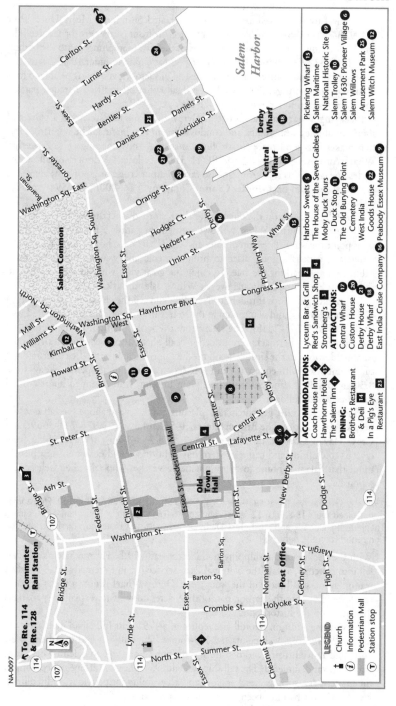

Salem Harbor

Derby Wharf

Central Wharf

Salem Common

Old Town Hall

ACCOMMODATIONS:
Coach House Inn **7**
Hawthorne Hotel **13**
The Salem Inn **1**

DINING:
Brother's Restaurant
& Deli **14**
In a Pig's Eye
Restaurant **23**
Lyceum Bar & Grill **2**
Red's Sandwich Shop **4**
Stromberg's **3**

ATTRACTIONS:
Central Wharf **17**
Custom House **20**
Derby House **21**
Derby Wharf **18**
East India Cruise Company **16**
Harbour Sweets **5**
The House of the Seven Gables **24**
Moby Duck Tours
- Duck Stop **11**
The Old Burying Point
Cemetery **8**
West India
Goods House **22**
Peabody Essex Museum **9**
Pickering Wharf **15**
Salem Maritime
National Historic Site **19**
Salem Trolley **10**
Salem 1630: Pioneer Village **6**
Salem Willows
Amusement Park **25**
Salem Witch Museum **12**

LEGEND
Church
Information
Pedestrian Mall
Station stop

To Rte. 114
& Rte. 128

Commuter
Rail Station

Post Office

NA-0097

To travel by sea as well as land, take a narrated 50-minute **Moby Duck Tour** (☎ **978/741-4386**) from New Liberty Street in front of the Visitor Center. The amphibious tour vehicle cruises the streets of the city, then plunges into the harbor. Tickets are $12 for adults, $10 for seniors, $8 for children under 12.

Should you find yourself in town at the end of October, you won't be able to miss **Haunted Happenings,** the city's 2-week Halloween celebration. Parades, parties, and tours lead up to a ceremony on the big day.

Pickering Wharf, at the corner of Derby and Congress streets, is a cluster of shops, boutiques, restaurants, and condos adjacent to a marina. The waterfront setting makes it a good place for strolling, snacking, and shopping. The **Pickering Wharf Antiques Gallery** (☎ **978/741-3113**) collects 40 dealers of all stripes under one capacious roof. You can also take a harbor cruise or go on a whale watch organized by the **East India Cruise Company** (☎ **800/745-9594** or 978/741-0434).

Three destinations on the outskirts of the historic district are worth the trip.

By car or trolley, the **Salem Willows** amusement park is 5 minutes away (many signs point the way). The strip of rides and snack bars has a honky-tonk air, and the waterfront park is a good place to bring a picnic and wander along the shore. Admission and parking are free. To enjoy the great view without the arcades and rides, have lunch one peninsula over at **Winter Island Park.**

Up-market gift shops throughout New England sell the chocolate confections of ✪ **Harbor Sweets,** and you can go to the source in Salem at Palmer Cove, 85 Leavitt St. (☎ **978/745-7648**). The retail store overlooks the floor of the factory—if you want to see the machinery in action, call ahead to see whether it's running. Recent additions to the sinfully good product lines include sugar-free offerings and candy embossed with equestrian and golf designs. The shop is open weekdays from 8:30am to 4:30pm and Saturday from 9am to 3pm, with extended hours around candy-centered holidays.

Finally, if you can't get witchcraft off your mind, several shops specialize in the necessary accessories. The **Broom Closet,** 3–5 Central St. (☎ **978/741-3669**), and **Crow Haven Corner,** 125 Essex St. (☎ **978/745-8763**), sell everything from crystals to clothing and cast a modern-day light on age-old customs—just bear in mind that Salem is home to many practicing witches who take their beliefs very seriously.

Salem Maritime National Historic Site. 174 Derby St. ☎ **978/740-1660.** Free admission. Guided tours $3 adults, $2 seniors and ages 6–16, $10 family. Daily 9am–5pm. Closed Thanksgiving, Dec 25, and Jan 1. Take Derby St. east; just past Pickering Wharf, the orientation center is on the right.

With the decline of the shipping trade in the early 19th century, Salem's wharves fell into disrepair, a state the National Park Service began to remedy in 1938 when it took over a small piece of the waterfront. **Derby Wharf** is now a finger of parkland extending into the harbor, part of the 9 acres dotted with explanatory markers that make up the historic site.

An exciting addition is a full-size replica of a 1797 East Indiaman merchant vessel, the *Friendship,* a three-masted 171-footer. The hull was laid in Albany, New York, and moved (using motors) during the spring of 1998 to Salem, where construction was completed. The tall ship is a faithful replica with some concessions to the modern era, such as diesel engines and accessibility for people with disabilities. Fees for visitors had not been determined at press time.

On adjacent **Central Wharf** is a warehouse that houses the orientation center. It dates from around 1800, and it was moved to the head of the wharf in the 1970s.

Ranger-led tours, which vary according to seasonal schedules, expand on Salem's maritime history. Yours might include the **Derby House** (1762), a wedding gift to shipping magnate Elias Hasket Derby from his father, and the **Custom House** (1819), where Nathaniel Hawthorne was working when he found an embroidered scarlet *A*. If you prefer to explore on your own, you can see the free film at the orientation center and wander around Derby Wharf, the West India Goods Store, the Bonded Warehouse, the Scale House, and Central Wharf.

The House of the Seven Gables. 54 Turner St. ☎ **978/744-0991.** www.7gables.org. Guided tours $7 adults, $4 ages 6–17, free for children under 6. July–Oct, daily 9am–6pm; Nov–Dec and Apr–June, daily 10am–4:30pm; Jan–March, Mon–Sat 10am–4:30pm, Sun noon–4:30pm. Closed Jan 1, Thanksgiving, Dec 25. From downtown, follow Derby St. east 3 blocks past Derby Wharf.

Built by Capt. John Turner in 1668, this building was later occupied by a cousin of Nathaniel Hawthorne's, and his 1851 novel of the same name was inspired by stories and legends of the house and its inhabitants. If you haven't read the book, don't let that keep you away—begin your visit with the audiovisual program, which tells the story. The house holds six rooms of period furniture, including pieces referred to in the book, and a narrow, twisting secret staircase. Tours include a visit to Hawthorne's birthplace (built before 1750 and moved to the grounds) and describe what life was like for the houses' 18th-century inhabitants. The costumed guides can get a little silly as they mug for young visitors, but they're well versed in the history of the buildings and artifacts, and eager to answer questions. Also on the grounds, overlooking Salem Harbor, are period gardens, the **Retire Beckett House** (1655), the **Hooper-Hathaway House** (1682), and a **counting house** (1830).

Combination discounted tickets (adult $10, child $6) for the House of the Seven Gables and Salem 1630 (see below) are available at both places.

✪ **Peabody Essex Museum.** East India Sq. ☎ **800/745-4054** or 978/745-9500. www.pem.org. Admission (good on 2 consecutive days) $8.50 adults, $7.50 seniors and students with ID, $5 ages 6–16, $20 family (2 adults, 1 or more children). Mon–Sat 10am–5pm, Sun noon–5pm. Closed Jan 1, Thanksgiving, Dec 25, Mon Nov–Memorial Day. Take Hawthorne Blvd. to Essex St., following signs for Visitor Center. Enter on Essex St. or New Liberty St.

The Peabody Essex Museum celebrates its bicentennial in 1999, with expanded exhibition space in the newly renovated library and even more growth in the works. Changes have been ongoing since the 1992 merger of the Peabody Museum and the Essex Institute, which combined fascinating collections that illustrate Salem's international adventures and domestic development.

The Peabody Museum, the nation's oldest in continuous operation, was founded in 1799 by the East India Marine Society, a group of sea captains and merchants whose charter included provisions for a "museum in which to house the natural and artificial curiosities" brought back from their travels. The collection of the Essex Institute (1821), the county's historical society, encompasses American art, crafts, furniture, and architecture (including nine historic houses), as well as dolls, toys, and games.

It all adds up to the impression that you're in Salem's attic, but instead of opening dusty trunks and musty closets, you find the treasures arranged in well-planned displays that help you understand the significance of each artifact. Trace the history of the port of Salem and the whaling trade; study figureheads of ships or portraits of area residents (including Charles Osgood's omnipresent rendering of Nathaniel Hawthorne); learn about the witchcraft trials; and immerse yourself in East Asian art and artifacts or the practical arts and crafts of the East Asian,

Pacific Island, and Native American peoples. The Asian Export Art Wing displays decorative art pieces made in Asia for Western use from the 14th to the 19th centuries. Sign up for a tour of one or more houses—the **Gardner-Pingree House** (1804), a magnificent Federal mansion where a notorious murder was committed in 1830, has been gorgeously restored. You can also sign up for a gallery tour or select from about a dozen pamphlets for self-guided tours on various topics.

The museum has an excellent gift shop and a cafe that serves lunch daily.

Salem 1630: Pioneer Village. Forest River Park, off West Ave. ☎ **978/745-0525** or 978/744-0991. www.7gables.org. Admission $4.50 adults, $3.50 seniors and ages 13–17, $2.50 ages 6–12. Daily Memorial Day–Halloween 10am–5pm. Closed Nov 1–late May. Take Lafayette St. (Rtes. 114 and 1A) south from downtown to West Ave., turn left, and follow signs.

A re-creation of life in Salem just 4 years after European settlement, this Puritan village is staffed by costumed interpreters who lead tours, demonstrate crafts, and tend farm animals. They escort visitors around the various dwellings—wear sneakers, because the village isn't paved—and explain their activities. As with any undertaking of this nature, it takes a while to get used to the atmosphere, but once you do, it's great fun.

When the 1996 film version of Arthur Miller's play about the witchcraft trials, *The Crucible*, was completed, the village inherited a large collection of authentic and reproduction props that have been put into use.

Combination discounted tickets for Salem 1630 and The House of the Seven Gables (adult $10, child $6) are available at both places.

۞ Salem Witch Museum. 19½ Washington Sq. ☎ **978/744-1692.** www.salemwitchmuseum.com. Admission $5 adults, $4.50 seniors, $3.50 ages 6–14. Sept–June, daily 10am–5pm; July–Aug, daily 10am–7pm. Closed Jan 1, Thanksgiving, Dec 25. Follow Hawthorne Blvd. to the northwest corner of Salem Common.

This is one of the most memorable attractions in eastern Massachusetts—it's both interesting and scary. Actually a three-dimensional audiovisual presentation with life-size figures, the Witch Museum is a former church surrounding a huge room lined with displays that are lighted in sequence. The 30-minute narration dramatically but accurately tells the story of the witchcraft trials and the accompanying hysteria. (One man is pressed to death by rocks piled on a board on his chest—smaller children might need a reminder that he's not real.) The narration is available translated into French, German, Italian, Japanese, and Spanish.

On the traffic island across from the entrance is a statue that's easily mistaken for a witch. It's really Roger Conant, who founded Salem in 1626.

ACCOMMODATIONS

Coach House Inn. 284 Lafayette St. (Rtes. 1A and 114), Salem, MA 01970. ☎ **800/688-8689** or 978/744-4092. Fax 978/745-8031. www.salemweb.com/biz/coachhouse. E-mail: coachhse@star.net. 11 units, 9 with bathroom (1 with shower only). A/C TV. $68–$75 double with shared bathroom; $75–$98 double with private bathroom; $125–$155 suite with kitchenette. Extra person $20. Rates include continental breakfast. Minimum 2–3 nights on weekends and holidays. AE, DISC, MC, V.

Built in 1879 for a ship's captain, the Coach House Inn is 2 blocks from the harbor. It's a good, thrifty choice if you don't mind the 20-minute walk or 5-minute drive from downtown Salem. The high-ceilinged rooms in the recently repainted three-story mansion have coffeemakers and elegant furnishings, and most have nonworking fireplaces, many of marble or carved ebony. Breakfast arrives at your door in a basket.

Hawthorne Hotel. 18 Washington Sq. (at Salem Common), Salem, MA 01970. ☎ **800/729-7829** or 978/744-4080. Fax 978/745-9842. 83 units (some with shower only). A/C TV TEL. $99-$182 double, $150-$275 suite. Off-season discounts available. Extra person $12. Children under 16 stay free in parents' room. Senior discount available. Minimum 2 nights on holiday weekends. AE, CB, DC, DISC, MC, V. Free parking. Small pets accepted; $15 charge.

This historic hotel, built in 1925 and nicely maintained—the lobby was remodeled in 1995, half of the guest rooms in 1997 and 1998—is both convenient and comfortable. The six-story building is centrally located. Some of the attractively furnished, decent-sized rooms overlook Salem Common. This is a busy neighborhood; ask to be as high up as possible. Guests have the use of an exercise room, and there are two restaurants on the ground floor, room service until 11pm, and dry cleaning and laundry service.

Salem Inn. 7 Summer St. (Rte. 114), Salem, MA 01970. ☎ **800/446-2995** or 978/741-0680. Fax 978/744-8924. www.salemweb.com/biz/saleminn. E-mail: saleminn@earthlink.net. 39 units (some with shower only). A/C TV TEL. Mid-Apr to mid-Oct double $109-$190; Halloween week $140-$190; Nov to mid-Apr $99-$179. Rates include continental breakfast. Minimum 2 nights during special events and holidays. AE, CB, DC, DISC, MC, V.

The Salem Inn occupies the comfortable niche between too-big hotel and too-small B&B. The hubbub of downtown falls away as you enter the inn, which consists of three properties. The 1834 West House and the 1854 Curwen House, former homes of ship captains, are listed on the National Register of Historic Places. The 1874 Peabody House is a newly restored Colonial mansion divided into luxury and family suites. The large, tastefully decorated guest rooms all have coffeemakers, and some have fireplaces, canopy beds, and whirlpool baths. Suites have kitchenettes. A peaceful rose garden and brick patio are at the rear of the main building, which also holds a meeting space. On the lower level is the Courtyard Café, where guests eat breakfast. It's open for dinner Wednesday through Sunday from 6 to 9:30pm.

DINING

Whether you're sitting down for three courses or grabbing a muffin and running, Salem offers a good selection. **Pickering Wharf** has a food court as well as a link in the **Victoria Station** chain (☎ **978/744-7644**), where the deck has a great view of the marina. **In a Pig's Eye,** 148 Derby St. (☎ **978/741-4436**), is a neighborhood tavern on the way to The House of the Seven Gables that serves great Mexican food and bar fare. For a quick bite, try **Brothers Restaurant & Deli,** 283 Derby St. (☎ **978/741-4648**), an inexpensive cafeteria-style family spot with home-cooked Greek meals that also serves breakfast all day.

✪ **Lyceum Bar & Grill.** 43 Church St. (at Washington St.). ☎ **978/745-7665.** Reservations recommended. Main courses $6–$10 at lunch, $10–$19 at dinner. AE, DISC, MC, V. Mon–Fri 11:30am–3pm, Sun brunch 11am–3pm; daily 5:30–10pm. AMERICAN.

Alexander Graham Bell made the first long-distance telephone call at the Lyceum, and you might want to place one of your own to tell the folks at home what a good meal you're having. The elegance of the high-ceilinged front rooms and glass-walled back rooms matches the quality of the food, which attracts local businesspeople and out-of-towners. Grilling is a favorite cooking technique—be sure to try the marinated, grilled portabella mushrooms, even if you have to order a plate of them as an appetizer. They're also scattered throughout the menu, for example in delectable pasta with chicken, red peppers, and Swiss chard in wine sauce, or with beef tenderloin, red pepper sauce, and garlic mashed potatoes. Spicy vegetable lasagna is also tasty. Try to save room for one of the traditional yet sophisticated desserts. The brownie sundae is out of this world.

Red's Sandwich Shop. 15 Central St. ☎ **978/745-3527.** Most items under $6. No credit cards. Mon–Sat 5am–3pm, Sun 6am–1pm. DINER.

This no-frills spot recently expanded, but it's still a place where locals and visitors feel equally comfortable. Hunker down at the counter or a table and be ready for your waitress to call you "dear" as she brings you pancakes and eggs at breakfast, or soup (opt for chicken over chowder) and a burger at lunch. **Red's Winter Island Grille** (☎ **978/744-0203**), under the same management, is open seasonally at Winter Island Park.

Stromberg's. 2 Bridge St. (Rte. 1A). ☎ **978/744-1863.** Reservations recommended at dinner. Main courses $6–$10 at lunch, $10–$15 at dinner; lobster priced daily. AE, DISC, MC, V. Tues–Thurs 11am–9pm, Fri–Sat until 10pm. Closed Tues after long holiday weekends. SEAFOOD.

For generous portions of well-prepared seafood and a view of the water, head to this popular spot near the bridge to Beverly. You won't care that Beverly Harbor isn't the most exciting spot, especially if it's summer and you're out on the deck enjoying the live entertainment (weekends only). The fish and clam chowders are excellent; daily specials are numerous; and there are more chicken, beef, and pasta options than you might expect. Crustacean lovers in the mood to splurge will fall for the world-class lobster roll. There's also a children's menu ($2.75 to $4.50).

EN ROUTE TO GLOUCESTER & ROCKPORT

If you approach or leave Cape Ann on Route 128, turn away from Gloucester on Route 133 and head west to **Essex.** It's a beautiful little town known for Essex clams, salt marshes, a long tradition of shipbuilding, an incredible number of antiques shops, and one celebrated restaurant.

Legend has it that ✪ **Woodman's of Essex,** Main Street (☎ **800/649-1773** or 978/768-6451), was the birthplace of the fried clam in 1916. Today the thriving family business is a great spot to join legions of locals and visitors from around the world for lobster "in the rough," steamers, corn on the cob, onion rings, and (you guessed it) fried clams. Expect the line to be long, even in the winter, but it moves quickly and offers a good view of the regimented commotion in the food preparation area. Eat in a booth, upstairs on the deck, or out back at a picnic table. Credit cards aren't accepted, but there's an ATM on the premises.

If this all sounds just plain uncivilized, make a reservation at **Tom Shea's,** 122 Main St. (☎ **978/768-6931**), which has table service, a more sophisticated menu, and a calmer atmosphere. You'll want to be well-fed before you set off to explore the numerous antiques shops along Main Street.

Just south of Gloucester on Route 127, you'll see signs for Magnolia and **Hammond Castle,** 80 Hesperus Ave., Gloucester (☎ **978/283-2080,** or 978/283-7673 for recorded information; www1.shore.net/~hammond). Eccentric inventor John Hays Hammond, Jr., designed the medieval castle, which was constructed of Rockport granite and cost more than $6 million when it was built from 1926 to 1929. Guided tours are no longer offered, so you're on your own with a pamphlet to direct you around the castle—not the most fulfilling way to explore such a peculiar place, but if you enjoy house tours or the medieval era, you'll definitely enjoy this. You'll see 85-foot towers, battlements, stained-glass windows, a great hall 60 feet high, and an enclosed "outdoor" pool and courtyard lined with foliage, trees, and medieval artifacts (including the whole wooden front of a butcher shop). Many

12th-, 13th-, and 14th-century furnishings, tapestries, paintings, and architectural fragments fill the rooms, and an organ with more than 8,200 pipes is used for monthly concerts. Admission to the museum is $6 for adults, $5 for seniors and students, $4 for ages 4 to 12, free for children under 4. Open daily Memorial Day through Labor Day from 10am to 6pm, Labor Day through October Thursday through Sunday from 10am to 4pm, and November through May weekends only from 10am to 4pm.

GLOUCESTER

33 miles NE of Boston, 16 miles NE of Salem

The ocean has been Gloucester's lifeblood since long before the first European settlement in 1623. The French explorer Samuel de Champlain called the harbor "Le Beauport" when he came across it in 1604, some 600 years after the Vikings, and its configuration and proximity to good fishing gave it the reputation it enjoys to this day.

On Stacy Boulevard west of downtown is a reminder of the sea's danger. Leonard Craske's bronze statue of the **Gloucester Fisherman,** known as "The Man at the Wheel," bears the inscription "They That Go Down to the Sea in Ships 1623–1923." More than 10,000 fishermen lost their lives during the city's first 300 years, and a statue honoring the women and children who waited for them is currently in the works.

GETTING THERE From Salem, follow Route 1A across the bridge to Beverly, pick up Route 127, and take it through Manchester (near, not on, the water) to Gloucester. From Boston, the quickest path is I-93 or Route 1 to Route 128, which runs directly to Gloucester. Route 128 is almost entirely inland; the exits for Manchester allow access to Route 127 if you want to combine speed and scenery.

The **MBTA** (☎ 617/222-3200; www.mbta.com) commuter rail runs from North Station in Boston to Gloucester. The trip takes about an hour. The **Cape Ann Transportation Authority,** or CATA (☎ 978/283-7916), runs buses from town to town on Cape Ann.

ESSENTIALS The **area code** is 978 (it recently changed from 508). The **Gloucester Tourism Commission,** 22 Poplar St., Gloucester, MA 01930 (☎ 800/649-6839 or 978/281-8865; www1.shore.net/~nya/gloucester.html), operates an excellent Visitors Welcoming Center. It's open daily from 9am to 5pm during the summer at Stage Fort Park, off Route 127 near the intersection with Route 133. The information center run by the **Cape Ann Chamber of Commerce,** 33 Commercial St., Gloucester, MA 01930 (☎ 800/321-0133 or 978/283-1601; www.cape-ann.com/cacc), is open year-round (summer, weekdays from 8am to 6pm, Saturday from 10am to 6pm, Sun from 10am to 4pm; winter, weekdays from 8am to 5pm). Call or write for the chamber's four-color map and brochure.

WHAT TO SEE & DO

Business isn't what it once was, but fishing is still Gloucester's leading industry (as your nose will tell you), and the fishermen need all the help they can get. Every year the fleet enjoys some divine intervention during **St. Peter's Fiesta,** a colorful 4-day event at the end of June. The Italian-American fishing colony's festival has more in common with a carnival midway than a religious observation, but it's great fun. There are parades, games, music, food, sporting events, and, on Sunday, the blessing of the fleet.

A Whale of an Adventure

The depletion of New England's fishing grounds has led to the rise of another important seagoing industry: whale watching. The waters off the coast of Massachusetts are prime whale-watching territory, and Gloucester is a center of whale-watching cruises. Stellwagen Bank, which runs from Gloucester to Provincetown about 27 miles east of Boston, is a rich feeding ground for the magnificent mammals, mainly humpback, finback, and minke whales, who dine on sand eels and other fish that gather along the ridge. Naturalists are on board the cruises to point out the various creatures. The whales often perform for their audience by jumping out of the water, and occasionally dolphins join the show. This is not the most time- or cost-effective activity you'll run across, especially if children are along, but the payoff is (literally and figuratively) huge.

Dress warmly, because it's much cooler at sea than in town, and take sunglasses, sunscreen, a hat, rubber-soled shoes, and a camera with plenty of film. If you're prone to motion sickness, take appropriate precautions (ginger, crystallized or in ginger ale, can help alleviate nausea), because you'll be out on the open sea for 4 to 6 hours.

Check the local marinas for sailing times, prices ($23 to $26 for adults, less for seniors and children), and reservations, which are always a good idea. This is an extremely competitive business—most companies guarantee sightings, offer a morning and an afternoon cruise as well as deep-sea fishing excursions, honor other firms' coupons, and offer AARP and AAA discounts. In downtown Gloucester, you'll find **Cape Ann Whale Watch** (☎ **800/877-5110** or 978/283-5110; www.caww.com), **Capt. Bill's Whale Watch** (☎ **800/33-WHALE** or 978/283-6995; www.cape-ann.com/captbill.html), and **Seven Seas Whale Watch** (☎ **800/238-1776** or 978/283-1776; www.cape-ann.com/whalewatch.html). At the Cape Ann Marina, off Route 133, is **Yankee Whale Watch** (☎ **800/WHALING** or 508/283-0313; www.yankee-fleet.com/whale.htm).

Moby Duck Tours (☎ 978/281-3825) are 50-minute sightseeing expeditions that travel on land before plunging into the water. The amphibious vehicles leave from **Harbor Loop** downtown, where tickets ($12 for adults, $10 for seniors, $8 for children under 12) are available. Also at Harbor Loop, you can tour the two-masted schooner *Adventure* (☎ 978/281-8079; www.cape-ann.com/adventure.html), a 121-foot fishing vessel built in Essex in 1926. The "living museum," a National Historic Landmark, is open to visitors from Memorial Day to Labor Day, Thursday through Sunday from 10am to 4pm. The suggested donation is $5 adults, $4 children.

To reach East Gloucester, follow signs as you leave downtown, or go directly from Route 128, Exit 9. On East Main Street, you'll see signs for the world-famous **Rocky Neck Art Colony,** the oldest continuously operating art colony in the country. Park in the lot on the tiny causeway, and head west along Rocky Neck Avenue, which abounds with studios, galleries, restaurants, and people. The draw is the presence of working artists, not just shops that happen to sell art. Most galleries are open daily in the summer, 10am to 10pm.

The **North Shore Arts Association,** 197 E. Main St. (☎ 978/283-1857), founded in 1922 to showcase local artists' work, is worth a visit before or after your excursion across the causeway. It's open June through September, Monday through

Saturday from 10am to 5pm, Sunday from 1 to 5pm, and admission is free.

Stage Fort Park (off Route 127 near the intersection with Route 133) offers an excellent view of the harbor and is a good spot for a having picnic, swimming, or just playing on the cannons in the Revolutionary War fort.

✪ **Beauport (Sleeper-McCann House).** 75 Eastern Point Blvd. ☎ **978/283-0800.** www.cape-ann.com/beauport.html. Guided tours $6 adults, $5.50 seniors, $3 ages 6–12. Tours on the hour mid–May to mid–Oct, Mon–Fri 10am–4pm; mid-Sept to mid-Oct, daily 10am–4pm. Closed mid–Oct to mid–May and summer weekends. Take East Main St. south to Eastern Point Blvd. (a private road), drive one-half mile to house, park on left.

The Society for the Preservation of New England Antiquities, which operates Beauport, describes it as a "fantasy house," and that's putting it mildly. Interior designer Henry Davis Sleeper used his summer residence as a retreat and a repository for his vast collections of American and European decorative arts and antiques. From 1907 to 1934, he decorated the 40 rooms, 26 of which are open to the public, to illustrate literary and historical themes. The entertaining tour concentrates more on the house and rooms in general than on the countless objects on display. You'll see architectural details rescued from other buildings, magnificent arrangements of colored glassware, an early American kitchen, the "Red Indian Room" (with a majestic view of the harbor), and "Strawberry Hill," the master bedroom. If you're visiting from June through September, call ahead to see whether afternoon tea is being offered while you're in town. Note that the house is closed on summer weekends.

Cape Ann Historical Association. 27 Pleasant St. ☎ **978/283-0455.** Admission $3.50 adults, $3 seniors, $2 students, free for children under 7. Tues–Sat 10am–5pm. Closed Feb. Follow Main St. west through downtown and turn right onto Pleasant St.; the museum is 1 block up on right. Metered parking available on street or in lot across street.

This meticulously curated museum makes an excellent introduction to Cape Ann's history and artists. It devotes an entire gallery to the extraordinary work of ✪ **Fitz Hugh Lane,** the American Luminist painter whose light-flooded paintings show off the best of his native Gloucester. The nation's single largest collection of his paintings and drawings is here, along with new galleries featuring works on paper by 20th-century artists such as Maurice Prendergast and Milton Avery, work by other contemporary artists, and granite quarrying tools and equipment. On display in the **maritime and fisheries galleries** are entire vessels (including one about the size of a station wagon that actually crossed the Atlantic), exhibits on the fishing industry, ship models, and historic photographs and models of the Gloucester waterfront. The **Capt. Elias Davis House** (1804), decorated and furnished in the Federal style with furniture, silver, and porcelains, is part of the museum.

ACCOMMODATIONS

Atlantis Oceanfront Motor Inn. 125 Atlantic Rd., Gloucester, MA 01930. ☎ **978/283-0014.** www.cape-ann.com/atlantis.html. 40 units (some with shower only). TV TEL. Late June–Labor Day $100–$120 double; spring and fall $65–$95 double. Extra person $8. Closed Nov to mid-Apr. Minimum 2 nights on spring and fall weekends, 3 nights on holiday and summer weekends. AE, MC, V. Follow Rte. 128 to the end (Exit 9, East Gloucester), turn left onto Bass Ave. (Rte. 127A), and follow a half-mile. Turn right and follow Atlantic Rd.

The stunning views from every window of this motor inn would almost be enough to recommend it, but it also has a heated outdoor pool and a friendly staff. The redecoration of the guest rooms in comfortable, contemporary style was completed in 1995. Every room has a terrace or balcony and a small table and chairs, and the coffee shop on the premises serves breakfast until 11am.

Cape Ann

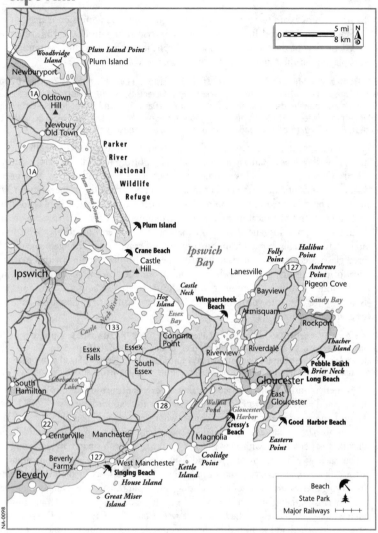

Best Western Bass Rocks Ocean Inn. 107 Atlantic Rd., Gloucester, MA 01930. ☎ **800/528-1234** or 978/283-7600. Fax 978/281-6489. 48 units. A/C TV TEL. Late Apr–late May $100–$130 double; Memorial Day–late June and early Sept–Oct $120–$155 double; late June–Labor Day $125–$165 double. Extra person $8. Rollaway bed $12. AE, CB, DC, DISC, MC, V. Rates include continental breakfast. Children under 12 stay free in parents' room. Minimum 3 nights on summer weekends, some spring and fall weekends. Closed Nov–late Apr. Follow Rte. 128 to the end (Exit 9, East Gloucester), turn left onto Bass Ave. (Rte. 127A), and follow a half-mile. Turn right and follow Atlantic Rd.

A family operation since 1946, the Bass Rocks Ocean Inn offers modern accommodations in a traditional setting. The spacious guest rooms overlook the ocean from a sprawling, comfortable two-story motel, with the office and public areas in a Colonial Revival–style mansion built in 1899 and known as the "wedding-cake house." The rooftop sundeck, balconies, and heated outdoor pool offer excellent views of the surf. Guest rooms have balconies or patios; each has a king bed or two double beds. Each morning a buffet breakfast is served, and each afternoon coffee, tea, lemonade, and chocolate-chip cookies are offered. A billiard room and library are available, and bicycles are at the disposal of the guests.

DINING

See "En Route to Gloucester & Rockport," above, for information about the celebrated **Woodman's of Essex.**

The Gull. 75 Essex Ave. (Rte. 133), at Cape Ann Marina. ☎ **978/281-6060.** Reservations recommended for parties of 8 or more. Main courses $6–$12 at lunch, $7–$21 at dinner. DISC, MC, V. Daily late Apr–Oct 6am–9pm. Closed Nov–late Apr. Take Rte. 133 west from intersection with Rte. 127, or take Rte. 133 east from Rte. 128. SEAFOOD.

The floor-to-ceiling windows show off the Annisquam River from almost every seat at the Gull. This big, friendly restaurant specializes in seafood but is also known for its prime rib, and it draws locals, visitors, boaters, and families for large portions at reasonable prices. Ask about the daily specials. The seafood chowder is famous (with good reason), appetizers tend toward bar food, and fish is available in just about any variety and style. At lunch, there's an extensive sandwich menu. The Gull has a full bar.

The Rudder Restaurant. 73 Rocky Neck Ave., East Gloucester. ☎ **978/283-7967.** Reservations required on weekends. Main courses $13–$20. DISC, MC, V. Memorial Day–Labor Day, daily noon–10:30pm; call for open hours and days spring and fall. Closed Dec to mid–Apr. SEAFOOD/INTERNATIONAL.

A meal at The Rudder is not just a meal—it's a party. Overlooking Smith Cove, in the heart of the Rocky Neck Art Colony, the 40-year-old restaurant is packed, floor to ceiling, with gadgets, colored lights, antiques, photos, menus from around the world, and other collectibles. Ask for a seat on the deck (if it's not low tide) and be prepared for anything, because The Rudder is known for its "spontaneous entertainment." You might hear live piano music or see Susan's invisible flaming baton twirling act. Yes, it's pricey, but you're also paying for the floor show. And the chefs are creative, making this one of the few places in the area where you don't have to stick to basic seafood. Try the shrimp farcis appetizer; main course offerings run the gamut from shrimp scampi over fresh linguini to chicken picatta. There's also a children's menu ($8).

ROCKPORT

40 miles NE of Boston, 7 miles N of Gloucester

This lovely little town at the tip of Cape Ann was settled in 1690, and over the years it has been an active fishing port, a center of granite excavation and cutting, and a thriving summer community whose specialty seems to be selling fudge and refrigerator magnets to out-of-towners.

There's more to Rockport than gift shops—you just have to look. It's popular with working painters (Winslow Homer is only one of the famous artists who have captured the local color), and for every year-round resident who seems genuinely startled when legions of people with cameras around their necks descend on Rockport each June, there are dozens who are proud to show off their town.

GETTING THERE   Rockport is north of Gloucester along Route 127 or 127A. At the end of Route 128, turn left at the signs for Rockport to take 127, or continue until you see the sign for East Gloucester and turn left onto 127A, which runs along the east coast of Cape Ann. Route 127 is a loop that cuts across the peninsula inland and swings around to follow Ipswich Bay.

The **MBTA** (☎ 617/222-3200; www.mbta.com) commuter rail runs from North Station in Boston to Rockport. The trip takes 60 to 70 minutes. **The Cape Ann Transportation Authority,** or CATA (☎ 978/283-7916), runs buses from town to town on Cape Ann.

ESSENTIALS The **area code** is 978 (it recently changed from 508). The **Rockport Chamber of Commerce and Board of Trade,** 3 Main St. (☎ 978/546-6575; www.rockportusa.com), is open daily in summer from 9am to 5pm, and winter weekdays from 10am to 4pm. The chamber also operates an information booth seasonally (mid-May to mid-October) on Upper Main Street (Route 127), about a mile from downtown—look for the "Welcome to Rockport" sign. At either location, ask for the pamphlet "Rockport: A Walking Guide," which has a good map and descriptions of three short walking tours. Out of season, Rockport closes up tighter than an Essex clam, and from January through mid-April, it's pretty but somewhat desolate.

If you can schedule only one weekday trip, make it this one. For traffic and congestion, downtown Boston has nothing on Rockport on a summer Saturday afternoon. Whenever you go, circle the square once to look for parking (mind the limits on many meters), and if there's no place to park, try the back streets, even if they're some distance from the center of town. Or use the parking lot on Upper Main Street (Route 127) on weekends. Parking from 11am to 6pm costs $6 to $7, and a free shuttle takes you downtown and back.

WHAT TO SEE & DO

The most famous example of what to see in Rockport has something of an "Emperor's New Clothes" aura—it's a wooden fish warehouse on the town wharf, or T-Wharf, in the harbor. The barn-red shack (often erroneously rendered in bright red), known as **Motif No. 1,** is the most frequently painted object in a town filled with lovely buildings and surrounded by rocky coastline. The color certainly catches the eye in the neutrals of the surrounding seascape, but you might find yourself initiating or overhearing conversations about what the big deal is. Originally constructed in 1884 and destroyed during the blizzard of 1978, Motif No. 1 was rebuilt using donations from the local community and tourists. It stands again on the same pier, duplicated in every detail, and reinforced to withstand storms.

Nearby is a phenomenon whose popularity is easier to explain. **Bearskin Neck,** named after an unfortunate ursine visitor who drowned and was washed ashore in 1800, has perhaps the highest concentration of gift shops anywhere. It's a narrow peninsula with one main street (South Road) and several alleys lined—no, crammed—with galleries, snack bars, antiques shops, and ancient houses. You'll find dozens of little shops carrying clothes, gifts, toys, inexpensive novelties, and expensive handmade crafts and paintings.

More than 2 dozen art galleries display the works of local and nationally known artists. The **Rockport Art Association,** 12 Main St. (☎ 978/546-6604), open daily year-round, sponsors major exhibitions and special shows throughout the year. Chamber music fans can contact the Chamber of Commerce for information about the **Rockport Chamber Music Festival,** an early summer highlight.

If the mansions of Gloucester are too plush for you, or if you want some tips on what to do with old newspapers, visit the **Paper House,** 52 Pigeon Hill St., Pigeon Cove (☎ 978/546-2629). It was built in 1922 entirely out of 100,000 newspapers—walls, furniture, even a piano. Every item of furniture is made from papers of a different period. It's open daily May through October from 10am to

5pm. Admission is $1.50 for adults and $1 for children. Follow Route 127 north out of downtown about three-quarters of a mile until you see signs pointing to the left.

To get a sense of the power of the sea in this part of the world, take Route 127 north of town to the very tip of Cape Ann. **Halibut Point State Park** (☎ **978/546-2997**) has a staffed visitor center, walking trails, tidal pools, and water-filled quarries (swimming is absolutely forbidden). You can climb around on giant boulders on the rocky beach, or climb to the top of the World War II observation tower. Guided tours (for $2.50 per person) are available on Saturday mornings in the summer, and this is a great place just to wander around and admire the scenery. On a clear day, you can see Maine.

And if you'd like to indulge the inexplicable craving for fudge that overwhelms otherwise mild-mannered travelers when they get their first whiff of salt water, you can give in to temptation and then watch taffy being made at **Tuck's Candy Factory,** 7 Dock Sq. (☎ **800/569-2767** or 978/546-6352), a local landmark since the 1920s.

ACCOMMODATIONS

When Rockport is busy, it's *very* busy, and when it's not, it's practically empty. If you haven't made summer reservations well in advance, cross your fingers and call the Chamber of Commerce to ask about cancellations.

Moderate

Old Farm Inn. 291 Granite St. (Rte. 127), Rockport, MA 01966. ☎ **800/233-6828** or 978/546-3237. Fax 978/546-9308. 10 units (some with shower only), 1 cottage. A/C TV TEL. July–Oct $88–$130 double, Apr–June and Nov $78–$125 double. Room with kitchenette $120, 2-room suite $130. 2-bedroom housekeeping cottage $1,125 per week July–Aug. Extra person $15. Rollaway bed $20. Room rates include buffet breakfast. Minimum 3 nights on holiday and summer weekends. AE, MC, V. Closed Dec to mid-Apr. Follow Rte. 127 north from center of town until signs point to right for Halibut Point State Park; inn is in front of you.

This gorgeous bed-and-breakfast is a 1799 saltwater farm with antique-furnished rooms in the Inn, the Barn Guesthouse, and the Fieldside Cottage. Each room is uniquely decorated with country-style furnishings (many have beautiful quilts on the beds), refrigerator, and coffeemaker, and innkeepers Susan and Bill Balzarini will make you feel at home. They serve a generous buffet breakfast in the first-floor sunroom. About 2½ miles from the center of town, the inn is in a beautiful location a stone's throw from Halibut Point State Park.

Peg Leg Inn. 2 King St., Rockport, MA 01966. ☎ **800/346-2352** or 978/546-2352. www.cape-ann.com/pegleg. 33 units (some with shower only). TV. Mid-June to Labor Day, holiday and fall weekends $85–$140 double, $160 two-bedroom unit. Off-season discounts available. Extra person $10. Rates include continental breakfast. Minimum 2 nights on weekends, 3 nights on holiday weekends. AE, MC, V. Closed Nov–Mar.

The Peg Leg Inn consists of five early American houses with front porches, attractive living rooms, and well-kept flower-bordered lawns that run down to a gazebo at the ocean's edge. It's not luxurious, but it is convenient and comfortable. Rooms are good-sized and neatly furnished in Colonial style, and some have excellent ocean views. Guests at the inn may use the sandy beach across the road.

Ralph Waldo Emerson Inn. 1 Cathedral Ave., P.O. Box 2369, Rockport, MA 01966. ☎ **978/546-6321.** Fax 978/546-7043. www.cape-ann.com/emerson. E-mail: emerson@ cove.com. 36 units. A/C TEL. July–Labor Day $99–$140 double; spring and fall $88–$128 double. Extra person $7. Crib or cot $7. Weekly rates available. Minimum 2 nights on summer weekends. DISC, MC, V. Closed Dec–March; open weekends only Apr and Nov. Follow Rte. 127 north from the center of town for 2 miles and watch for sign; turn right at Phillips St.

Somewhere in the old guest register of the Ralph Waldo Emerson Inn you might find the name of Emerson himself—the distinguished philosopher was a guest in the original (1840) inn in the 1850s. The oceanfront building was expanded in 1912, and it still has an old-fashioned feel—with the exception of the heated outdoor saltwater pool, a most enjoyable modern convenience. Furnishings such as spool beds and four-posters grace the nicely appointed, though not terribly large, rooms. There's no elevator; rooms that require a climb and face the street or have indirect views of the water are less expensive than the more accessible accommodations. If you can manage the stairs, though, the view from the top-floor rooms is worth the exertion and expense. Recreation rooms include areas for playing cards or table tennis, or watching the wide-screen TV. The indoor whirlpool and sauna is available for a fee.

The dining room opens to the public when tables are available. Breakfast is served from 8 to 10am, dinner from 6 to 9pm.

Yankee Clipper Inn (Romantik Hotel). 96 Granite St. (Rte. 127), Rockport, MA 01966. ☎ **800/545-3699** or 978/546-3407. Fax 978/546-9730. www.yankeeclipperinn.com. 29 units. A/C TEL. Memorial Day to mid-Oct, $109–$269 double; weekends spring and fall $115–$157 double; weeknights spring and fall $83–$115 double. Extra person $26. Rates include full breakfast in summer, continental breakfast in spring and fall. Minimum 2 nights on weekends. AE, DISC, MC, V. Closed mid-Dec to mid-Mar.

Just north of town, this luxurious lodging sits on extensive lawns overlooking the sea. The three-story main inn—with its Georgian architecture, outdoor heated saltwater pool, and rooms with private balconies—is the most beautiful of the hotel's four buildings. Rooms are attractively furnished; most are large, and many have views of the water. The least expensive rooms offer neither, but you might not mind feeling like a poor relation at a place this nice. Many common rooms within the inn face the water, notably the large and attractive dining room, which is open to the public. Reservations are required of guests as well as the public.

Inexpensive

Captain's Bounty Motor Inn. 1 Beach St., Rockport, MA 01966. ☎ **978/546-9557.** www.cape-ann.com/capt-bounty. 24 units. TV TEL. Apr to mid-May $65 double, $68 efficiency, $70 efficiency suite; mid-May to mid-June and late Sept–Oct $80 double, $85 efficiency, $90 efficiency suite; mid-June to late Sept $98 double, $110 efficiency, $120 efficiency suite. Extra person $10, rollaway bed $5. All rates based on double occupancy. Minimum 2 nights on weekends, 3 nights on holiday weekends. DISC, MC, V. Closed Nov–Mar.

To get closer to the beach than this modern, well-maintained motor inn, you'd have to sleep on a houseboat. Ocean breezes provide natural air-conditioning—each rather plain room in the two-story building overlooks the water and has its own balcony and sliding glass door. It's hardly plush, but you can't beat the location. Rooms are spacious and soundproofed, and kitchenette units are available.

✪ Inn on Cove Hill. 37 Mt. Pleasant St., Rockport, MA 01966. ☎ **888/546-2701** or 978/546-2701. 11 units (9 with bathroom, 4 with shower only, 1 with tub only). A/C TV. $68–$110 double with private bathroom, $50 with shared bathroom. Extra person $25. Rates include continental breakfast. Minimum 2 nights July–Aug and weekends June, Sept–Oct. Closed Nov to mid-Apr. MC, V. No children under 11 accepted.

This three-story inn was built in 1791 using the proceeds of pirates' gold found a short distance away. It's an attractive Federal-style home just 2 blocks from the head of the town wharf. Although it's close to downtown, the inn is set back from the road and has a delightful hideaway feel. Innkeepers Marjorie and John Pratt have decorated the guest rooms in period style, with at least one antique piece in each room. Most rooms have Colonial furnishings and handmade quilts, and some have canopy beds. In warm weather, a continental breakfast with home-baked breads and muffins is served on china at the garden tables; in inclement weather, breakfast in bed is served on individual trays.

If you're coming by train from Boston, the hosts will meet you at the station; if you drive, parking is provided.

DINING

Rockport is a "dry" community where the law prevents restaurants from serving alcoholic beverages, but you can bring your own bottle, sometimes subject to a corking fee.

On Bearskin Neck, the **Portside Chowder House** (☎ **978/546-7045**) serves Southern barbecue—no, seriously, it serves delicious fresh chowder by the cup, pint, and quart. For deli sandwiches during the day and sit-down service of Italian specialties Wednesday through Saturday evenings, **LoGrasso's,** 13 Railroad Ave., Rte. 127 (☎ **978/546-7977**), is a good choice.

Brackett's Oceanview Restaurant. 29 Main St. ☎ **978/546-2797.** Reservations recommended at dinner. Main courses $5.75–$15. AE, DC, DISC, MC, V. Mid-Apr to Memorial Day, Thurs–Sun 11:30am–8pm; Memorial Day–Oct, Sun–Fri 11:30am–8pm, Sat 11:30am–9pm. Closed Nov to mid-Apr. SEAFOOD/AMERICAN.

From the dining room at Brackett's, there's a gorgeous view of the water you glimpsed between buildings as you walked along Main Street. The nautical decor suits the seafood-intensive menu, which offers enough variety to make this a good choice for families—burgers are always available. The service is friendly, and the fresh seafood quite good, if not particularly innovative. Try the codfish cakes if you're looking for a traditional New England dish. The most exciting offerings are on the extensive dessert menu, where anything homemade is a great choice.

✪ **The Greenery.** 15 Dock Sq. ☎ **978/546-9593.** Reservations recommended at dinner. Main dishes $6.25–$12 at lunch, $9.25–$16 at dinner; breakfast items $1.25–$7. DISC, MC, V. Mid-Apr to Nov Mon-Fri 9am–10pm, Sat–Sun 8am–10pm. Closed Dec to mid-Apr. SEAFOOD/AMERICAN.

This is the best restaurant in Rockport, a place that could (but doesn't) get away with serving so-so food because of its great location at the head of Bearskin Neck. The cafe at the front gives no hint that at the back of the building is a dining room with a great view of the harbor. The terrific food ranges from crab salad quiche at lunch to lobster at dinner to steamers anytime, and the huge salad bar is available on its own or with many entrees. Breakfast is served on weekends. All baking is done in-house, which explains the lines at the front counter for muffins and pastries. This is a good place to launch a picnic lunch on the beach, and an equally good spot for lingering over coffee and a delectable dessert and watching the action on and near the harbor.

My Place By-the-Sea. 68 South Rd., Bearskin Neck. ☎ **978/546-9667.** Reservations recommended at dinner. Main courses $5–$13 at lunch, $13–$19 at dinner. AE, CB, DC, DISC, JCB, MC, V. Apr–Nov, daily 11:30am–9:30pm. Closed Dec–Mar. SEAFOOD.

The lure of My Place By-the-Sea is its location at the very end of Bearskin Neck, where you'll find Rockport's only outdoor oceanfront deck. There are excellent views of Sandy Bay from the two decks and shaded patio. The menu is reliable if not exactly inspired, with many options dictated by the daily catch. The baked fish and seafood pasta entrees are good choices, and you can also have chicken or beef. The dessert menu includes excellent homemade fruit pies.

Peg Leg. 18 Beach St. ☎ **978/546-3038.** Reservations recommended. Main courses $7–$19. AE, MC, V. In season, nightly 5:30-9pm. AMERICAN/SEAFOOD.

This pleasant restaurant serves tasty, uncomplicated American food in a garden-like setting, with plants in hanging baskets, geranium trees, and flowers all around. The greenhouse, very romantic in the evening with its recessed spotlights and candles, is behind the cozy main restaurant. Entrees include the house special chicken pie, seafood "pies" (casseroles), fresh fish, steaks, and lobster. All baking is done on the premises, and bread baskets always include sweet rolls. There is also a children's menu ($7).

3 Plymouth

40 miles SE of Boston

Everyone educated in the United States knows at least a little about Plymouth—about how the Pilgrims, fleeing religious persecution, left Europe on the *Mayflower* and landed at **Plymouth Rock** in December 1620. Many also know that the Pilgrims endured disease and privation, and that just 51 people from the original group of 102 celebrated the first Thanksgiving in 1621 with Squanto, a Pawtuxet Indian associated with the Wampanoags, and his cohorts.

What you won't know until you visit Plymouth is how small everything was. The *Mayflower* (a replica) seems perilously tiny, and when you contemplate how dangerous life was at the time, it's hard not to be impressed by the settlers' accomplishments.

Capt. Bartholomew Gosnold named Cape Cod in 1602, and 12 years later Capt. John Smith sailed along the coast of what he named "New England," calling the mainland opposite Cape Cod "Plymouth." The passengers on the *Mayflower* had secured the title for a tract of land near the mouth of the Hudson River in "Northern Virginia" from the London Virginia Company; in exchange for their passage to the New World, they promised to work the land for the company for 7 years. However, on November 11, 1620, rough weather and high seas forced them to make for Cape Cod Bay and anchor there, at Provincetown. The captain then announced that they had found a safe harbor, and he refused to continue the voyage farther south to their original destination. They had no option but to settle in New England. With no one to command them, their contract with the London Virginia Company became void, and they were left on their own to begin life in a new world.

Today, Plymouth is a manageable day-trip destination particularly suited to families traveling with children. It also makes a good rest stop between Boston and Cape Cod.

GETTING THERE   By car, follow the Southeast Expressway (I-93) from Boston to Route 3. Take Exit 6, then Route 44 east, and follow signs to the historic attractions. The whole trip takes about 45 minutes if it's not rush hour. Or continue on Route 3 to the **Regional Information Complex** at Exit 5 for maps, brochures, and information. To go directly to **Plimoth Plantation,** take Exit 4.

The **MBTA** (☎ **617/222-3200;** www.mbta.com) reinstituted service on the **Old Colony Railroad line** in 1997. The new commuter rail serves Plymouth from South Station, a 1-hour trip, during the day on weekdays and all day on weekends (at peak commuting times, service is to nearby Kingston). It's an especially pleasant ride when the fall foliage and cranberry bogs are at their colorful peak.

Plymouth & Brockton buses (☎ **617/773-9401** or 508/746-0378) leave from the terminal at South Station. You can also make connections at Logan Airport, where buses take on passengers at all airline terminals. The bus is more expensive than the commuter rail but runs more often.

ESSENTIALS   The **area code** is 508. If you haven't visited the Regional Information Complex, you'll want to stop in and at least pick up a map at the **Visitor Center** (☎ **508/747-7525**), 130 Water St., across from the town pier. To plan ahead, contact **Plymouth Visitor Information,** P.O. Box ROCK, Plymouth, MA 02361 (☎ **800/USA-1620** or 508/747-7525; www.visit-plymouth.com).

WHAT TO SEE & DO

The logical place to begin (good luck talking children out of it) is where the Pilgrims first set foot—at **Plymouth Rock.** The rock, accepted as the landing place of the *Mayflower* passengers, was originally 15 feet long and 3 feet wide. It was moved on the eve of the Revolution and several times thereafter before assuming its present permanent position at tide level, where the winter storms still break over it as they did in Pilgrim days. The McKim, Mead & White–designed portico around the rock was commissioned in 1920 by the Colonial Dames of America. It's not much to look at, but the accompanying descriptions are interesting, and the sense of history is curiously impressive.

Plymouth Rock Trolley, 22 Main St. (☎ **508/747-3419**), offers a narrated tour and unlimited reboarding privileges daily Memorial Day through October and weekends through Thanksgiving. It's a good idea if young children are along. Tickets are $7 for adults and $3 for ages 3 to 12. Trolley markers indicate the stops, which are served every 20 minutes.

To put yourself in the Pilgrims' footsteps, take a **Colonial Lantern Tour** offered by New World Tours, 98 Water St. (☎ **800/698-5636** or 508/747-4161). Participants carry pierced-tin lanterns on a 90-minute walking tour of the original settlement under the direction of a knowledgeable guide. It might seem a bit hokey at first, but it's fascinating. Tours run nightly, late March through Thanksgiving. The standard history tour leaves the New World office at 7:30pm; the "Legends and Lore" tour leaves from the lobby of the John Carver Inn, 25 Summer St., at 9pm. Tickets are $9 for adults, $7 for children. The same company offers a 2-hour "Lunch on Burial Hill" tour at noon daily in July and August. The price ($15 adults, $10 children) includes a picnic lunch, and reservations are required.

To get away from the bustle of the waterfront, you might want to relax at **Town Brook Park** at Jenney Pond, across Summer Street from the John Carver Inn. Across from the tree-bordered pond is the **Jenney Grist Mill,** 6 Spring Lane (☎ **508/747-3715;** admission $2.50 adults, $2 ages 5 to 12), a working museum where you can see a reconstructed early American water-powered mill that operates in the summer, daily from 10am to 5pm. The specialty shops in the same complex, including the excellent Jenney Grist Mill Ice Cream Shoppe, are open year-round, daily from 10am to 6pm. There is plenty of parking.

EXPLORING THE HISTORIC HOUSES

You can't stay at Plymouth's historic houses, but they're worth a visit to see the changing styles of architecture and furnishings since the 1600s. Costumed guides explain the homemaking and crafts of earlier generations. Most of the houses are open Memorial Day through Columbus Day weekends and during Thanksgiving celebrations; call for schedules. And if you're sightseeing with children, pretend the next sentence is written in capital letters: Unless all of you have a sky-high tolerance for house tours, pick just one or two from eras that you find particularly interesting. Each tour has something to recommend it; the Sparrow and Howland houses are most interesting for those curious about the original settlers.

Six homes are open to visitors: the 1640 **Sparrow House,** 42 Summer St. (☎ **508/747-1240;** admission $1); the 1666 **Howland House,** 33 Sandwich St. (☎ **508/746-9590;** admission $3 adults, 75¢ ages 6 to 12); the 1677 **Harlow Old Fort House,** 119 Sandwich St. (☎ **508/746-0012;** admission $3 adults, 75¢ ages 6 to 12); the 1749 **Spooner House,** 27 North St. (☎ **508/746-0012;** admission $3 adults, 75¢ ages 6 to 12); the 1754 **Mayflower Society Museum,** 4 Winslow St. (☎ **508/746-2590;** admission $2.50, 75¢ ages 6 to 12); and the 1809 **Hedge House,** 126 Water St. (☎ **508/746-0012;** admission $3 adults, 75¢ ages 6 to 12).

Mayflower II. State Pier. ☎ **508/746-1622.** www.plimoth.org/mayflowe.htm. Admission $5.75 adults, $3.75 children 6–12, free for children under 6. Mayflower II and Plimoth Plantation admission $18.50 adults, $16.50 seniors, $11 children 6–12, free for children under 6. Apr–Nov, daily 9am–5pm.

Berthed a few steps from Plymouth Rock, *Mayflower II* is a full-scale reproduction of the type of ship that brought the Pilgrims from England to America in 1620. Even at full scale, the 106½-foot vessel, constructed in England from 1955 to 1957, is remarkably small. Although little technical information is known about the original *Mayflower,* William A. Baker, designer of *Mayflower II,* incorporated the few references in Governor Bradford's account of the voyage with other research to re-create as closely as possible the actual ship. In 1997, 2 to 3 years of extensive reconstruction and renovation work began. The exhibit changes regularly as renovations proceed, incorporating the workers' explanations and interpretations of their efforts. (Ordinarily, costumed guides provide first-person narratives about the vessel and voyage.) Other displays describe and illustrate the voyage and the Pilgrims' experience, including 17th-century navigation techniques, and the history of the *Mayflower II.* The vessel is owned and maintained by Plimoth Plantation, which is 3 miles south of the ship. Alongside the ship are museum shops that replicate early Pilgrim dwellings.

○ **Plymouth National Wax Museum.** 16 Carver St. ☎ **508/746-6468.** Admission $5.50 adults, $5 seniors, $2.25 ages 5–12, free for children under 5. Mar–June and Sept–Nov, daily 9am–5pm; July–Aug, daily 9am–9pm. From Plymouth Rock, turn around and walk up the hill or the steps.

Across New England (and probably across the United States), adults who visited the Plymouth National Wax Museum as children can still tell you all about the history of the Pilgrims. More than 180 life-size figures are arranged in the galleries, and dramatic sound tracks tell the story of the move to Holland to escape persecution in England; the harrowing trip across the ocean to the New World; the first Thanksgiving; and even the tale of Myles Standish, Priscilla Mullins, and John Alden. This museum is a must if children are in your party, and adults will enjoy it, too. On the hill outside is a monument at the gravesite of the Pilgrims who died during the settlement's first winter.

Pilgrim Hall Museum. 75 Court St. ☎ **508/746-1620.** www.visit-plymouth.com/pilgrimhall. Admission $5 adults, $4.50 seniors and AAA members, $3 children. Feb–Dec, daily 9:30am–4:30pm. From Plymouth Rock, walk north on Water St. and up the hill on Chilton St.

This is a great place to get a sense of the day-to-day lives of Plymouth's first white residents. Many original possessions of the early Pilgrims and their descendants are on display, including an uncomfortable chair that belonged to William Brewster (alongside a modern-day model—that's how you can tell it's uncomfortable), one of Myles Standish's swords, and Governor Bradford's Bible. Regularly changing exhibits explore specific aspects of the settlers' lives, such as home construction or the history of prominent families. Among the permanent exhibits is the skeleton of the *Sparrow-Hawk*, a ship wrecked on Cape Cod in 1626 that lay buried in the sand and undiscovered until 1863. It's even smaller than the *Mayflower II*. Built in 1824, the Pilgrim Hall Museum is the oldest public museum in the United States and is listed on the National Register of Historic Places.

Plimoth Plantation. Rte. 3. ☎ **508/746-1622.** www.plimoth.org. Admission $15 adults, $9 children 6–12, free for children under 6. Plimoth Plantation and *Mayflower II* $18.50 adults, $16.50 seniors, $11 ages 6–17, free for children under 6. Apr–Nov, daily 9am–5pm. From Rte. 3, take Exit 4, Plimoth Plantation Highway.

Allow at least half a day to explore this re-creation of the 1627 Pilgrim village, which children and adults find equally interesting. You enter by the hilltop fort that protects the villagers and walk down the hill to the farm area, visiting the homes and gardens, which have been constructed with careful attention to historic detail. Once you get over the feeling that the whole operation is a bit strange (we heard someone mention Pompeii), it's great fun to talk to the "Pilgrims"—actors who, in speech, dress, and manner, assume the personalities of members of the original community. You can watch them framing a house, splitting wood, shearing sheep, preserving foodstuffs, or cooking a pot of fish stew over an open hearth, all as it was done in the 1600s. And they use only the tools and cookware available then. Sometimes you can join in the activities—perhaps planting, harvesting, a court trial, or a wedding party. Wear comfortable shoes. There's a lot of walking involved, and the plantation isn't paved.

The community is as accurate as research can make it: accounts of the original Pilgrim colony were combined with archaeological research, old records, and the history written by the Pilgrims' leader, William Bradford, who often used the spelling "Plimoth" for the settlement. There are daily militia drills with matchlock muskets that are fired to demonstrate the community's defense system. In fact, little defense was needed, because the local Native Americans were friendly. Local tribes included the Wampanoags, who are represented at a homesite near the village, where members of the museum staff show off native foodstuffs, agricultural practices, and crafts. Admission to the plantation includes a visit to the homesite.

At the main entrance, you'll find two modern buildings with an interesting orientation show, exhibits, a gift shop, a crafts center, a bookstore, and a cafeteria. There's a picnic area nearby.

Cranberry World. 225 Water St. ☎ **508/747-2350.** Free admission. May 1–Nov 30, daily 9:30am–5pm. Guided tours available; call for reservations. From Plymouth Rock, walk north for 10 minutes right along the waterfront.

Cranberries aren't just for Thanksgiving dinner, as Ocean Spray's interesting visitor center will remind you. Displays include outdoor demonstration bogs, antique harvesting tools, a scale model of a cranberry farm, and interactive exhibits. There are daily cooking demonstrations and free cranberry refreshments. September and October are harvest time.

ACCOMMODATIONS

On busy summer weekends, it's not unusual for every room in town to be taken. Make reservations well in advance.

Moderate

Governor Bradford on the Harbour. 98 Water St., Plymouth, MA 02360. ☎ **800/ 332-1620** or 508/746-6200. Fax 508/747-3032. 94 units (some with shower only). A/C TV TEL. $89–$124 double in season. Extra person $10. Off-season and AAA discounts available. Children under 16 stay free in parents' room. AE, CB, DC, DISC, MC, V.

This three-story motor inn is across the street from the waterfront and only 1 block from Plymouth Rock, the *Mayflower II,* and the center of town. The rooms, each with two double beds, have attractive, modern furnishings, wall-to-wall carpeting, refrigerators, and coffeemakers. Twenty-two rooms were redecorated in 1997. More expensive rooms are higher up and have clearer views of the water. There are a small heated outdoor pool and coin laundry facilities.

☯ **John Carver Inn.** 25 Summer St., Plymouth, MA 02360. ☎ **800/274-1620** or 508/746-7100. Fax 508/746-8299. 79 units. A/C TV TEL. Mid-Apr to mid-June $75–$95 double; mid-June to mid-Oct $85–$105 double; mid-Oct to Nov $75–$95 double; Dec to mid-Apr $65–$85 double. Children under 19 stay free in parents' room. Passport to History package rates change seasonally. Senior and AAA discounts available. AE, CB, DC, DISC, MC, V.

A three-story Colonial-style building with a landmark portico, the John Carver Inn offers comfortable, modern accommodations, a large outdoor pool, and all the amenities, including room service and conference rooms. The good-sized guest rooms are newly renovated and decorated in colonial style. The inn is within walking distance of the main attractions, and the staff is friendly and helpful. A **Hearth 'n' Kettle** restaurant is on the premises. The hotel offers a good deal (the Passport to History Packages) that includes a 2-night, 3-day stay for two, four breakfast tickets to the restaurant, two $10 discount dinner tickets at the restaurant, two Plimoth Plantation or whale-watch tickets, and two tickets to the trolley or Wax Museum.

Pilgrim Sands Motel. 150 Warren Ave. (Rte. 3A), Plymouth, MA 02360. ☎ **800/ 729-SANDS** or 508/747-0900. Fax 508/746-8066. www.pilgrimsands.com. E-mail: thebeach@pilgrimsands.com. 64 units, 2 two-bedroom suites. A/C TV TEL. Summer $93–$123 double, spring and early fall $80–$105 double, Apr and late fall $60–$80 double, Dec–Mar $50–$70 double; $90–$175 suite. Rates might be higher on holiday weekends. Extra person $6–$8. AE, CB, DC, DISC, MC, V.

This attractive motel is on a private beach 3 miles south of town, within walking distance of Plimoth Plantation. If you want to avoid the bustle of downtown and still be near the water, it's a fine choice. The good-sized, modern units have individual climate control and tasteful furnishings. If you can possibly swing it, book a beachfront room—the view is worth the money. In the summer, guests have access to the sundeck, whirlpool spa, and outdoor and indoor swimming pools. Most rooms have two double or two queen-size beds, and many have refrigerators. They're divided into smoking and no-smoking wings. There's a coffee shop on the premises.

Sheraton Inn Plymouth. 180 Water St., Plymouth, MA 02360. ☎ **800/325-3535** or 508/747-4900. Fax 508/746-2609. 175 units. A/C TV TEL. Apr–Oct $100–$205 double; Nov–Mar $85–$160 double. Children under 18 stay free in parents' room. Extra person $15. AE, CB, DC, DISC, JCB, MC, V.

This attractive, four-story hotel sits on a hill across the street from the waterfront. If you need the amenities of a chain and want to be near the historic sights, this is your only choice—happily, it's a good one. Rooms are tastefully furnished in contemporary style and have climate control and in-room movies, and guests have the use of a laundry room. Some rooms have small balconies that overlook the indoor swimming pool and whirlpool. The first floor (41 rooms) was renovated in early 1998.

The hotel also has an exercise room, a business center and conference rooms, room service until 11pm, weekday newspaper delivery and dry cleaning, baby-sitting, a restaurant, and a pub.

Inexpensive

Cold Spring Motel. 188 Court St. (Rte. 3A), Plymouth, MA 02360. ☎ **508/746-2222.** Fax 508/746-2744. 31 units (some with shower only), 2 two-bedroom cottages. A/C TV TEL. $59–$79 double, $69–$89 cottage. Off-season discounts available. Extra person $5. Rates include continental breakfast. Closed Dec–Mar. AE, DISC, MC, V.

Convenient to downtown and the historic sights, this pleasant, quiet motel and the adjacent cottages surround a nicely landscaped lawn. Its location, a bit removed from the water, makes it a great deal. The two-story building is 2 blocks inland, not far from Cranberry World, and set back from the street in a quiet part of town. There's parking at your door.

DINING

Lobster Hut. Town Wharf. ☎ **508/746-2270.** Fax 508/746-5655. Reservations not accepted. Luncheon specials $4.50–$8; main courses $5–$13; sandwiches $1.75–$6. MC, V. Summer daily 11am–9pm; winter daily 11am–7pm. SEAFOOD.

The Lobster Hut is a self-service restaurant with a great view. Order and pick up at the counter, then take your food to an indoor table or out on the large deck that overlooks the bay. For starters, have some clam chowder or lobster bisque. The seafood "rolls" (hot dog buns with your choice of filling) are excellent. You can choose from a long list of fried seafood—including clams, scallops, shrimp, and haddock. Or you might prefer boiled and steamed items, burgers, or chicken tenders. Beer and wine are served, but only with meals.

McGrath's Harbour Restaurant. Town Wharf. ☎ **508/746-9751.** Reservations recommended at dinner. Main dishes $10–$15. AE, DC, DISC, MC, V. Summer daily 11:30am–9pm. Closed Mon in winter. SEAFOOD.

McGrath's is a big, busy place, the choice of many families, local businesspeople, and tour groups. In addition to fish and seafood dinners, the extensive menu features poultry (including turkey—this is Plymouth, after all), prime rib, sandwiches, and children's offerings. Ask for a table overlooking the water because the room facing inland is on the gloomy side, and be sure you're in good company because service can be slow.

Run of the Mill Tavern. Jenney Grist Mill Village. ☎ **508/830-1262.** Reservations recommended at dinner. Main courses $6–$12. AE, MC, V. Mon–Sat 11:30am–10pm, Sun noon–10pm. AMERICAN.

This friendly restaurant is near the waterwheel at Jenney Grist Mill Village in Town Brook Park. It's an attractive setting, surrounded by trees, and the wood-paneled tavern offers good, inexpensive meals. The clam chowder is fantastic. Other appetizers include nachos, potato skins, buffalo wings, and mushrooms. Entrees are standard meat, chicken, and fish, and there are also seafood specials. The children's menu is a great bargain, with burgers and fish-and-chips at $2.50 to $3.50.

Appendix: Useful Toll-Free Numbers & Web Sites

AIRLINES

Air Canada	800/776-3000	www.aircanada.ca
American Airlines	800/433-7300	www.americanair.com
British Airways	800/247-9297	
	0345/222-111	
	in Britain	www.british-airways.com
Canadian Airlines		
International	800/426-7000	www.cdair.ca
Continental Airlines	800/525-0280	www.flycontinental.com
Delta Air Lines	800/221-1212	www.delta-air.com
Northwest Airlines	800/225-2525	www.nwa.com
Southwest Airlines	800/435-9792	iflyswa.com
Tower Air	800/34-TOWER	
	outside New York	
	718/553-8500	
	in New York	www.towerair.com
Trans World Airlines (TWA)	800/221-2000	www2.twa.com
United Airlines	800/241-6522	www.ual.com
USAirways	800/428-4322	www.usair.com
Virgin Atlantic Airways	800/862-8621	
	in Continental U.S.	
	0293/747-747	
	in Britain	www.fly.virgin.com

CAR RENTAL AGENCIES

Advantage	800/777-5500	www.arac.com
Alamo	800/327-9633	www.goalamo.com
Auto Europe	800/223-5555	www.autoeurope.com
Avis	800/331-1212	
	in Continental U.S.	
	800/TRY-AVIS	
	in Canada	www.avis.com
Budget	800/527-0700	www.budgetrentacar.com
Dollar	800/800-4000	www.dollarcar.com
Enterprise	800/325-8007	www.pickenterprise.com
Hertz	800/654-3131	www.hertz.com
Kemwel Holiday Auto	800/678-0678	www.kemwel.com
National	800/CAR-RENT	www.nationalcar.com
Payless	800/PAYLESS	www.paylesscar.com
Rent-A-Wreck	800/535-1391	rent-a-wreck.com
Thrifty	800/367227	www.thrifty.com
Value	800/327-2501	www.go-value.com

MAJOR HOTEL & MOTEL CHAINS

Best Western International	800/528-1234	www.bestwestern.com
Clarion Hotels	800/CLARION	www.hotelchoice.com/cgi-bin/res/webres?clarion.html
Comfort Inns	800/228-5150	www.hotelchoice.com/cgi-bin/res/webres?comfort.html
Courtyard by Marriott	800/321-2211	www.courtyard.com
Days Inn	800/325-2525	www.daysinn.com
Doubletree Hotels	800/222-TREE	www.doubletreehotels.com
Econo Lodges	800/55-ECONO	www.hotelchoice.com/cgi-bin/res/webres?econo.html
Fairfield Inn by Marriott	800/228-2800	www.fairfieldinn.com
Hampton Inn	800/HAMPTON	www.hampton-inn.com
Hilton Hotels	800/HILTONS	www.hilton.com
Holiday Inn	800/HOLIDAY	www.holiday-inn.com
Howard Johnson	800/654-2000	www.hojo.com/hojo.html
Hyatt Hotels & Resorts	800/228-9000	www.hyatt.com
ITT Sheraton	800/325-3535	www.sheraton.com
La Quinta Motor Inns	800/531-5900	www.laquinta.com
Marriott Hotels	800/228-9290	www.marriott.com
Motel 6	800/4-MOTEL6	
Quality Inns	800/228-5151	www.hotelchoice.com/cgi-bin/res/webres?quality.html
Radisson Hotels International	800/333-3333	www.radisson.com
Ramada Inns	800/2-RAMADA	www.ramada.com
Red Carpet Inns	800/251-1962	
Red Lion Hotels & Inns	800/547-8010	www.travelweb.com
Red Roof Inns	800/843-7663	www.redroof.com
Residence Inn by Marriott	800/331-3131	www.residenceinn.com
Rodeway Inns	800/228-2000	www.hotelchoice.com/cgi-bin/res/webres?rodeway.html
Super 8 Motels	800/800-8000	www.super8motels.com
Travelodge	800/255-3050	
Vagabond Hotels	800/255-3050	www.vagabondinns.com

Index

See also separate Accommodations and Restaurant indexes, below.
Page numbers in italics refer to maps.

GENERAL INDEX

ACCOMMODATIONS

FROMMER'S® COMPLETE TRAVEL GUIDES

(Comprehensive guides with selections in all price ranges—from deluxe to budget)

Alaska	France	Portugal
Amsterdam	Germany	Prague & the Best of the
Arizona	Greece	Czech Republic
Atlanta	Hawaii	Provence & the Riviera
Australia	Hong Kong	Puerto Rico
Austria	Honolulu, Waikiki & Oahu	Rome
Bahamas	Ireland	San Antonio & Austin
Barcelona, Madrid & Seville	Israel	San Diego
Belgium, Holland &	Italy	San Francisco
Luxembourg	Jamaica & Barbados	Santa Fe, Taos &
Bermuda	Japan	Albuquerque
Boston	Las Vegas	Scandinavia
Budapest & the Best of	London	Scotland
Hungary	Los Angeles	Seattle & Portland
California	Maryland & Delaware	Singapore & Malaysia
Canada	Maui	South Pacific
Cancún, Cozumel & the	Mexico	Spain
Yucatán	Miami & the Keys	Switzerland
Cape Cod, Nantucket &	Montana & Wyoming	Thailand
Martha's Vineyard	Montréal & Québec City	Tokyo
Caribbean	Munich & the Bavarian Alps	Toronto
Caribbean Cruises &	Nashville & Memphis	Tuscany & Umbria
Ports of Call	Nepal	USA
Caribbean Ports of Call	New England	Utah
Carolinas & Georgia	New Mexico	Vancouver & Victoria
Chicago	New Orleans	Vermont, New Hampshire &
China	New York City	Maine
Colorado	Nova Scotia, New	Vienna & the Danube Valley
Costa Rica	Brunswick &	Virgin Islands
Denver, Boulder &	Prince Edward Island	Virginia
Colorado Springs	Oregon	Walt Disney World &
England	Paris	Orlando
Europe	Philadelphia & the Amish	Washington, D.C.
Florida	Country	Washington State

FROMMER'S® DOLLAR-A-DAY GUIDES

(The ultimate guides to comfortable low-cost travel)

Australia from $50 a Day	Israel from $45 a Day
California from $60 a Day	Italy from $50 a Day
Caribbean from $60 a Day	London from $70 a Day
England from $60 a Day	New York from $75 a Day
Europe from $50 a Day	New Zealand from $50 a Day
Florida from $60 a Day	Paris from $70 a Day
Greece from $50 a Day	San Francisco from $60 a Day
Hawaii from $60 a Day	Washington, D.C., from
Ireland from $50 a Day	$60 a Day

FROMMER'S® MEMORABLE WALKS

Chicago	New York	San Francisco
London	Paris	

FROMMER'S® PORTABLE GUIDES

Acapulco, Ixtapa/
  Zihuatenejo
Bahamas
California Wine
  Country
Charleston & Savannah
Chicago

Dublin
Las Vegas
London
Maine Coast
New Orleans
New York City
Paris

Puerto Vallarta, Manzanillo
  & Guadalajara
San Francisco
Sydney
Tampa Bay & St. Petersburg
Venice
Washington, D.C.

FROMMER'S® NATIONAL PARK GUIDES

Grand Canyon
National Parks of the American West
Yellowstone & Grand Teton

Yosemite & Sequoia/
  Kings Canyon
Zion & Bryce Canyon

THE COMPLETE IDIOT'S TRAVEL GUIDES
(The ultimate user-friendly trip planners)

Cruise Vacations
Planning Your Trip to Europe
Hawaii

Las Vegas
Mexico's Beach Resorts
New Orleans

New York City
San Francisco
Walt Disney World

SPECIAL-INTEREST TITLES

The Civil War Trust's Official Guide to
  the Civil War Discovery Trail
Frommer's Caribbean Hideaways
Israel Past & Present
New York City with Kids
New York Times Weekends
Outside Magazine's Adventure Guide
  to New England
Outside Magazine's Adventure Guide
  to Northern California

Outside Magazine's Adventure Guide
  to the Pacific Northwest
Outside Magazine's Guide to Family Vacations
Places Rated Almanac
Retirement Places Rated
Washington, D.C., with Kids
Wonderful Weekends from Boston
Wonderful Weekends from New York City
Wonderful Weekends from San Francisco
Wonderful Weekends from Los Angeles

THE UNOFFICIAL GUIDES®
(Get the unbiased truth from these candid, value-conscious guides)

Atlanta
Branson, Missouri
Chicago
Cruises
Disneyland

Florida with Kids
The Great Smoky
  & Blue Ridge
  Mountains
Las Vegas

Miami & the Keys
Mini-Mickey
New Orleans
New York City
San Francisco

Skiing in the West
Walt Disney World
Walt Disney World
  Companion
Washington, D.C.

FROMMER'S® IRREVERENT GUIDES
(Wickedly honest guides for sophisticated travelers)

Amsterdam
Boston
Chicago

London
Manhattan

New Orleans
Paris

San Francisco
Walt Disney World
Washington, D.C.

FROMMER'S® DRIVING TOURS

America
Britain
California

Florida
France
Germany

Ireland
Italy
New England

Scotland
Spain
Western Europe

WHEREVER YOU TRAVEL, *H*ELP IS NEVER FAR AWAY.

From planning your trip to providing travel assistance along the way, American Express® Travel Service Offices are always there to help you do more.

Boston

American Express Travel Service
One Court Street
617/723-8400

American Express Travel Service
222 Berkeley Street
617/236-1331

American Express Travel Service
170 Federal Street
617/439-4400

Travel

http://www.americanexpress.com/travel

American Express Travel Service Offices are located throughout Massachusetts. For the office nearest you, call 1-800-AXP-3429.